KIERKEGAARD:
A kind
of Poet

University of
Pennsylvania Press
Philadelphia

KIERKEGAARD:
A kind
of Poet

By LOUIS MACKEY

Selections from Concluding Unscientific Postscript, by Søren Kierkegaard, translated by David F. Swenson and Walter Lowrie (copyright 1941 © 1969 by Princeton University Press), Princeton Paperback, 1968; from Philosophical Fragments, by Søren Kierkegaard, originally translated and introduced by David Swenson; New Introduction and commentary by Niels Thulstrup; Translation revised and commentary translated by Howard V. Hong (2d ed. copyright © 1962 by Princeton University Press), Princeton Paperback, 1967, are reprinted by permission of Princeton University Press and the American Scandinavian Foundation. Selections from Fear and Trembling and the Sickness Unto Death, by Søren Kierkegaard, translated with an Introduction and Notes, by Walter Lowrie (copyright 1941, 1954 by Princeton University Press: Princeton Paperback, 1968), and from Either/Or, by Søren Kierkegaard (copyright 1944, © 1959 by Princeton University Press; Princeton Paperback, 1971): passages from Vol. I, translated by David F. Swenson and Lillian Marvin Swenson, and from Vol. II, translated by Walter Lowrie, are reprinted by permission of Princeton University Press.

All selections from Edifying Discourses, Vols. I and II, 1962, by Søren Kierkegaard, translated by David F. and Lillian M. Swenson, are reprinted by permission of Augsburg Publishing House, Minneapolis, Minnesota, copyright owner.

All selections from Johannes Climacus, or De Omnibus Dubitandum Est, and A Sermon, by Søren Kierkegaard, translated by T. H. Croxall (Stanford: Stanford University Press and London: A. & C. Black Ltd., 1958), are reprinted with permission.

All selections from The Journals of Søren Kierkegaard, translated by Alexander Dru (London: Oxford University Press, 1938), are reprinted by permission of Mr. Dru.

FOR
LINDA

CONTENTS

PREFACE

The thesis of this book is neither difficult nor novel. Quite simply, it argues that Søren Kierkegaard is not, in the usual acceptation of these words, a philosopher or a theologian, but a poet. Quite unoriginally, it repeats what Kierkegaard often and in diverse ways said of himself, that he is "only a peculiar kind of poet or thinker," not the philosophic skald whose penetrating eye scans the ramparts of Being, nor the theological "witness for the truth" of Christianity who authoritatively propounds the Faith.

Old and obvious as it is, the thesis still needs to be defended. For though the interpreters of Kierkegaard have all conceded it in principle—they could scarcely do otherwise in view of his own abundant declarations—they have almost all abused it in fact. It is no part of my purpose, and it is certainly not my desire, to pick quarrels with these worthy exegetes, many of whom have made substantial contributions to my understanding of their master. But it is worth a paragraph's passing to reflect upon the *kinds* of books and essays that are written about Kierkegaard. There is first of all what might be called the "survey and summary" that runs through Kierkegaard's works, offers précis of each, and rounds out with a résumé of the whole. Such books are useful for students, especially when it is a question of introducing a new and difficult writer to the public, and more especially when the survey and summary are not overlaid with the summarist's *ad hoc* evaluations. But the misleading feature of such works is that, though mention may be made of "indirect communication," they cannot avoid becoming compendia of Kierkegaardian teaching, that teaching which Kierkegaard insisted he did not have to offer and which he went out of his way to avoid offering. To write a compendium of Kierkegaard's doctrines by means of a review of his works is like summarizing the philosophy of Shakespeare by means of a survey of the plays.

Then again, there are the books that are almost pure

evaluation, the attacks and the appreciations. Generally theological, but occasionally philosophical, these books also have their uses. They can coax an antagonistic reader into a more sympathetic rapport with a writer who certainly merits appreciation. Or, in the case of attacks, the reader who is too prone to be intoxicated by Kierkegaard can be sobered with a bit of critical objectivity. But in either case, the attack or the appreciation presumes a doctrinal statement to be applauded or decried, an argument to be accepted or refused. And that makes about as much sense as agreeing or disagreeing with *Hamlet*.

Finally, there are the books and monographs and essays on special topics in Kierkegaard. For such detailed examinations of a complex and involved corpus every student of Kierkegaard has reason to be grateful. But even if we overlook the dangers involved in considering members of a closely articulated body out of context, there is still the misleading presumption of a Kierkegaardian system whose parts can be clarified toward a pending elucidation and ultimate espousal or rejection of the whole.

What it all comes to is this: Kierkegaard has been treated, even by those otherwise sensitive to the poetic dimension of his work, as if he were a straightforward philosophical or theological writer. He has been studied almost exclusively with the help of those means of analysis that are presumed appropriate to philosophical systems and theological essays. And this inevitably skews the perspective of the student who is trying to understand him. Kierkegaard's writings are storehouses of philosophical and theological materials, and it is only prudent that modern philosophers and theologians should go into Egypt to replenish their own barns. There is no private property in the realm of spirit, so that it is even proper for them to reap where they have not sown. But the fact is that if Kierkegaard is to be understood *as Kierkegaard*, he must be studied not merely or principally with the instruments of philosophic and theological analysis, but also and chiefly with the tools of literary criticism. That is what this book tries to do; or rather, since I am inadequate to the task and therefore bound to humility as Adam was bound to perspire, that is what this book says the student of Kierkegaard ought to try to do.

I have not attempted a survey or an epitome of Kierkegaard. Rather, I have selected a few of his cardinal works and tried to read them closely and sensitively, with a view not only to what they say but even more to how they say it. I have focused on the pseudonymous works and the edifying discourses, neglecting for the most part the journals and the late writings that Kierkegaard published over his own name. The journals are important for an understanding of Kierkegaard's intellectual and artistic development; but my concern has been philosophic and critical, not genetic in any sense. The late writings I have passed over, largely because they are not part of the series of writings that Kierkegaard called his "literature." I have, in other words, restricted myself to the published canon and treated it as an independent literary whole. There are doubtless purposes which are not served in this way. But I believe that my approach is (a) acceptable critical practice, (b) in line with Kierkegaard's own intent, and (c) illuminating. I have tried to read the works he wanted read in the way he wanted them read.

I have not been particularly concerned to commend or to chide Kierkegaard or any of his pseudonyms, though I am sure my valuations will be obvious to everyone but me. And I have tried to see the whole Kierkegaard in the parts selected for analysis. But most of all I have endeavored, in chapters 1 through 5, to read the Kierkegaardian corpus as the "poetry of inwardness" he meant it to be. I have tried to make it clear that whatever philosophy or theology there is in Kierkegaard is sacramentally transmitted "in, with, and under" the poetry. I can claim no competence as a critic, but I have tried to keep myself alert to those characteristics of the literary form of the writings which are designed, in Kierkegaard's program, to "reduplicate" the content. In other words, I have tried to take him quite literally and quite simply when he described himself as "a peculiar kind of poet and thinker who . . . would read the fundamental document of the individual, human existence-relationship, the old, well-known, handed down from the fathers. . . ."

The detailed analyses and close readings of chapters 1 through 5 are meant to provide the evidence on which the conclusions and projections of chapter 6 rest. Chapter 6, by way of advancing the thesis of the whole book, argues that the artistry of Kierkegaard, while often praised, has seldom been sufficiently appreciated, and that its integral relationship to his thought has never been clearly seen. In particular, his use of pseudonyms, of metaphor, and of more complex literary forms to convey his ideas dictates the way in which these ideas are to be understood and appropriated. Like the unity of the corpus of a poet, the unity of Kierkegaard's writings is a metaphoric rather than a literal unity; his thought is analogically one rather than univocally one; and his dialectic is a dialectic of images (in the largest critical sense) rather than a dialectic of concepts in the abstract. His argument, therefore, like the argument of the poet, cannot be taken as the ground of a merely theoretic assent. It must be imaginatively re-lived by the reader and, to have its full effect, must be met with a personal response, an existential "reduplication" or an equally existential refusal.

This is what I have tried to show, by the analyses of the first five chapters, and by the conclusions of chapter 6, with respect to the proper reading of Kierkegaard. I am persuaded that the study of Kierkegaard can throw a new light on the meaning of poetry and—in view of his conjunction of "poet and thinker"—on the relationships between poetry and philosophy. It seems to me—and I have tickled this point toward the end of chapter 6—that a "poetic" reading is the best reading of any philosophy that still professes to love wisdom. Philosophers all too typically emphasize the dialectical aspect of their enterprise, at the expense of its rhetorical and poetic dimensions. Philosophy is not only dialectric, producing conviction. It is also rhetorical, aimed at persuading. All actual philosophical discourse is addressed, not to a putative pure rational "anyone," but to a particular "someone" in a particular context. It takes account, as pure dialectic would not, of the diversity of persons and situations: witness Socrates in the dialogues of Plato. Moreover, in order to effect persuasion and conviction, philosophic discourse must first produce understanding, in the sense of imaginative and affective comprehension. This is its poetic aspect. Witness again Plato. In the work of Kierkegaard the dialectic and the rhetoric are united in the service of poetry, as I believe they are in the major philosophical tradition of the West.

Nothing, of course, could be less poetic—nor, I suspect, less philosophical—than those philosophies that prefer the mechanical clatter of logical symbols, the abstemious one-upmanship of language analysis, or the jejune solemnities of the epoché, to the untidy and rather dangerous mysteries of the *philosophia perennis*. But every philosopher worthy of his birthright is also "a kind of poet." So, at least, I believe; and I hope this book will indicate that I believe it with reason. With far greater humility and certainly less irony than Johannes Climacus introducing the *Philosophical Fragments*, I can say of this book that it "does not make the slightest pretension to share in the philosophical movements of the day, or to fill any of the various roles customarily assigned in this connection: transitional, intermediary, final, preparatory, participating, collaborating, volunteer follower, hero, or at any rate relative hero, or at the very least absolute trumpeter." But at the very, very least it is worth while to understand Kierkegaard as he wanted to be understood. And if this has the further effect of broadening and deepening someone's appreciation of the philosophical tradition, that cannot be altogether without value. It has been of value for me, and if it should be of value for someone else—whom "with joy and gratitude" I should certainly call "*my* reader"—then I have my reward.

LOUIS MACKEY, Austin, Texas

KIERKEGAARD:
A kind
of Poet

1
SOME VERSIONS
OF THE AESTHETE:
Either/Or
And Others

Infandum me jubes, Regina, renovare dolorem: these words, which Kierkegaard set as an epigraph over the account of his unhappy betrothal to Regine Olsen, might stand for an epitaph over the man and his work.[1] His entire life was a retelling—to his journals, to himself, to God, and to posterity—of a grief inexpressibly out of proportion to the events that occasioned it. The public circumstances of Kierkegaard's life were inconsiderable: a troubled devotion to his father, a broken engagement, a squabble with a tabloid paper, and a flurry of pamphlets flung at a Church so secure in its Establishment that it scarcely stirred itself to reprove him. Yet at the bidding of these—an old man confused by guilt, a guileless girl half in love and half mesmerized, a brightly irresponsible journalist, and a pair of comfortable bishops—he renewed daily the anguished self-examination that was his real life. This self-scrutiny appears poetically transformed in the fourteen volumes of his published writings, and lies pathetically naked before the reader of the eighteen volumes of his journals.

Kierkegaard's life was spent "in the service of the Idea."

1

Whatever befell him was reflected and doubly reflected, translated almost before it happened from experience into idea. His every overt action—and they are few—had been so prepared and doubly prepared in advance that the actual performance was but a tired epilogue to the exhausting ideational drama. In his youth he was told by one of his professors that he was "completely polemical"; in the year before his death he was still shining this remark into the dark corners of his personality, looking for the goblins. His assault on the Danish Church had deployed inwardly through persecution and martyrdom before he ever uttered a critical word; when he did finally "speak out," the proper episcopal indignation he aroused could not begin to measure up to the epic crucifixion projected in his journals.[2]

He was, as he himself might have said, infinitely dialectical. Things that move ordinary men to a simple readjustment of their circumstances necessitated in Kierkegaard a total upheaval of the personality. Every event, every action or passion, every concern, required a recasting *de novo* of his image of himself. The result was that these same events, actions, passions and concerns, given absolute significance as ideal possibilities, lost all meaning as realities.

For this reason, the substance of his life was a pervasive melancholy formed in the crucible in which he transmuted all experience into reflection. Living as he did in possibility, out beyond the real, there was no one to whom he could express that unutterable grief, the being of which nonetheless was its own everlasting reiteration. He could find no contemporaries, because he was in truth a man without a present. His life was essentially over and done with before it had begun: in the midst of life he was as one already dead. *"Periissem nisi periissem,"* he wrote, "is and always will be the motto of my life. Therefore I have been able to endure what would long ago have killed another who was not already dead."[3]

It is understandable that this motif should thread through his writings. Kierkegaard's melancholy produced and reproduced itself by a kind of superfetation of the spirit; by its own dialectic it destroyed the innocence it mourned and made impossible the "repetition" it yearned for. Virginity, of the spirit as of the flesh, is never loved until it is lost, and by then it cannot—short of a miracle—be restored. So Kierkegaard's "spheres of existence" are determined by the round of recollections, pains, and longings that articulate his inner life.

Periissem nisi periissem is the motto affixed to Quidam's diary ("Guilty?/Not Guilty?") in *Stages on Life's Way.* The anonymous author of "The Unhappiest Man" and other essays in the first volume of *Either/Or* belongs to a nocturnal society lugubriously and synthetically named *symparanekromenoi,* "the fellowship of the deceased." All of Kierkegaard's writings lament an immediacy hopelessly lost in reflection, a youth-that-never-was recollected in the impuissance of eternal old age. His vision of Christian consummation is a miraculous and elusive *redintegratio in statum pristinum,* a new immediacy, a contemporaneity with self possible only by virtue of the absurd. Between paradise lost and paradise regained he pitches an ethical struggle to fuse the actual and the ideal, a struggle whose desperate issue is the everlasting recollection of guilt. [4]

Immediacy—never possessed but always forfeit, vainly sought and paradoxically bestowed—is the *cantus firmus* about which the polyphonic Kierkegaardian literature shapes its varied and often dissonant counterpoint. In order to hear the strange music ringing from this Phalarian bull, [5] it is necessary to attune oneself first of all to Kierkegaard's understanding of immediacy.

The word "immediacy" itself is a bit of jargon that Kierkegaard picked up from Hegel and the Hegelians. It would be tedious and pointless to pursue the technical meaning of this term in Hegel's system, but it is important to get the general sense of the word as a way into Kierkegaard's mind. It is common to equate *immediate* experience with *direct* experience, experience as it is *simply given* and *simply had* before the onset of reflection. Sensation and feeling are immediate as opposed to thought; first impressions are immediate as opposed to second guesses; life as it is before it doubles back on itself in the "mediation" of self-consciousness is "immediate existence." If nature be opposed to the reflexive operations of freedom, then a man's immediacy is what he is "by nature."

Traditionally "aesthetic" has come to mean "pertaining to beauty and the fine arts," but in Kierkegaard it retains its etymological sense of *aisthesis,* "sense perception." He defines what he calls the "aesthetic"—as a dimension of existence and as

3

an overall design for living—by means of the immediate. "The aesthetic in a man is that by which he immediately is what he is."[6] If we could discover what human nature is, then we could catch ourselves in our immediacy, and we would understand what Kierkegaard means by the aesthetic.

But the difficulty with immediacy (remember Kierkegaard's own case) is that it never *is* where it is asked about. Asking about immediacy is already an act of reflection once removed from the immediate. Just as a man cannot look himself straight in the eye, so immediacy cannot be got at directly (immediately); it can only be divined as the prelapsarian origin mirrored but never substantially present in every condition of self-awareness. This alienation of the self from its immediacy infects the philosophical attempt to comprehend human nature categorially, but it is more arresting in the case of the man who tries to *be* his immediacy.

Kierkegaard's "A" is such a man. The anonymous dilettante whose dilations fill *Either/Or* I, A is offered as a representative aesthetic personality. In view of the identity of the aesthetic with the immediate, one might expect him to be a sensual man, a man whose overriding aim is the direct satisfaction of his native wants. It is true that he lives for pleasure. And yet he is canny enough to know that no human life is lived on the strength of impulse alone. No man can turn and live with animals, for the turning would imply a prior disengagement from the unconscious mass of beasthood. The placid and self-contained innocence of the brute is a dream of the poet, not the situation of man. True to the paradox of immediacy (that it never is where it is sought), desire and gratification are presented not as A's life but as the chief *preoccupation* of his life.

A is a perfervid admirer of Mozart's *Don Juan*. In his essay "The Immediate Stages of the Erotic or the Musical Erotic" he praises Mozart's opera as a perfect work of art, "classic and immortal," on the grounds that it realizes a total fusion of form and content. In *Don Juan*, as A hears it, the musical form is so happily and inseparably wedded to the passional content that together they body forth sexual desire in its immediacy. Don Juan's sensuality is pure undifferentiated desire. He craves *woman*, wholesale and without discrimination of age or beauty: *purchè porti la gonella, voi sapete quel chè fà*. His passion is a "force of nature," unriven by reflection and undisturbed by moral misgivings. Mozart's music is the artistic analogue of this passion, an aural energy not yet articulated into the intelligible forms of speech. There are words, of course, but their very absurdity ("one thousand and three in Spain . . .") negates their significance as language and hurls them back into the floodtide of sound.[7]

A thinks it appropriate that the legendary figure of Don Juan issues from that medieval Venusberg where thought and speech had no home. For he is not, like the Greek Eros, a tutelary spirit who prospers the amours of others but is not himself in love. Nor is he, like his counterpart Faust, a highly individualized intellectual doubter of demonic proportions who seduces one maiden and despairs. He is the type of sensuality *an sich*, paradoxically chartered as an independent and sovereign power by the attempt of early Christianity to banish it from the realm of spirit. While Faust is properly portrayed on the tragic stage, Don Juan, A believes, is the natural subject of music, and of comic opera in particular. The vitality without individuation of Don Juan corresponds exactly to the form without intellectual content which is the essence of Mozart's musical expression. In Mozart's opera A finds *immediacy immediately presented*, the content of immediacy interfusing and interfused by immediate form. In this exquisite alchemy art (reflection) *is* nature (the immediate).

Yet there is ambiguity in this achievement. *Don Juan* is after all *art*. One must go to art if he wants to find the immediate given in its immediacy. Don Juan could never happen in real life: one thousand and three in Spain! Global sexuality is a fictive biology of the heroes of imagination. Pure immediacy cannot be experienced as the content of an actual life; it can only be savored as fantasy.

This contradiction is implicitly recognized in A's analysis of *Don Juan*. He is fascinated by the Don because he is a pure type, and by the opera because it is the pure presentation of a pure type. Mozart's masterpiece is the embodiment of the most abstract idea (sensuality) in the most abstract medium (music). Sensuality is "abstraction" because, as immediate, it is not yet parcelled out into specific preferences for discreet objects (*purchè porti la gonella . . .*), and not yet constrained by moral necessity to accept the discipline of a part within an ordered whole. Sensuality *simpliciter* is only the abstract dynamic, the "exuberant joy," of life. Music is similarly abstract. Language—naming, defining, judging, and discoursing—is the spirit's vehicle for the tenor of the concrete. Music with its moving and interacting tonal patterns mimics the syntactic form of language but altogether lacks its semantic commitment: it is the abstract dynamic of spirit without the content of spirit. [8] By A's logic of inversion, that which appears to be most concrete—sensuality and its expression—evaporates into the airiest of abstractions.

It is this logic that prompts A's genuflection in the presence of pure types purely enshrined in a pure medium. Men often voice a vague desire to enjoy life in all its forms and to experience everything. They are only saying in their cruder way what A says with superior consistency: "I want to *be life*, not this life or that life, but *all* life, indeed vitality itself." But Kierkegaard's paradigmatic aesthete is also disenchanted by superior wisdom: he knows that this desire is unattainable. Too sophisticated to be a sensualist himself, he is reconciled to *admiring*, in its artful and only possible realization, that perfection which he cannot *be*. The man who endeavors to live wholly out of nature, the man who wishes to be only what he immediately is, will, if he is honest, be driven by the logic of immediacy to the antithesis of immediacy: bootless enthusiasm for a beautiful but impossible ideal. The internal nexus joining "aesthetic" in its etymological sense to "aesthetic" in its traditional connotation is hereby exposed: art is the transfiguration of nature by self-consciousness.

But A is not done yet. He is too thorough a dialectician and too determined an aesthete to repose in admiration at the expense of enjoyment. If he cannot make immediacy his life, he will make life itself an art. This reversal takes place already in the essay on *Don Juan.* No sooner has A declared the essential abstractness of the opera and its theme than he turns around to deliver an encomium of the infinite richness of every work of art. In a passage reminiscent of Kant's doctrine of Aesthetical Ideas, he speculates: *because* the unity of form and content in a consummate work of art precludes any *definitive* critical analysis, the work is an inexhaustible vein from which infinite reflections can be mined. No understanding of the work is ever final, therefore the possibilities for understanding it are infinite. A's rationale is quasi-Hegelian: because it is wholly abstract, immediacy is fecund with every possible concretion. That which lacks all determinacy is receptive to any and every determination. For if the most concrete, by reason of its density, is the most abstract, then the most abstract, by reason of its emptiness, is potentially the most concrete.

This turn in his theory of art offers A a way out of his personal impasse. The aesthete (etymological sense) wants pleasures; the aesthete (traditional connotation), knowing that he cannot have his pleasures by instinct, seeks to contrive them by craft. His immediacy becomes the infinitely pliable medium in which he fabricates his delights. He cannot attain to the condition of nature; he will therefore aspire to the condition of art. A's *diapsalmata* or "refrains," and his paper on "The Rotation Method" are ventures in the art of living. [9] The aphorisms, directed *ad se ipsum*, are the fruits in his own person of the counsel advanced in his "essay in the theory of social prudence."

The burden of A's moods is clearly heard in these typical *diapsalmata:*

I do not care for anything. I do not care to ride, for the exercise is too violent. I do not care to walk, walking is too strenuous. I do not care to lie down, for I should either have to remain lying, and I do not care to do that, or I should have to get up again, and I do not care to do that either. *Summa summarum:* I do not care at all.

Let others complain that the age is wicked; my complaint is that it is paltry; for it lacks passion. Men's thoughts are thin and flimsy like lace, they are themselves pitiable like the lacemakers. The thoughts of their hearts are too paltry to be sinful. For a worm it might be regarded as a sin to harbor such thoughts, but not for a being made in the image of God. Their lusts are dull and sluggish, their passions sleepy. They do their duty, these shop-keeping souls, but they clip the coin a trifle, like the Jews; they think that even if the Lord keeps ever so careful a set of books, they may still cheat Him a little. Out upon them! This is the reason my soul always turns back to the Old Testament and to Shakespeare. I feel that those who speak there are at least human beings: they hate, they love, they murder their enemies, and curse their descendants throughout all generations, they sin.

The essence of pleasure does not lie in the thing enjoyed, but in the accompanying consciousness. If I had a humble spirit in my service who, when I asked for a glass of water, brought me the

7

world's costliest wines blended in a chalice, I should dismiss him, in order to teach him that pleasure consists not in what I enjoy, but in having my own way.

The last of these is the root and reconciliation of the first two. Prerequisite for the practice of any art is the absolute freedom of the artist. What the aesthete is after—the condition of all subsequent pleasure—is "having his own way." On the one hand, then, he does not care to do anything; for anything he does puts him under the compulsion to do something else. At the same time he despises the paltry caution that shortchanges its vices for the sake of higgled virtues; to balk at *les grandes passions* is to stop short of a full realization of one's possibilities. It is necessary both to enjoy everything and to care about nothing. The essence of freedom, aesthetically conceived, is to enjoy having one's own way, or by simple substitution, enjoying oneself enjoying oneself. Desire and enjoyment are only free if they are indifferent to what is desired and enjoyed. One must want without needing and enjoy without being gratified.

The aesthete's attitude toward the passions and their ambiguity is epitomized by the mottos prefixed to various parts of the first volume of *Either/Or*. On the title page of the volume the editor of A's papers, Victor Eremita, remarks the question of the English poet:

> Are passions, then, the pagans of the soul?
> Reason alone baptized?

A's own choice of mottos betrays his answer. At the head of his *Diapsalmata* he sets the words:

> Grandeur, savoir, renommée,
> Amitié, plaisir et bien,
> Tout n'est que vent, que fumée:
> Pour mieux dire, tout n'est rien.

"Shadowgraphs," A's lecture on notable deceived women of literature, is delivered under German auspices:

> Abgeschworen mag die Liebe immer sein;
> Liebes-Zauber wiegt in dieser Hohle
> Die berauschte, überraschte Seele
> In Vergessenheit des Schwures ein.

* * *

8

Gestern liebt' ich,
Heute leid' ich,
Morgen sterb' ich;
Dennoch denk' ich
Heut' und Morgen
Gern an Gestern.

Paralyzed disillusionment and intoxicated involvement are the poles of A's passional life. The tactic by which he arbitrates their conflict is a step backward into the provisional detachment of bliss remembered and doom disdained.

In an "ecstatic lecture" A defines the "sum and substance of all philosophy" by a series of monotonous dilemmas: if you marry, you will regret it, and if you do not marry, you will regret that; if you trust a woman, you will regret it, and if you do not trust a woman, you will regret that; hang yourself and you will regret that, don't hang yourself and you will likewise regret that, *ad infinitum*. Either/or: for any x, either you do x or you do not do x, and in any case you will be sorry. Therefore—and this is the wisdom by which A consoles himself—: neither/nor. Every decision and every action entail regret for the alternate possibility concurrently and irrevocably renounced. Therefore, one should so live *aeterno modo* that he abrogates the law of contradiction in advance by—doing nothing. No decisions, no regrets; no actions, no consequences. The path to free self-enjoyment is the way of *dolce far niente*. [10]

But the sweet life of aesthetic indolence calls for the most delicate management. One cannot, for example, *resolutely* do nothing and survive the resolution unscathed. To do nothing in an affirmative way is just as constraining as doing something: if you do something, you will regret it, and if you do nothing, you will regret that. Strictly speaking, one should not even do nothing. But this is also, strictly speaking, impossible: like it or not, one will either ride or walk, lie down or stand up. Some practical expedients are required.

One course that recommends itself is romantic frenzy: let yourself go. Since it is really a matter of indifference what a man does, then anything he goes at is fine and beautiful if he does it with total abandon. But the romantic is a very poor counsellor. Wiser by an eternity, A knows that if he lets himself go, he will *certainly regret that*. The secret of enjoyment is neither to do nothing nor to do anything with all one's might. The secret is to do *everything* in such a way that one rigorously *avoids all commitments.* The art of living is neither an impossible self-denial nor a prodigal self-squandering, but the most fastidious self-discipline.

Self-discipline as a technique for maximizing pleasure and minimizing boredom: this is the prescription of A's disquisition on the rotation-method. The artful hedonist rotates his pleasures as the farmer rotates his crops. To this end he must be prepared to allow any or all of his desires to lie fallow at any time. The first precept of this strangely skewed ascesis is the counsel of despair: *nil admirari.* "It is impossible to live artistically before one has made up one's mind to abandon hope; for hope precludes self-limitation." Hope exposes the hopeful to the possibility of frustration; therefore walk circumspectly that you may forget the unsettling at will and redeem the tedious with recollection. The art of recollection—the imaginative revision of a delightful past—and the art of forgetting—the sidestep by which one diverts himself from the path of a disgruntling present—together compose the dear desperation that shields the aesthete forever *(aeterno modo)* from the threat of the future.

> One who has perfected himself in the twin arts of recollecting and forgetting is in a position to play at battledore and shuttlecock with the whole of existence. . . . The art of recollecting and forgetting will also insure against sticking fast in some relationship of life, and make possible the realization of a complete freedom.

From this synderesis follow the particular maxims of aesthetic praxis: take fullest advantage of people, but beware the obligations of friendship; enjoy love, but shun marriage; cultivate the arts, but see that you reap no profit therefrom. Whatever the situation, stay in control. Now there is only one way a man can stay in control of every situation, and that is by first assuming complete control of himself. He cannot produce at will the events and environs of his life; he cannot even create his own moods. But he can determine the *meaning* these circumstances will have for him by the practice of systematic *arbitrariness.* [11] Suppose, for example, he goes to church (no experienced aesthete would neglect the charming possibilities offered by the practice of religion): he will so attend to the sermon that he refuses the pastoral edification in order to beatify himself with

10

observations of the pastoral Adam's apple. In an erotic *pas de deux* he will be the curious *voyeur* of his own athletic love-making.

An example of A's literary employment of the method of arbitrariness is his unpublished review of Augustin Scribe's one-act play, *Les premiers amours.* Commentators have several times noted that Scribe's farce is unworthy of the attention—not to mention the pages!—that "Kierkegaard" has lavished on it. [12] But it is a product of *A*'s ingenuity, and a typical product at that. He knows that the play is trivial, and reviews it for precisely that reason. Otherwise wholly nugatory, the little comedy serves as an occasion on which A can display to himself his own poetic cleverness—and revel in the conceit of doing something worthless in the most exquisite style. By seizing the occasion—*any* occasion—and turning it to capricious ends, he makes and unmakes his situation as it pleases him. He is at once the donor and the recipient of his delights. By his hopeless withdrawal from immediacy he perfects his freedom; by his arbitrary return to immediacy he keeps his independence and simultaneously gives his life content. The varied round of pleasures is enabled by the larger "rotation method," the dialectical circle of withdrawal and return.

Thus the pattern of A's life duplicates the structure of *Don Juan.* As in the aesthetic unity of the opera the most vacuous abstraction is by implication the most teeming concretion, so in the aesthetic unity of A's existence the kenosis implied in his *nil admirari* is the emancipation by which he releases himself for the arbitrary pursuit of every pleasure. The practical dilemma of the hedonist is resolved in the light of the art theorist's analysis of immediacy. However circuitous the route, A comes at last to the land of heart's desire.

Yet the solution is suspect, if for no other reason then at least because it does not match A's character as this is delineated in *Either/Or* I. In spite of his asseverations in "The Rotation Method," his life is no carrousel of joys; he is not just an exceptionally refined playboy. The discussion so far, intent on the rationale by which A orders and justifies his life, has overlooked several important aspects of the life itself. It has slighted, for example, the heavy sadness that palls the *diapsalmata,* and the fascination with death and dereliction in essays like "Shadowgraphs," "The Ancient Tragical Motif as Reflected in the Modern," and "The Unhappiest Man." In particular it has said nothing of A's membership in the *symparanekromenoi*, the "fellowship of the deceased." These are strange themes and strange predilections for a hedonist, and yet they follow irresistibly from the aesthetic presupposition that life consists in enjoyment: "There are well-known insects which die in the moment of fecundation. So it is with all joy; life's supreme and richest moment of pleasure is coupled with death." The familiar connection between sexual consummation and death—a standard pun in the English of the sixteenth and seventeenth centuries—is the more obvious consequence of a less obvious but more intimate and fundamental conjunction of death and delight.

"Death," says A, addressing the *symparanekromenoi*, "is for us the greatest happiness." In his lecture on "The Ancient Tragical Motif," subtitled "an essay in the fragmentary," he outlines the metaphysical and artistic tenets held by the brotherhood of defunct men. Reality, in their view, is a show of accidental events, of which the only thing one can confidently say is: it passes. Reality is essentially *pastness.* But it is a pastness without finality or fulfilment: reality is as desultory as it is fleeting. That which is past without being perfected is dead. Reality aesthetically conceived is death. [13]

Significantly this "fellowship of buried lives," as one commentator has called it, holds it meetings on Friday evening, the memorial of the Passion of Christ and the traditional time for the weekly celebration of Holy Communion in the Danish Church. They celebrate instead the descent of darkness, and at the end of the longest day of the year hold festivities to herald "the approaching victory of night." As their most fervent longing is for death, the beatific blindness to being, so A apostrophizes for them the temporary surcease offered by night:

> In this toast I hail thee, silent Night, eternal mother from whom all things are! From thee they come, to thee they return. Again have mercy upon the world, open thine arms wide to receive all things in thy embrace, and hide us safe in thy bosom! Dark Night, I hail thee, I hail thee victor! And this is my solace, for thou dost shorten all things: day and time and troublesome memory in an eternal forgetfulness!

Theory of art follows ontology. The literati of the *symparanekromenoi* are dedicated to the production of works marked by a "gleaming transitoriness." Their essays are "anacoluthic," "fragmentary pursuits;" or as A finally sums it up, "Let us then describe our purpose as an attempt . . . in the art of writing posthumous papers." Since for these aesthetes art is not distinct from life, their art of living is an imaginative dying before their death. The fellowship of the deceased are those who have chosen death as a way of life. In keeping with their one and only passion, a sympathetic dread that searches out the secrets of sorrow, and in execution of their choice, which is to "love only grief," the members of the *symparanekromenoi* listen enrapt to A's "enthusiastic address" on the question, Who is the unhappiest man in the world? "The unhappiest man," he tells them, is the man who absents himself from experience, whose hope and whose memory are equally vain, because his future is already past in anticipation and his past forever imminent in recollection. A man without a present, his life a possibility never tried and never to be overtaken, but ever cherished, he is embalmed before his birth. "But what do I say: the unhappiest, the happiest I ought to say, for this is indeed a gift of the gods which no one can give himself." [14]

The unhappiest man's anticipation—by which he neutralizes his future in advance—and his recollection—by which he improves his past after the fact—are identical. They come to the same thing as A's *nil admirari*—a total *dégagement* from the pressure of immediate existence—and are sometimes covered by the single term "recollection." Commenting on A's belief that "the love of recollection is the only happy love," the author of *Repetition* remarks, "In that he is perfectly right, too—if one will only remember that it first makes a man unhappy." As he explains a few pages later, "Recollection has the great advantage that it begins with the loss, hence it is secure, for it has nothing to lose." The "young man" of *Repetition*, confidant of the author, is a case in point. Newly enamored of a willing maiden, he does not press the point of his love but chooses rather to pace the floor and repeat the words of Poul Møller's "Aged Lover:"

> From the spring-time of my youth there comes a dream
>> To my easy chair,
> And I feel an ardent longing for thee,
>> Thou sun among women.

By imagining himself old enough to recollect his love, the youth loses his girl but raises his experience to the "second power." [15]

Only the man who is dead to reality is eternally secure in the possession of imaginative bliss. Only that which is irrevocably lost may safely be enjoyed. The unhappiest man, and paradoxically the happiest, the man whose life is death, is the aesthete himself. Whence the *symparanekromenoi,* for whom death is the greatest happiness.

The paradox is illumined by a recapitulation of the aesthetic project and its execution. The aesthete wants enjoyment, but enjoyment cannot simply be had, it must be arranged. Life must be made an art, but the art of living requires a total detachment from everything merely given and possibly unpleasant, as well as a disinterested arbitrariness in the concoction of actual pleasures. The perennial threat to this insouciance is misfortune, and the supreme misfortune is death. Fate, in its double role of chance and necessity, and especially death, inevitable in its outcome but inconstant in its choice of time and place and manner, seem to constitute the absolute frustration of aesthetic freedom. The one gift that cannot be refused is death. Suicide will not work: its apparent defiance is really capitulation. The aesthete could not consistently kill himself unless he could survive to enjoy the event. More than that: his pride would not permit him thus vulgarly to snatch at this most sublime *piéce de resistance* of destiny.

Two consequences follow: first, the aesthete worships fate. In the *ultimatum* of death it sets the outer limit to his *nil admirari* and his caprice; it is the one power he cannot transcend or overwhelm. A's devotion to tragic literature is the offering he lays on the altar of his god. But (and this is the second consequence) the tragic corpus itself is the divine liturgy in which death is transubstantiated to art. In the celebration of this liturgy the aesthete receives the bread and wine of his own communion with life. The holy mystery of aestheticism is that everything—even misfortune and death—can be enjoyed. "Pleasure disappoints, possibility never." In possibility, Kierkegaard liked to say, everything is possible. In the grace of this possibility the aesthete consumes his god and enters into his beatitude. [16]

But it must not be forgotten that this is a black mass. The aesthete's communion is a foretaste of death. His beatitude—prefigured already in his initial retreat from life and now perfected in his tragic necrolatry—is *melancholy.* Melancholy is the ultimate and only consistent form of aesthetic enjoyment. The artful life is the life of imagination, and "imagination as such always makes melancholy." [17] Over the entrance to the aesthetic life burn the prophetic words: *lasciate ogni speranza, voi ch 'entrate.* [18] The art of living is the art of enjoying despair. It is not surprising, then, to find among A's aphorisms passages like these:

> In addition to the rest of the numerous circle of my acquaintances, I still have one intimate confidant—my melancholy. In the midst of my job, in the midst of my work, she beckons to me and calls me aside, even though physically I do not budge. My melancholy is the most faithful mistress I have known; what wonder, then, that I love in return.

> I say of my sorrow what the Englishman says of his house: my sorrow is my castle.

> My life is like an eternal night; when at last I die, then I can say with Achilles:
> *Du bist vollbracht, Nachtwache meines Daseyns.* [19]

Not the slightest statue but requires for its beauty the scarring of a mountain; what wonder that the art of life demands the forsaking of a world. Not *Weltschmerz* but a *schmerzliche Weltlosigkeit*, not world-weariness but a weary worldlessness, are the melancholy outcome of A's assault on immediacy.

But if the prospect is dreary, the achievement is magnificent. A is unequivocally intent on living aesthetically, and he accepts the consequences of his project with matchless consistency. To say that he is effete is no refutation: he embraces vanity with the enthusiasm of despair. To complain that he is gloomy is beside the point: he savors the wormwood and the gall with bittersweet relish. Seen from inside his skin, any protest against his way of life—in the interests of sanity, sound sense, morals, or piety—is bound to seem philistine. He is, to give him his proper name, the *poet* par excellence. His medium is not words, but himself: he is the living *poiesis,* the root and branch of which all merely verbal making is but the flower.

Unlike Don Juan, who must vanish when the house lights go up, A might really exist, does in fact exist as the father of us all. Like most men most of the time and all men some of the time, he seeks (but with exemplary single-mindedness) the

15

richest satisfaction of desire compatible with the widest exercise of freedom. That this involves him in paradox is a fact he sees and welcomes, because he is more honest and more thorough than the rest of us. His life is the indefatigable process of reconciling its own contradictions. Each stage of the Hegelian dialectic is driven by its inner contradictions into another and higher stage. In the Kierkegaardian dialectic, each of the "stages on life's way" *contains* its contradictions—is, in fact, the *project* of so containing them. While the typical Hegelian protagonist is the abstraction of an abstraction *(Herrschaft* and *Knechtschaft)*, the Kierkegaardian "existence-spheres" come to focus in *dramatis personae* who struggle to assimilate their problems into the abiding integrity of their individual personalities.

The poet is Kierkegaard's usual paradigm for the aesthetic life, the specimen according to which all the other versions of the aesthete are declined. Appropriately *Either/Or* begins with a despairing definition of the poet: "An unhappy man who in his heart harbors a deep anguish, but whose lips are so fashioned that the moans and cries which pass over them are transformed into ravishing music."[20] Like the victim roasted in Phalaris' bull, the poet is caught in the collision of his inner wretchedness with the splendor of its outward expression. His life is a thing of beauty and a joy forever, but the price he pays for this excellence is a hollow melancholy at his life's core. This pattern of the aesthetic character is repeated again and again in Kierkegaard, for the aesthete who appears as poet in *Either/Or* shows up in different costumes in Kierkegaard's other works. His guises are many, but the form beneath them is the same. In particular it is worth while to note two of his chief epiphanies: the *lover of recollection,* and the *experimental psychologist* or *observer.*

That A is a lover of recollection is already clear, but the most explicit champion of the art—its theorist, so to speak—is William Afham of the *Stages on Life's Way.* The *Stages* consists of three parts, standing respectively for the aesthetic, ethical and religious existence-spheres: *In Vino Veritas,* an account of a banquet adorned with speeches on woman by the symposiasts; a polemic against the enemies of marriage, by a husband; and *Guilty?/Not Guilty? A Passion Narrative,* the diary record of an unhappy love affair. *In Vino Veritas* is subtitled "a recollection, subsequently related by William Afham." William's prefatory

16

note (*Forerindring* = literally "prerecollection") is an essay on the significance of the recollective power.

The essay begins by distinguishing the power of recollection *(Erindring)* from that of memory *(Hukommelse)*. One may, William says, remember something with great accuracy without recollecting it. Memory is only the minimal condition of recollection, by means of which "the experience presents itself to receive the consecration of recollection." If memory is the power of bringing the past back into the present, then recollection "consists in removing, putting at a distance" that which is recalled. The distance achieved by recollection is the distance of ideality, for whereas memory is the immediate recoil of the then upon the now, recollection is the reflective reinterpretation of that immediacy.

By means of the ideality of recollection, William hopes to achieve the kind of aesthetic immortality to which A also aspires. "Recollection seeks to assert man's eternal continuity in life and to insure that his earthly existence shall be *uno tenore. . . .*" For recollection effects a purification of what is recollected in accordance with the recollector's "Idea" of himself and his life:

> Properly speaking, only the essential is the object of recollection . . . . The essential is not simply essential in itself, but it is such by reason of the relation it has to the person concerned. He who has broken with the idea cannot act essentially, cannot undertake anything essential. . . .

To "live for an Idea" which one has given oneself is— essentially!—to sever all communication with ordinary men. The words of Ovid—*bene vixit qui bene latuit*— are a maxim for the recollecting aesthete, so that, as William astutely perceives, "every recollection is a secret." Thus he says apropos of his choosing a secluded sylvan glade as the locale in which to recollect the banquet,

> Certain it is too that the world and all that therein is never appears to better advantage than when it is seen from a nook and one must take a look at it by stealth; certain it is too that all one hears in the world or is able to hear sounds most enchanting and delicious when heard from a nook where one gives ear to it by stealth. [21]

All the aesthetic categories cluster around the concept of recollection:

17

As the labor of recollection is always blessed, so it has this blessing as well, that it becomes itself a new recollection, which in turn enthralls. For he who has once understood what recollection is is captivated for all eternities, and is captivated in that very moment. And he who owns one recollection is richer than if he possessed the whole world. Not only the expectant mother, but above all the recollector, is in the family way. [22]

The Danish idiom for "in the family way" is *i velsignede Omstaendigheder,* which literally means "in blessed circumstances." But William is not merely punning. The woman with child is a symbol for the fecundity of recollection by which the aesthete is everlastingly ("for all eternities") and blessedly possessed. The proprietor of a single recollection, like the wife of a devoted and insistent husband, is repeatedly fruitful. His labors, like hers, produce riches unmatched by any worldly affluence, for they are the fruit of his fancy's womb.

In a word, the recollective power is the poetic power, and William Afham, the lover of recollection, is one at heart with A, the aboriginal poet. His emotion recollected in the tranquillity of a forest nook is A's reflective enjoyment sequestered in the hermitage of despair. William himself allows that "it is an art to recollect" and later adds that "the ability to recollect is the condition of all productivity." Of his own recollection of the banquet he says, "I sometimes feel as though I had not experienced it, but had poetically invented it." That he did invent it *(digte)* it is further suggested by his name, for *Af ham* in Danish simply means "by him." The aesthetic reader would also attend to the hint from Lichtenberg printed on the obverse of William's title: *Solche Werke sind Spiegel: wenn ein Affe hinein guckt, kann kein Apostel heraus sehen.* [23] He would take from this clue the knowledge that the essential meaning of this latter-day *Symposium* is the meaning he poetically invents in his own recollection of William's narrative—that meaning of which every reader can justly say that it is "by him." *In vino puerisque veritas:* in the heady wine of imagination and in the poetic offspring begotten in the intoxicated ardor of recollection is latent the truth of the aesthetic way of life.

Like the lover of recollection, the *observer* is also a figure of the poet. Kierkegaard liked to think of himself as a spy in the service of God. His pseudonym, Constantine Constantius, spies on the human race—though not precisely on God's behalf—in his book *Repetition.* He describes his book as "an essay in experimental psychology" and so identifies himself as an experimental psychologist. As confidant of the "young man" of the book his function is to observe the behavior of his subject in various situations—some of them situations he has himself contrived—in order to enrich his speculative enjoyment of human nature thereby.

At first glance Constantine's kinship with A is not obvious. He takes A to task for his view that the love of recollection is the only happy love, and in the opening pages of his book retails the praises of repetition in opposition to hope and recollection. Hope is a garment stiff and untried, recollection a garment outgrown and discarded, but repetition is a comfortable and imperishable garment; hope is a lovely but elusive maiden, recollection a beautiful but exhausted old woman, but repetition is a faithful and unaging wife; hope is an alluring fruit which does not satisfy, recollection a pittance which does not satisfy, but repetition is the bread that satisfies with blessing; and so on. Yet the difference between A and Constantine Constantius is not as great as it seems. For A, though he says that the love of recollection is the only happy love, knows what Constantine knows: that the joy of recollection is a melancholy joy. And Constantine, though he affirms that repetition "is reality, and . . . the seriousness of life," a manly way of life in opposition to the cowardice of hope and the *luxuria* of recollection, is not himself a practicer of repetitions. Disillusioned by a vain attempt to repeat his own remembered delights—he is an aesthete, and it is the repetition of *pleasures* he seeks for himself—he has abandoned every hope of recreating the joys of the past. His life at the time of the novel is a retreat into the eternity of recollection in spite of his theoretical misgivings. Saddened by his experience, he has become a wistful, somewhat whimsical observer of life, an "experimental psychologist."

The young subject of Constantine's experiment has, when the reader and Constantine first meet him, fallen in love with a girl who returns his love. But because of his melancholy temperament—Constantine calls him "the woeful knight of the only happy love of recollection"—he cannot marry her; nor does he dare to initiate her into the secret of his melancholy. He has not the heart for Constantine's proposal: to trick the girl into thinking him a faithless scoundrel, so that she will detach herself

19

of her own accord. In spite of his love for her he is forced to break off relations, and so becomes the unwilling agent of her unhappiness. His problem then defines itself in terms of "repetition:" How can he free himself of guilt and if possible assuage the misery of his beloved? Can he effect a *redintegratio in statum pristinum?* He very nearly receives a religious answer to his question by a study of the trials of Job. But at the crucial moment, his desolate beloved consummates a happy marriage with another man and by her "magnanimity"—a theme on which the bitter youth plays the most dissonant variations—he is released from his responsibility. Released, however, into the service of the Idea; so that he who would not be a deceiver, could not be a husband, and narrowly missed being a man of faith, becomes at last a poet through the exhilirating emancipation of disillusionment. There is a patent likeness between this young lover, who is made a poet by the magnanimity of woman after an infatuation with the constancy of Job, and the archpoet A, who understands the consolations of religion and refuses them out of fidelity to his Idea of "the unhappiest man." Perhaps here as elsewhere the child is father of the man: the young man of *Repetition* is seen at the moment when he first enters into that tragic stasis in which A is eternally caught and fixed.

The character of Constantine Constantius, consonant with that of A and the young man, is more sharply delineated in the light of his relations with the latter. He is at first attracted to the youth by his natural charm, and then drawn into greater intimacy with him by sympathy with the sufferings of unhappy love. Soon, however, his theoretical propensity asserts itself: "Great God! thought I, such a melancholy has never before presented itself in my practice." Before long, "against his will," he begins "to behave toward him as an observer." Not that he is cold and indifferent to his subject: "I really suffered a great deal on account of the young man, who was fading away daily." At one point in their association he reports that he was disarmed of his detachment, too moved by the young man's passion to make observations. But he has a significant motive for sharing the young man's grief: "And yet I did not in the least regret participating in his sufferings, for in his love at least *the idea* was stirring." Constantine's commitment to the Idea is elaborated in his divagations on the theater, which he regards as a panoramic

20

display of human possibilities that pleasures the observer without demanding of him any personal involvement in their ephemeral shadow-play. He is particularly fascinated by the farce, the form of comedy which conjoins the generic and the accidental in a way that entrances the imagination but does not satisfy the intellect nor engage the will. [24]

His attitude toward woman—a theatrical attitude that combines imaginative fellow-feeling with scientific objectivity—focuses Constantine's theory and practice of observation. Woman, he believes, though she may be loved for her beauty, must always be treated in a spirit of jest. For in spite of the allure of individual women, woman as such represents the accidental in human nature as compared with man, who embodies the essential. [25] His relations with women are true to this form. A strange girl whom he meets in the country requests a ride in his coach. She gets her ride, and on the way Constantine enjoys the thought of the intriguing possibilities of such an encounter; in fact he had been on the verge of approaching her with such intrigues in mind before she begged a seat in his carriage. But in the end she is delivered intact to her home, while Constantine takes the precaution of leaving the coach two miles out of Copenhagen and walking to his own house—in order that his companion may not be made the subject of unpleasant rumors. In the theater he admires a pretty maiden in the box opposite his own; but he does not address her, for he would not embarrass her innocence with the intrusion of even his purest thoughts. He drives long miles through sleepless nights to content his insomniac soul with the sight—and no more—of the nocturnal walks of a handsome peasant lass. He is attentive to—and savors—all the moods and forms of woman, from unconscious innocence, through healthy natural openness, to the most urbane versions of worldly experience. But touch them he will not. The one ostensible exception to this rule turns out to be another instance of it on closer inspection. By way of facilitating his young friend's exit from his love affair, Constantine engages the services of a moderately good-looking seamstress. She is to take up residence in an apartment he has rented; the young man is to enter her front door and leave privily by the back door every night for a year. The youth will acquire a reputation for immorality which will persuade his beloved, who will then discard him. The plan does not appeal to the young man, and it never comes off. But what is important is Constantine's detachment throughout the whole affair. For all his affection for the young man he is willing to destroy his reputation, and that of the seamstress into the bargain, in the interest of his science of observation. His actual intercourse with other persons is that of a decently humane psychologist with his experimental animals. They are in his eyes *Versuchspersonen,* to be treated—in a spirit of jest—with delicacy and sympathy so far as these do not disturb the necessary objectivity of the experimentalist. His curiosity about people—and his affection for them, which is quite genuine in its own way—stops just short of responsible relations with them. For as he says:

> This is the way I am built. At the first shudder of presentiment my soul has in an instant followed through the whole chain of consequences, which in reality often require a long lapse of time to come to evidence. The concentration of presentiment one never forgets. So it is, I believe, an observer ought to be built, but when he is built in this fashion he will also suffer much. The first moment may overwhelm him almost to the point of fainting, but in this fit of pallor the idea has impregnated him, and from now on he is in an apt mood for discovery. When a man does not possess this feminine quality which permits the idea to come into the right relation to him, which always is a fructifying relation, he is of no use as an observer, for he who does not discover the totality discovers nothing.[26]

The rapid vacillation between pathos and intellectuality is reminiscent of A; the obstetrical metaphor, brought into connection with "the Idea," harks back to William Afham and his familial identity with A. And indeed Constantine Constantius—out of a hundred possible translations "Steadfast Self-possession" suggests itself—is but another version of the poet. He is a *psychologist* in the Platonic sense the word still carried in the early nineteenth century: that is, he is a student of souls and of the kinds of souls.[27] He is an *experimental* psychologist insofar as he sets people in controlled situations where he can observe their typical behavior. On some occasions he produces not only the situations but also the types—imaginatively—for the sake of more exact observation. But to make and record controlled observations of controlled people, to create figures of soul for the purpose of contemplation, is a way of poetizing (*at digte*). The experimental psychologist in the Kierkegaardian shadow-play is a poet, and his "essay in experimental psychology" is a poem in the genre novel, species farce-comedy. It is, as another author describes it, a "whimsical book."[28]

Repetition concludes with a letter from Constantine Constantius to the reader, in which he casually admits that the young man and his story are his own poetic invention. Just as William Afham really creates the banquet he "recollects," so Constantine creates the young man he "observes." The letter is addressed "To N. N., this book's real reader." Who that reader may be is a hard question—Constantine suspects that he is a "fictitious figure"—but there is no question that the proper aesthetic reader will be he who in "observing" the book achieves a repetition of his own personality in the eternity of his imagination. The reader's psychological experiment will have himself as subject, and will recreate that self poetically in reading the book. That may be why Constantine concludes:

> Thou wilt perhaps from time to time be disturbed by an apparently idle witticism or by an indolent expression of defiance, but afterwards perhaps thou wilt be reconciled to this.
>
> Devotedly thine,
Constantine Constantius

"On wild trees," runs the motto of *Repetition,* "the flowers are fragrant; on cultivated trees, the fruits."[29] The imaginative resourcefulness and versatility that the aesthetic author expects of his reader are no more than he regularly demands of himself; they are the same as those attitudes and techniques by which A keeps his personal yawl afloat on the sea of fortune. The aesthete is the poet, whether his medium be language, other people, himself, or all three. The name is not important. What is important is the essential structure of the Kierkegaardian *aisthesis* which is most richly revealed in A, but which also informs the activities of such superficially diverse but analogically identical types as William Afham and Constantine Constantius. This long digression from the case of A is no digression after all; for there is only one *dramatis persona* under all these costumes, the lived poetry which in Kierkegaard's view constitutes the aesthetic way of life, the life which all men—though crudely and with little or none of A's ingenuity—immediately live.

A then is a poet. He is also a man, or, as he is ensconced in

23

his literary productions, an "existential possibility." The excellence of his poetic achievement is validated by the cogency of his *modus vivendi:* he exists his poetry and poetizes his existence. To call him "aesthete" is to acknowledge the hypostatic union of immediacy and freedom where art is incarnate in life and life is redeemed in art.

At the end of the first volume of *Either/Or,* hard on the heels of "The Rotation Method" and balancing in bulk the long essay on *Don Juan* with which the book opens, stands the "Diary of the Seducer."[30] Apparently alien to the rest of the book, the Diary is also somewhat deceptive. Allegedly found among the papers of A, who in turn claims to have copied it out on the sly, it purports to be the private journals of one Johannes nicknamed "the seducer." It was the first of Kierkegaard's writings to be translated (almost too predictably: into French), and that in a meretricious interest. But while the Diary is indeed the record of a seduction, any salacious expectations raised by the title are laid in the perusal. The carnal climax occurs in the interval between the ultimate and penultimate entries, while the remaining 140-odd pages detail the intricate procedure by which the seduction is accomplished. Having sighted and fancied Cordelia Wahl, Johannes determines upon her undoing, lays his snares, and takes his prey. Once he has her he immediately releases her (having introduced her, as he puts it, into a "higher sphere" of consciousness)[31] for her interest is gone with her maidenhood.

More interesting than the story itself is Johannes' theory of seduction and the techniques by which the theory is implemented. The principal thing, Kierkegaard noted in his own copy of the book, is the *method.* This is not *a* seducer's diary, but *the* Seducer's diary.[32] Seduction, as Johannes understands it, is not the act of defloration, nor does it presuppose an excessive concern with sex. To seduce a woman means: with no force but with much art to secure the free capitulation of her mind to yours. That sexuality will be the normal context for such an enterprise is obvious; but it is strictly incidental to the real objective, which is the conquest of the spirit and not the congress of the flesh. It is difficult but not impossible to imagine Johannes a eunuch. When a woman has acknowledged herself captivated, be her body never so intact, she is possessed more effectively than if she were captured by rape.

   The character and the escapades of Johannes the Seducer suggest a comparison with Don Juan. The Don is sensuality pure and simple, to the exclusion of intellect. He is no more a seducer than is the force that through the green fuse drives the flower. Johannes is an intellect that can become sensual at will: "He lived far too intellectually to be a seducer in the common understanding of the word. Sometimes, however, he assumed a parastatic body, and was then sheer sensuality." *Purchè porti la gonella, voi sapete quel chè fà* describes the amorphous longings of Don Juan; the Seducer's more discriminating desire is presaged in the motto of his Diary, *Sua passiòn predominante è la giovin principiante.* The texts are from the same libretto, and it is not surprising to find A, in his commentary on *Don Juan,* imagining another kind of seducer, a seducer who will enjoy not the satisfaction of desire, but the "deception," the "cunning," the "how, the method" of seduction. Johannes is this "reflective Don Juan," whose pleasure is the seducing and not the rewards of seduction. Don Juan wants women, and for his purposes they are all sisters. His Teutonic namesake wants the excitement of a contest of minds, and for this end he needs a very particular woman: *la giovin principiante,* old enough to have a mind of her own, woman enough to want to give it away, and young enough to be unscarred by previous combats.
   Johannes is after Cordelia's mind and the thrill of beguiling it. As he is scrupulous in his choice of victims, so he is ingenious in the selection and use of his weapons. He brings to his task resources of cunning, psychological insight, and patience— especially patience; Cordelia is five months in the making—that would tax and tire the ordinary sensualist. He shifts his moods in Cordelia's presence with calculated randomness: bewilderment begets attraction. He drones for hours with her old aunt about the high price of butter: boredom gives franchise to erotic fancy. He arranges to have her courted by an obliging boor: contempt of Edward becomes a bond that ties Cordelia to Johannes. He is betrothed to Cordelia, and promptly breaks the engagement: transferred from public trust to clandestine adventure, her desire burns sweeter and stronger. Whatever his tactics, Johannes never makes a move to seduce, and by that fact is made more seductive. His strategy, consistent with his theory of seduction, is to make himself an object at once terrifying and fascinating, *mysterium tremendum et fascinans.* He makes himself—to adduce

25

the rubric under which he himself classifies his activities as a seducer—*interesting*. Bewitched at last, Cordelia throws herself into his arms, unable any longer to deny him the love he has evoked but never demanded.

When she finally succumbs, it is not clear to her just who has done what and to whom. It is almost, in retrospect, as if she had seduced him. And this, of course, is exactly the effect Johannes has wanted and so faultlessly prepared: that his desire should become hers, that she should freely but helplessly surrender herself to her destroyer. It is not without reason that self-accusation alternates in Cordelia's mind with accusation of Johannes, for he has made her an active accomplice to her own seduction. Because of her education by Johannes she can curse, she can plead, and she can abase herself in a way that heaps coals of fire on the head of her deceiver. She has, in short, become intrigued and intriguing. As A remarks, she may not have the compass that she admires in Johannes, but she is "not without modulation." Her complicity does not alter the fact that Johannes is the *primum movens* by whose agency Cordelia is relieved of her innocence, but it does exhibit the extent to which the seducer is able to confound his victims in the process of destroying them. [33]

His journal gives us primarily Johannes' view of Johannes, and from within he looks very much like A. He is, by his own admission, a poet. Seduction is a kind of *poiesis* worked in the medium of woman's sexuality. If Johannes is careless of Cordelia and her feelings, it is only because he is so painstakingly careful of his artistry. He is faithless with Cordelia the girl, but only because of a higher fidelity to Cordelia "the Idea," who is privileged to be immortalized in his art. His pact is with the aesthetic, and that involves, as the case of A has already shown, detachment and arbitrariness in relation to actual persons and events. Like A and his "unhappiest man" the Seducer is a lover of recollection. But the passion for recollection—for the translation of actuality into ideal possibility—proscribes any nice consideration for the actuality so translated. That other friend of recollection, William Afham of *Stages on Life's Way*, observes:

> If it were not in bad taste to use a human being as a means to an end, a favorable contrast for recollecting an erotic relationship might perhaps be found by getting oneself into a new love affair—just for the sake of recollecting.

No respecter of persons, and not afflicted with William's rather squeamish good taste, Johannes does just that: he uses his victims in order that he may keep faith with the Idea. Even before he has his way with Cordelia he is plotting his next escapade, in a series of preliminary flirtations *(actiones in distans)* with which his Diary is punctuated. One can imagine him speeding from his tryst with Cordelia to pick up these other threads he has previously knotted and begin sewing a new erotic situation—savoring the most delicate recollections of Cordelia all the while. His exquisite detachment from the whole affair is a matter of record. Speaking somewhat after the fact, he remarks:

> Whether Edward, e.g., would think it over and fall in love again with Cordelia, or would recite his love affair by heart, I leave to him. Why should I get mixed up in other peoples' affairs? [34]

It goes without saying that Johannes shares with Constantine Constantius a dedication to "experimental psychology." The last words of his Diary, written scarcely twenty-four hours after his enthusiastic defloration of Cordelia, show a rapid recrudescence of disinterested objectivity:

> It would, however, really be worth while to know whether or not one might be able to poetize himself out of a girl, so that one could make her so proud that she would imagine that it was she who was tired of the relationship. It could become a very interesting epilogue, which, in its own right, might have psychological interest, and along with that enrich one with many erotic observations. [35]

All the features of the poetic syndrome are present in Johannes' Idea; seduction, which is a kind of poetry and a means of recollection, is no less emphatically a species of psychological experiment. Johannes' character and his conduct offer incontrovertible proof of his thesis that all love, poetically viewed, is essentially faithless.

Johannes could if he wished offer justification for his practice, though he is far too pure an aesthete to defend himself morally. The qualities by which he seduces girls are just those qualities of tact, diplomacy, and skill in the handling of people which are universally honored among men of affairs. If from a certain perspective he seems cold, cruel, inhuman, it is only because he does successfully what most men bungle: he manipulates people exclusively for his own purposes. If it be objected that he has after all deceived Cordelia, he can reply: Yes, but for her own good; I found her a girl, I left her a woman. She is not ruined by her seduction, but made; and she has become for the first time free, self-conscious, and mature. "So it is not so great a misfortune for a woman to be seduced, and she is lucky to be so. A girl who is admirably seduced may make an admirable wife." Since marriage (lifelong constancy to a vow) and seduction (the once-for-all destruction of innocence) are incompatible, it stands to reason that a girl's husband and her seducer may not be the same man. That every girl *needs* a seducer goes with saying. Thus Johannes theorizes:

> If I were not so good at seducing. . . , and if I wanted to be a married man, I would always choose a seduced woman, so that I might not have to begin by seducing my wife. . . . A marriage. . . ought never to be planned to begin as if it were the beginning of a story of seduction. This much is certain, that for every woman there is a corresponding seducer. Her good fortune consists in encountering precisely him. [36]

Cordelia's husband—if she finds one—will be indebted to Johannes for his services. The seducer, by norms and devices commonly approved, but with much greater expertness in the application, is the benefactor of mankind.

Cordelia, however, is differently impressed. Her letters (four of them are incorporated in Johannes' Diary) speak alternately horror, outraged innocence, pathos, self-pity, and—preeminently—confusion. Undone and abandoned, she continues to love Johannes, with a wounded fidelity that pleads for his mercy, and with a vengeance that, mercy not forthcoming, attaches her to him for all eternity as his everlasting curse. A must have had Cordelia in mind when he drew his shadow-graphs of Marie Beaumarchais, Gretchen, and Donna Elvira. These "heroines of reflective grief" have, like Cordelia, experienced deception, and "a deception is for love an absolute paradox." A girl whose love is egoistically rooted will be too proud to believe that anyone would *dare* deceive her, while a girl whose devotion is sympathetically fixed on her lover has in despite of all evidence an unswerving faith that he *could* not deceive. There is no way out of the vicious circle of reflection so generated, A suggests, but the way of ethical resolve. [37]

For that, however, Cordelia is not yet prepared. Her hurts

are too new, her love too warm, and her heart too young for that. She is—the balance of her moods comes to this—traumatized by her experience. She shudders at the awareness that she has been possessed by a demon, she has made love to a "parastatic" body! Her lover dwells in splendid and terrible isolation in a phantom realm behind the real world. In the whimsicality of his moods he appears suddenly out of nowhere and as quickly vanishes again, so that Cordelia has often found herself "embracing a cloud." Because he willed to be her god, Johannes has become her devil. The aesthetic integrity of his personality is, from Cordelia's point of view, the dreadful vacuity of one who does not *practice* deception but *is* deceit itself. Johannes is betrayal as a way of life; his fidelity in the "service of the Idea" necessitates a renunciation of every real relationship. He declares to the world—and to Cordelia in the very act of making love to her—"What have I to do with thee?" (Mark 5:7; cf Matthew 8:28 ff.*)*

That Cordelia should feel this way about her experience is hardly astounding. More important is the fact that A himself is aghast at Johannes. The account of his transcription of the Diary begins in Gothic mystery ("I cannot conceal from myself, scarcely can I master the anxiety which grips me at this moment . . . "), moves to the realization that Johannes is a "depraved personality," and concludes in a prediction of derangement. A, who is a confidant of Cordelia and sees the desolation of her virginity, prophesies that Johannes will eventually outsmart himself:

> As he has led others astray, so he ends, I think, by going astray himself. . . . He who goes astray inwardly. . . soon discovers that he is going about in a circle from which he cannot escape. I think it will be this way with him later, to a still more terrible extent. I can imagine nothing more excruciating than an intriguing mind, which has lost the thread of its continuity and now turns its whole acumen against itself, when conscience awakens and compels the schemer to extricate himself from this confusion.

It is strange to hear A speaking of conscience, and ominous that he does so only in the presence of Johannes the Seducer. He confesses that he is

> never quite able to control the anxiety that grips me every time I think about the case. I, too, am carried away into that nebulous realm, that dream world, where every moment one is afraid of his

own shadow. Often I seek in vain to tear myself away; I follow along like a menacing shadow, an accuser who is mute. How strange! He has spread the deepest secrecy over everything, and yet there is an even deeper secret, and that is the fact that I am privy to it. . . . There is really nothing else which involves so much seduction and so great a curse as a secret.

A man who wills mystification as an end may wind up caught in the springs and elastics and false bottoms of his own legerdemain; the secrecy that is a condition of seduction may become a solitary confinement in which the seducer goes mad for want of another against whom he can rectify his wild imaginings.

Yet it is not Johannes who is on the brink of madness, but A; it is not Johannes in whom conscience starts with a cry of pain, but A. Of Johannes, A says:

Conscience exists for him only as a higher degree of consciousness, which expresses itself in a disquietude that does not, in a more profound sense, accuse him, but which keeps him awake, and gives him no rest in his barren activity. Nor is he mad; for the multitude of finite thoughts are not petrified in the eternity of madness. [38]

Not Johannes' secret life, but A's privy involvement in *l'affaire* Cordelia—as an observer tranced in fascinated terror—is the beginning of insanity. *Johannes is the omen of madness and the awakening of conscience in A.*

Johannes sees himself as an artist, a poetizer of girls. To Cordelia he is an incubus with whom she has lain to her soul's damnation. For A Johannes is just *himself looked at from without.* The "Idea" of seduction is a principled infidelity that excuses itself from every concrete involvement for the sake of the recollected possibility. Viewed *ab extra,* the seducer's systematic irresponsibility has the aspect of fundamental deceit. But this is not essentially different from A's practice of the "rotation method," its outward caprice and its inner *tristesse.* If A is the Romantic ironist, then Johannes the Seducer may well be Kierkegaard's most ironic commentary on that irony and its practitioners. Victor Eremita, the pseudonymous editor of *Either/Or,* begins his general preface to the work by voicing his doubt concerning the Hegelian maxim that inner essence and outer expression are ultimately identical. Of A in particular he says that "his external mode of life has been in complete contradiction to his inner life." This discrepancy between inner and outer is the burden of Romantic irony. And yet in A's shudder at the Seducer is revealed a doubly ironic identity underlying and supporting this diversity. Between the whimsical sadness of A and the desolate inconstancy of Johannes there is the most perfect—and most terrifying—unity. The demonia of the seducer is the melancholy innocence of the aesthete seen from the other side, the side of his relations to other people with whom, willy nilly, he is involved, and whom, willy nilly, he draws into the vortex of his own confusion. A, who knows both Johannes and Cordelia, is granted this double recognition of himself and the awful wisdom it brings: the wisdom of fear and of a conscience born in fear.

But the intimacy between A and Johannes goes even deeper. Victor Eremita argues his conviction that A is the author, and not as he claims the pilferer, of the "Diary of the Seducer." For

> the dominant mood in A's preface in a manner betrays the poet. It seems as if A had actually become afraid of his poem, as if it continued to terrify him, like a troubled dream when it is told. If it were an actual occurrence which he had become privy to, then it seems strange that the preface shows no trace of A's joy in seeing the realization of the idea which had so often floated before his mind . . . . [The reference is to the reflective seducer imagined in the essay on *Don Juan*.] I find no trace of such joy in the preface, but rather, as was said, a certain horror and trembling, which might well have its cause in his poetical relationship to this idea.

The suggestion that Johannes is a possibility projected by A is confirmed by the latter's remark that the Diary is a "poetic reproduction" of experience, and "therefore neither historically exact nor simply fiction, not indicative but subjunctive." It is written in the mood of "as if," the mood of contrary-to-fact; Johannes looks so much like A because he is only a poetic elongation of A's personality. The madness and the moral upheaval on which he is verging are but the unfolding of possibilities already latent in A himself. In the "Diary of the Seducer" A has imaginatively pushed his way of life beyond its extreme limit, and he is appalled when he sees where it is leading him. [39]

31

But Johannes *is* a *persona*, not a person. Just as pure sensuality (Don Juan) is possible only in art, so also is pure reflection (Johannes the Seducer). In *Don Juan* the unity of form and content is perfect because the distinction between them has not yet been drawn. In the journals of Johannes (the ghostly lover who assumes on occasion a parastatic body) the separation between nature and freedom is so complete that it can never be healed. It is no accident that Don Juan and the Seducer have names—indeed the same name—univocal names appropriate to pure types, whereas A is as anonymous and equivocal as immediacy itself. For neither Don Juan nor Johannes is a possibility that can be actualized. They are, rather, the ideal *terminus a quo* and the equally ideal *terminus ad quem* of the aesthetic life, which A alone and ambiguously *lives.* In Don Juan art is impossibly submerged in life; in Johannes life is impossibly lost for the sake of art. Inspired to enthusiasm by the one, recoiling in dread from the other, the aesthete strikes between them the precarious unhappy equilibrium of his own life in art. His existence is such stuff as dreams—bad dreams—are made of, and his little life is rounded with the sleep of unconscious nature. But that is merely to say that he is man—man as he immediately, aesthetically *is,* haunted by memories of bestial innocence and nightmares of demonic experience, melancholy in the assumption of his uncertain destiny.

That this pattern of relationships among Don Juan, A, and Johannes the Seducer is to be found in *Either/Or* I there is no doubt. Yet the identification of A as a man existing his immediacy is facile and premature. Victor Eremita, who supervises the publication of both volumes of *Either/Or,* suspects that the papers of A and those of B (the moralist of the second volume) may be the contrivance of a single author. He does not urge the point. But if it is true, then *Either/Or* becomes a novel and not—as it purports to be—an interchange between two men; A (ignoring B for the moment) becomes another *persona* in the Kierkegaardian repertory; and the whole work is transported into the impersonal eternity of poetic fancy. As Victor says, "When the book is read, then A and B are forgotten, only their views confront one another, and await no finite decision in particular personalities."[40]

As a matter of fact there are rather strong suggestions in

other places that Victor himself in the author of *Either/Or*, and that he only hides in the wings of editorial irresponsibility in order to allow greater independence to the creations of his pen. In the banquet of *Stages on Life's Way*, Victor delivers a panegyric on Mozart which is a microcosm of A's essay.[41] A note to the *Concluding Unscientific Postscript* by Johannes Climacus underlines this fact.[42] But who then is Victor Eremita? A poet, surely, and blood-brother of A, William Afham, and Constantine Constantius. But who is the poet? He is, it becomes increasingly and insistently clear, *everyone* and *no one*. The poet, which is to say, the aesthete in any of his sea-changes, is "an existential possibility tending toward existence," "not existence," but "an existential possibility which cannot win through to existence." That is why Johannes Climacus correctly observes that in *Either/Or* "there is no author."[43] Not only the admittedly fictive characters like Don Juan and Johannes the Seducer (or for that matter the young man of *Repetition*), but their creators as well, lack flesh-and-blood reality. The poet, who represents man's attempt to live his immediacy, is like immediacy itself eternally presupposed but never present. He is the flickering shadowgraph of human possibilities, the everlasting equivocator who wears an infinite number of masks but never appears *in propria persona*. He *has* no proper person, for he is himself only the possibility of manhood, imaginatively entertained and intellectually contemplated, but not yet consolidated in an actual personality.[44]

The partakers of the banquet in *Stages on Life's Way* are five: Johannes the Seducer, Victor Eremita, Constantine Constantius, an otherwise unidentified *couturier*, and a young man (not, presumably, the young man of *Repetition*). At a coffee-house meeting of the group prior to the banquet itself, the matter of planning and executing such an entertainment is broached, and well nigh honored in the breach for the difficulty of the observance. The young man declares himself unqualified to arrange a banquet, and the *couturier* has no time for such things.[45] The *couturier* is a man of business who labors day and night, prostituting woman-kind to the mercenary lusts of the fashion-merchants. The young man has not yet, at the time of the banquet, had a love affair. Moreover, he has an anxious forboding of the contradiction of flesh and spirit that is imminent in a love-relationship, and would, he fears, painfully declare itself in the first kiss. His lack of experience is testimony to his youth; his manhood is displayed by his dread in the face of possibility. [46]

Johannes the Seducer is ready for a symposium, but on one condition, that it be "accomplished all of a sudden." The locale and its furniture must appear out of nowhere and be destroyed immediately after the feast, even as he himself materializes and vanishes with diabolic rapidity on his errands of seduction. His companions agree to the desirability of such an arrangement, but Victor Eremita makes a long speech explaining that no banquet can possibly be planned on these lines, so that, *ergo*, no satisfactory banquet can be planned at all. Victor believes that the *thought* of a banquet is more to be desired than the reality, since "everyone is sufficiently sated merely by the talk about the banquet, for the good Lord satisfies the stomach before the eye is satisfied, but imagination acts inversely." He agrees that a banquet must happen "at once" *(ex templo)*, but that which happens at once obviously cannot be planned in advance. Especially since the cooperation of good fortune—which can never be coerced—is required, and since the details of a proper banquet—the number and character of the guests, the quality and the amount of wine, the illumination, the dinner music, the table service, and so on—are prohibitively difficult to provide for. Therefore, Victor concludes, a banquet is a *pium desiderium*, the attainment of which is an impossibility delicious to meditate.

The banquet would not have taken place at all had it not been for the quiet and mysterious efficiency of Constantine Constantius, the "experimental psychologist," which in this instance might be rendered, the "practical aesthete." It is Constantine who makes the necessary arrangements, sends the guests their invitations—suddenly, on the morning of the day the banquet is to occur—and engineers the destruction of the setting at once upon the cessation of festivities. Even Constantine allows that he would never risk attempting a repetition of his feat: so precarious a thing it is to introduce the Idea into reality!

Perils of a like refinement attend the conduct of the banquet itself. When it is proposed that speeches be made *inter pocula* on the subject of woman and love, Johannes protests that he "never could get drunk, and when he had reached a certain point he became more and more sober the more he drank." Again it is

34

Constantine who breaks the vicious magic circle and initiates the actual drinking and the actual speaking.

The tenuous character of the aesthete's ties with reality is again evident in the content of the speeches of the symposiasts. The young man, after much troubled reflection on the possibility of love, sorrowfully renounces the real thing. Constantine regards woman as "a jest" who may be enjoyed but never taken in earnest. Victor Eremita: woman is "immediacy" and for that reason a vanishing negativity; a temporary erotic liaison is occasionally inspiriting for a man, but a responsible and permanent alliance with a woman would be a dreadful mistake. The *couturier:* women are giddy fools who deserve the treatment they receive at the hands of *couturiers.* Johannes the Seducer: woman is a savory bait the gods have prepared for men, to distract them from storming Olympus; only the seducers are clever enough to eat the bait and elude the tender trap in which husbands are caught. [47]

Finally and most significantly: the "authors" and "editors" of *In Vino Veritas, Repetition,* and *Either/Or,* like their literary fictions, dissolve in fantasy when the reader tries to pin them down. William Afham, who observes and later recollects, i.e., creates the banquet-episode, inexplicably takes no part in the feasting and speech-making himself. At the conclusion of his narrative he bows out with a flourish of Hegelian dialectic:

> But who then am I? Let nobody ask. If it has not occurred to anybody to ask, I am relieved, for then I am over the worst of it. Besides, I am not worth asking about, for I am the most insignificant of all things, it makes me quite bashful to have people ask about me. I am pure being and therefore almost less than nothing. I am the pure being which is the accompaniment of everything yet never observable, because I am constantly *aufgehoben.* I am like the line above which is written the task for the pupil to reckon out, and below it the answer—who cares about the line? [48]

William is to be taken at his word. The aesthetic immediacy is *aufgehoben* the moment it is asked about—though not precisely *à la mode hegelienne*—so that the poet fades to sheer transparency before his equally evanescent fancies. Constantine Constantius' letter to the reader of *Repetition* turns on a similar bit of self-abnegation, this time tied to the imagery of maternity:

> My dear reader, thou wilt understand that the young man is the focus of interest, whereas I am a transitory figure, like a midwife in relation to the child she has brought to birth. And such, in fact is my position, for I have as it were brought him to birth, and therefore as the older person I do the talking. My personality is a presupposition psychologically necessary to force him out. . . .

Constantine insists that he is not a poet, and indeed he is not a poet in the way that his young man is. But at the same time he manages to confound his own personality with that of his subject and that of his "real reader" so that the three are fused in the ideal unity of a "fictitious figure:"

> I have brought my own person into the theme; but if thou, my dear reader, wilt look more closely, thou wilt easily see that I am only a serviceable spirit and am far from being indifferent to the young man, as he fears . . . . Every movement I have made is made only in order to throw light upon him; I have constantly had him *in mente*, every word of mine is either ventriloquism or is uttered with reference to him . . . . For this reason all movements take place lyrically, and what I say about myself one is to understand obscurely of him, or by what I say one is to understand him better. Thus I have done for him what I could—just as now in what I am about to say I try to be of service to thee, dear reader, by being again a different person. [49]

The attempt of William Afham and Constantine Constantius to draw their readers into the imaginative texture of their works has already been sufficiently noted. The gambit is nowhere more subtly and effectively proposed than in the closing words of the Preface by the editor—author?—of *Either/Or*:

> I have nothing further to say except that the honored authors, if they were aware of my project, might possibly wish to accompany their papers with a word to the reader. I shall therefore add a few words with them holding and guilding the pen. A would probably interpose no objection to the publication; he would probably warn the reader: read them or refuse to read them, you will regret both. What B would say is more difficult to decide. He would perhaps reproach me, especially with regard to the publication of A's papers. He would let me feel that he had no part in them, that he washed his hands of responsibility. When he had done this, then he would perhaps turn to the book with these words: "Go out into the world then; escape if possible the attention of critics, seek a single reader in a favorable hour, and

should you meet a feminine reader, then would I say: 'My fair
reader, you will perhaps find in this book something you ought
not to know; other things you might well profit from knowing;
may you so read the first that having read it, you may be as one
who has not read it; may you read the other so that having read it,
you may be as one who cannot forget it.'" I, as editor, only add
the wish that the book may meet the reader in an auspicious hour,
and that the fair reader may succeed in following B's well meant
advice.[50]

With these words and this amphibolous wish Victor Eremita
takes the genuine aesthetic stance, slipping with his characters
and his reader into the *ubique et nusquam* of imagined possibility.
The "conquering hermit," who is every other Kierkegaardian
poet as well, lies concealed in the everyone-and-no-one that is
the hidden life of immediate human nature.

That is why A, though he is in a sense all of us, is in
another and equally crucial sense, none of us. The metaphoric
unity of all the versions of the aesthete, from Don Juan to
Johannes the Seducer, and their intersection in A, have been
documented in abundant detail. It has likewise become clear that
A, the prototypical aesthete, and everlasting equivocator, is a
mirror for Everyman in his immediacy. And it has been shown
by the evidence just cited, but also by the impossible consistency
of A's life conjoined with its arbitrariness, by the sensuality of
Don Juan which is perfect abstraction, and by the poetic
integrity of the Seducer which encloses a personal vacuum, that
the aesthetic cannot be lived, or rather, that it can only be lived
by equivocation on the actual and the ideal. "A's papers contain a
number of attempts to formulate an aesthetic philosophy of life.
A single, coherent, aesthetic view of life can scarcely be carried
out."[51] Every aesthete is, and declares himself to be, an infinite
regress into unreality.

A's anonymity and ambiguity, his tendency to disperse into
his myriad masks, while it identifies him as infinitely adaptable
materia prima of the human, also indicates the other side of this
truth: that immediacy as such can never be the substance of an
actual human life. That is the twofold sense of the solemn
admonitions which the ethicist of *Either/Or* II levels at A. A is a
persona that cannot fill out to a person; therefore B accuses him of
inhumanity. Yet A is the dramatic potentiality for every person;

therefore in addressing A, his moral nemesis is accusing all of us. In more than one sense is the reader of *Either/Or* (or of *Repetition,* or *In Vino Veritas,* or any of Kierkegaard's "aesthetic" works) engaged by the work itself. If he is drawn by the aesthetic authors and editors into collaboration on the poetic structure of their works, he is also, by the larger plan of these books, thrown back onto the resources of his own will to achieve that selfhood which the aesthete can only dream.

But this is proleptic. "Will" is not in the aesthete's active vocabulary, nor does it stand for anything in his character or in the conduct of his life. A *is,* without qualification of freedom, the attempt to *be* that immediacy which is the universal substrate of human existence. His pursuit of pleasure is an attempt simultaneously to explore the full range of human possibilities and to arrest that pursuit at the instant of enjoyment just short of the crisis of realization. He is everyone in the imaginative versatility with which he plans and executes his exploration; he is conscious that he is no one in the melancholy moment when he shrinks from the claims of actuality. For B it is this "no one" that is decisive and damning. For A himself it is the attempt at "everyone" that matters regardless of the cost; to live as an aesthete is to declare in effect that the versatility is worth the melancholy.

2
WORLD ENOUGH
AND TIME:
The Letters of
Judge Wilhelm

Volume II of *Either/Or* consists of a brace of very long letters and a sermon. The sermon (of which more later) is by an unnamed priest. The author of the letters is called B, to distinguish him from A, the author of Volume I; but his letters tell us that his name is Wilhelm, that he is married and a father, and that he is an Assessor in the lower courts. The letters are addressed to A, who is a friend of Judge Wilhelm and a frequent visitor in the latter's home. The first letter defends "The Aesthetic Validity of Marriage" against the casual eroticism of the aesthete. The second bears the formidable title "The Equilibrium between the Aesthetical and the Ethical in the Composition of Personality." Under this prodigious head, the Judge mounts an attack on A's way of life and constructs a rationale for his own ethical mode of existence.

He is not, however, a philosophical moralist, nor for that matter an overly acute thinker. His approach is in keeping with his status in society and his epistolary form. He writes expansively and at his ease, from the security of an official position and the warmth of an idyllic marriage. His attitude is never argumentative and his concern never theoretical. Though his form permits him occasional digressions into philosophy, he is at bottom always the judge and paterfamilias, and his letter is appropriately compounded of advice and counsel, fireside wisdom, friendly exhortation and occasionally sharp accusation. His purpose is exclusively practical: to get A to change his way of life.

Indeed the whole point of his critique of aestheticism is just that: it is not *practical*. Seizing on the catchword "either/or," which A had used as a pretext for idleness, the Assessor throws it back in his face. For an ethical man this motto epitomizes the utter seriousness with which he confronts a choice between two exclusive alternatives. For A it is a retreat into that eternity of imagination where all contraries are reconciled in a harmony of indifference. For the speculative fancy the opposition of good and evil has no force. Considered only as ideas they are so far from contradictory that they are mutually interdependent: he who thinks good must therewith think evil, and vice versa. The idea of one is no better and no worse than the idea of the other, and there is no choice to be made between them. The aesthete, insofar as he lives *aeterno modo*, makes no choices; and since a man's character is constituted by the choices he makes, the aesthete has no self. His identity is at best the abstract identity of an unrealized possibility. The Judge remarks A's predilection for "the first sensation of falling in love"—and his hatred of marriage. His psychological interest in observing people, because it stops short of any responsible concern for them, is at worst "treacherous" and at best "a hypochondriac curiosity." "Your life," the Judge tells him, "is wholly given over to preliminary runs" which never end in the leap of decision by which possibilities are translated into actualities.

But such a stasis cannot be sustained. A recognizes that he must do something; and so he acts, but he acts arbitrarily and without commitments. Ideally he is detached from life; actually he samples everything life has to offer—with the proviso that he is not buying. This means, in ethical terms: ideally his self is a vain imagination, while actually it is dissolute in the etymological sense of *dissolved*. His virtuosity, his ability to acquit himself in any situation and to play at everything, means that he is nothing but a *poseur*. His life is an endless series of masks in an endless masquerade, dissipated in its own external relations. Even his well-doing—Judge Wilhelm recalls a street-scene in which A had overheard a poor woman wishing for five dollars, grandly presented her the coveted note, and vanished with mercurial rapidity—is but a capricious experimentation, a will to "play the part of fate" which the Judge can only describe as "prodigiously faithless."

> Ah! you are indeed a strange being, at one moment a child, at another an old man, at one moment you are thinking with prodigious seriousness about the loftiest scientific problems, proposing to sacrifice your life to them, the next moment you are an amorous fool.

The aesthete so vacillates between the moods of youth and age, gravity and folly, that he disintegrates altogether. "Your life resolves itself completely into interesting particulars of this sort," and never acquires the solidity and consistency of a real human personality.[1]

A's life has neither ideal integrity nor actual continuity. The aesthete is trying to combine Don Juan (pure immediacy) with Johannes the Seducer (pure reflection), but the project is impossible and he constantly comes apart at the seams. On the one hand he withdraws to demonic vacuity, on the other he returns in a plenitude of chaos; but never shall the two meet in the identity of a single personality informed by a fixed and steady character. You are impractical, the Judge tells A, in the radical sense that you cannot be a self on your own terms.[2] A's attempt to live his immediacy makes him, as we have seen, everyone in possibility and no one in reality:

> You are an epitome of every possibility. . . . Every mood, every thought, good or bad, cheerful or sad, you pursue to its utmost limit, yet in such a way that this comes to pass rather *in abstracto* than *in concreto*; in such a way that this pursuit itself is little more than a mood from which nothing results but a knowledge of it, not even so much that the next time it becomes harder or easier for you to indulge in the same mood, for you constantly retain a possibility of it. Hence, one can reproach you almost for everything and for nothing, because it is and is not chargeable to you.[3]

The same futility can be observed in the aesthete's attempts to deal with time. The connection between time and personal identity is clear from a consideration of the nature of choice. A's "choices" do not commit him to anything, which is to say that they are all for the moment. Decisive choosing binds the chooser

41

to the consequences of his choice, either permanently or for a specified period of time. Ethical choice takes the form of vow or public contract; it is decisive because it decides a man's character for the future, it defines him in advance. Only that man has a self whose personality is continuous through time, and this requires that he be willing to put his future in trust by means of his choices. So it is that the Assessor takes marriage (the vow) and vocation (involving contractual obligation) as paradigm cases of ethical choice.

Another pseudonym, the dialectical lyricist John of Silence, observes that "aesthetics does not trouble itself greatly about time, whether in jest or seriousness time flies equally fast for it." The aesthete lives, in his own words, *aeterno modo*, a dubious vantage point from which time and the events that transpire in time become matters of indifference. Therefore, "the aesthetical idea contradicts itself as soon as it must be carried out in reality," for the aesthete's negative ideality makes it impossible for him to fit temporal existence consistently into the pattern of his life. Perhaps that is why the same pseudonym dwells at some length on the category of "the interesting" and calls it the *discrimen rerum* between the aesthetical and the ethical. It was "the interesting" in the *persona* of Johannes that seduced Cordelia, that is, confounded her real existence by means of a visionary and romantic ideal; it was "the interesting" in Johannes that intrigued and terrified A, and nearly made him a man of conscience. For "the interesting" is the place at which the imagined ideal erupts disturbingly into the realities of time, and the encounter with it therefore necessitates either an advance to ethical responsibility (A has said that the only salvation for a deceived woman lies in ethical resolve) or a demonic retrenching on the part of the aesthete in the manner of the Seducer himself. It is his preoccupation with "the interesting" that attracts Constantine Constantius to lovely young women and pathetic young men—and sends him glancing off from them into the cool detachment of psychological observation.

John of Silence contrasts the atemporal effeteness of the aesthetic with the ethical demand for "revelation," the demand that a man make public avowal of his character and assume public responsibility for his actions. The aesthetic eternity is locked in the secrecy of private fantasy: both A and William Afham, not to mention Victor the Hermit, are connoisseurs of solitude, and Johannes the Seducer is the incarnation of absence. The insistence of the ethicist on the importance of coming to terms with time is in effect a requirement for publicity and participation in the open and ongoing life of a community. The vow and the contract, which in Judge Wilhelm's view spell out the terms of an ethical commitment to time, are also public guarantees that the ethical man means to stand revealed among his fellows. [4]

Moreover, it is natural that *Judge Wilhelm* should adduce the problem of time. As a judge he is daily encountering the necessity of decision. Making a decision requires preliminary deliberation, and in the course of this deliberation, there is a moment of indifference, the moment in which several alternatives are present and the will can incline any way. But whereas the aesthete wants to remain poised in this indifference lest some pleasure elude him, the ethical man knows that the moment of indifference is also the instant of resolution, which must be seized or lost forever. Life moves forward, and this movement prohibits everlasting deliberation about alternatives. At some point one alternative must be chosen to the exclusion of its opposite, or both of them are irrecoverably gone. For the aesthete, a possibility is an ever-present opportunity for enjoyment; for the ethical man, it is the now-or-never demand for decision. Therefore the Judge can say, I am fighting for possibility, for freedom, and for the future. [5]

The aesthete, however, has no future; his existence is a recollection of eternity, never a resolution in time. He loses his possibilities in the attempt to preserve them inviolate, for he never actualizes them, and a possibility unactualized is as profitable as miser's gold. His ideal of non-involvement is a freedom suspended from decision, not a freedom engaged to decide, and it is therefore barren. Yet—the other side of the paradox returns—the aesthete does face a future, he does actualize his possibilities, he does choose. But he does it *malgré lui*. Lost to the world in deliberation, he acts on impulse, he vacillates, he chooses by default or by accident. But the possibilities he actualizes in this way are not his own, they are things that happen to him. And the actions he arbitrarily elects to perform show by their arbitrariness that they are actions to negate action, chosen for the express purpose of avoiding the consequences of choice. By his choice of an aesthetic way of life he assumes an irresponsibility for his actions, which prevents him from choosing in an ethical sense.

A's choices, to use Judge Wilhelm's language, lack earnestness, energy, and pathos. [6] His character wants constancy and permanence. He cannot meet the future in serious resolve so as to give his personality continuity throughout time. But that is just another way of saying that he is no one. A is torn in contradiction between the rich but abstract ideality of his imagination and the pointless hither-and-thither of his actual life. From an ethical point of view, his anonymity signifies not concreteness, but the extremes of emptiness and formlessness to which his way of life alternately compels him. The two halves of his life are perpetually alienated from each other. His either/or is at the level of theory an indifferent both/and, and at the level of action an equally indifferent neither/nor. The ethical either/or—a resolute choice shaping the personality through time by reference to an ideal apprehended in the instant of reflection—forever exceeds the compass of his aestheticism.

The aesthete has no self, then, because he cannot come to terms with the temporal dimension in which human personality must necessarily be worked out. The accusation can be further generalized: the aesthete confuses the theoretical and the practical domains. In a long digression on Goethe's *Aus meinem Leben*, the Assessor remarks with indignation on the fact that the hero of that book "distances" every human *Wahrheit* by means of a recollective *Dichtung:*

> What does it mean to poetize a life-relationship? . . . To poetize an actual life-relationship by the aid of distance . . . is neither more nor less than to falsify the ethical element in it and to stamp upon it the counterfeit impression of a casual happening and a mere problem for thought. . . . It is no more than the ostentatious parade of the natural and pleasure-loving man in defiance of the ethical. . . . As a matter of course, not everybody who poetizes poetizes masterpieces. Who would be so foolish as to affirm such a thing? But from the ethical point of view, this distinction, that one is a hero, yes, perhaps even the only one who counts as a hero, and the other a bungler, has nothing to do with the case. [7]

To reproduce one's experience in the medium of poetry may, in the hands of a master, be the way to create works of excellence. But if a man's life consists of this reproduction, then he betrays experience by reducing it to the occasion of his creativity, prefers his own appetite for pleasure to the demand for responsible action, and inverts the order of reality by confounding the essential (ethical) with its accidental adornment (aesthetic).

The aesthete takes for the whole of life what is at best a part of it, the idealizing activity of imagination and intellect. There is no doubt, Judge Wilhelm tells him, that "if to deliberate were the proper task for a human life, you would be pretty close to perfection." The Judge acknowledges A's superiority as a dialectician and for that reason does not question the logic of his position. What he questions is the propriety of logic as a way of life. If a man makes a career of theorizing, he identifies his existence with the "instant of deliberation," which, however, "like the Platonic instant, has no existence, least of all in the abstract sense in which you (A) would hold it fast."[8] The instant of deliberation is the momentary withdrawal from existence in which the ethical man surveys his possibilities and gathers his forces for a return via decisive choice and action. But the aesthete, striving to hold the moment fast in contemplation, makes his whole life a withdrawal. Since his choices are only choices in an equivocal sense, since his arbitrariness is a synonym for dissoluteness, he remains essentially outside actual existence. His eternity, which does not inform his existence but abandons it, is a false eternity; his freedom, which never commits itself, is a false freedom. He has—the conclusion is monotonous but inescapable—no self.

The man who confuses theory and practice can go mad in his theoretical isolation, as the case of the Seducer has shown. But he can also be tripped up in practice. Suppose, says the Judge, a charming and gifted young man, for whom you feel a simple and genuine affection, should come to you for advice on how to conduct his life. (Perhaps Judge Wilhelm is familiar with the young man whose sufferings momentarily engaged the sympathies of Constantine Constantius, or that other young man whose innocence charmed William Afham!) You initiate him into the mysteries of your aestheticism, he disappears from your society for a time, and then reappears older and wiser. Wiser, however, with your own wisdom: cynicism, hatred of life, and melancholy. Is it not conceivable that you might be taken aback? Might you not deplore your own personality reflected in another whom you love? If you are able to be affected in this way by another human being, then your aestheticism is not wholly consistent. A perfectly consistent aestheticism would amount to the demonia of the seducer; this is a possibility A has shrunk from in horror. Judge Wilhelm asks him to imagine, not a fanciful extension of his personality, but an actual *alter ego* who might show him what sort of man he really is. And this, the Judge adds, is a consummation devoutly to be wished:

> Some day the circumstances of your life may tighten upon you the screws in its rack and compel you to come out with what really dwells in you, may begin the sharper inquisition of the rack which cannot be beguiled by nonsense and witticisms.

The only hope for the aesthete is that he may be caught off guard and moved to acknowledge the extremity of his condition. [9]

The Assessor knows that it will take more than a disturbing personal experience to dislodge A from his aestheticism. But the example of the young friend clears the way for a devastating conclusion. The art of living requires that the aesthete stay in control of himself and his situation; to this end A advocated hopelessness and arbitrariness. However, the case of the young man suggests that he is not in control after all. His aim is enjoyment. "*But,*" Judge Wilhelm counters, "*he who says that he wants to enjoy life always posits a condition which either lies outside the individual or is in the individual in such a way that it is not posited by the individual himself.*" That this is the case with health, beauty, love, wealth, fame, status, talent, pleasure, and the like is obvious. It is obvious to A, and he has given up hoping in such things. But it is also the case with that view of life which Judge Wilhelm describes as "the most refined and superior" of all aesthetic views, a view which is recognizable in the Judge's utterances as the view of A himself:

> Your thought has hurried on ahead, you have seen through the vanity of all things, but you have got no further. Occasionally you plunge into pleasure, and every instant you are devoting yourself to it you make the discovery in your consciousness that it is vanity. So you are constantly beyond yourself, that is, in despair. . . . You are like a dying man, you die daily, not in the serious significance usually attached to this word, but life has lost its reality, and, as you say, you always count your days by the number of times notice is served on you to quit your lodging.

The Assessor perceives that A's melancholy, the cultivation of despair for its own sake, is the final and most sophisticated form of aestheticism. But it is nevertheless desperate, and it betokens the loss of a world. The aesthete aims at enjoyment, and his melancholy makes that enjoyment as intense as possible. Judge Wilhelm does not begrudge A his achievement: "In case enjoyment were the chief thing in life, I would sit at your feet as a pupil, for in this you are a master." But the very intensity with which he gorges his pleasures is the aesthete's undoing, for that intensity, the Judge comments, "has a good deal in common with the intense enjoyment of the Strasbourg geese which costs them their lives." However consistent it may be in itself (in possibility all things are possible), aestheticism cannot be made consistent with reality, even when reality is conceived aesthetically as fate. The aesthete, who thinks to conquer fate by anticipating and transforming in tragedy the worst it can bring, may still be shattered by the best. It does no good to proclaim oneself the unhappiest man:

> He who says that sorrow is the meaning of life has joy outside him in the same way that he who would be joyful has sorrow outside him. Joy may take him by surprise in exactly the same way that sorrow may take the other by surprise. His life view thus hinges upon a condition which is not in his power, for it is really just as little in a man's power to give up being joyful as to give up being sorrowful. But every life view which hinges upon a condition outside itself is despair.

If he is surprised by joy, the aesthete has lost the mastery of life on which the success of his aestheticism depends. That he can be so surprised is clear. Though he is prepared to transport everything that happens to him into the never-never land of reflection, he must nevertheless wait for it to happen. However effete, he is always liable to be taken unawares by immediacy, by some mood or happenstance that he did not and could not neutralize *a priori* and in the concrete—and that on the terms of his own metaphysic. He may make a garden of his melancholy and water it with poetic tears, but the flowers and the weeds still grow where they list. That his life, even in its most tragic and poignant moments, is only a pose is made evident by the fact—surely disconcerting to a member of the *symparane-kromenoi*—that there are days when he is happy in spite of himself.

In his very joy the aesthete is in despair, a paradoxical despair quite different from the hopelessness which he recommends as a condition of freedom. The despair of which Judge

47

Wilhelm speaks is a consequence of unfreedom, of the aesthete's unconditional dependence upon conditions beyond his control.

> So it appears that every aesthetic view of life is despair, and that everyone who lives aesthetically is in despair, whether he knows it or not. But when one knows it (and you indeed know it), a higher form of existence is an imperative requirement.

The words in parentheses are important, for they mark the possibility of a transition to a "higher form of existence." The life of the aesthete is *perdition;* he is *lost* in the sense that he has missed the possibility of becoming himself. *But this perdition is of his own choosing.* He knows that he is sick unto death, and still persists in his aestheticism. His choice—the one real choice that the aesthete makes—is the election of a way of life whose inevitable end is despair. That is why Judge Wilhelm reminds A of the teaching of the Church that melancholy *(acedia)* is a sin, and adds that "a man may have sorrow and distress, yea, it may be so great that it pursues him throughout his whole life, and this may even be beautiful and true, but a man becomes melancholy only by his own fault." Stifling though it be, *the aesthete's unfreedom is an unfreedom that he has freely undertaken* by choosing to live aesthetically. It is an unfreedom, therefore, from which he can by another free choice emancipate himself. The way of emancipation is the passage from an aesthetic to an ethical mode of existence.

To characterize the ethical life is to move from the Assessor's accusation of A to the advice and counsel which he, still judge and husband, has ready to hand. His first admonition, and the first step toward a higher "stage" on life's way, is: Despair! The initial movement toward the ethical is the same as the terminal moment of the aesthetic. The same and yet different; for the despair which Judge Wilhelm recommends is not the despair which the aesthete nurtures as the last end of a life of enjoyment. It is a *despair of the life of enjoyment as such,* and thus *the gateway into a new kind of life.* You can see, says the Judge to A, that your life is desperate. Accept this fact and break with aestheticism altogether, give up without reservation your impossible attempt to achieve freedom and selfhood at the level of immediacy. You will *ipso facto* have elevated yourself to the true freedom and the concrete selfhood of the ethical man. "The aesthetical in a man is that by which he is immediately what he is; the ethical is that whereby he becomes what he becomes." By giving up the vain endeavor to *be* himself (aesthetic), a man is first enabled to *become* himself (ethical).

This election of despair is the critical breach with immediacy that distinguishes the aesthetic from the ethical. For the aesthete, in spite of all his reflection, remains "in his immediacy." His art of living is at most an attempt so to arrange or to edit the given that it can be (reflectively, to be sure) enjoyed as it is. The ethical man on the contrary undertakes the wholesale reconstruction of his nature in the light of his duty and in the power of his freedom, to the end that he may thereby make himself what he is obligated to become. "So then," the Judge repeats,

> choose despair, for despair is a choice; . . . one cannot despair without choosing. And when a man despairs he chooses again— and what is it he chooses? He chooses himself, not in his immediacy, not as this fortuitous individual, but he chooses himself in his eternal validity. [10]

The aesthete's life is always subject to some condition over which he has no control, for no man every wholly catches up with himself, and no man can sever all the ties that bind him to his given existence. His eternal flight from this *conditio sine qua non* of his life constitutes that "hysteria of the spirit" which is his melancholy. [11] His quest for enjoyment is essentially desperate. This is not to say that enjoyment is not possible; it *is* possible. But it is *only* possible (fortuitous), for there is nothing a man can do by himself to assure it absolutely. Therefore, enjoyment is *im*possible as a way of life individually and personally his own. The life he enjoys is never perfectly his, and he is consequently without hope of securing for himself the pleasure and the freedom he desires. "The poet's life," Kierkegaard said, "is despair of being able to become the thing he wishes." [12] Infinitely resourceful, the aesthete reconciles himself to enjoying the hopelessness of his existence. Insofar as he recognizes his own nullity, he has verged on a profound truth, *the* truth of aestheticism, that the life of enjoyment is a living death. But this recognition is not sufficient by itself to resurrect the aesthete's defunct personality. That can only happen by a free choice of the will, and if this is withheld the aesthete remains strung up on his melancholy, and need never give in to the promptings of his despair.

What the aesthete must do is to give up his whole way of life. And then he will be in a position to become himself. In fact, by this first authentic act of freedom, he will already have become for the first time a real person. By despairing of himself *qua* aesthetic he will at once have chosen himself *qua* ethical in his eternal validity. For his eternal validity as a self is nothing other than the freedom by which he chooses himself, the act by which he appropriates and engages himself as a self-determining human being. The "absolute" self of which Judge Wilhelm speaks, the self which a man becomes by decisively resolving against a life of enjoyment, is just freedom.[13]

To equate the self with the freedom whereby it chooses itself may seem like vain circularity. And so it would be if it were the *idea* of the self and the *idea* of its freedom that were meant. But the Assessor speaks always with reference to actual individuals actually taking charge over their actual individual lives. And in such case the choice of one's self in its eternal validity is exposed to concrete alternatives which give the choice, and the self, a distinctive content. In a polemic not addressed to A, a defense of marriage against the objections of its sophisticated despisers, the Judge examines the two principal alternatives so encountered.[14] What he calls in this essay the ethical "resolution" *(Beslutning)* is equivalent to the self-choice which he urges on A.

There are, the Judge recognizes, two basic forms of the resolution, the positive and the negative. In a positive resolution (e.g., marriage) a man affirms the constitution which is his by natural endowment and historical inheritance, and undertakes the task of molding this immediacy in the forms of ethical accountability. In a negative resolution (e.g., monastic celibacy) a man refuses this immediacy, to the extent that this is possible, and affirms his moral freedom in independence of nature and history. This negative form of the resolution, because it is deliberately, consistently, and responsibly taken, is not to be confused with the thoughtless and irresolute manner in which the aesthete "fools life away" in "fastidious picking and choosing." The latter is the "wishful ideality" with which Judge Wilhelm reproaches A. The negative resolution is a legitimate form of self-choice whose claims cannot be disallowed by an

50

ethical court of inquiry. Either form of the resolution is to be preferred to the dreaming and drifting of the aesthete, for as the Judge says, "All of a man's ideality consists first and last in resolution."

Yet for all his theoretical breadth of vision, the Judge cannot in fact condone any but a resolve in the affirmative. The positive resolution "is secure in its happy result," while the negative resolver has declared a war on his immediacy that will not be over until life itself is. Life sustains the positive resolve, but the negative has only the barren force of will to uphold it. The positive resolution has only the anxiety that it will not remain true to itself; the negative has a double peril, for besides the difficulty of preserving his choice intact, the negative chooser can never know whether his choice was right or horribly wrong until, at the earliest, life itself is over and done. In brief, the positive resolution is daily verified in experience; the negative resolution is like an hypothesis that is never verified in this world. The married man eats every day the fruits which are the proof of his love; the monk makes a lifelong painful fast in preparation for the far-off heavenly banquet. Therefore, although "resolution" in either direction "is man's ideality," the "more perfect ideality," the "true idealizing resolution," is the positive resolve.

The duality of immediacy and reflection in human existence may be designated by any number of oppositions. The Assessor pins his case for the positive resolution on a selection of these contraries. The negative resolution denies the temporal for the sake of the eternal; the positive, which works at introducing the eternal into the temporal, is "signed in heaven and countersigned in time." The negative resolver has no outlet for his human feelings, for he has cut himself off from the common life of his fellows; the positive resolve is just as "sympathetic" as it is "autopathic." The positive resolve is concrete while the negative is abstract, and "abstraction is the first expression of ideality, but concretion is its essential expression." The positive resolution makes its peace with destiny (which may be, the Judge adds, divine providence) when it accepts fate as the burden and the task of freedom: the negative resolve, in the solitude of freedom, "readily becomes proud, supercilious, inhuman, and more particularly all the arguments of fate are regarded as legally invalid." The Judge could go on forever, but, mercifully, he does not.

The sum of the matter is, in words calculated to catch the attention of an aesthete, that the positive resolution of the ethicist is the true art of living. Of conjugal love Judge Wilhelm writes:

> It is poetic, ineffably poetic, as love is, but resolution is the conscientious translator who translates enthusiasm into reality, and this translator is so precise, oh, so precise!

Marriage, and by extension the fundamental choice of self on which it rests, is poetry translated into reality. By the power of freedom, the ethical man picks his self out of the clay of its immediacy, shapes it in the image and likeness of freedom itself, and breathes into it the breath of its eternal validity. [15]

The self so chosen both comes into existence with the choice and exists prior to the choice as something to be chosen. What exists before the choice is the self as immediately given. The self that comes to be by the choice is the same self lifted from nature to self-consciousness by means of freedom.

> In this case choice performs at one and the same time the two dialectical movements: that which is chosen does not exist and comes into existence with the choice; that which is chosen exists, otherwise there would not be a choice. For in case what I chose did not exist but absolutely came into existence with the choice, I would not be choosing, I would be creating; but I do not create myself, I choose myself. Therefore, while nature is created out of nothing, while I myself as an immediate personality am created out of nothing, as a free spirit I am born of the principle of contradiction (either/or), or born by the fact that I choose myself. [16]

The freedom by which a man chooses himself in his eternal validity is not abstract, like that of the aesthete, but as concrete as possible; for the self which is chosen is the self that is given in the whole of its natural and historical determinations. Likewise the choice itself is not a once-for-all bit of derring-do (the sort of thing an aesthete might try off and on), but a daily reengagement of the whole personality in the terms and consequences of the original decision. Self-choice is thus not only the entrance to the ethical life; it is also the constitutive principle by which that life is structured. As such it is compounded of two essential moments, the moments, in the Assessor's language, of *repentance* and *duty*. In the *present* resolution of self-choice a man takes all of his *past* into his freedom (repentance) and freely programs his entire *future* (duty).

The centrality of time in human existence demands recognition at each stage on life's way, and it is not surprising to find that Kierkegaardian *personae* who occupy widely different existence-spheres nevertheless parcel out their temporality into analogous categories. The aesthete apprehends his past in recollection and his future in hope; repentance and duty are the ethical correlates of these temporal modes. But the recollection and the hope alike of the aesthete merge in a retreat to an imaginary eternity that empties his existence of temporal content and consistency: the unhappiest man in the world, the man without a present, is vanity before and behind and throughout. The ethical man, on the contrary, whose choice is a choice of himself in all his temporal concretion, unites his past (repentance) and his future (duty) in the instant of resolution. At one point in his correspondence Judge Wilhelm addresses A in his own language:

> You. . . will certainly grant that I am right in making the general observation that men are divided into two great classes: those who predominantly live in hope; and those who predominantly live in recollection. Both have a wrong relation to time. The healthy individual lives at once both in hope and in recollection, and only thereby does his life acquire true and substantial continuity.

"The true present," he adds, "is a unity of hope and recollection."[17] But that unity is more accurately expressed in ethical terms as a unity of duty and repentance. Over against the hero of the *symparanekromenoi*, the unhappy man of forlorn hope and melancholy recollection, bereft of his present, stands the ethical hero, the happy hero of resolution, in the true present, his past mastered in repentance and his future secure in the bond of duty.

The necessity and the significance of repentance in an ethical mode of existence are obvious if it is noted that a man who chooses himself ethically chooses to be absolutely responsible for whatever he is and becomes. But the self for which he assumes total responsibility stands in a natural and historical nexus, it has a spatial and temporal spread; in particular it has a past. This past becomes his when he freely accepts the liability for it, and he cannot reject it without going back on his self-choice. Yet there is much in any man's past that cannot be affirmed as good. It must therefore be affirmed as guilty. The affirmation of oneself as guilty is the ethical meaning of repentance. Repentance is the movement of freedom by which a man gets under the whole weight of his past and shoulders it for the future. For "my life does not begin in time with nothing, and if I cannot repent the past, freedom is a dream."[18]

It is only if he is willing to undertake his guilt that the ethical man can say he chooses himself as "absolute." He does not create himself as a natural and historical being: in this sense he is not absolute but relative, not independent but contingent. But he is free with a dependent freedom and he becomes a contingent absolute just insofar as he is able to get hold of himself as a whole. And this he can do only if he will repent himself back through his whole history.

Free self-choice is the choice of oneself as guilty. Any other understanding of freedom is either paltry or abstract, the paltriness which the aesthete despises or the abstraction that he is condemned to remain. Judge Wilhelm wants to make clear to A that any qualifications or limitations introduced at this point would be no more than a craven attempt to get an easy acquittal for aestheticism.

It is easy to see why Kierkegaard entrusts the commendation of the ethical life into the hands of Judge Wilhelm; for to live ethically is to sit in judgment on oneself and hand down the bitter verdict, Guilty. Anyone who cannot declare himself guilty in this way has not yet accepted himself completely. Anything less than a choice of oneself as guilty is only a form of "self-defense" by which a fundamentally aesthetic personality protects itself against the intrusion of the ethical demand. Only by repentance does one choose himself concretely. Only by repentance does one acknowledge the double truth, that evil belongs necessarily to his self (else he could not choose it) and that it does not belong necessarily to his self (else he could not choose it freely and absolutely).

The greater the freedom the greater the guilt, and this is one of the secrets of blessedness, and if it be not cowardice, it is at least faintheartedness not to be willing to repent the guilt of the forefathers; if not paltriness, it is at least pettiness and lack of magnanimity.[19]

Repentance, however, is but one moment of the ethical choice; the correlative movement in the opposite direction, first empowered by repentance, is duty. The aesthetic life was structured by a dialectic of withdrawal and return. The same dialectic repeats itself in the ethical life, but at the level of freedom, and therefore, in radically altered form, now concretely temporal rather than abstractly eternal. Having attained the level of freedom by despairing of aestheticism, the ethical man concurrently chooses himself in his eternal validity. The movement of repentance is the element of withdrawal in this self-choice; by repentance he gets all the way outside himself, behind his own past. In the life of duty he returns to himself and advances into his future.

The self that is repented is the concrete self. It is the past actuality of the individual who chooses; but insofar as he chooses it, it becomes his future possibility. Nature overtaken by freedom and considered in relation to the future becomes task. The task of the ethical man is to become himself, to take his given nature in hand and make it his responsibility. And to accept oneself as one's own responsibility is to acknowledge the claim of duty. "For as soon as in despair a person has found himself, has absolutely chosen himself, has repented himself, he has himself as a task under an eternal responsibility, and thus duty is posited in its absoluteness." Duty, like repentance, expresses the identity of dependence and freedom in human personality.

Duty conceived is of course utterly abstract. But duty acted on is as concrete as the individual himself. The principle of duty can be stated in a form applicable to every man without exception: Thou shalt become thyself. But particular duties cannot be defined in theory, they can only be discovered in situation. Particular duties arise, for each person, out of the exigencies of his particular nature and the particular circumstances in which he finds himself. Judge Wilhelm, as a married man, a father, and a civil servant, has no difficulty descrying the duties that are appropriate to his station in life. And neither, he suggests, will anyone who is seriously committed to the principle of duty, who has not kept back some little aesthetic reservation by which he hopes to get himself an occasional moral holiday. That is why the Assessor does not represent the primary ethical choice as a choice *between* good and evil, but as a choice *of* good and evil as the constitutive categories for one's life.

The distinction between good and evil does not exist for the aesthete; morality is not an immediate qualification of human nature nor of the reflection of that nature in the mirror of imagination. To choose to lead one's life in terms of the opposition of good and evil is to elect the ethical as against the aesthetic mode of self-understanding. But for that reason the choice of the ethical *is* the choice of the good; for the good in an abstract sense is just the free resolution to become oneself by the way of repentance and duty. "As soon as one can get a man to stand at the crossways in such a position that there is no recourse but to choose, he will choose the right." Not that the ethical man does what is right in every case; but even when he does wrong in some particular, his commitment to the principle of good is still primary. The fundamental orientation of his will, which shows itself in his repentance and his recognition of duty, is right. In this respect he is opposed to the demoniac like John the Seducer, who is imprisoned in evil even though he may incidentally do good.

Ethics, for Judge Wilhelm, is not a matter of values but of being. It is not in the first place a question of following a certain set of moral rules; it is the determination to become a certain kind of person. As over against the aesthete, who drifts through life neutrally occupied with imaginative possibilities and therefore never becomes a self, the ethical man sustains in day-to-day exercise of will the resolution by which he ever consolidates his personality around the either/or: good/evil. If by repenting the past a man can assume the burden of responsibility for himself, and if by daily facing the future in dutiful resolve he can build the integrity of this self, then it may be added that his

> eternal dignity consists in the fact that he can have a history, the divine element in him consists in the fact that he himself, if he will, can impart to this history continuity, for this it acquires only when it is not the sum of all that has happened to me or befallen me but is my own work, in such a way that even what has befallen me is by me transformed and translated from necessity to freedom.

The Assessor's conception of history, which has more than a suggestion of Hegel about it, implies a perfect mutuality of subject (freedom) and object (immediacy) which is attained only in ethical choice. Speaking *in casu amoris* the Judge declares that only conjugal love is authentically historical. Romantic love gives itself out to be wholly immersed in the beloved, but the lover's concern with his object reduces to a cherished and fragile feeling of himself that cannot enter into responsible involvement with the beloved. Similarly, seduction (which the Judge calls "experimental love") pretends to be absorbed by the vicissitudes of the victim, while in reality it is no more than an imaginary self-manipulation of the seducer. But married love

> shows itself to be historical by the fact that it represents a process of assimilation which works its way through its experience and refers the experience back to itself. Thus, it is not a disinterested witness of what occurs but is essentially a sympathetic participant, in short, it experiences its own development.

Like the Hegelian consciousness making historical experience of its object, the ethical resolve of freedom so communicates with the "other" of its givenness that while the other is "posited" by the self-choice and so not independent of it, nevertheless the self allows the other its own development and is a "sympathetic participant" in it. Thus the married man assumes dominion over his erotic desires by means of the vow in which his choice of himself is already presupposed as perfected; but within the dimension of that vow he can allow his desire its natural development and throw himself with a whole heart into its movement. Generalizing, the Judge concludes:

> In the resolution *(Forsaettet)* is posited *(er sat)* an other, but at the same time this other is posited as overcome; in the resolution this other is posited as an inward other, inasmuch as even the outward is visible by means of the reflection in the inward experience. The historical factor here consists in the fact that this other comes forth and acquires its validity, but precisely in its validity is seen to be something which ought not to have validity, so that love (the content of the resolution), tested and purified, issues from this movement and assimilates the experience.

In this *Aufhebung* of nature by spirit, accomplished in the twofold movement of repentance and duty, the discrepancy between inner and outer is repaired. What the wishful longing of the aesthete could not achieve—the reconciliation of immediacy and freedom—is experienced as a living historical reality by the ethical man.

Therefore, although the choice of the ethical way of life entails the rejection of the aesthete's way of life, the aesthetic element in existence remains. A man does not eliminate his immediacy by choosing to live his life in other than immediate categories. That was the point of the Assessor's fable of the young man: to indicate that the aesthete could not even neutralize his immediacy nor escape the shocks to which it might expose him, much less deal honorably with it. It is now incumbent on Judge Wilhelm to show that the ethical life *does justice to* this aesthetic component of existence. And he does so at length. "Personality," he says, "manifests itself as the absolute which has its teleology in itself"; or as we might translate: personality is an end in itself. But this intrinsic value is exactly what the aesthete is after when he seeks to live "beautifully" and "artistically." Ethical personality, the one thing in the world that is of inherent worth, is also the one thing truly beautiful. The ethical choice is far from negating the aesthetic element of life: it is in fact the necessary condition of genuine aesthetic enjoyment. For example, suppose a man possesses great wealth. As long as he continues to live aesthetically his wealth is his fate. He is dependent upon it for his enjoyment; it, not he, constitutes his life; his wealth owns him, he does not own it. If he then makes the ethical choice of himself, he becomes free with respect to his wealth. His life no longer depends upon it or upon any gift of fortune; good fortune or bad, he is master of himself. Now for the first time he can enjoy his wealth and enjoy it freely, because it has become a thing of indifference to him. This indifference may sound like the aesthete's hopelessness, but there is a new twist. In his hopelessness the aesthete remains enslaved to the fate he flees. In ethical self-choice a man buys his immediacy back out of slavery to nature and fate, and makes it his own. The ethical choice is the condition of the possibility of pleasure, for it does not destroy the aesthetic but redeems it. [20]

The prospect is inviting. But the Judge's letters in *Either/Or* do not detail the resources of freedom by means of which this rehabilitation of immediacy takes place. Possibly he was conscious of this deficiency when he later included such a statement in his "Various Observations about Marriage in Reply to Objections." This statement is important for an understanding of the ethical point of view, because it exhibits that viewpoint in its furthest reaches.

There is a kind of reflection, the Judge says, which is "the destroying angel of immediacy." Such a reflection is that of the Seducer: as the critic of immediacy it holds against it the norm of an abstract ideal to which no immediacy can accommodate itself, and which, therefore, annihilates that immediacy as the Seducer annihilates Cordelia. Were all reflection of this sort, none but the unhappy "negative resolution" would ever be possible. Fortunately for the ethical enthusiast, there is another kind of reflection that is good medicine for the immediate, a reflection whose purpose is not to demean reality with the rod of the ideal, but to introduce the ideal as a shaping and stabilizing influence into the real. It is not unlikely that the Judge is thinking of the two functions of the law: its governing power by which it brings about justice among men as opposed to its punitive power by which it can only excise injustice. The reflection that all but prevented the aesthetes of *In Vino Veritas* from tasting the perfect banquet is the angel of devastation; the reflection by which Judge Wilhelm earns the daily bread of conjugal bliss is the spirit of reconciliation.

The constructive reflection proper to the positive resolution concerns itself with the relationship of the ideal to the real. It does this by first perfecting itself as reflection. A man cannot call himself rational nor claim to order his actions by reason until he has consumed all the energies of reason in philosophic questioning and recoiled from the surds of existence onto the necessity of order, however arbitrary its ultimate foundations. So also,

> In a purely ideal reflection the resolution has ideally exhausted reality, and the conclusion of this ideal reflection is something more than a *summa summarum*, in short it is precisely resolution; resolution is the ideality brought about by a purely ideal reflection, it is the earned capital required for action.

Unpacking: a man about to undertake an ethical choice anticipates, naturally, certain difficulties that will arise from the side of his immediacy when it comes to working out the details of his choice in daily life. A man on the brink of matrimony will think of the discouraging possibilities that lie in his way: his wife may lose her affection for him or vice versa, infidelity may threaten, business failure and poverty may lurk around the corner, disease and death may take their toll of his family, the in-laws may be intolerable, etc., literally *ad infinitum*. There is no end to possibilities when one is reflecting. If our bridegroom-to-be is not to give up in cynical despair and pronounce marriage far too risky a business in view of the frailty of nature, if, that is, he is not to become the woeful hero of the negative resolution, he must somehow arm himself to do battle with these dreadful possibilities. He does this, according to the Assessor, simply by facing the matter out. The possibilities are infinite. But freedom is as infinite as possibility. Indeed, freedom is the *source* of infinite possibility, for it is only a *free* being who *has* possibilities. Freedom, therefore, is able to set all these heads on a single neck and sever them with a single stroke of resolve. A "purely ideal reflection" neutralizes the terrors of reality by "ideally exhausting" it, that is, by forseeing all the possibilities (not severally, of course, but in the principle that anything is possible) and steeling itself to face them. This is resolution's "earned capital for action." The man who has ideally vanquished infinite possibilities is not likely to be unsettled by the finite selection, however grisly, with which reality is able to try him. The point of the exertions of repentance and duty is to gather up all the possibilities issuing from the past and the future, sum them in an ideal reflection and counter them with resolution. Such a resolution, the Judge concludes, will hold fast to the ideal, triumph over all the dangers and temptations of reality, and put the resolver in relationship with God through the universal.[21]

The last phrase is loaded with echoes of other pseudonyms, *personae* who stand for a religious way of life that goes beyond the limits of the ethical. In the passage under discussion Judge Wilhelm makes use of the characteristic Kierkegaardian religious categories in order to bolster the ethical resolve and to explain how it manages to bridge the gap of possibility between freedom and nature. "The resolution," he says, "is not man's strength, it is not man's courage, it is not man's talent . . . , but it is a religious starting point." Reflection, he writes, "is brought to a conclusion in faith, which is precisely anticipation of the ideal infinity in the form of resolution."[22] Johannes Climacus in the *Philosophical Fragments* had already declared that faith conquers doubt (which like possibility is infinite upon reflection) by including it within itself as a constantly *aufgehoben* moment.[23] His contrapositive Anti-Climacus was to define God as infinite possibility, so that the encounter with infinite possibility is an encounter with God.[24] Vigilius Haufniensis, the watchman of

60

Copenhagen and guardian of the ramparts of Christian theology against the rationalistic attack force, defines faith in terms almost the same as the Assessor's: "By faith I mean what Hegel somewhere in his fashion calls very rightly the inward certainty which anticipates infinity."[25] Judge Wilhelm characterizes the resolution as a "new immediacy attained through the ideally inexhaustible reflection," which new immediacy is the reconciliation of God and man, the second "immediacy of religion." Finally, the Assessor's venture that the man preparing for the resolution of marriage "must either let go of love . . . or believe in God," since the "absurdity of love" can only be secured against the trials of time by the "absurdity of religion,"[26] harks back to the faith of father Abraham, which Johannes de Silentio says is had only "by virtue of the absurd."[27]

Judge Wilhelm, then, means to be a religious man and he means to advocate a religious view of human existence. Especially is he driven to religion by the challenge which a recalcitrant immediacy and a restless reflection throw down to each other: religious faith is the only power by which the two may be united in peace. Yet it is strange that the Judge combines with his piety a more than conventionally Protestant suspicion of monasticism (of which more later), and a more than strictly Pauline optimism about marriage (of which also much more later). The Assessor's religion relates man to God *through the universal*, as opposed to the faith of Abraham, which is initially alienated from the universal (=the ordinary human) situation and only restored to it by the miraculous interposition of God. His religion is in reality "a religious life-view constructed upon ethical postulates,"[28] and his appeal to God—like any consistent ethical faith—is an appeal to the only power in heaven that is capable of repairing on earth the breach of freedom and nature. Judge Wilhelm's God, like the God of Immanuel Kant, is a supersensible guarantor of the validity of his moral position and its invisible harmony with the seemingly independent domain of natural desire. Though the point of reference is transcendent, the act of referral (resolution or faith) is the immanent act of a human will, and the import of the act and its object lies wholly within the sphere of worldly ethical activity. Religion, for Judge Wilhelm, is not a distinct way of life, but a dimension of the ethical life, essential if the strength of resolution is to be equal to the task of redeeming its (also essential) dimension of immediacy.

The transfiguration of the aesthetic by the ethical is the theme of much of Judge Wilhelm's second letter to A, and works itself out in a series of contrasts between the aesthetic and the ethical ways of life. The ethical, he says, is the *universal*, as opposed to the aesthetic, which is *differential*. While the aesthete's personality is always built on his possession of some talent that differentiates him from the mass of men, the ethical man refuses to take any moral advantage from such gifts. He will not let his personal fate separate him from other men; the fact that one is a genius or "the unhappiest man" in the world is ethically irrelevant, and no man devoted to duty would claim any virtue either from his excellence or his wretchedness. The ethical choice equalizes men in a way that most men, their lives aesthetically determined, find hard to tolerate. It is difficult to resist the temptation to hold back from the universal some little difference, be it only one's misery, that sets one apart from the herd. Yet it is ethically intolerable that there should be essential differences among men, that a man's character should depend on luck, good or bad, or that men should be distinguished as men from each other by aesthetic accidents. Of course, all the aesthetic differences remain within the context of the ethical choice; but there they exist as freely appropriated, non-essential, and therefore redeemed and given their rightful status. [29]

It may seem inconsequent that Kierkegaard presents the aesthete as a figure of human nature—man in his immediacy— and yet allows Judge Wilhelm to classify the aesthetic as the "differential" and claim for the ethical the rights of "universal human." But the rationale is not far to seek. Immediately men are what they are; what they are, however, is not one and equal, but different and diverse. Universal humanity is a vestment to which only he is entitled who has received the consecration of freedom. This is a self-ordination to which all men have vocation, for a man acquires his universal humanity by means of his ethical self-choice, whereby he relates himself to the eternal and makes this eternal validity effective in time. Immediacy is but a tissue of "givens" from which the human is to be made by the techniques of resolution. The man who, like the aesthete, wants to *be* his immediacy wills to hold on to his difference from others, a potentiality toward the universal, but never the universal itself in full reality, "signed in heaven and counter-signed in time," sharing with all men their common filiation from divinity and their common destiny as mortals on earth.

The aesthetic is *secrecy* (the secrecy of the peculiar and the differential), the ethical is *revelation* (the revelation essential to the universal human). It is the duty of every man to become manifest, the Judge insists.[30] Commenting on this dictum, Kierkegaard writes that it is "really the opposite of the whole of the first part [of *Either/Or*]."

> The aesthetic is always hidden; insofar as it expresses itself it is coquettish. It would, therefore, have been wrong to allow "A" to speak out his inmost heart directly, or even among "B's" papers. From his papers one suspects what is inside "A", one knows the outside with which he is accustomed to deceive from "B's" papers.[31]

Characteristically A expresses himself archly to a nonesuch audience, while B pours out his heart for hundreds of pages in letters addressed to A, and aimed at his conversion to the universal. The ethical universal demands community—and demands it openly—just as the aesthetic difference craves privacy —and speaks only by a kind of ventriloquism that will not betray its hermitage.

But this is only to repeat (the Judge is as repetitive as the simplicity of his message and the volume of his enthusiasm can make him) what has already been said: the ethical universal (duty) is a *concrete* universal as opposed to the *abstract* or poetic universal. For duty works intimately into and through the temporal finite world, while poetry can only retreat from it. The poet may be the child of eternity, but he has not the seriousness of eternity, which is its ability to incarnate itself in time. Mysticism, asceticism, monasticism the Asesssor regards as a kind of aesthetic *contemptus mundi* masquerading as religious; intrusive in their relation to God, they take the ethical decision in vain and deceive themselves out of a world. The ethical man by contrast takes his place in the world in the midst of the community of men; he knows that it is his duty (to the universal) to reveal himself to others, while the aesthete—whether poet, demon, or mystic—always remains in the concealment of his aesthetic differentia. Though he can conceive of a man who, because of some unique vocation, finds it impossible to "realize the universal," the Judge can see nothing in the life of such an "exception" but unrelieved misery. If such a man is reconciled to the universal at all, it will only be by remorse over his inability to actualize the universal directly.[32]

In the later and more polemical essay, in which he brushes against the religious limits of his moralism, the Assessor goes more particularly into this question: Is there a justified exception to the universal? Marriage is of course the case in point of the universal. "I do not say," the Judge begins, in epilogue to his defense of the wedded estate, "that marriage is the highest, I know a higher; but woe to him who would skip over marriage without justification." If a justified exception to the universal is to occur, it must occur "in the direction of the religious, in the direction of spirit, in such a way that being spirit makes one forget that one is also man."[33]

Constantine Constantius indulges in not a little mystifying talk about the exception in *Repetition,* in keeping, no doubt, with his determination to speak in riddles so that the heretics will not understand him. Constantine's concern is with the dialectical wrestling-match in which the exception champions against the universal its claim to be justified. "On the one side," he writes,

> stands the exception, on the other the universal, and the strife itself is a strange conflict between the wrath and impatience of the universal at the hubbub the exception causes, and its amatory predilection for the exception. . . . On the other side the insubordination and defiance of the exception is in conflict with its weakness and morbidity.

The universal breaks with the exception in this strife and in so doing strengthens it, like the angel that wrestled Jacob into Israel and blessed him by breaking him. Thus empowered, the exception sustains its case against the universal and receives the paternal benediction.

> The situation is as follows. The exception thinks also the universal when it thinks itself, it labors also for the universal when it elaborates itself, it explains also the universal when it explains itself. If one would study the universal thoroughly, one has only to look for the justified exception, which manifests everything more clearly than does the universal itself. The justified exception is reconciled with the universal; the universal is fundamentally polemical against the exception, for it will not evince its predilection before the exception, so to speak, compels it to admit it. If the exception does not possess this power, it is not justified, and therefore, it is very shrewd of the universal not to evince its predilection too early.

Constantine is thinking of Job, who is "sensible only of Heaven's wrath" until by his insistent forensic he "compels heaven to speak out" and is reconciled to his Maker. But he has room in his categories for another justified exception: his young friend, who against his will is made a poet. For any poet is, according to Constantine, a justified exception who "represents the transition to the more properly aristocratic exceptions, namely, the religious exceptions."[34]

Not so generous as the experimental psychologist is the legal mind of Judge Wilhelm. He will allow but one exception to the universal, a religious one, and that of a very special sort. Monasticism he cannot countenance: the monk is inhumane, and presumptuous into the bargain. Inhumane, because he "will not have any concrete comprehension of that which for the majority of men is their life's reality," to wit, marriage and the daily round of communal existence. Presumptuous, because he insinuates himself into "a sort of over-forward comradeship" with God. Ignoring entirely that vocation which at least in theory is a precondition of the monastic vow ("everyone is able to do [it]"), the Judge rejects holy chastity out of hand.

Neither can he countenance the man who by reason of his melancholy temperament begs to be excused from the toils of marriage and socially useful employment. A burden to himself, he would not be a burden to others, and so he "underbids" the universal. But such a man, an object of pathos in his own imagining, is in reality a theme for comedy. Like the man who bargained for reduced fare on a towboat ride and was given half-price on the condition that he would help pull the boat, the melancholic "believes that he is slipping through for half-price, but does not observe that he is pulling as hard as the crew, and has to pay out money besides." He does not in fact avoid life, but only suffers from his abstract relationship to it. Insofar as he must continue to take part in human life whether he likes it or not, he makes his contribution to the whole and reaps no profit but an increase of sorrow.

If there is to be a justified exception to the universal (marriage), he must meet the following rigorous requirements laid down by the Judge: (1) he must be deeply in love, and compelled to break with the beloved; (2) he must be married and a father, compelled to forsake wife, children, and kin; (3) he must love life itself, especially in giving it up, for "he who would renounce something universal must know it more thoroughly than does the man who lives securely in it"; (4) "he must comprehend the after-pains of the breach as punitive suffering," though he cannot find himself guilty in a single point as against the life he renounces; for (5) no man can make himself the justified exception by his own will, but rather he must be forced to it by something that happens to him from without; so that (6) he acknowledges himself the most miserable of men; and to cap the thing (7) he cannot explain his plight to others, for since he has broken with the universal "no one can understand him" and "human language has for him naught but curses, and the human heart has for his sufferings only the one feeling that he is guilty." "This," the Assessor concludes, "is the beginning of becoming an exception, if there be such a thing; if all this is not given, then he is without justification." There is one more turn to the screw: the justified exception "never gets to know definitely in this life if he is such." "I do not know," the Judge sighs, "whether there is a justified exception, and if there be such a man, neither does he know it, not even at the instant when he sinks down, for if he has the least presentiment of it, he is not justified." The sealed dispatch which contains his orders from God may not be opened until he is too far out at sea to turn back, too far even for a last longing look at the shore he has left forever behind him. [35]

This terrible figure, from whom Judge Wilhelm shrinks in eloquent horror, has all the lineaments of Abraham, as he is portrayed by John of Silence. Married and a devoted father, executor of the covenant, in love with the life of his tents, Abraham is brought into conflict with his God, his people, his family, and his own heart by the divine command to sacrifice Issac. He cannot even confide to Sarah the purpose and reason of that trek to Mt. Moriah which is to deprive her of the beloved fruit of her aged and blessed womb. By his faith, and by the absurd power of God, Abraham receives Isaac again; but in the moment of his renunciation he is without comfort or community, a man isolated in contradiction to the universal, justified only by counsels hidden beyond the reach of human reckoning in the inscrutable purposes of God. [36]

The poet of *Fear and Trembling* admires in his silence that faith which he cannot comprehend. Judge Wilhelm, committed to the universal, sees the same possibility, but turns his eyes from the dreadful vision to the happier scenes of his parlor and the reassuring order in the courtroom. In the Diary of the Seducer the aesthete gets a presentiment of the ethical life, but he contrives to poetize the threat of conscience into a bittersweet disquietude that bodes no crisis but only adds a new tang to his *vita ante acta*. So in the thought of the justified exception the possibility of a religious breach with the universal looms before the Judge; but he disqualifies the notion as a remote and improbable bogey, so that he may return to the security of "what I definitely know . . .

> The happiness of my marriage. . . . The terror is now far off, I am no longer sitting as examining magistrate, but in my library; and as a thunderstorm makes the landscape smile again, so is my soul again in the humor to write about marriage. . . . [37]

Which presumably he would have done had not his wife at that moment passed his door and dropped a hint that she would welcome his attentions. To which pleasant husbandly duty he hastens with eager and confident steps.

In the light of these observations, it is easy to see why the Judge exults in the view that every man has a calling and is obliged to work in order to live; whereas the aesthete, for whom the necessity of working would be burdensome, requires (the accident of) opulence in order to carry out his project of enjoyment. The contractual obligation involved in work points up the ethical conviction that there is an order of things in which every man can find a place, a place where he can accomplish the universal (by earning . . .) in his own individuality (. . . his living). Such a man is his own providence, and that is no more than to say that he lives ethically.

The ethical view of work may be summed up in three propositions which Judge Wilhelm elaborates in this second letter. (1) It is every man's duty to work for his living. The aesthete hopes to escape the curse of Adam, whether by fortune or by artifice, but the ethical man rejoices to labor in the service of the universal. The gift of wealth is an exception to the normal condition of man, a special favor, which for the aesthete is a blessing, but which for the ethical man constitutes an exceptional humiliation to his freedom and an exceptional addition to his duty. For it is in work that man perfects his dignity and his autonomy. "It is precisely by working that man makes himself free, by working he becomes lord over nature, by working he shows that he is higher than nature." This last, with its rumor of Hegel, reveals that work for Judge Wilhelm is part of the total process of self-formation by which the ethical man enthrones his eternal validity in the kingdom of nature and history. Thus the struggle for bread, because it takes a man in his essential humanity, is at once more difficult and nobler than those heroic ventures in the exceptional at which the poet marvels. The unusual and the extraordinary prove nothing. But the fact that a man can, and is obliged to, earn his own living shows that the ethical personality "has its teleology in itself." The ethical view of work has a double advantage over the aesthetic:

> In the first place, it is consonant with reality and explains something universal in it. . . . In the second place, it construes man with a view to his perfection, sees him in his true beauty.

For the ethical hero, work is no *"dura necessitas,"* but rather "the most beautiful thing and the most perfect."

(2) It is every man's duty to have a calling. This proposition defines the ethical man's attitude toward his natural abilities. For the aesthete, work, when it is not a sordid drudgery for subsistence, can only be understood as the unfettered and unproductive development of his talents, for which, of course, a fortune is required. For the ethical man a "talent" is a "call," and his work is the activity of freedom by which he transforms a gift into a vocation. The man who has found his calling has

> at the same time a more significant expression for its relation to his personality: it is his calling, and so the accomplishment of it is associated with a satisfaction of his whole personality; he has got also a more significant expression for the relation of his work to other men, for since his work is his calling, he is thereby put essentially on an equal footing with all other men, he is then doing by his work the same thing that every other man does, he is performing his calling. He claims recognition of this, more he does not claim, for this is the absolute.

Like the duty to work, the duty to regard one's work as a call has the twofold advantage that "it explains talent not as something accidental in existence, but as the universal," and so "it exhibits the universal in its true beauty," that intrinsic *telos* that only the realization of the "universal human" can lay claim to.

(3) It is every man's duty to do his job and not fret himself about what he may have accomplished over and beyond the simple fulfillment of his duty. The aesthete may insult humanity and flatter himself (or console himself!) with the view that only a few really great men are ever elected to change the course of history. The ethical man prefers the humane consolation of duty, for which the only accomplishment that matters is "doing one's job," and in relation to which every other impression that a man may make on his contemporaries or on posterity is a bit of luck, to be accepted with gratitude if good and forgone without envy or self-pitying malice if bad.

> So our [ethical] hero works in order to live; this work is at the same time his pleasure; he fulfills the duties of his calling, he accomplishes his job—to say it all in one word, and with a word which inspires you [A] with dread. . . he has a living.

But though A shudder at the thought, Judge Wilhelm is moved to enthusiasm by the simple moral consideration that he can always do well (earn his daily bread) by doing good (following the call of duty to perfect the universal in his daily employment). [38]

Finally, Judge Wilhelm's ardent advocacy of marriage, as against romantic love and seduction, expresses to perfection the way in which the ethical self-choice works itself out in time and transfigures a man's immediacy. Biologically bound to the bearing and rearing of children, the life of woman is limited and defined by the cycle of conception, gestation, parturition, and maturation. She therefore understands time more intimately than any masculine philosopher; she and not man deserves to be called the lord and master of nature. Her ethical role, consequently, is to be man's finitude, and this she achieves only in her capacity as wife and mother. To treat her as an ideal (seduction) or as an occasion (romance), is to defraud her and oneself of destiny. It is only in marriage, where it becomes duty via the solemn vow, that love achieves actuality in time. Whence "the aesthetic validity of marriage." Any other view of love treats it as an abstraction or as an accident, betrays it or loses it by default. The freedom that is vainly sought in seduction, and the pleasure that is vainly demanded of romance, first become realities in the ethical context of marriage, where immediacy ("falling in love")

69

is taken up in freedom (the vow) and made concrete in the public trust and private devotion of family life.[39] .

This matter of marriage will bear further consideration. In the Assessor's first letter to A, it bears more than 150 pages of close analysis. It is not surprising to learn that marriage has the same virtues as the calling:

> It elucidates the universal, not the accidental. It does not show how a couple of very singular people with extraordinary traits might become happy, but how every married couple may become so. It regards the relationship as the absolute, and so does not apprehend the differences as guarantees, but comprehends them as tasks. It regards the relationship as the absolute and hence beholds love with a view to its beauty, that is, its freedom; it understands historical beauty.[40]

To the maxims on work, quoted above, we must add the proposition, It is every man's duty to marry. The defense of this position, plus a demonstration of the perennial beauty of the married estate, constitutes the bulk of the Judge's brief for "the aesthetic validity of marriage." "Validity" *(Gyldighed)* is a legal term, and it is the Assessor's purpose to show that marriage can maintain its rights before the judgment seat of aesthetics.

As a solid citizen of the nineteenth-century Danish middle class, Judge Wilhelm has naturally soaked up, from the pulpit and the popular press as well as from his more scholarly reading, the Hegelian habit of thinking in threes: thesis, antithesis, and synthesis. He is critical of the prevailing tendency to construe life in hyper-intellectual categories, but though his content is everyday life, his form is straight Prussian academy. The trinity is this case is romantic love (immediacy), intellectual anti-love (reflection), and marriage (the synthesis of immediacy and reflection).

Romantic love the Judge identifies with the feeling of "falling in love," and quite correctly regards it as the wholly abstract possibility of a real love-relationship. He speaks of the unreality of the period of engagement, in which the lovers, not yet permitted to taste the meat and potatoes of marriage, live only upon "the sweet confectionary of possibility." Though dear to the poet, because of its innocence of all responsibility and involvement, the engagement (like the Hegelian immediacy) is only a presupposition that is annulled when one acts on it. (In the Judge's day, fornication and adultery were not yet the normal novelistic expressions of love, though they were rapidly becoming so; nor did the nineteenth century, like the twentieth, suppose that experience of sex was a necessary preliminary to the feeling of love.)

Romantic love is immediate because it is abstract; at the same time it is immediate in the sense that it is based on natural necessity (think of the dialectic of *Don Juan*). "Falling in love" is the natural response to physical beauty and to the inner spiritual beauty that is hidden in the body and is "constantly on the point of expressing itself, peeking out through the sensuous form." (Has the Judge perhaps read Plato's *Phaedrus* and *Symposium?*) This very inner beauty, which is active behind the scenes of romance, is a "presumptive eternity" which "ennobles" love, sets it in relation to the "true eternity" of morality, and fits it to be delivered out of bondage to the senses by a resolute decision of the will.

But before the harbor of matrimony is reached, the lovers (at least the more intellectual male) must navigate the shoals of reflection. It will be recalled that A had taken *Les premières amours* of Scribe as the occasion not only to rehearse the playwright's jibes at romance, but also to remark on the importance of the "accidental" for the exercise of his own genius. Judge Wilhelm takes him up on this. Identifying "first love" with "romantic love," he avows that he knows "a much deeper appreciation of the significance of the accidental in life," to wit marriage, the joy of which is "to renew constantly the first love." The poet's ironies at the expense of romance are like a parasite on love, living on what they destroy. That love itself, evacuated by satire, is likened to an exanimate body that continues with tragicomic persistence to perform its customary functions during the brief moment before death overtakes it entirely. [41]

An incomplete reflection (anything short of resolution) will necessarily become cynical and disillusioned with romance. Its deadly works are seduction or—more respectable but no less dreadful—the *marriage de convenance*. Both are "convenient arrangements" which, for all the precise calculation that may triumph in them, are permeated by the deepest melancholy and the most complete dearth of love. Like morality and unlike romantic love, they have an abundance of reflection; but they lack the "true eternity" of the ethical and the eternity *in potentia*

71

of first love. Love is scarcely born in feeling before it is murdered in infancy by reflection.

The only agency that can unite the opposites of romance and reflection is Christian marriage. The same Protestant this-worldliness that hallows gainful employment also sanctifies the marriage bond. Marriage, says the Judge, "is the true transfiguration of romantic love," as well as "the most beautiful task proposed to men." For "all the beauty inherent in the pagan erotic has validity also in Christianity, insofar as it can be combined with marriage." As the resolution is a new immediacy which mates obligation with pleasure in higher unity, so the Christian wedding vow is a higher synthesis of duty and desire.

The basis for the reconciliation of first love and reflection, the ground of the possibility of marriage, is that eternity which is potentially present in feeling and actually realized in ethical choice. Love, as opposed to simple lust, has in it "precisely the characteristic of eternity," albeit latent and undeveloped. Therefore, love is "the substantial factor in marriage." Love is the matter whose potencies are elicited by the supervening form of the resolution. Love and ethics are connatural, and this is the preestablished harmony which secures the marriage vow. Love is untried by time and circumstance, but it is armed against all the sieges of misfortune by that resolve, approaching faith, which is refined in the fires of infinite possibility. Therefore, "marriage contains an ethical and religious factor, as love does not; for this reason marriage is based upon resignation, as love is not."

The dialectic by which Judge Wilhelm explains the "eternity" of first love and defends its compatibility with resolute reflection is exceedingly difficult, but absolutely important. It is the "firstness" of "first love" that is the key to his mind here. When it is experienced, each man's first love is a present reality. For the fact that it is the first, and therefore to date only, love, it contains its own entire past. And because it is in itself a possibility to be realized, it is pregnant with its entire future. This is its eternity, that it unites past, present, and future in itself. "In 'the first' the whole is present implicitly, hiddenly . . .; the first love comprises the whole content." This accounts, to the Judge's satisfaction, for the all-engrossing power of romantic love which makes the lovers oblivious to the world around them. It explains the perennial theme of poets, "that the lovers even at first sight feel as if they had already loved one another for a long while." And it makes sense of the sentiment that love is outside of time. [42]

Viewed in this light, first love manifestly cannot be repeated: there is no second, third, fourth, love. Love can be lost, if carelessly handled by a cynical reflection like that of Scribe; and if once the first love is lost, all love is lost, for the first contains the whole. Or, a consummation devoutly to be wished, love can be forever preserved if it is "reflected upon eternally" by the vow of marriage.

Thus it is that the love which is first in time is also eternal. This unity of the temporal and eternal is, of course, an immediate unity; it is the given of love, as opposed to that mediate synthesis which is achieved in the resolution of freedom. Similarly love has been seen to embrace an immediate harmony of the sensuous and the ideal (beauty). It is the unity of freedom and necessity; for in the very inevitability of his passion, the lover "feels himself free, is sensible in this of his whole individual energy, precisely in this he senses the possession of all that he is." Finally, love unites universal and particular; every instance of love displays the same generic nature, and yet each such instance also "has the particular up to the limit of the fortuitous." But all these unities, the Assessor recalls, "it has, not by virtue of reflection but immediately."

Now then: the project of marriage is to make first love historical, that is, to effect a synthesis of subject and object, the self and its experience, and so on. But first love has shown itself upon dissection to be already a synthesis of this sort, immediate to be sure, but needing only to be unfolded in the concrete and not requiring to be violated or reformed. It may, as the Judge puts it, be "assumed into a higher concentricity" without passing through the valley of the shadow of a doubt. Reflection is, as we have seen, able not only to destroy, but also to save; and the discussion of first love has now shown that it is ripe for salvation, like the baptized infant ready to be rapt to heaven, needing no preliminary ordeal of repentance and purgation.

The higher concentricity is naturally a wedding ring; and since matrimony in Judge Wilhelm's circle is a Christian institution, he finds himself in contradiction with A's views on flesh and spirit. In his *Don Juan* essay A theorized that Christianity had instituted an absolute enmity between the spirit and the flesh. The Judge, an illumined theologian worthy of the twentieth century, corrects his exegesis. The "flesh" of which the Scriptures speak is not, he says, sensuousness,

> it is selfishness, and in this sense even the intellectual which you call "spiritual" may be sensual; for example, if a man takes in vain his intellectual gifts [who could that be?] he is carnal.

Therefore, the joy and fullness of the body, provided it is innocent, can easily be fitted into a Christian life. If A's interpretation of Christianity were correct, then, says the Judge, we ought to begin forthwith on a course of mortification like that practiced by the extremest ascetics; good health would be a parlous spiritual state; the lepers should have refused to be healed. But all this is plainly out of keeping with a religion whose great Physician went about healing the sick. It is as bad to be too spiritual as it is to be too sensual. Johannes the Seducer is no closer to God than Don Juan; if anything he is yet farther off. [43]

Given this understanding of the relation of body and soul, first love may be wound into the "higher concentricity" of holy wedlock without the intervening shock of an eccentric reflection. First love is simply "referred to God" by the lovers when they give Him thanks for their love, as they might give Him thanks for the bread they eat and the good health they enjoy. By this act of thanksgiving "an ennobling transformation is effected" in their love. It is straightway set in the circle of eternity just as the diamond is set in the golden wedding band. When love is brought to the altar to be consecrated, nature is received into the hallowing community of grace; every good thing in love is sanctified; love is rendered immune to all the natural shocks that flesh is heir to; and the beauty of romance is led unscathed out of the abstraction of feeling into the concreteness of history. The matrimonial "Mine!" re-echoes "not only in the seductive eternity of the instant, not only in the illusory eternity of fantasy and imagination, but in the eternity of clear consciousness, in the eternity of eternity." The reality of married love, founded not "upon obscure forces, but upon the eternal itself," is simply the content inherent potentially in first love, made actual by its subsumption under the rubric of duty. Love becomes a reality when the lovers acquire "resolute purpose and the sense of obligation"; and this they do when they thankfully and resolutely refer their love to God in the marriage vow.

That there is a contradiction in the aesthete's attitudes

toward love—and so in his character as aesthete—is nowhere more clearly seen than in his refusal of the holy estate of matrimony. As a romantic worshipper of *das ewige Weibliche,* he will have none of that mastery over the female with which Christian marriage invests him (I Corinthians 11:3,8–9; Ephesians 5:22–24); and yet, as seducer, it is precisely the most complete hegemony he seeks. As romantic he rejects the dogma of original sin, with which inheritance of their primal parents the wedding ceremony unambiguously enriches the couple at the altar; yet to a "reflective" love it is the "sinful" woman who is aesthetically most interesting. The aesthete will not make a duty of faithfulness, but as romantic he will swear oaths of eternal fidelity which as seducer he cynically finds meaningless. The Judge concludes: your [A's] love demands the transfiguration of marriage, but you thwart it; you feel the need of the "third power" of religion to harmonize and consolidate your personality, but you will not satisfy this need. Therefore, "the death of your love is certain."

The Judge's next task is to show how marriage retains, reinforces, and redeems the aesthetic qualities of romantic love. These qualities are two: first, that "infinity" or "apriority" which has already been remarked, and second, the immediate unity of opposites—sense and spirit, necessity and freedom, time and eternity—that has been shown to be latent in first love. Beginning with the second: marriage also unites the sensuous and the spiritual, after having first put the distance of a "truly idealizing" reflection between them. The spirituality of first love is only a pagan "soulishness," a sensuousness naturally permeated by spirit; the spirituality of marriage, which with greater Christian incisiveness distinguishes body and soul, with equally greater profundity reclaims the body for the soul: "the further one is removed from the sensuous the more aesthetic significance it acquires, for otherwise the instinct of the beast would be the most aesthetic." Similarly: the freedom of first love is but "the soulish freedom of an individual not yet clarified from the dregs of natural necessity," while the more complete ethical and religious freedom of the married couple makes possible a more complete "abandonment of devotion, and only he can be lavish of himself who possesses himself." And not least: marriage has the unity of time and eternity in the true present of resolution, while first love has only a perishing instant that ever disintegrates into a specious present and an equally specious "forever."[44]

What marriage does for the oppositions implicit in love it also does for love's infinity. Judge Wilhelm has the most chilly contempt for all the "finite reasons" that are usually urged in behalf of marriage: one should marry because marriage is a great school for character, one should marry in order to propagate the species, one should marry because it is good to settle down and have a home, etc. All these things are factually true, but if they are taken to justify marriage, they are immoral and unaesthetic, wholly out of order because so much less than the "inward infinity" of marriage itself. Marriage, because it harmonizes all the contradictions of life, "has . . . its teleology in itself; it exists because it constantly presupposes itself, and hence, every question about its 'why' is a misunderstanding. . . ."

The Assessor's claim makes sense only if one realizes that he is using "finite" and "infinite" with a thoroughly Hegelian meaning. A finite reason for marriage would be an external and limiting reason: one does X for the sake of some Y which, as external to the nature of X, puts limitations on X. If one marries in order to propagate the race, then it is the race that matters and not the marriage. The "inward infinity" of marriage, by contrast to the finitude of reasons, is the "good" infinite:

> As an outcome of this investigation I can emphasize here the fact that marriage in order to be aesthetic and religious must. . . have no finite "why." But this was precisely the aesthetical feature of first love; and so here again marriage is on a level with first love, and the aesthetic feature of marriage is that in itself it conceals a multiplicity of "whys" which life gradually brings to light in all their blessedness.[45]

"Infinite" means: self-contained and, therefore, self-justifying, having its teleology in itself. Marriage, according to the Judge, is the highest *telos* proposed to men, because it contains in itself all the boundless diversity of life, including the factors valued by the aesthete. And it includes this diversity in such a way that it is not limited by it, but rather informs it and so gives life meaning, purpose, and unity. The aesthetic lover is desperately subject to restraint by that which he desires and cannot control: favorable circumstance. The conjugal lover, abetted by the "third power" of eternity, has taken his circumstances in tow and beautifully abides in the security of the higher concentricity, the infinite intrinsic teleology of his vow.

The wedding ceremony itself symbolizes this infinity or marriage and so, aesthetic protests to the contrary not withstanding, is a "glorification"[46] of love. The ceremony at the foot of the altar (1) surveys the history of the human race back to Adam and Eve, (2) confronts the espoused couple with original sin and its consequences—for woman, childbirth in pain and subjection to her husband; for man, toiling and sweating for sustenance, (3) demands that the couple counsel with God and conscience before acting, and (4) requires the solemn vow "before God and this congregation." By these means it (1) presents the couple with the universal in the particular and installs *this* marriage in history as the concrete universal (the self-contained infinite), (2) imparts to man and woman their greatest dignity: that they are sinners before God, a state incomparably higher than that of nature, (3) by reminding them of the curse incurred by the first parents, exposes them candidly to the challenge and the dangers of life, and (4) by demanding a vow in the presence of God and man, confronts the bridal pair with their freedom. No better token could be forthcoming, the Judge thinks, that marriage does not despoil the beauty of life, but enhances it.

Judge Wilhelm's defense of "the aesthetic validity of marriage" amounts in effect to a complete inversion of A's view of what is truly beautiful; for

> the aesthetic does not lie in the immediate, but in the acquired— but marriage is precisely the immediacy which has mediacy in itself, the infinity which has finiteness in itself, the eternal which has the temporal in itself.

As the struggle which contains its own victory, marriage is the fulfillment of both the ethical and the aesthetic ideals. "It is, therefore, not true that marriage is a highly respectable estate, but a tiresome one, while love is poetry. No, marriage is properly the poetical thing." Judge Wilhelm plays continually, in his letters to A, on what he takes to be the principal weakness in the aesthete: his incapacity to unite the moments of the actual and the ideal. And he proposes to replace this metastable poetic with a more consistent aestheticism, a poetry of life empowered by and contained with the ethical resolve. Because it has the "law of motion," the capacity to develop historically, conjugal love gives husband and wife the concrete opportunity to achieve gradually a complete mutuality of understanding. For the same reason—that it need not hide from the realities of time—conjugal love does not fly from society, from the congregation before which its vows are taken, nor from the ever-enlarging life of family and acquaintances. While thus involved, conjugal love is also free: it can do without society, without children and family reunions, even, if need be, without romance and sensual gratification, for its enjoyment is conditional upon nothing but the autonomous resolve of husband and wife. Marriage is paradigmatic for the ethical life and salutary for the aesthetic because it unites the fullest freedom with the richest content of natural pleasure in the totality that the aesthete desires, but in his indecision always misses.

The aesthete may still protest against what he regards as the wearisome monotony of married life, with the contention that his "is a nature designed for conquest and not capable of possessing." The Judge counters that everyone is "made for conquest," for the capacity to seize and enjoy the moment is a predicate of the natural man. Possession, however, is an art:

> True art generally takes the opposite direction to the course which nature follows, though without annihilating the process of nature; and so true art will exhibit itself by possessing, not by conquering.

Once again the Assessor inverts A's understanding of the aesthetic, so as to imply that the aesthete remains "stuck in his immediacy," laden with the weight of raw nature, while the ethical man rises to the level of freedom and art. The ethical, he says, recalling the anacoluthic essays of the *symparanekromenoi*, has both an antecedent and a consequent clause, while the aesthetic has only a protasis followed by a suspicious dash. The "external history" of the aesthete is a struggle for conquest, but after the conquest comes only the vain inability to possess, and the ashen taste of regret. The "internal history" of the married man armed with his vow "begins with possession, and history is the development through which one acquires possession." And this "internal history" is, as we have already seen, the "only true history."

The Assessor accuses A of succumbing to the popular

misunderstanding "which confounds what is aesthetically beautiful with the representation of aesthetic beauty." The artistic representation concentrates on ". . . the happy, the indescribable moment, the moment of infinite significance. . . ." But for this reason it must omit everything that is genuinely historical and cannot be represented as condensed in the moment; for example, patience, humility, and conjugal love, the essence of which is that they take time and involve much repetition in time. It is true that the highest art form is that which allows the greatest significance to time, which art form Judge Wilhelm, following Lessing, thinks is poetry. But even the poem when completed must be read as a unity whose parts react on each other indifferent to before and after. Every poem is a spatial construction and only incidentally an event in time; no poem can re-present temporal succession in its structure without foreshortening to the moment. Temporal succession can only be lived, it cannot be depicted without falsification. And yet, the temporality of married love, by virtue of its identity and its historicity, has been shown to be the most beautiful, the only truly beautiful, form of love.

> When, then, I willingly admit that romantic love lends itself more aptly to artistic representation than does conjugal love, this is not by any means to say that the latter is less aesthetic than the former; on the contrary, it is more aesthetic.

Art and poetry cannot represent marriage because in marriage the essential factor is just time itself and its reconciliation with the eternal—"as long as you both shall live"—; but time itself cannot be represented in art, and so to the poet, marriage is repetitious, monotonous, boring. But in reality—as opposed to "in poetry"—the most beautiful of all things is the lifelong daily struggle of love with time and in time. The happiest man alive (as opposed to the "unhappiest man") is the man who lives in eternity and hears the striking of the clock in the hallway measuring out the hours. "Here I have reached the highest concept of the aesthetic," says the eulogist of marriage and the common life:

> And truly he who has enough humility and courage to let himself be transfigured to this degree; who feels that he is, as it were, a character in the drama which the Deity composes, where the poet and the prompter are not different persons, where the individual,

79

like a practiced actor who has lived himself into his part and into his lines, is not disturbed by the prompter, but feels that what is whispered to him is what he himself would say, so that it almost becomes doubtful whethher he puts the words in the prompter's mouth or the prompter in his; he who in the deepest sense feels that he is poet and poetized, who at the moment he feels himself to be the poet possesses the primitive pathos of the lines, at the moment he feels himself poetized has the erotic ear which picks up every sound—that man, and that man alone, has realized the highest ideal of aesthetics.[47]

Then let the aesthete of whatever stripe rage in impotent polemic; the poet of matrimony has a calm and assured reply out of the repose of his heart to the wild protestations of an overingenious head. Is there a young man who is put off from love by the promised warfare of the flesh against the spirit? The Judge will remind him that love is a given which cannot be thought, and chide him that he has lost his immediacy in reflection. Let the youth forbear trying to understand love and instead submit himself to it as to a miracle of nature. Are there connoisseurs of women, seducers, to whom woman is but a lovely apparition meant to be a moment's ornament? The Judge will reprimand him for his insult to the sex; for woman, subject to the categories and capable of the satisfactions of the universal human, is "quite as good as man." Are there men so demented that they make a joke of the idiosyncracies of women? The Assessor will reply that the true humor—which laughs in sympathy with its object—is only to be found in the married estate, where no comedian would dream of finding himself. Romantic love is so dreadfully serious about itself that it cannot laugh; and the laughter of the cynic is a gallows laughter. Are there those who superficially believe that a woman's beauty is but the fading flower of her youth? The Judge will argue that a woman's beauty, provided she be wife and mother, increases with the years. And he will prove his proposition by a series of vignettes from life: a young woman unwearied and unfrayed carries her tired child with poise and dignity down the boulevard of a busy city; a matron in church, unembarrassed, divides her attention charmingly between the edifying words of the preacher and the squirming of the impatient youngster at her side; an old woman at fireside, surrounded by her family, sums in her loving and contented glance the achievements of a domestic lifetime.

Are there men who, in their pride, demean woman as "the weaker sex?" Far from it, Judge Wilhelm answers; as wife and mother, woman's strength is equal to that of man, though it be expressed in patient endurance and with delicate grace rather than in the heavy plodding of business and in outbursts of heroic energy. It requires no great art to insult the female, but much and truer art to let her come into her own in her role as the entrepreneur of the finite. It is no great achievement to disdain the wedded state, or to play at the *game* of love, but it is the sublimest aesthetic achievement as well as the loftiest moral venture to make a happy marriage. For marriage is and will ever be the highest privilege and the gravest responsibility, the extremest duty and the most satisfying *telos* assigned to man. [48]

So Judge Wilhelm concludes—or rather does not conclude, for he is as garrulous as time itself. The length of his letters suggests that his wife's expert management of his finitude leaves him infinite leisure for distributing extra-professional counsel. But that in a way is his point: only by advancing to an ethical understanding of himself does a man find world enough and time to achieve a stable equilibrium of the aesthetical and the ethical in the constitution of his personality. When the Judge is not firing broadsides against the scoffers at marriage, he is writing letters to A. The writings of the aesthete are fruitless divagations (his unpublished review of Scribe), lectures to defunct men, maxims *ad se ipsum* (the deadest of the dead), or aimless meditations. They are meant as poetic and dialectical exercises to be enjoyed, esteemed, admired. But a letter, as the Assessor himself points out, is addressed to a particular person at a particular Post Office. [49] It has the purpose of admonishing and moving its recipient. Like the wisdom of Nathan the prophet addressed to David the King, the wisdom of Judge Wilhelm addressed to A the poet must not be critically evaluated, but personally appropriated: Thou art the man! So the Judge means to lay down the law in a way that will require A to give the verdict and pass sentence on himself. The very habiliments of the two volumes of *Either/Or* are not without significance: A writes on fine vellum letter paper in quarto, the Judge on legal foolscap in folio; A's papers are so disparate that they cannot be ordered except arbitrarily, the Judge's letters have their own order. [50] In sum: A can be anything consistently except *sincere*, which sincerity would be the consistency of life, not the consistency of thought and imagination. The Judge abounds in sincerity (sometimes at the expense of logical consequence and literary elegance), a sincerity that was no doubt *ad nauseam* to A, but which also might have been *ad emendationem vitae suae* had he chosen to get the point.

"What I wanted to do," the Judge writes by way of rounding off A's lesson in morals,

> was to show how the ethical, in the regions which border on the aesthetical, is so far from depriving life of its beauty that it bestows beauty upon it. It affords peace, assurance, and security, for it calls to us constantly: *quod petis, hic est.*[51]

Judge Wilhelm can address A as he does because they are struck by a common perplexity: the contradiction between immediacy and reflection, nature and freedom, in the human self. And they are engaged by a common problem: how to work these conflicting elements into a single personality. A, as aesthete, wants simply to be himself as he is. And the Assessor's reply is that this cannot be done, for what a man is immediately is just this contradiction of immediacy and reflection. The equilibrium which A tries to maintain is worse than precarious, it is an impossible ideal.

> So you are through with life, and, as you say, you have no need to make a will, for you have nothing to leave. But you are unable to hold yourself erect on this pinnacle, for it is true that your thought has taken everything from you, but it has given you nothing in place of it.[52]

Forever vacillating, losing nature for the sake of freedom, and losing freedom for the sake of nature, the aesthete ends by losing himself as the particular worldly and temporal person he is bound to become. The "composition" *(Udarbejdelse)* of personality which the Assessor presses upon him is etymologically a "working-out" or "elaboration" of the self in the temporal order of the world.

In his own copy of *Either/Or* Kierkegaard wrote:

> The first part always comes to grief upon time; which is why the second part first and foremost establishes its worth, by showing in the essay (on the aesthetic validity of marriage) that the aesthetic resolves itself in time, and in the second essay (on the

equilibrium . . .) that to be capable of becoming history, of acquiring history is the significance of the temporal and finiteness.[53]

Volume II of *Either/Or* bears a motto from Chateaubriand's *Atala: Les grandes passions sont solitaires, et les transporter au desert, c'est les rendre a leur empire.*[54] With these words the Judge answers the question posed (and otherwise treated) by the first volume: "Are passions, then, the pagans of the soul? Reason alone baptized?"[55] The Assessor's contention is that only if "passion is brought out of isolation in the solitary individual and brought into communal life with the marriage partner and children is it sanctified, baptized."[56]

The epigraph from Gorgias with which Judge Wilhelm prefaces his *Observations* on marriage makes the same point: "The deceived is wiser than the not-deceived."[57] The Judge and A contend over the same bone: How can it be brought about that reflection shall not violate immediacy? How can freedom and nature be united in such a way that each is given its rights? A will not be put off with any deceptively simple solution to this agonizing problem, and so he despairs of all solutions. The Assessor is no more simple-minded than A, but he is prepared to accept what the latter cannot stomach: a solution which is effective in the days of his life and the world of his daily concern even though it defy theoretical analysis and defile poetic fancy with common sense.

> Is my wealth perhaps less considerable because I possess it in one security which is the only safe one? Is my claim upon life less because I have it on stamped paper? . . . Is not the marriage service itself such a "dark saying" that it needs more than a poet to understand it? Is not its language so astonishing that he who understands the half of it might lose his wits entirely? To talk about duty to a pair of lovers!—to understand this and yet be in love, be bound to the beloved by the tightest bond of immediacy! . . . To hear this, to see the resolution, to hold the mind intent upon it, and at the same time to be able to see the myrtle crown upon the head of the loved one—verily a married man, a proper married man, is himself a miracle![58]

Marriage is the miracle of everyday. Wiser he who is deceived out of the illusions of fancy and speculation by the miracle of reality than he who with matchless consistency and immaculate poesy is tough-minded to the point of effeteness. The latter gives himself in exchange for a wealth that profits him nothing; the former pays a great price, but he buys in an acceptable time the only pearl worth having: his own irreplaceable self.

That is why there are in Kierkegaard's books many versions of the aesthete, and yet no aesthete in reality: his equilibrium is a dance on the tight rope strung between freedom and nature, and though he think himself poised, his foot invariably slips in due time. But there is one and only one ethical man in Kierkegaard: Assessor Wilhelm with his commonplace name, his commonplace marriage, and his commonplace calling. For the victory that Judge Wilhelm wins in the arena of the finite is more than an equilibrium: it is the concrete opportunity—world enough and time—to reconcile what he is and what he can be in the integrity of what he becomes.

3
THAT GOD MAY BE ALL IN ALL:
The World of the Edifying Discourses

Judge Wilhelm means to be a practical man. Consideration of his theories is fittingly supplemented by a scrutiny of his practice. His extravagant praise of connubial love suggests in particular a closer look at his marriage. That marriage, he is quick to boast, is as nearly perfect as an earthly union can be. I have never, he says, experienced any conflict between love and duty, nor for that matter any serious marital conflicts at all.[1] One need not be a cynic (though perhaps one needs to be married) to remark that such an idyllic relationship could only be imagined by a bachelor like Kierkegaard. Even if we allow for nineteenth-century conventions about the place of woman in home and society, Judge Wilhelm's marriage is *prima facie* suspect.

It is suspect for its tidiness and facility. The Assessor's wife has presumably "chosen herself in her eternal validity"; otherwise she would not have been capable of the marriage vow. And yet, by her husband's theory, her reality consists in being his "finitude." She organizes the Judge's finitude for him in a way that is perfectly consonant with his will. Her "absolute" self is identical with her relationship to her man. Woman, the Judge says, is immediacy through and through: her makeup is purely aesthetic in distinction from that of the troubled male. Luckier than her husband, she can soar directly from the first immediacy of romance to the second immediacy of the resolution. Broken in man by a crisis of reflection, the continuum of personal development in woman flows smoothly from love into marriage.[2] For this reason the Judge can write, without presuming to compromise his marriage or his wife's humanity, "In truth, she owes me nothing, and yet I am everything to her."[3] Because she attains by nature to the higher concentricity of resolve which her husband must take by freedom, the Assessor's wife is at once independent of him and wholly immersed in her devotion to him. She is all freedom *qua* human, and all nature *qua* woman and wife.

It appears that the Judge has protested too much. At one and the same time he affirms his wife's freedom and the nice compliance of her freedom with his. Is this not, in a very subtle way, just what Johannes did with Cordelia? Judge Wilhelm says that sentimentality, because it is unrealistic, is the same as heartlessness.[4] Is it not sentimental of him to base "the aesthetic validity of marriage" on his wife's docility? Has he not handled her rather heartlessly by presuming that her freedom is his nature? To the extent that he makes of his wife's humanity a willing plasticity to his own prerogative the Judge, like the Seducer, appears sentimentally calloused.

And if he is not quite fair to his wife, neither does he seem to be wholly on the level in his dealings with nature generally. If he assumes that the world will never assault him with forces too powerful to defeat, then he may well be counting too much on a deeper harmony of nature and freedom that has not always been evident to hungry and tormented people. And if his techniques of "internalization" are meant to cut the Gordian knot of affliction by simply removing to the ideal, then does he not run the risk of making conjugal love quite as abstract as "first love" or seduction? "I cannot blame the Judge," says the voice of another pseudonym,

> for his enthusiastic zeal in behalf of marriage; but nevertheless I think that the Judge, supposing I could get hold of him and whisper a little secret in his ear, will concede that there are difficulties he did not take into account.[5]

Difficulties, that is, concerning ethical freedom and its relation to immediacy: how is it that a man acquires himself "in his eternal validity" simply by deciding to, and how by the power of this decision is nature rendered wholly tractable, so that the Judge and his obliging little wife continue forever transparent to themselves in the new immediacy of their vow?

The suspicion that there is a dishonesty lurking in the upright heart of Judge Wilhelm is borne out by the "Ultimatum" that concludes *Either/Or* II. As the Diary of the Seducer draws the ultimate consequences of aestheticism, so this ultimatum exposes the presuppositions of the ethical life. In form it is a sermon, composed by an old classmate of the Assessor, now priest of a lonely parish on the northern moors of Jutland. The sermon has been sent by its author to Judge Wilhelm, who in turn passes it along to A. The priest in his religious solitude reminds the Judge of his young friend's aesthetic isolation. The sermon says briefly all that Judge Wilhelm said at length in his letters; indeed it says more (". . . also what I was desirous of saying") and says it more felicitously. In the note which accompanies the sermon, the Judge advises A to read it and think of himself, for, he adds, "I have read it and thought of myself."[6] Just as A was unsettled by the vision of his extremity in the Seducer's Diary, so Judge Wilhelm is disturbed by this sermon, which is no more than the last word on his own life. It is an ultimatum issued to the ethicist by a representative of the religious.

The title of the sermon is "The Edification Implied in the Thought that As Against God We Are Always in the Wrong." Its text (Luke 19: 41–48) describes the prophetic lamentations of Jesus over Jerusalem. From the conclusion of the innocent with the guilty in the sack of Jerusalem, the priest infers: Are we not all guilty as over against God? And is this not the most edifying (*opbyggelige*, literally "upbuilding" or "constructive") thought a man can have? Trying to calculate one's moral worth by reference to human standards leads to disquietude and doubt of self, never to certainty and self-assurance. But measured against God we are always in the wrong, and in this knowledge we find rest and peace.

The words of Jesus to the doomed city of Jerusalem may be an oblique complaint of the fluency of Judge Wilhelm's self-understanding:[7] "If thou hadst known in this thy day, even thou, the things which belong unto thy peace! but now they are hid from thine eyes. . . . Thou knewest not the time of thy visitation." The Judge confidently builds his peace (edifies himself) on the conviction of the essential rightness of his life: when a man lives ethically he is always good in principle even though he occasionally does wrong. The Jutland priest counters: whatever the relative rights and wrongs of a man's conduct, he can find repose in the understanding that he is always guilty as against the Absolute.

Kierkegaard's priest suggests that dogged persistence in an ethical way of life will bring a man to the point where he must either choose to acknowledge himself absolutely in the wrong or lose himself in a maze of casuistries. If he does not reach this point he deceives himself and shortchanges his principles. The sermon strikes at the assumptions that underlie Judge Wilhelm's views, especially his assumption of an easy harmony of freedom and nature in human action. Typically the argument of Kierkegaard's discourses begins as fable, turns sharply to simile, and ends as an analogue of the man-God relationship. This sermon is no exception. To make his point, the priest examines a relationship between two lovers. Love is the Judge's specialty, but the priest considers a possibility that never arises in the Assessor's life or thought. Suppose, he says, a radical conflict between lover and beloved. How can such a conflict be reconciled? Will the lover spend himself computing the rights and wrongs of each party to the relationship? Even if that were not an impossible task, such pettiness would hardly bespeak a deep and sincere love. Will he assert his own right as against the beloved? If he does, then it is not the beloved but his rectitude that he loves. The true lover will neither defend himself nor bargain for advantages; the true lover will without reservation put himself in the wrong that his beloved may be right and their love secured.[8]

Judge Wilhelm had written, "The highest expression of love is that the lover feels himself as nothing in the presence of the beloved, . . . for to feel oneself as something conflicts with love."[9] But for him this is only a sentiment that intensifies his marital contentment without qualifying his moral integrity. It is one of the numerous fringe benefits of his resolution. The priest, however, moving this proposition from the fringes of feeling to the center of freedom, draws from it a conclusion that undermines the Judge's whole way of life: when a lover who has chosen to bring his love under the dominion of the categories good/evil finds himself in discord with his beloved, he can honor his love and respect his duty only by pleading guilty without extenuation. And in so doing he has removed the ethical self-confidence that was the keystone of his *modus vivendi*.

It may be objected that a human relationship is a thing compounded of relativities and appropriately judged by less than absolute standards. No man is absolutely right or absolutely wrong over against another man. There will be a comparative right and a comparative wrong, but no total guilt. The objection would be valid were it not that Judge Wilhelm's ethic makes an absolute claim; he must either make good the claim—which cannot be done by a calculus of relativities—or relapse into the "paltriness" which both he and the aesthete disdain. What is more, guilt in all crucial instances is "dialectical"; that is, it is not a "clear and well ascertained" fact, but a *dubium* about which a man might debate with himself forever.[10] Guilt cannot be ascertained, it must be *assumed*. And the final significance of the act of repentance—which is the act of assuming one's guilt—is that it effects the transition from ethics to religion. The ethical question, raised in earnest and resolved in the bitter earnest of repentance, has a religious answer.

According to Judge Wilhelm a man *chooses himself absolutely* when in repentance he takes his whole past and in duty his whole future under the lordship of his freedom. It is his freedom assuming responsibility for his nature that constitutes his ab- solute worth as a human being. The priest does not contest the notion that a human being has absolute worth or that he has it by freedom. His doubts, reflected in the story of the unhappy lovers, concern man's ability to master his own life as completely as the Judge's theory requires. If the Judge supposes that conflicts are impossible in his own marriage, that marriage is built on an illusion. And when conflicts occur, they cannot be resolved by moral computation in a way that meets the Judge's ethical demand. No man acquires his "eternal validity" by coming off better in a quarrel with his wife. If the ethical man is in earnest about choosing himself in his eternal validity, he will have to choose himself as he is in relation to the Absolute. And if the true lover would not wish to be right as against his beloved, what man could will to be anything but absolutely in the wrong before God?[11] If Judge Wilhelm means what he says, he will make the leap from an ethical to a religious mode of existence.

Among Kierkegaard's notes in his own copy of *Either/Or* there is one that is portentous for Judge Wilhelm, suggested to Kierkegaard by his reading in the Koran:

> The twelfth sura of the Koran deals with Joseph. He is successful, his innocence in relation to Potiphar's wife is perfectly established, and still he says: *Doch will ich mein Herz nicht ganz frei sprechen von Schuld.*

> If a man is most completely in the right, yet over against God he must always have a higher expression: that he is in the wrong. *For no man can absolutely penetrate his own consciousness.*[12]

Judge Wilhelm thinks that a man can get behind his whole history and push. He claims to do by means of repentance what he finds the aesthete unable to do by means of imagination: to overtake himself and take himself over completely. But he cannot get himself in hand, as the case of his marriage shows. He may persuade himself of the malleability of his own—and his wife's!—immediacy. But the slightest discord in their marital harmony will reveal obscurities of nature not illumined by freedom. The attempt to explore these recesses will issue either in the degradation of marriage into moral horse-trading, or in the hardening of sentimentality into self-deception.

The act of repentance, as the Judge understands it, does not solve all the concrete problems to which a man may be exposed in daily life. Nor does devotion to duty guarantee a man against the contingency of future moral impasse: the judge may yet encounter actual duties he cannot perform and particular obligations he cannot fulfill. He may, for example, find himself presented by his children, for whom he has assumed responsibility by begetting them, with unsurmountable barriers to his own rectitude. If the aesthete can be surprised by joy, Judge Wilhelm may be brought up short by guilt. Aesthetic freedom flees from life; ethical freedom takes life as a task. But ethical freedom can no more empower a man to control his destiny than aesthetic freedom can shield him from it.

Of course the Judge is no stranger to guilt. But he takes his guilt as a moral challenge, when in fact he would be better advised to see it as moral defeat. For the affirmation of guilt does nothing to get rid of it, and this is the tragedy of the ethical life. If a man is to achieve selfhood by freedom, he must shoulder responsibility for the past, even for "the sins of the fathers." But he is incapable of eliminating or reforming that past and therefore barred from meeting the absolute demand of duty. The ethical battle is lost before it begins. A man may recognize this and console himself with that "worldly wisdom" which the priest caricatures in the words, "One does what one can."[13] But who knows what he can do? He may either assume that he can do all that he should, which is presuming too much; or he may conclude that he only can do what in fact he does, and by this he gets rid of repentance, duty, and his title to absolute worth at one stroke. In any case, freedom, which is potent to make a man guilty, is impotent to remove guilt. In the words of Frater Taciturnus,

> The ethical sphere is only a transitional sphere, and hence its highest expression is repentance as a negative action. The aesthetic sphere is that of immediacy, the ethical is that of requirement (and this requirement is so infinite that the individual always goes bankrupt). . . .

Repentance, since it expresses the determination to be responsible for one's whole self, is the highest expression of an ethical way of life. But at the same time it is a confession of ethical insolvency, it declares the bankruptcy of him who repents. The ethical stage on life's way is thereby narrowed to a transitional sphere, a strait which by its "negative pressure"[14] can force a man out of the aesthetic and into a religious way of life, but which cannot itself be his continuing city. All that a man can build for himself in the realm of ethics is confusion. The evil that he does is his own doing, and he is answerable for it. But since it has become an ineradicable part of his past, he cannot answer to one in a thousand. A man can no more consolidate his self ethically than he can compose it poetically, for immediacy conspires to righteousness as little as it does to beauty. The ethical man is involved in a complicity with evil and a duplicity in himself from which he can find release nowhere but in religion. When he admits defeat, his personality is constituted absolutely (. . . as against God) in the only way it can be (always in the wrong . . .).

So long as he continues to be satisfied with what he ekes out by his own freedom, Judge Wilhelm knows not the things that belong to his peace. In the despair which he commends to A and enacts as the prelude to his own life he is close to apprehending his predicament. But he identifies despair with self-choice, and so reveals that the despair was incomplete. A thoroughgoing despair would exhaust the self and leave it no strength with which to make reprise of itself. Speaking *in persona* Johannes Climacus, Kierkegaard says:

> The difficulty is, that the ethical self is supposed to be found immanently in the despair, so that the individual by persisting in his despair at last wins himself. . . . But this avails nothing. When I despair, I use myself to despair, and therefore I can indeed by myself despair of everything; but when I do this, I cannot by myself come back. In this moment of decision it is that the individual needs divine assistance. . . .[15]

But Judge Wilhelm does not discern the time of his visitation and misses the *divinum auxilium* to sink back into the comfortable fiction of his own competence.

To be fair to him, Judge Wilhelm is a pious man. The name of God occurs frequently in his letters; he even speaks of learning about God through pain and distress. But where his piety is not a vague surcharge of feeling, it tends to be a vague support for his self-confidence. He writes, for instance, of his delight that he "can come to the aid of the Deity" by freely appropriating everything that happens to him, the joyful as well as the sorrowful. For there is, on his view, no enmity between flesh and spirit, man and God, that would prevent the religious from rooting and flowering in the soil of immediacy watered by ethical freedom. The terrors which the aesthete (perhaps wiser in his way than the child of light) apprehends in the marriage relationship are pooh-poohed by the Judge on the most lovable exegetical grounds, so that the happy bride and groom may "refer" their love to God, thank Him for it, and take it directly and innocently to bed. "Religion," the Assessor says, "is not so foreign to human nature that a rupture is necessary in order to awaken it."[16] If in his later writings he is more sensitive to the possibility of such a rupture, if as he grows older the religious pretensions of his world view become more evident, its demand more stringent, and his employment of religious categories more frequent and more insistent, it is also true that in his "Observations" he rejects the religious "exception" to the universal with far greater passion than he shows in his letters to A. The ethicist in this essay is not only "militant, fighting *ancipito proelio* against the aesthetic . . .; he seeks also to defend himself against the religious. In rounding out his position as an ethicist, he does his utmost to defend himself against the decisive form of a higher standpoint."[17] His replies are addressed to religious as well as to aesthetic objections against marriage. The more articulate his understanding of the nature of the religious, the more intense his refusal of it. That he uses the language of faith to package and market an ethical commodity is no proof to the contrary. For as Johannes Climacus remarks in another connection, the important thing is not that one uses the decisive categories, the important thing is whether one means anything decisive by them. For all his emphatic devotion—granting its sincerity—Judge Wilhelm's religion functions essentially as a reinforcement and a refinement of his ethics. And it is a long way from religion as ethical prop and ethical decor to the knowledge of God of which the Jutland priest is speaking. The God of the religious way of life appears not in ethical victory, but only in the shipwreck of freedom on the shoals of guilt. Judge Wilhelm's religion is as sentimental as his marriage. It too easily becomes a cavilling with God, a will to be always in the right and to have the world on his own terms. His distrust of those unfortunate people who cannot put body and soul together in the ethically approved fashion, his satisfaction with his own familial and social life, and his ever-sanguine conscience show that he has not chosen himself with utter honesty. His ethic succeeds aesthetically as well as it does because he cheats a little here and there—which is to say, given his absolute ethics, that he cheats absolutely. A serious choice of himself would not automatically bring him to a lovely concord of freedom and nature, man and wife, individual and society. It would isolate him before God in the awareness of his inadequacy to render account of himself.

"Poetry is glorious," says Frater Taciturnus, "religion is still more glorious, but what lies between them is prattle, no matter what talent is wasted upon it." The power of immediacy is broken only by the infinite, and not by the finite, reflection. But an infinite reflection—devotion to "the Idea" exacting its last full measure—is in principle a relationship to God. Poetry can only be replaced by religion as the master passion of the soul.

Ethics in the manner of Judge Wilhelm is an inglorious compromise, and it is therefore prattle no matter how well he brings
it off. His own appeal to infinite reflection, by which he believes
he can disarm all possibilities in advance of the fact, is not
entirely lucid. "The aesthetic is higher than actuality before
actuality, that is to say, in illusion; the religious is higher than
actuality after actuality, that is, by virtue of a God-
relationship."[18] The aesthete cannot endure either the harmony
of the ideal and the actual (Don Juan) nor their contradiction
(Johannes the Seducer), and so he settles for an equivocal
melancholy. The ethical man should know that he cannot make
himself virtuous by making himself happy, and he will when
pressed acknowledge that he cannot always manage to bring
happiness out of virtue. But like a practical Kantian, striving for
his own moral perfection with the assurance that the universe
would not be so irrational as to deny him his due reward, and
bestowing happiness on others to a degree that accords with his
own rational idea of their moral perfection, he tries to keep his
cake and eat it: he does what he can. In the case of Judge
Wilhelm this means that he will on occasion rob the fact (usually
his wife's) to pay the principle (usually his own), and on other
occasions rob the principle (usually his wife's) to satisfy the fact
(usually his own.) If he were in real earnest about the infinite
resolution by which he claims to choose himself in his eternal
validity, he would stop playing at put and take with the actual
and the ideal, and choose God, *pereat mundus.* In the light of the
religious *Ultimatum,* the ethical life of Judge Wilhelm is but a
more respectable version of the old aesthetic pose: he is masquerading as destiny, and that is prattle and self-deception. The
religious man knows that the only real choice he has is the choice
of God.

Therefore, the priest tells his hearers, choose yourself. But
choose yourself as you are: in the wrong against God. You lose
yourself eternally as long as you continue to absolutize your
freedom. You gain yourself eternally as soon as you recognize
your nothingness. The decision for absolute guilt—and it is a
decision, not reached by calculation but taken in freedom—is the
only edifying (constructive) decision available. This is the act of
freedom by which a man's self acquires absolute worth: the
choice of his self as worthless in relation to God. "What I gain by
resignation" of the ethical endeavor and choice of the religious

is, according to another pseudonym, "my eternal consciousness, . . . for my eternal consciousness is my love to God,
and for me this is higher than everything."[19] If a man would not
pamper himself with a tender notion of himself, let him abandon
the hope that he can justify his life, and prefer the sober
consolation of guilt. If he would not stultify himself with the
thought that he can always do well by doing good, let him
inspire himself to action by the thought of guilt, unencumbered
by the necessity to be right or to become ever and ever righter. If
he would not be reduced to the jejune expedient of making
himself up as he goes along ("One does what one can"), let him
take the painful but redeeming option of religion.

Summarizing the "stages on life's way", Kierkegaard wrote,
"while aesthetic existence is essentially enjoyment, and ethical
existence, essentially struggle and victory, religious existence is
essentially suffering, and that not as a transitional moment, but
as persisting."[20] An aesthete's life is organized around pleasure,
an ethical life around the opposition of good and evil. The
religious life is a life in which *God* is acknowledged as the sole
sufficient point of reference for human existence. Reflection on
the idea of God shows that such a life is necessarily a life of
suffering.

God may be called Absolute Reality, Absolute Power, *id
quo majus cogitari non potest, ipsum esse subsistens, Qui est*—or any of
an indefinite number of comparable names. And they are all
correct. Certainly a slighter epithet would be inadequate. But
not even these superlatives define or describe God. For if God is
the *Absolute*, then He transcends everything that can be known
by men, all of which is but relative. God is modally *other* than
man and man's world. His existence, therefore, cannot be
proven nor His nature conceived. To demonstrate or delineate
God would bring Him within the ambit of finite reason and
demean His absoluteness. In a word, anything that is said about
God discredits Him, except this confession itself.[21]

Nevertheless God can be experienced. Because He is
wholly other than man, He can be encountered as the negation
of everything human. This is what happens in the experience of
guilt; when a man admits the impossibility of legislating and
warranting his own conduct, he is exposed to God. Whenever
some finite hope or finite assurance breaks down, there is an

access to God. Whenever all human possibilities—aesthetic, intellectual, moral—are exhausted, there God is present. This is true especially of man's religiousness; human attempts to make contact with God must be frustrated before God Himself can break through. For if God is God, then every endeavor to edify oneself on anything less than the recognition of God—be it so crass as pleasure, so respectable as duty, or so sublime as piety—is an idol interposed between man and God. It is only when his idols crumble that a man can know God.

This knowledge of God, attained in the disaster of everything taken in lieu of God, is *identical with* the experience of the nothingness of man. Though He is in Himself the fullness of reality, *ens realissimum*, God is only known to man as man's emptiness. He is experienced as the infinite nothingness that appears in the failure of the finite. Where there is uncertainty, despair, the consciousness of guilt, suffering without relief— there also is the experience of God. There *is* God, for the meaning of God in human experience is just the suffering implicit in the renunciation of man's self-assurance. God *is* without qualification or limitation; man is, without qualification or limitation, *nothing* as against God. The suffering of this truth is essential and persistent in the religious life.

But God, whom no man can see and live, is also the source of all being, the creator and revivifier of men. The thought of guilt is the edifying thought, because it provides the solid ground on which life can be founded without fear of ruin. There is, as Climacus says, a necessary misunderstanding between man and God, since they are opposites. But there is also the possibility for man of an enthusiastic endurance of this misunderstanding.

> The edifying reflection at the close of *Either/Or*, "that over against God we are always in the wrong," . . . is merely the discrepancy of the finite and the infinite brought to rest in an enthusiastic reconciliation in the infinite. It is the last enthusiastic cry in which the finite spirit appeals to God, within the sphere of freedom: "I cannot understand Thee, but still I will love Thee, Thou art always right; even if it seemed to me as if Thou didst not love me, I will nevertheless love Thee." Hence it was that the theme was so worded: the edification that lies in the thought etc.; the edifying is not sought in the annulment of the misunderstanding, but in the enthusiastic endurance of it, and in this final act of courage as if bringing about its annulment. [22]

This endurance, which Climacus calls "worship," is the other side of the encounter with God. Worship, in this context, means the recognition in practice of the "qualitative difference" between man and God, the everlasting recollection of guilt. Such a worship is entirely private, since God and his relation to man exceed all liturgical representation and devotional expression. Nevertheless it is the reservoir from which the religious man draws the waters of life. When he owns himself guilty, he is not confessing that he broke some of God's rules; the consciousness of inevitable and total guilt could not be arrived at by drawing up a balance sheet. Kierkegaard's word for guilt *(Skyld)* means originally "debt." To know oneself guilty in a religious sense is to know oneself *in debt to* God. The religious man *owes himself* completely to God. [23] He is aware that the self which is reduced to impotence in the presence of God is also upheld by the divine power. In his weakness he is sustained by a power not his own, for he has dried up his own sources in despair. Unlike the aesthete, who poetizes himself, and the ethical man, who sits in judgment on himself, the religious man *receives* himself as a gift from God. Outwardly he does not differ from other men: he enjoys life like the aesthete, and he works at his responsibilities like the ethical man. Yet he is inwardly supported neither by fate nor by freedom, but by the consciousness that all he is or does is a divine gratuity. In his suffering he gives thanks continually, for "there is always reason to give thanks to God," since "every human being is in debt to Him, and in debt forever." [24]

God's annihilation is creation, and the suffering of guilt by man is one with the sufferance of guilt by God. This is the unique "withdrawal and return" of the religious life paralleling but transcending like movements in the aesthetic and ethical spheres. Kierkegaard's *Edifying Discourses*, which he published under his own name and in which he speaks directly from the religious point of view, portray this dialectic of annihilation and restoration over and over again, from the perspectives provided by a wide diversity of human concerns, human situations, and human problems. Brief readings of a few of these discourses will display the utter simplicity and the infinite adaptability of the religious way of life.

a) "Every good and every perfect gift is from above."

One of three discourses with the same title and the same text, this devotional extracts the implications of the religious man's belief in the goodness and the sovereignty of God the Creator. The relevant portions of the text are worth citing:

> Let no man say when he is tempted, I am tempted of God: for God cannot be tempted with evil, neither tempteth He any man: But every man is tempted when he is drawn away of his own lust, and enticed. . . . Do not err, my beloved brethren. Every good gift and every perfect gift is from above, and cometh down from the Father of lights, with whom is no variableness, neither shadow of turning. Of his own will begat he us with the word of truth, that we should be a kind of firstfruits of his creatures. . . . Wherefore lay apart all filthiness and superfluity of naughtiness, and receive with meekness the engrafted word, which is able to save your souls. (James 1:13-21)

God tempts no man, and cannot himself be turned aside by evil. Therefore life itself, whatever it may contain of happiness or of misery, is a gift of God, good and perfect, which man should receive with gratitude. The man who so accepts his life acquires also the best and most perfect gift of a constant soul, by which he is conformed to the likeness of God, the Father of lights with whom is no variableness nor shadow cast by turning.

Though God tempts not and is not tempted, men are enticed perpetually by their own lust for dominion. Prosperity can be the occasion on which a man tempts himself to ignore God by the complacent impudence of assuming His favor. The aesthete requires good fortune for the success of his endeavor in the art of living; the ethical man prides himself on his indifference to fortune and his ability to "make his own living." Jealous of his devotion and mindful of the lures of pride, the religious man may actually draw back from good fortune in suspicion, and welcome the onslaught of adversity.

Yet this too is an occasion of falling, for there is no more security in bad fortune than in good. Adversity can inspire a man to the despair of self-rejection and defiance of God just as prosperity can allow him to lose God by default. Even a humble enduring of poverty may signify more devotion to the humility of the endurer than to the bounty of the Giver of want. The man who banks on either happiness or misery for his piety has willed to dispense with God.

You wished (the *Discourses* always address an imagined "listener", that "single individual" whom Kierkegaard liked to call "*My* reader") that God's ideas about what was profitable to you might be your ideas, but you also wished that He might be the almighty Creator of heaven and earth, so that He might rightly fulfill your wish. And yet if He were to share your ideas, then must He cease to be the almighty Father. You would in your childish impatience, as it were, corrupt God's eternal Being, and you were blind enough to delude yourself, as if it helped you if God in heaven did not know better what was profitable to you than you yourself; as if you would not sometime discover with terror that you had wished what no man would be able to bear if it came to pass.

What such a man wills is the death of God. To conjure the image of God out of human notions of bane and benefit is to annihilate God by reducing Him to an adjunct of man, closing the infinite qualitative gulf that separates them. The true worshipper will in spirit and in truth remember that

> As God's all-powerful hand made everything good, so He, the Father of lights, still constant, makes everything good in every moment, everything into a good and perfect gift for everyone who has the heart to humble himself, heart enough to be confident.

Yet confidence is hard come by. Doubt springs eternal in the human breast, and the human mind demands an explanation and a reckoning. What *is* a good and perfect gift? What—of all the things that happen in this world—really comes *from God?* How can one distinguish good from evil, Godly from unGodly? The religious explanation is not calculated to satisfy these doubts, but to challenge them. The counter to these questionings is that "everything which comes from God is a good and perfect gift, and that everything which is a good and perfect gift is from God." Or in the words of the Apostle, "All of God's creation is good, if it is received with thankfulness." Doubt, which is suspicious of creation, and faith, which gives thanks for it, are opposites between which *tertium non datur.* The believer cannot *answer* the suspicions of doubt, even those that disquiet his own mind and heart; he can only displace them with his thanksgiving. To thank God for his gift of life leaves no room for attempts to figure out what He meant by pain and evil, only for the edifying recognition that, whatever happens, God is the Father of lights, with whom is no change or shadow of turning. The inclination to theodicy is natural enough, "for every man will readily be thankful for the good he receives, but every man's heart is also weak enough to wish to determine for itself what the good is." The weakness is not overcome by catering to it. The cornerstone of the religious life is the conviction that *God is;* and this is the stone which the doubter refuses in favor of the architecture of reason. That all creation is good can only be understood by one who believingly wills to understand it, which the doubter on implicit principle does not; that God is the almighty and immutable Giver of good can only be attested by the man who has swallowed his doubts and thanked God for his life through weal and woe, pain and pleasure, poverty and plenty, until his life's end. Only the perfected believer has earned the right to doubt, and he will not claim it. It is of him that the Apostle says, all things work together for his good, because he loves God (Romans 8:28). [25]

Assuming that doubt is subdued, yet another obstacle to faith offers itself. A man may be so conscious of his own unworthiness before God, whether by specific fault or only by circumstance and temperament, that he feels himself bound to a life of penitence. For such a man life must seem a punishment from God, the more severe as it is decked with success and earthly joy. Yet even this man loves God, as his sense of unworthiness proves. To love God is to thank God and he who loves God "according to his own imperfection" thanks Him most perfectly because he loves Him most selflessly. In no merely rhetorical sense is the penitent's worship the most perfect worship. For God is most exalted where the worshipper feels himself most abased; in penitent thanksgiving the worshipper receives everything from God, even his thanksgiving, for he knows that he himself can offer nothing to God. The penitent in his lowliness understands that "this is love, not that we love God, but that God loves us." Penitence indeed *is* God, the Good and Perfect Gift Himself, alive and active in the human spirit precisely when that spirit knows itself to be nothing but a land of emptiness and need. [26]

The man who understands his imperfection in this way may still regard his life as a punishment from God. But emboldened by this understanding, he will humble himself for the further and more difficult understanding: that this punishment is also a good and perfect gift. As long as he withholds this supreme act of devotion, he is still tempting God, insisting on his own reality over against God: he *will be* the one whom God finds it worth His while to punish. Acquiescence once made, he has conformed his will to the will of the unchangeable God, and attained to the essence of worship and the religious life. He has made himself nothing that God may be all in all.

Kierkegaard's prayers characteristically capsulize the discourses they attend:

> *Every good and every perfect gift is from above and cometh down from the Father of lights, with whom is no variableness nor shadow of turning.* These words are so beautiful, so eloquent, so moving [in prosperity]; they are so soothing and so comforting [in adversity], so simple and comprehensible [as against the elaborate scruples of doubt], so refreshing and so healing [to the broken and penitent spirit]. Therefore we will beseech Thee, O God, that Thou wilt make the ears of those who hitherto have not regarded them [the prosperous ignorers of God], willing to accept them; that Thou wilt heal the misunderstanding heart [the man distraught with adversity] by the understanding of the word, to understand the word; that Thou wilt incline the erring thought [doubt] under the saving obedience of the word; that Thou wilt give the penitent soul [the poor in spirit] confidence to dare to understand the word; and that Thou wilt make those who have understood it [the true worshippers] more and more blessed therein, so that they may repeatedly understand it. Amen. [27]

He who, in the darkness of need, receives with meekness the engrafted word of truth, preserves his soul from the temptations of prosperity, adversity, doubt, and despair. He prepares in his own spirit a constant dwelling place for the saving and illumining presence of the eternal God.

b)   "To acquire one's soul in patience."

The Gospel according to St. Luke provides Kierkegaard with the text and the theme for this discourse. In a passage that predicts the sack of Jerusalem and prophesies the end of time, Jesus warns his disciples of the tribulations they must suffer in these last days before the coming of the Kingdom. But in the midst of this tale of eschatological terror He offers them an encouraging word. "In your patience," He tells them, "ye shall win your souls." So every man, Kierkegaard expands, can and must acquire his soul in patience, amid the toil and trouble of this mortal life:

Man is born naked and brings nothing with him into the world; whether the conditions of life stand like friendly figures who have everything in readiness, or he must toilsomely discover them, still every man, in one way or another, must acquire the conditions for his own life. Even if this view of life makes an individual impatient, and thereby incapable of action, yet the better men know how to understand this, and to adapt themselves to the idea that life must be acquired, and that it must be acquired in patience.

If the previous discourse taught that life is a gift to be received with thanksgiving, this one argues the equal and opposite truth, that life is a goal to be attained by means of patience.

Patience *(Taalmodighed)* is the courage *(Mod)* to endure *(at taale),* and as such it is "the strength of soul which every man needs to attain his wish in life." Courageous endurance is the condition necessary for the acquisition of selfhood. But this sort of talk breeds contradiction. Is not a man's self (=life=soul) the condition presupposed by everything else he does and has, including patience? Is not patience an accident of soul rather than its premise? Kierkegaard sharpens the paradox:

> Nevertheless, if a man owns his soul, does he then need to acquire it; and if he does not own it, how can he acquire it, since the soul becomes the final condition which is presupposed in every acquirement, and hence too in acquiring the soul? Can there be a possession such that it exactly indicates the condition of being able to acquire the same possession?

This is not only a problem in New Testament exegesis, nor a perplexity generated by certain peculiarities of "religious language." This is a difficulty indigenous to the dialectic of freedom and nature by which human life is essentially wracked. For while the self is in one sense given, it is as surely true that every man is responsible for his own personality. No worldly commodity can serve for such a paradoxical possession, for every temporal good bears its properties according to the law of excluded middle. It is either owned, in which case it cannot be acquired; or it must be acquired, in which case it is not owned. Much less can the eternal enter into contradiction, for the eternal has the predicate of identity: it simply *is.* Only of the soul may it be said that it is

> the contradiction between the eternal and the temporal, and for that reason it can be possessed and acquired at one and the same

time. Furthermore, if the soul is this contradiction, it can only be owned in that it is acquired, and acquired in that it is owned. [28]

The remainder of the discourse proceeds to unravel this paradox with dialectical rigor.

The reality of the soul is presupposed by the acquisition of it. And yet it is not in the hands of the man whose soul it is, else he could not be asked to win it. Who then possesses it? Where is it? The human self, Kierkegaard says, is initially (naturally or aesthetically) immersed in the life of the world. The man who sets out to acquire property in the world—whether it be the extra-human world of natural things or that sub-human realm of artificial things and values created by the superficial commercial intercourse of men—is so concerned with these things and so contingent upon them that his self is owned by his property. This is the immediate heritage of the naked and newborn, an inheritance which is refined (but not essentially altered) as it is perpetuated by the normal processes of education and civilization. Only if a man has extirpated his concern for the world, become utterly indifferent to it, can he really own it; for only thus does his self achieve the independence required for ownership.

> If a man cares only about the external, the worldly, the temporal, then are not the world and the temporal existence unconditionally stronger than he? Therefore a man can truly own the imperfect only by relinquishing it, which really indicates that he does not own it, even if he owns it. [29]

Or in the words of another discourse, "he who, when he has the world, is as one who does not have it, then he has the world, otherwise the world has him."[30] In a passage reminiscent of Hegel and even more ominous of Heidegger Kierkegaard continues:

> At the very beginning, then, a man is at the point to which men later aspire as the acme of glory; he is lost in the life of the world, he owns the world, that is to say, he is owned by it. But at the same time he is distinct from the whole world, and he feels an antipathy which is not in harmony with the processes of the worldly life. If he now wishes to acquire the world, he must overcome this disquietude, until he once more vanishes like the wave in the sea of the worldly life; then he has won the world. If, on the contrary, he wishes to acquire his soul, he must allow this antipathy to become more and more explicit, and in this acquire

his soul; for his soul was exactly this distinction from the worldly life: it was the infinitude of the worldly life in its distinction from itself. [31]

The self is enclosed in the world by its own concern. Yet this very *concern with* the world reveals that the self is *in potentia distinct from* the world. The distinction is at first, even in the "natural" man, *felt* in such "antipathetic" moods as anxiety, shame, and transcendent longing. But how is this antipathy to be made "more and more explicit," so that a man may "acquire his soul" in full consciousness of its difference from the world?

That there is a distinction between the soul and the world, of which every man is aware, however vaguely, means that the soul does not ultimately depend upon the worldly cares to which it is given. The world's "ownership" of the soul is an unlawful possession, which it has by default of spirit. But neither does the soul belong to the man who might claim it, for he has yet to acquire it. Even at the limit of his appropriation *he* could not bring his *soul* into stable identity with *himself.* In *making it his own* he relies upon the distinction of freedom, which, at the same time that it severs his soul from the world, introduces duplicity and contradiction into the human condition itself. The self is a dependent variable which nevertheless depends neither upon the world of its concern nor upon the man to whom it pertains. The *lawful* owner of the soul, He whose legitimate possession it is, the Being upon whom the reality of the human self depends in fee simple, is "no other than the Eternal Being, than God Himself." [32]

This is to reiterate the paradox:

> The human soul is a contradiction between the external and the inward, the temporal and the eternal. It is a self-contradiction, because that which makes it what it is, is the fact that it wishes to express the contradiction in itself.

This paradox is the limit of the independent reality of the soul and the condition of the possibility of its acquisition.

> If it were not in contradiction, it would be lost in the earthly life; if it were not self-contradiction, then movement would be impossible. It must at the same time be owned and acquired; it belongs to the world as its unlawful possession; it belongs to God as his true possession; it belongs to man as his true possession,

that is as the possession which he must acquire. Consequently he then acquires, if he actually does acquire it, *his soul from the world, of God, by himself.*

His soul is the only thing a man can genuinely own, for it is the only possession he receives as a gift from the only Giver who is empowered and entitled to give it, the possession

> which does not belong to any other soul in the world, whose acquisition does not make him a debtor to luck or fate or accident or men or friends or enemies or the world, since, on the contrary, in this acquisition he discharges his debt to the world by giving it what belongs to it, and only remains as God's debtor, which is not to be a debtor, since God is the one good and Himself affords the possibility of *becoming* His debtor.

A man must acquire *his* soul, *from* the world, *of* God, *by* himself. But how does a man acquire *his* soul *by* himself, if God *has* it in eternal security and disposes it at His pleasure? "In *patience* ye shall win your souls." Patience is the human agency, the condition with which a man must equip himself if he is to acquire his soul. In connection with worldly affairs, patience is an external instrument sometimes necessary (though often unpleasant) for the attainment of a sometimes real (but often only apparent) good, a condition that is laid aside when the thing sought is finally possessed. Not so when the soul is the good to be acquired. Here the condition and the conditioned, the means of seeking and the thing sought, are the same. To have patience—the courage to hold out for one's soul's sake against the intrusive distractions of the world, in the belief that God is the soul's source and surety—*is* to acquire one's soul.

> In this acquirement . . . the condition is also the object of the acquirement, and it does not depend on anything external. Therefore the condition, after it has served for the acquirement, remains as the thing acquired. . . .

Patience is a condition always and unconditionally needed, for only when it is present can one own—that is, constantly acquire—his self. The other side of the paradox with which the discourse began is that "the condition was precisely the ownership of the soul which made its acquisition possible." To *become* oneself (the ethical ideal) and to *be* oneself (the aesthetic self-possession) amount to the same thing from the perspective of

105

religion: the "enthusiastic endurance" of patience in which a man preserves his soul independent of the world by submitting it in total surrender to God. From the religious point of view, to acquire oneself in patience is simply to have the courage to endure the truth of the situation.

The ultimacy of patience and its identity with the soul are evident from the fact that, like the soul, patience is presupposed by the acquisition of itself: one must have patience in order to learn patience. The religious life is a closed circle centering in God. Because it is a *closed* circle there is no way to break down the paradox on which this discourse is mounted. Because it centers in *God*, there is no need to do so: a circle centered in God comprehends all reality, including the human soul.

> In patience the soul comes to terms with all its owners: with the worldly life when the sufferer acquires himself from it; with God when the sufferer receives himself from Him; with himself when he retains what at the same time he gives to both, without anyone being able to take it from him: patience. . . . This self-contradiction is here again the expression of the fact that the soul is stronger than the world through its weakness and that it is weaker than God in its strength, that it can acquire nothing except itself, unless it wishes to be deceived, and it can only acquire itself by losing itself.

Because God is all in all, the acquisition of one's life as a task is the same as the reception of one's life as a gift. That is the divine circularity. It is in the passivity of patience—in suffering and in the courage of endurance—that a man acts so as to earn his soul, from the world where he finds it, of God who eternally owns it, by himself as he day by day humbles himself to accept it. [33]

The two discourses, on life as gift and life as task, reflect on Judge Wilhelm's ethical project of self-choice. In choosing myself, the Assessor writes, I choose that which already exists: else I should be creating myself, which is manifestly false. But in choosing myself I also bring that self into being, for until it is appropriated by freedom it exists only as a potency locked in the grip of nature. The dialectical circle of ethical self-choice is retraced by the circle of religion—to receive oneself is to achieve oneself—but with an absolute difference. The self-choice of Judge Wilhelm turns on human freedom, for which God's creation provides the matter, the locale, the opportunity, and the demand. The religious life centers, begins, and ends in God. Something—be it only a fragment of unmanageable immediacy or suppressed reflection—always falls outside the circle of ethics, only to intrude itself from time to time in the self-shattering experience of guilt. The circle of God—its center everywhere and its circumference nowhere—has no outside. God is all the world that matters for the religious man, and the only obligation laid on his freedom is that he endure with thanksgiving his secure inclusion in the divine milieu. At the limits of his exertion he enjoys the blessed recognition that even his gratitude and his patience are the *opus Dei*. His soul, wholly occupied and possessed by God, is for the first time and forever, his own.

In other discourses Kierkegaard locates particular problems and preoccupations that beset men in general and the ethical man in particular. Against the backdrop of the letters of Judge Wilhelm the discourses on time and on the good stand out with special pertinence.

c)   "The expectation of faith"
Kierkegaard's first edifying discourse, designated for New Year's Day, meditates the problem of time, especially the future, for, as the occasion itself recalls, "The past is completed; the present is not; only the future is, which yet is not." Faith is the weapon with which the religious man arms himself against every threat, and it is in faith that "he possesses the only power which can triumph over the future." Faith is the religious man's *summum bonum*; it is the ultimate gift which he would give, if he could, to the person he loves. It is supreme among human goods because it can be shared by all on equal terms and without diminution. Because it is an inner object of will and not an outer term of wishing, faith is a locus of duties—the category of futurity in the universal human ethic of Judge Wilhelm. But for this very cause it cannot be transmitted from one man to another; it can only be learned by each man alone, on his own initiative and under the tutelage of God. As the Apostle says, in the words that furnish the text for this discourse, "But before faith came, we were kept under the law, shut up unto the faith which should afterwards be revealed. Wherefore the law was our schoolmaster. . . . But after that faith is come, we are no longer under a schoolmaster. For ye are all the children of God by

faith. . . . " (Galatians 3:23–26) Latent in every man, available to all who will it—and only to those who will it—faith, like the "soul" of the previous discourse, "is the only unfailing good, because it can only be had through being constantly acquired, and can only be acquired through being constantly developed."

Faith is so essentially an inward and private boon that could it be imparted to one man by another, it would cease to be the highest good:

> "If I," said [one who wished to give faith to another], "with my wish or with my gift could present him with the highest good, then could I also take it from him, even if he need not fear this; aye, what is worse, if I could do this, then I should in the same moment that I gave it to him, take it from him; for in the fact that I gave him the highest good, I took the highest good from him; for the highest would be that he should give it to himself."

To have no human schoolmaster in faith is to have in God a diligent Father and Teacher. The highest good can be given by God without reduction, for God is Himself the highest and self-giving Good of every man. Faith is the "universal human" in a sense Judge Wilhelm would not have understood, nor allowed had he understood it; open to all, it nonetheless severs each man from the other, removes him from the discipline of the law, and exposes him to that isolation in which he meets and receives God. [34]

Kierkegaard's eulogy of faith is a simple deduction from the premise that faith is the highest good. It is another thing to exhibit the efficacy of faith which empowers a man to master his future. [35] Consideration of the "expectation of faith" must begin with the recognition that futurity is a dimension peculiar to *human* time, and anxiety for the future a distinctive feature of *human* life. The complaint, unique and pervasive among men, that they are too much preoccupied with tomorrow, may overlook the fact that

> it is precisely man's greatness, the proof of his divine heritage, that he can occupy himself with the future; for if there were no future, neither would there have been a past, and if there were neither past nor future, then would man be enslaved like the beasts, his head bent toward the earth, his soul ensnared in the service of the moment. [36]

Man has a future only because he is able to transcend the present temporal moment into the realm of possibility. Futurity may even be defined as possibility appearing in the realm of temporality, and the fact that it can so appear is a sign of that freedom by which man is filiated from the divine omnipotence.

No man can "live in the past" without defrauding his freedom. But neither can he dwell in the present until he has met and conquered the threat of possibility that looms in his future. This would seem to be an impossible demand, insofar as the future is conjured into being by the very freedom that is asked to tame it.

> He who fights with the future has a . . . dangerous enemy, . . . for he fights with himself. The future is not; it borrows its strength from the man himself, and when it has tricked him out of this, then it appears outside of him as the enemy he must meet. Let a man then be as strong as he will, no man is stronger than himself. . . . When a man strives with the future, then he learns that however strong he is compared with the rest, there is one enemy who is stronger, that is himself; one enemy he cannot conquer by himself, that is himself.

The future is not a person or an object lying in ambush around the next corner of life. The future is possibility perspectived by time and rooted in human freedom. But no man so transcends himself that he can lay all the possibilities which his own freedom has raised. His powers are never greater than his possibilities. Not experience nor conjecture nor supposition nor logic nor strength of will is sufficient to remove the threat of tomorrow. [37] Freedom, which dignifies human existence, also bids fair to dissolve it in futile anxiety.

Only by the power of the eternal can the disintegration of the temporal be arrested:

> Through the eternal can one conquer the future, because the eternal is the foundation of the future; therefore through this one can understand that. What then is the eternal power in man? It is faith. What is the expectation of faith? Victory, or as the Scriptures have so earnestly and so movingly taught us, it is that all things must work together for good to those that love God. But an expectation of the future which expects victory has indeed conquered the future. The believer is therefore done with the future before he begins on the present; for what one has conquered no longer has power to disturb one, and this victory can only make one more powerful for the present. [38]

Not man's freedom alone, but pre-eminently the eternal, is the "foundation of the future." The future, which is the *possible* appearing in time, is also the *eternal* appearing in time. That which *is* (the eternal), viewed from the temporal moment, is that which *may come to be* (the possible). Man's freedom is not creative *ex nihilo*; his possibilities not only arise from his subjective transcendence of the present moment, but ultimately rest upon an objective ground, which is "the eternal" or, in the words of the pseudonym Anti-Climacus, God, who *is* the sum and source of all possibility.[39] Were human possibility not rooted in being itself, were the temporality of man not hung from the eternity of God, the future could not terrify. For if a man is not stronger than himself, he is at least no weaker than himself. But it is God and not himself alone with whom he wrestles when he locks with the future. And God, who gives the battle, must also give the victory.

Man is the being *for whom* there are the future possibilities; God is the dimension *in which* and the power *by which* the reality of these possibilities is guaranteed. Man is the intersection of now and forever, the projection of time into eternity and of eternity into time. His temporality, which is both his grandeur and his misery, is his transcendence from the focus of freedom toward that field of possibilities everlastingly sustained in being by the divine omnipotence. He is threatened by his future because he is at once *not* God and yet *related to* God by his freedom in what Kierkegaard calls a "possibility-relationship." Faith is "the eternal power in man," the apprehension of omnipotence by freedom and of freedom by omnipotence. It is man's "possibility-relationship" to God understood in the light of God's creator-relationship to man. Faith is the power of God effective in man, drawing him beyond the future into the fortress of eternity, where every possibility is victoriously countered by a superabundance of power. That is what the author of *The Concept of Dread* means when he says that "every man's life is religiously planned":[40] no man comes to himself until he has perfected his union with God in faith, the "ideal anticipation of eternity" that subdues the future and restores him to peace in the present. *Aeternitas est interminabilis vitae tota simul et perfecta possessio.*[41] Only God is truly present to Himself, without nostalgia for yesterday or dread of tomorrow; only that man lives "whole and undivided" in the moment who is uplifted above it "in divine jest" by his projection into the eternal Now. The man of faith is so educated by possibility, the divine schoolmaster, that he has nothing to fear in the examination of life. The battle of time is already decided in eternity, and the combatant has only to await the eventual victory that is assured on the other side of the future.

There is a wisdom born of human experience that would counsel against the temerity of "expecting victory" in the engagements of this world. Experience teaches those who attend to it that they must be prepared for some good but also for some evil in the days to come. Experience never teaches more than this. With whatever semblance of quantitative precision it is tricked out, experience yields only an indecisive approximation to the future: there will be some of this and some of that. It offers no sure guidance or reliable aid in dealing with possibility, but only starts the workings of doubt and despair. If a man had only his experience to go on, Kierkegaard remarked in his diary, he would go mad. [42] What certainty he learns from his uncertain experience issues not from experience itself but from his decisions in the face of it: one man may learn patience and another resentment from the same hardship, just as the one may learn humility and the other arrogance from the same good fortune. If a man has really drawn from experience the lesson of doubt, he will not broadcast it to others as the wisdom of experience, but will rather sink into the deathly silence of despair:

> Doubt is a profound and cunning passion, but he whose soul it did not grip so intensely that he became speechless, only falsely imputes this passion to himself; what he says, therefore, is not only untrue in itself, but especially so on his lips. [43]

The expectation of faith need pay no attention to the voice of experience, for if it does not put him off with useless recommendations of moderation, experience will only lead a man into frustration. Where there is no certainty forthcoming, it is wiser to be deceived by faith than to tempt oneself into despair.

A positivist would still demur: this faith which is to see a man through the perils of possibility is so indeterminate a thing that it might as well be a fairy ring, an enchanted circular hypothesis that solves all problems ideally because it has no factual implications and could not conceivably be shaken by any datum of experience. The believer, previously tried in the

111

encounter with doubt, is not enticed by a sophistication that would deprive him of the timeless good of faith he presently possesses and endow him with an insatiable longing for the niggardly and inconstant satisfactions of the world:

> "I am not deceived; [he might say] for what the world seemed to promise me, that promise I still did not believe that it would keep; my expectation was not in the world, but in God. This expectation is not deceived; even in this moment I feel its victory more gloriously and more joyfully than all the pain of loss. If I lost this expectation, then would everything be lost. Now I have still conquered, conquered through my expectation, and my expectation is victory."

Unhappy the man who falls outside the circle of faith, for it is the girdle of divinity that arms and defends the soul. The positivist's lust for empirical verification is a desolate and sterile passion that subjects him helplessly to the aimless vicissitudes of the world. Faith cannot be deceived, for its claim is secured by the unchangeable God, not the changing world. Only the believer himself can render his faith vain, by ceasing to believe. There are but two terms in the relation of faith: the divine omnipotence and man's freedom. God, the source of all potency, is eternally faithful. Only man's ambiguous freedom can falter and fail and lose the victory of the expectation of faith.

Rather than seek impossible validations of God, the believer will examine his own convictions:

> We so often fall into error because we look for an assurance of our expectation, instead of an assurance of faith that we believe. The believer demands no proof for his expectation; "for," he says, "if I could assume something to be a proof, then, when it proved my expectation, it would also disprove it. My soul is not insensible to the joy or pain of the individual, but, God be praised, it is not thus that the individual can prove or disprove the expectation of faith. God be praised! Nor can time prove or disprove it; for faith expects an eternity. . . ."[44]

Beyond all signs and wonders, the expectation of faith is the victory that overcometh the world. For the reality of that highest good is God present in the soul, the eternal immanent in the temporal, God's power in man's weakness, triumphing over the threat of possibility amid the wrecks of time.

Judge Wilhelm to the contrary notwithstanding, the ethical

life never has world enough nor time. For ethics, consistently understood, is all principle.

> The ethical inquires only about guilty/not guilty, it is man enough to hold its own with anybody, it has no need of anything outward or visible, not to speak of anything so ambiguously dialectic as fate and chance, or of the judgment of any formal tribunal. The ethical is proud and says, "When I have passed judgment nothing more is needed."

The Assessor makes out as well as he does by cheating, padding out his principles with a bit of aesthetic stuffing here and there. More consequent is the connoisseur of conscience who will not be tempted to set any finite end in place of his categorical duty, nor calculate his moral worth in terms of goods enjoyed. Yet even he will expect such goods—sooner or infinitely later—and accept them as his due. The very fact that a thoroughly honest ethical mode of life is impossible—that it must either regard temporal existence as a distraction from principle or illicitly appropriate its satisfactions as rewards of duty—is a datum of religion.

> The principle of the spirit is that the outward and visible (the glory of the world or its wretchedness, an outward result or the lack of it for the agent) exist in order to test faith, and hence not to deceive, rather that the spirit may be put to the test by setting all this at zero and withdrawing itself. The outward counts neither one way nor the other. . . . The religious outcome, indifferent to the outward result, is only assured in the inward sphere, that is, in faith.

The religious man has all the time in the world. Since nothing in the world or in time counts for or against God, the life of faith is at once a perpetual struggle without illusive assurance of temporal conquest, and a constant victory over the temporal by virtue of its anchor fixed in eternity. That is why the "good infinity" which Judge Wilehlm found in his marriage is a myopic illusion. The religious man, because he knows that God is all and the world by comparison nothing, must be content with a "negative infinity," a lifelong striving to perfect his faith, the sole and absolute significance of which is that it binds him to God.[45] Precisely because the world counts for nothing he can engage it to the limit of his strength without fear that it will ever prove too much for Him by whom he is everlastingly sustained. The aesthetic life is desire in quest of enjoyment, the ethical is struggle with hope of conquest, but the religious life is a suffering which, because it is never finished in time, is at every moment eternally transmuted to joy in the victorious expectation of faith.

d)   "Every good and every perfect gift is from above"

The first edifying discourse on this text drew attention to the *gift;* this second exploration of the Apostle's words pinpoints the *good* and the *perfect.* A lyric prelude depicts the mythic prelapsarian state of man, that age of innocence before the first parents had eaten of the fruit of the tree of the knowledge of good and evil. "Heaven would have been upon earth, . . . the image of God . . . stamped upon everything in a splendor of glory . . . and He . . . invisibly present in everything." In this peaceable kingdom all the good and perfect gifts of Creation were enjoyed without anxious questions about the Giver.

But the peace is broken, "the serpent deceived Eve, and thus through a deception knowledge came as a deception into the world." For

> the fruit of knowledge always seems pleasant, and it is pleasant to look at, but when one has enjoyed it, then it brings tribulation, forces the man to labor in the sweat of his brow, and sows thorns and thistles before him.

The fall of Adam and Eve is repeated by every man in every generation. One bitter fruit of the tree of knowledge is *doubt,* the anxiety of the intellect, which "twines itself clingingly" around the fallen heart and binds it in distress and contradiction. Innocence is ignorance, but the knowledge of good and evil—not the knowledge acquired by contemplative gazing, but the knowledge that is tasted and consumed—entails a loss of immediacy and a bondage to perpetual doubt. For this disillusion that follows in the wake of reflection cannot be shaken by him who has called it upon himself:

> And is it not the cunning of doubt which makes a man imagine that by himself he can overcome himself? As if he were able to perform a miracle such as has never been heard of, either in heaven or upon earth or under the earth, that in a struggle with himself, a man can be stronger than himself!

114

So the discourse turns to a consideration—a disquieted and doubtful human consideration, suited for a child of Adam—of the word from the Gospel: "If you who are evil know how to give good gifts to your children, how much more shall your heavenly Father give good gifts to them who ask him?" A comforting thought, until one notices the concessive "if" and the condition which it sweepingly, casually, as a mere matter of fact, presupposes: that man is evil. And if man is evil, then all earthly life is evil, or becomes so as it passes through his darkened heart and tainted hands. If man is evil, then he has no good gifts to give to his children, nor the knowledge of how best to give them. No father whose child begged bread would give him a stone, nor a serpent if he cried for fish. But the very bread and fish are qualified by the need that calls for them and the imperfect solicitude that gives them:

> But was the bread or the fish in itself a good gift, or was it not so only insofar as it was needed? And again, is not the fact of needing it an imperfection in human nature? And even if a man did need it, might it still not be better for him that it was refused him; may he not, in a higher sense, have needed this refusal, as when the prodigal son asked for bread, and husks of the field were given him, so that he might come to himself and turn from the error of his ways?

A man may know what is good, but not know how to give it to those who need; or he may know how to give, but not be able to tell the good from the evil gift in the time of necessity. Or he may, caught in the entire ambiguity and confusion of the fallen human estate, sorrowfully draw the conclusion doubt demands:

> So, then, nothing good and perfect exists in the world; for the good either only exists so that in existing it becomes a doubtful good, but a doubtful good is not a good, and the good which can only be so in that it cannot exist, is not the good; or it exists so that it is conditioned by a presupposition which must exist, and which is not itself the good.

But that very conclusion is the point toward which the Gospel is driving: man is not good, but *God is.*

> Has the word ever concealed the fact that men are not able to give good gifts? If this were not so, then no man would need God's gifts. . . . Because the whole world is evil, is God therefore not

115

good? . . . Is not this the one thing needful, and the only blessed thing both in time and eternity, in necessity and in joy—that God is the one good, that no one is good except God?

So understood the word of the Lord becomes the word of His Apostle: Every good and every perfect gift is from above.

> What the earthly life does not possess, what no man possesses, that God alone possesses, and this is not a perfection in God that He alone possesses it, but a perfection in the good, that a man, insofar as he becomes a participant therein, becomes so through God. What then is the good? It is that which is from above. What is the perfect? It is that which is from above. Whence comes it? From above. What is the good? It is God. Who is it who gives it? It is God. Why is the good a gift, and this expression not a figure of speech, but the only real truth? Because it is from God. For if it were through the man himself, or through some other man, that it was conferred on the individual, then it would not be the good, or a gift, but only apparently so; for God is the only one who gives so that He gives the condition with the gift, the only one who when He gives has already given. God gives both to will and to do, He begins and He perfects the good work in a man.

This, for all his cherished religiosity, is the antipode of the orientation of Judge Wilhelm, who aims to effect the good by his own freedom, to impart its overflow to his wife and fellows, and to receive benefits from them in his turn. God is good when man no longer knows what the good is, or even if it exists: this truth of faith disables doubt completely. It cannot be understood by a doubter, for so it would become doubtful. It reverses and nullifies doubt because it abides in God who is beyond doubt. And if a man will abide in God, in whom he lives and moves and has his being, then he *will not* doubt. For:

> The thought of man knows the way to much in the world, it presses even into the darkness and the shadow of death, into the interior of the mountain, it knows the way thither where no fowl knows it, and his eye sees every precious thing; but the way to the good, to the secret place of the good, he does not know; for there is no way thither, but every good and every perfect gift comes *down* from above.

The mind of man is full of doubt. Therefore the truth of this word cannot be proven; not by signs and wonders, for doubt will never agree to miracles; nor by experience, for it is doubt that makes experience unreliable; nor in the witness of flesh and

116

blood, for *all* men are the confidants of doubt. Even if the doubter could be given the proof he wants, this testimony would only be an indulgence of his disease that would feed and batten it, not the medicine that could heal it. What the doubter needs is not more doubt nor the reinforcements of doubt, but the word of faith, which will not fight doubt with its own weapons but will first bind it and then disarm it. Only faith answers to God. Not human knowledge, which is doubt, nor human effort, which is futility, can reach as far as the good. The good is God and from God, and it can only be received by faith.

But doubt is a dialectician who will not be put off by the recommendation that he stop thinking and start believing. The doubter wants to know the *condition* on which he may confidently relax his vigilance and comfortably believe. But the religious discourse cannot reassure the doubter without first abashing him:

> God Himself has given this condition, for otherwise the good would not be a gift; this condition is itself again a perfection, for otherwise the good would not be a perfect gift. Earthly need (which conditions and compromises all earthly goods) is not a perfection, but rather an imperfection. Therefore, even if a man's gift were perfectly able to satisfy one, the gift would still be an imperfect gift because it was needed. But the fact of needing the good and perfect gift from God is a perfection; therefore the gift in itself is also thereby a perfect gift because it is needed.

The condition on which a man may receive in faith the Good which is God is just his *need* of it. This need, which is evident enough in the confusion of ethical knowledge and the failure of ethical endeavor, is given by God himself in the act of creation: of his own will begat He us with the word of truth. The sophistries of doubt—themselves the stings of finitude and Fall—may cover this need, but they cannot eradicate it; "for is this not an imperfection in yourself that you do not quite need God, and consequently you do not quite need His good and perfect gift?" And though they can drive a man from the Paradise of the first creation, these fruits of his infidelity cannot curtail the power of God to make all things new in the Eden of the spirit: for the engrafted word is able to save your souls. [46]

The doubter's only recourse, and his only need, is to cease tormenting himself with the instruments of his damnation. In the terms of the Apostolic admonition, he must be swift to hear,

117

slow to speak, and slow to wrath, quick to expunge the tarnish of evil and abundance of bitterness, that he may receive in meekness the engrafted word of faith. The ultimate capability of man is the power to empty himself of everything but that need of God with which he was created, so that, discovering the image defaced by sin, he may receive the Good which comes down from the Father of lights, whose clarity no shadow can obscure and whose holiness no trace of evil can defile.

The reading of these discourses has revealed that a simple argument threads them all, whatever the terms and tactics required by particular texts or occasions. The nerve of religion is that the existence of God, taken as the premise of a way of life, abruptly and overwhelmingly becomes the whole content and conclusion of that life. Johannes Climacus, who has a humorist's profound understanding of religion, writes that the believer may begin with the idea of God as

> a postulate, but not in the otiose manner in which this word is commonly understood. It becomes clear rather that the only way in which an existing individual comes into relation with God, is when the dialectical contradiction brings his passion to the point of despair, and helps him to embrace God with the "category of despair" (faith). Then the postulate is so far from being arbitrary that it is precisely a life-necessity. It is then not so much that God is a postulate, as that the existing individual's postulation of God is a necessity. [47]

Kierkegaard never stated that necessity more directly than he did in his summary discourse on the theme:

e)   "Man's need of God is his highest perfection"

Unlike most of Kierkegaard's discourses, which take a Biblical text or an "imagined occasion" as their point of departure, this one begins as a musing over a pair of everyday utterances. The first is the Danish equivalent of the proverb, "Man wants but little here below nor wants that little long." The second, which like the first is frequently offered as a consolation to men in excess of suffering and extremity of need, is the all-too-commonplace, "You must try to be content with the grace of God."

This latter is strange comfort, for "if a man were really to think this thought in its eternal validity it would at once nullify all his worldly thinking, imagining, and desiring, and turn everything upside down." God and His grace are the best and greatest of gifts. How strange to have to "try"—or to recommend to another that he "try"—to "be content" with the grace of God! Our commonplace commendation of God is a rejection of God; when God has become *pis aller,* He has ceased to be God.

> The more one thinks about it, the stranger does the earthly life and the human language become. Intermingled with all of life's earthly and worldly differences, which are already quite sufficiently insistent upon being taken at their own evaluation, we thoughtlessly permit the distinction of the divine also to make its appearance, and in such a manner as to show that it is at bottom really excluded.

The relationship of God and man is inverted in everyday thought and speech by the impatient and inordinate self-assertion of the human spirit.

> When we speak of being content with the grace of God, the reason doubtless is that the grace of God does not express itself in our experience as a human being would like, or finds it easy to understand, but speaks instead a more difficult language. . . . It is because of man's impatience that the language speaks of trying to rest content with the grace of God.

This analysis postulates an understanding of the proper ordering of God and man; it is such an understanding that the body of the discourse attempts to produce by a consideration of the sentiment, Man needs but little, and that not for long. If we imaginatively relieve a man of his possessions, one by one, we find that he does indeed need but little in the way of earthly goods. Self-sufficiency is his strength. But in the spiritual domain his need is total, and this absolute neediness is his perfection:

> In the case of the earthly goods of life the principle obtains that man needs but little, and in proportion as he needs less and less he becomes more and more perfect. . . . But in the relation between a human being and God this principle is reversed: the more a man needs God the more perfect he is.

Every man needs the consolation of the grace of God. But no man can apprehend his need, much less embrace the consolation, so long as he continues to cherish the deceitful symbols of autonomy. In a passage that could stand as a précis of all the edifying discourses Kierkegaard writes:

"Before this consolation can be yours, you must learn to understand that you are absolutely nothing in yourself. You must cut down the bridge of probabilities which seeks to connect the wish, the impatience, the desire, the expectation, with that which is wished, desired, and expected; you must renounce the intercourse which the worldly mind has with the future; you must retire into your self, not as into a fastness that still bids defiance to the world, while the individual keeps his most dangerous enemy with him in the fortress, aye, while it was perhaps precisely on the advice of this enemy that he shut himself in—but a man must retire into himself so as to sink down into his own nothingness, making an absolute and unconditional surrender."

Kierkegaard means "nothingness," and in no hyperbolic sense. Man is *in himself* nothing; it is the miracle of God's might and the mystery of His goodness that man is *at all*. For this reason, "the highest of human tasks," like that stripping of himself that was asked of the rich young man in the Gospel, "is for a man to allow himself to be completely persuaded that he can of himself do nothing, absolutely nothing."

Man's truth is his annihilation. Yet it would suppose too much to imagine that any man could be persuaded that he is literally nothing in and by himself, and so become the "sole instrument of his annihilation." The rich young man demurred to the truth because of his many possessions, and so does every man shrink from self-denial in anxiety for the supposed goods of his spirit. This is not moral cowardice, but a fact of human nature. Man cannot immolate himself; he "can at the most will to understand that this fire only burns until the fire of the divine love lights the flames in that which the first fire could not consume." For the truth about man is that he can do *nothing* of himself, not even understand his nothingness. God is, and His Being implies man's non-entity; His omnipotence entails man's impotence.

But in the heavens above . . . dwells the God who can do all things; or rather, He dwells everywhere, though men fail to perceive His presence. . . . God in heaven can do all things, and man can do absolutely nothing.

This non-being and this impotence constitute man's real greatness and his only power: he is admirably suited to be the creature of God, who is all, by virtue of the fact that he himself is nothing.

120

Does it not seem to you, my hearer, that these two, God and man, are well suited to one another? . . . Or would you rather be as one who is not at all suited to God, or as one who can himself do something, and hence is not altogether suited to God? . . . It is in this sense that man is great; and he arrives at the highest pitch of perfection when he becomes suited to God through becoming absolutely nothing in himself.[48]

What Kierkegaard proclaimed in the nineteenth century, to the scandal of his Christian contemporaries, is at bottom the common medieval teaching that man's desire for self-fulfillment can be satisfied by nothing less than union with God. Man is *capax Dei*, and in this negative capability reposes his dignity. There is thus an equation between man's want and God's abundance. Omnipotence and creaturely dependence, reconciling grace and sinful defection, are the same reality seen from opposed perspectives. Therefore, to know that one's need of God is his highest perfection is the only reliable self-knowledge.

The prudential accounting of his own capacities which a man can make by considering himself in relation to the world and to other men is absolutely undependable.[49] For the world is varying and unsettled; man's best knowledge of the world is only probable, and since there is no finite proportion between mere probability and absolute certainty, all knowledge of the world is absolutely uncertain. What holds of the world holds of the other men one meets within it. Moreover, a man's relation to the world and to his fellows is never more than an unedifying external relationship which cannot compose his existence. Let a man know that in relation to external things and persons he can literally be sure of nothing and literally accomplish nothing with assurance: by this knowledge he will be weaned from the distentions and foreshortenings of time, the blind alleys of finitude and the will-o-the-wisp of probability. Secured against deception from without he will have achieved, not self-knowledge, but the first prerequisite of authentic self-knowledge.

No man can understand himself or define himself in relation to the world and other men. Neither can he hope, by a retreat from these external involvements into the hermitage of his own heart, to perfect his self-knowledge and his self-determination. From an engagement in solitude with himself, a man learns that he can do absolutely nothing to bring himself into existence, nor to order, direct, or reform the existence he is given. Another discourse has demonstrated that no man is stronger than himself. He can at the most withstand himself; he can never overcome, exceed, surpass himself.[50] Power is exhibited and exercised only against opposition. When his struggle is not with the world or with other people, but with himself, a man discovers very quickly that he is powerless.

By this discovery he passes from the porch into the holy place of self-knowledge.

> In so far as a man does not know himself, nor understand that he can of himself do nothing, he does not really become aware, in any deeper sense, that God exists. . . . But whoever knows in himself that he can do nothing, has each day and each moment the desired and indubitable occasion to experience the living God.

Though he is nothing in himself, yet he goes on living; and though he is powerless of himself, yet he persists in action. Can he then be oblivious to the divine visitation? "Whoever can do nothing of himself, cannot undertake the least enterprise without God's help, or without coming to notice that there is a God." To know oneself is to know God in one and the same act of cognition. God exists only in and for inwardness, and "whoever knows himself in the manner described above . . . also knows that God is with him. . . ." In and with the understanding that a man can do absolutely nothing of himself "God is immediately present."[51]

This self-knowledge, which is also a knowledge of God, is not a speculative venture nor a beatific vision. It is in the humble service of *worship* that God and man are at one and known to be at one. Johannes Climacus defines this inner act of piety theoretically:

> Precisely because there is an absolute difference between God and man, man will express his own nature most adequately when he expresses this difference absolutely. *Worship* is the maximum for the God-relationship of a human being, and hence also for his likeness with God, because the qualities are absolutely different. But the significance of worship is, that God is absolutely all for the worshipper; and the worshipper is again one who makes the absolute distinction.[52]

It is man's capacity to worship which, according to another discourse, is "the glory of our common humanity."

122

> Man and God do not resemble each other directly, but conversely: only when God has infinitely become the eternal and omnipresent object of worship, and man always a worshipper, do they then resemble one another. . . . To worship is not to rule, and yet worship is precisely that whereby the man resembles God, and the fact of being able in truth to worship, is the superiority of the invisible glory above all creation.[53]

When he has acknowledged his impotence in the lowliness of worship, a man is lifted up again by the grace of God, so that he who can do nothing of himself is yet able with God's help to do all things, even to "gain a victory over himself." Knowing and loving God he knows and is filled with the "power that makes all things work together for good." He who is conscious that he is nothing in himself is in God sanctified and recreated:

> Just as the self-knowledge which reveals one's own nothingness is the necessary condition for knowing God, so the knowledge of God is the condition for the sanctification of each human being in accordance with his specific end. Wherever God exists in truth there He is always creative. It is not His will that men should bask in the contemplation of His glory in spiritual sloth; but He wishes, through coming to be known of man, to create in him a new man.

This new man is the *imago Dei,* once covered over and defiled by the sin of self-sufficiency, now uncovered and refurbished in the crisis of man's agon with God.

> Whom should the striving soul wish to resemble except God? But if he is himself something or desires to be something, then is this something sufficient to prevent the likeness. Only when he himself becomes nothing, only then can God shine through him, so that he resembles God. However great he is, he cannot express this resemblance to God. God can only imprint Himself upon him when he has himself become nothing.

So the discourse concludes, returning once more to the *cantus firmus* of the religious life:

> The knowledge of God is the most decisive factor in every human life, and without this knowledge, a man would become absolutely nothing. Without God he would perhaps scarcely be able to grasp the most elementary secret of the truth, that he is of himself absolutely nothing; even less would he be able to understand that it is his need of God that constitutes his highest perfection.[54]

123

The world of the *Edifying Discourses* might seem to be the world upside down. It is a world in which every value honored among men is subverted, every thought that passes for consequent among men undermined. Yet this world, apparently so bizarre and unnatural, is perfectly rational given the fundamental law of its nature: *God is.* This law, which is normative for the religious life, does invert the world that men inhabit most of the time. For the life that most men live, even their formal piety and their official theology, is a frantic and single-minded flight from the dreadful reality of God. Understandably so. If God is, then all finite knowledge and valuation is rendered anxiously uncertain. In the world of Kierkegaard's discourses there is no counting on anything but God; any reliance on lesser securities than Omnipotence is radical impiety. To say, as Kierkegaard does, that man is infinitely insecure ("There is no immediate health of the spirit")[55] and to add, as he also does, that man lives by faith, is to say the same thing in two ways. The only foundation on which a man can safely build his life is the foundation of faith, love, and trust in God. And this very surrender *to* God is simultaneously a surrender *of* all those earthly and human idols which are the gods of Everyman, and which in the presence of the Holy One Himself crumble to dust.

This is a hard saying, and the religious life is a hard life. Yet it is a consolation as well as a despair. Kierkegaard never tried to prove the reality of God or the value of the religious life—that would have been an impious veneration of reason—but he did point out, again and again, that the reality of God, while it makes prosperity and happiness doubtful, and self-confidence impossible, also alleviates adversity and suffering, and precludes despair. And he recurred without fail to the lucid simplicity and sufficiency of a life lived in the exclusive but all-comprehending presence of God, as opposed to the perilous complexity of the aesthetic life and the wearisome routine of an immanent ethic.

The aesthetic life is infinitely dialectical; but its infinity is spurious. Enthusiastically mediating one contradiction and thereby desperately generating another, A is never done and always lost. The ethical life, for all the Assessor's Hegelian apparatus, is not dialectical at all. Judge Wilhelm is rather a simple-minded and soft-hearted rationalist, for whom each occasion is a fresh example of duty and a new opportunity for his freedom; his life consists in picking these challengers off one by one as they come along. The religious life is again dialectical, but it follows the circular dialectic of the "good" infinity. There can be no typical religious *persona* or cast of *personae:* only a speaker, out of his God-relationship addressing "my hearer" in the solitude of his inwardness, with the direct and monotonous intelligence: all roads lead to God. For the religious man particular persons, places, events, and circumstances are of no moment except as they one and all reduce to the God-man reciprocity. These differences are signalized by the very diversity that marks these chapters: the aesthetic life is the subject of a sinuous and self-perpetuating argument of ever-renewed interest and labyrinthine intrigue. The ethical life can only be portrayed as one thing after another, strung on a thread of identity. The characterization of the religious life, whatever special occasions elicit variety in its terms, is essentially the same edifying thing over and over again.

But for all these differences there is a larger pattern of unity in the interrelationships of the stages on life's way. The argument of the discourses should have made it evident that the religious life is a repetition, at a higher level, of the structural moments of the aesthetic life. Like the aesthete, the religious man receives rather than makes himself; but whereas the aesthete is at the mercy of a fate which he frantically tries to elude, the religious man is at the mercy of God, which he embraces with enthusiasm. For he knows that he is "always in the wrong" against God, which is to say that he has no rights *(have altid Uret)* to maintain against God. God's claim on man is absolute, but man has no claim on God or the world or himself. His self and his world, like every good and perfect gift, come down from above. That is why, though his commitment to God is no more than any man might undertake and is indeed an obligation laid on all men by the very being of God, the religious man is still an exception to the "universal human" ethic by which men propose to govern their own lives.

Judge Wilhem allowed the possibility of such an exception to the universal, though he recoiled from the thought of it in principled horror. The "someone" (Quidam) of *Guilty/Not Guilty?* is a man on the way to becoming a religious exception, but arrested demonically this side of decision in the moment of his crisis. In one respect he is the realization, or almost-realization, of the religious sufferer imagined by the Assessor in his essay on marriage immediately preceding Quidam's diary in *Stages on Life's Way.* But in another sense he stands as a refutation of the

Judge's idea of religion. For Quidam meets none of Judge Wilhelm's requirements for a "justified exception" to the universal: he is not married or domiciled in the world of everyday, he does not love life as the Assessor thinks a proper exception should, and he is tormented by that melancholy disposition for which Judge Wilhelm has no pity. The Judge, when he considers religion as sympathetically as he knows how, cannot avoid thinking of it in ethical categories. His justified exception to the ethical is a man who will nevertheless be able to justify himself *to* the ethical. But the authentic religious life is a "teleological suspension of the ethical," a forsaking of every attempt to justify one's life to the universal, at the beck of a singular conviction of the inexplicable, incommunicable, and overriding authority of God.

The case of Job is a parable of the religious man's exceptional dependence on God, as well as an illustration of the kinship between the religious and the aesthetic. Apostrophized in the letters of Constantine Constantius' young friend, Job lies just off the poetic center of *Repetition:* Constantine writes in jests and in riddles, so that heretics who may read will get nothing to run with. But his significance is pivotal; he illumines with a religious light the two phases of aestheticism represented in the novel by the quasi-demonic observational detachment of Constantine and the melancholy poetic destiny of his young man. Job, the youth exclaims, "lies upon the confines of poetry." And he clarifies: "Nowhere in the world has the passion of pain found such an expression." Job's "passion of pain" is not so much the consequence of his afflictions as of his "noble human dauntlessness." For "the passion of freedom within him is not stifled or tranquilized by a false expression." Job suffers because he insists on bringing his afflictions into the presence of God and pleading his right before the Judge: "O that a man might go to law with God, like a son of man with his fellow!" In thus taking his case to God Job is in the right, for his torments are not the penalty of sin, but a trial that will prove both his humanity and his fealty to God. It is his humanity that will not suffer without protest, and his humanity is herein justified. But that humanity is also put in its place by the Voice out of the thunderstorm, so that Job's finding is the terrible verdict: guilty before God, and the justice he receives is the terrible equity laid down with the foundations of the world: that God is all and Job is nothing.

126

Did Job lose his case [*faa Uret*]? Yes, eternally; for he can appeal to no higher court than that which judged him. Did Job win his case [*faa Ret*]? Yes, eternally . . . for the fact that he lost his case *before God.*

When he receives himself again from God, after "all *conceivable* human certitude and probability pronounced it impossible," Job experiences a repetition of that initial gift of life for which he is eternally indebted to God's bounty. It is in this sense that religion is a "second immediacy" and a new birth: the religious man, by his return to God and to that nothingness out of which he was at first created, gains a new and spiritual understanding of the original and natural disposition of his being by the divine gratuity. Constantine's young man is a poet, *capax Dei* and readied by the misery of his unhappy love for a divine thunderstorm. But he is snatched from the lightnings of the grace of God by a maiden's generosity. Had he set aside the consolations of woman's magnanimity and gone on like Job to the ultimate encounter, he

> would have gained a fact of consciousness to which he could constantly hold and which would never become ambiguous to him but would be profound earnestness because he himself had posited it by virtue of a God-relationship.

For the consciousness of the religious man is the aesthetic consciousness of the poet "raised to the second power," the melancholy covenant of immediacy devastated and rehabilitated in the new dispensation of grace.[56]

Like the aesthete in a second respect, the religious man is a spiritual hermit; but whereas the aesthete is demonically shut up in himself, the religious man is alone with God, the giver of all good. In the course of these chapters we have repeatedly had occasion to remark the dialectical interplay of the inner life with the outer world in the structure of *Either/Or.* The reconciliation of the religious and the aesthetic standpoints, as well as the sharp antagonism that sets them against each other, is distilled into the opening and the closing sentences of that work. Victor Eremita introduces his general preface with the words:

> Dear Reader: I wonder if you may not sometimes have felt inclined to doubt a little the correctness of the familiar philosophical maxim that the external is the internal, and the internal the external.[57]

127

That he himself has such doubts is clear not only from the rest of his preface, but also from the contradiction between inner melancholy and outer gaiety that continually afflicts the aesthetic poet-hero of Volume I. Judge Wilhelm is confident that he has adjusted the claims of body and soul, self and world, by the omnicompetent agency of his freedom. But the *Ultimatum* of the Jutland priest exposes the Judge's patchwork for the motley it is and returns the reader once again to the oubliette of his self-consciousness with its concluding words: "Only the truth which edifies is truth for you."[58] The priest would have concurred in the opinion of the Quiet Brother that ". . . such categories as 'the outward is the inward and the inward is the outward' are, when applied to religion the inventions of Münchausens who have no understanding of religion. . . . "[59]

Yet in the edifying solitude of religion the disparity of inner and outer is healed, whereas in the loneliness of the poet it is perpetuated and in the extraversions of the ethical man merely hidden. For all the virtuosity of imagination and the adamantine determination of freedom, the power of God is the power that created heaven and earth and the soul of man; and it is therefore the only power that can keep them in order. This order is preserved by God within the single soul that commits itself and its world to His will and is content to have them back again at His good and perfect pleasure. Kierkegaard hoped that the reader of his edifying discourses would read them aloud to himself in the privacy of his closet; for there his voice would sound as a symbol of the voice of conscience, which in its deepest tones resounds with the voice of God.[60] So might the perusal of *Either/Or* edify, as Kierkegaard remarked in a note explaining the significance of his pseudonym:

When the reader has independently produced the title 'Either/ Or,' then would come an instant perhaps when he would be inclined to characterize himself as *Eremita*, for serious contemplation always makes one feel solitary. Perhaps there would come a next instant when he would call himself *Victor*, however he may be disposed to understand this victory more particularly.[61]

This last is a refusal to undertake the responsibility for any reader's peculiar self-understanding. But there is no doubt that the victory for which the religious reader will give thanks is the triumph of God within him over the recalcitrance of his soul and the snares of the world. The only truth that edifies—"for you"—is that Truth *against* which you are always in the wrong and *with* which you are eternally founded in and built upon the right. And that Truth exists—and is victorious—only in the inner man.

Like the aesthete, finally, the religious man suffers; but whereas the aesthete suffers his own vanity, the religious man is oppressed by the excess of divine bounty. "The aesthetic hero is great for the fact that he *conquers,* the religious hero is great for the fact that he *suffers.*" Sufferings of a spectacular sort may well engage the aesthete's interest and sympathy: A is a connoisseur of suffering, though it is essential to the preservation of his way of life that he *master* his misfortunes; the ennobling afflictions of the tragic hero, which border on the kingdom of ethics, are the poet's finest theme. These are the exceptional sufferings of exceptional men, who by their elevation above the ordinary achieve sublimity in their very downfall. But

> since the religious is only qualitatively dialectic and is commensurable for everything, and equally commensurable, every suffering may therefore *eo ipso* acquire interest, precisely for the reason that everyone may acquire a relationship to the idea. . . . But what is the idea-relationship here in question? Naturally it is a God-relationship.

Before God there are no greater or lesser men, no ordinary and no exceptional men. The religious is qualitatively dialectical only, for where God is all and man is naught the infinite qualitative difference between them precludes calculation of more and less. Therefore every suffering of every man opens for him an avenue to God. Every affliction, regardless of its rank in the grim hierarchy of human afflictions, is absolutely edifying when it is apprehended as a divine visitation.

Such a suffering relationship to God is an "idea-relationship" raised to the power of infinity because it is situated wholly within the self-consciousness of the sufferer.

> Aesthetics says quite rightly that suffering itself has no significance and no interest, and only when suffering is related to the idea is it concerned with it. . . . But when aesthetics has to explain to itself more precisely what it means to be related to the

> idea, it must again become evident . . . that it is only an im-
> mediate relationship which concerns aesthetics, in other words,
> that suffering must come from without, be visible, not having its
> origin and expression in the individual himself.

The trials of the tragic hero are visited upon him from without—he is the elect of destiny—and it is only for that reason that
he can surmount them in his agony. Moving from aesthetic
representation to aesthetic life, the aesthete can treasure his
suffering as A does only to the extent that the suffering and the
treasuring are separate quantities, the one external, the other
internal. Were the suffering to have its origin in his own spirit, it
would by that fact crowd out the melancholy triumph of
treasuring it. That is why fate and death are the *loci classici* of
aesthetic suffering. Only if the aesthete himself is *integer* can he
sustain his "Idea" and securely bring his affliction in relationship
to it. Once the suffering becomes inward, an agony of the inner
man, then the integrity of his ideal self is broken, and his game is
up. Therefore, "aesthetics keeps the hero in an undamaged state
by reason of the direct proportion between strength and suffering (the one within, the other from without)."[62]

But because God exists only inwardly—is encountered
only in the depths of personal despair—the suffering of the
religious man is not something he can relish or transform. For
the only power that can uphold him in his desolation is the very
power that lays waste his spirit. His suffering and its meaning
are the same thing; he and God are of one accord, that he is
nothing and God everything.

Yet his suffering is not without its own peculiar joy. Indeed
his suffering his own nothingness is the religious man's joy over
the reality of God. Frater Taciturnus writes that "in danger,
above seventy thousand fathoms of water, many, many miles
from human help, there to be joyful"[63]—that is the greatness
of the religious life. A himself understands the Frater's conviction
that poetry—especially at its tragic maximum—and religion are
glorious, but ethics merely twaddle. "The tragic," he says, "has
in it an infinite gentleness; it is really in the aesthetic sense with
regard to human life, what the divine love and mercy are. . . .
The ethical, that is strict and harsh." He might have had Judge
Wilhelm in mind when he wrote in his essay on tragedy ancient
and modern:

130

In a certain sense . . . it is an entirely correct tactic of the age to hold the individual responsible for everything; but the misfortune is that it does not do it deeply and inwardly enough, and hence its vacillation. It is self-complacent enough, to disdain the tears of tragedy, but it is also self-complacent enough to dispense with the divine mercy. But what is human life when we take these two things away, what is the human race? Either the sadness of the tragic or the profound sorrow and profound joy of the religious.[64]

If Judge Wilhelm often appears pedestrian and mock-solemn by comparison with A and the other aesthetes in Kierkegaard's repertoire, it is not because he is incapable of aesthetic levity. It is rather the case that he is not absolutely serious. That kind of earnestness would make him a religious man. And it would also release him from care about the things for which the aesthete— and in a different way, he—are anxious. The Assessor's gravity reveals that he is not sufficiently serious to be carefree.

A man's self is defined by his concerns: only the man concerned exclusively with God can afford to be utterly careless of the world and of himself. The poet is a melancholy being whose life is devoted to the pursuit of joy. The religious man is a sufferer who has the joy of knowing that God is glorified in his suffering. The difference and the similarity are due to the fact that the religious man has passed through the crisis of ethical freedom and its demise in guilt. He is able and willing to receive himself because he knows the futility of trying to create himself. He can repose in solitude because he has been disabused of the idea that he can effect a neat consonance of freedom and nature. He can sorrow joyfully, because he knows that his abasement is God's exaltation.

Yet what Judge Wilhelm said of immediacy—that it is given its rightful place by ethics—can be said of the ethical by the religious man. The life that is received from God includes moral striving as well as enjoyment; from his private understanding with God the religious man is ennabled to return to the life of community. The pleasures of love and the daily responsibilities of marriage—which in his heart he sacrifices to God— are given back to him with the cup of his religious suffering. He knows that he has them as moratoria from God. They are not his fate, but neither must he accrue them out of his own resources. That he is in debt to God means that he is released by God to the

131

possession of his life without concern lest he lose it and without the anxiety of failure; for he has already failed, indeed, he has given up succeeding. Woe to the man, Kierkegaard says, who succeeds against God! Blessed the man who is strong enough to be weak and poor in spirit before God![65]

"A man has only one God, and if he cannot reach an understanding with Him, to whom, then, shall he go?"[66] That he himself is nothing means that God is all in all. This is the unfailing certainty that emancipates the religious man from slavery to nature and himself, and delivers him to his anguished freedom. The self which he could not find in nature or in flight from nature, the self that he could not earn for himself, he first receives—in its eternal and absolute validity—when he abandons it to God. By the decision to be in the wrong as against God he is armed against despair and inspired to action. No longer tormented by the bad dreams of the aesthete nor defeated by the illusions of the ethicist, he seizes the time of his visitation, and learns in his day the edifying things that belong to his peace.

4
ALMOST IN EARNEST:
The Philosophy of
Johannes Climacus

On his own allegation Kierkegaard's writing was coerced from him by two urgent questions: What is it to be a man? and What is it to be a Christian? Not that there was in his day a shortage of answers to these questions; on the contrary, he felt there were too many and too facile answers, but not enough understanding of the questions. The voracious Hegelian philosophy had dialectically devoured human existence and Christian faith, and was regurgitating their speculative meaning in compendia predigested for popular consumption. Kierkegaard distrusted the agility with which speculation explained everything, and set himself to make things hard that everyone else was making easy.[1] His program in books like the *Philosophical Fragments* and the *Concluding Unscientific Postscript* was to rehearse the difficulty of the questions by means of a polemic against the ready speculative answers.

This chapter will consider the first and more general of Kierkegaard's leading questions. The specific problem of Christian belief will be aired in chapter 5. For Kierkegaard was convinced that the questions—What does it mean to exist? What does it mean to believe?—were so ordered that the latter could not be discussed until the sense of the former had been clarified. It is after all a *man* who *believes.* Moreover, the question of the meaning of human existence had to be raised existentially before the attack on speculation could have its effect.[2] In the stages on life's way Kierkegaard prepares an existential setting for the philosophical consideration of this question. The stages, not described by a disinterested observer but dramatized by representative *personae,* suggest that human existence is amenable to a diversity of living interpretations, each consistent in itself, each provident of a unique perspective on the others, and each irreducibly distinct from the others. For in spite of the ascending scale in which he presents them (aesthetic, ethical, religious), and in spite of his own commitment of the religious, Kierkegaard never lost sight of the fact that each existence-sphere is a way of life eligible and enactable by a human being, and that the only passage from one stage to another is an utterly free choice entailing a wholesale revision of the personality and its world.

To the question, What is man? there are as many existing answers as there are existing men. That is the "message" of Kierkegaard's "aesthetic" writings. The stages on life's way are the larger categories into which the answers fall, but each man by living his own life works out his unique solution to the problem of the meaning of human existence. This fact supplied a motif for Kierkegaard's critique of speculative philosophy. If life has an indefinite plurality of meanings in the concrete, then it has no one definitive meaning in the abstract, and it is perverse of the theorist to "discover" such a meaning and package it for retail distribution. A philosophical theory of human nature is like a suit of clothes made to the measure of the average man: it may approximate everyone, but it fits no one.

With this consideration and the previous discussion in mind it is possible to unravel passages like this:

Man is spirit. But what is spirit? Spirit is the self. But what is the self? The self is a relation which relates itself to its own self, or it is that in the relation, that the relation relates itself to its own self; the self is not the relation, but *that* the relation relates itself to its own self. Man is a synthesis of infinity and finitude, the temporal and the eternal, freedom and necessity, in short a synthesis. A synthesis is a relation between two. So regarded man is not yet a self.

134

> In the relation between two the relation is the third term as a negative unity, and the two relate themselves to the relation, and in the relation to the relation; such a relation is that between body and soul, when man is regarded as soul. If on the contrary the relation relates itself to its own self, then this relation is the positive third term, and this is the self.[3]

This is not the gobbledygook it seems to be, though there is good reason why it must seem so.

By classical philosophers the human self was interpreted as a psycho-physical duality. Plato takes man to be a synthesis of reason and appetite. What he calls "spirit" is merely the togetherness that unites the other two. It is "the third term as a negative unity" of *eros* and *nous,* in and to which they are bound. Allied in the good man with reason and in the bad man with desire, "spirit" is *nothing but* the ascendancy of one over the other in a given personality. The pagan, Kierkegaard says, always conceives the self as *nature.* For Plato the soul, like any other object or event, is a point of engagement for the cosmic forces of form and dynamic. For Aristotle the human self like any other entity, is a substantial juncture of form (soul) with matter (body). It is in either case the nature of the universe, writ small in human nature, that determines man to be what he is.

Suppose now the self is understood as *spirit.* According to Kierkegaard, this is the view of Christianity. In this version the union of psychic and somatic elements in the self is effected not by the nature of things, but by some "positive third term." This third term that positively joins body and soul ("that in the relation, that the relation relates itself to its own self") is the *self-consciousness* by which the psycho-physical synthesis transcends itself as nature and asserts itself as spirit. The self as spirit is the natural synthesis of body and soul become conscious of itself and *free* with respect to itself.

Freedom (or self-consciousness: the terms are finally synonymous in Kierkegaard) does not fit the naturalistic understanding of man at all. It is not the substantial essence of man (as such it would be determined) nor an attribute or operation of man (it is the *sine qua non* of selfhood) nor an essential property or power of man (as such it would be causally implicated in his essence and so determined). It cannot be defined, derived, or demonstrated by a study of human nature, for definition, derivation, and demonstration are equivalent to determination, and a freedom determined by nature is a contradiction in terms. Presupposed in every human act, self-consciousness is necessarily inscrutable; it is always behind the thinker and within him, never wholly outside him or before him. Freedom can only be conceived *via remotionis* as the original undemonstrable source, the undefinable insubstantial essence, and the continuing self-initiating act of spirit.[4]

This is the "relation which relates itself to its own self:" freedom, self-consciousness, or (which is the same thing) the self understood as spirit. Its reality is indicated by men's moments of ultimate self-surpassing—e.g., suicidal despair and self-sacrificing love—and by the ostensible difference between man and beast—such as the ubiquity of culture among men and its total absence among animals; that fact that the beast never gives himself an image of himself whereas man is always trying to live up to the self he thinks he is or wants to be; the circumstance that man, the adverbial creature, lusts shamefully, loves beautifully, and kills cruelly, while the beast can only mate, tend its young, and prey. But though it is everywhere hinted at, the self remains a mystery that eludes the understanding. That is why Kierkegaard "defines" it in impossibly tortured paradoxes. He is holding the jargon of his Hegelian contemporaries against them, to show that when one tries to grasp human nature categorially, he comes up with nonsense.

Yet the irony is soberly drawn, and the paradoxes mean just what they say. Human existence is not a unity of form and matter embedded in nature. Existence as spirit is the collision in man of nature (the psycho-physical synthesis) and freedom (the self-consciousness of this synthesis which robs it of substantiality and negates it as nature). "The self is not the relation, but *that* the relation relates itself to its own self."

Kierkegaard often describes human existence as a passion (*Lidenskab, passio*) inflicted by the straits in which the self is placed: man must forge his self by freedom, but the very capacity of transcendence that makes him a man upsets the stability of any self so achieved. To be spirit is to forfeit the security of nature; to be free is to lack the solace of natural determination. Unlike the animal who simply *is* what he *is*, man suffers as spirit the need and the contradiction of *becoming* what he *can be*.[5]

The rationale for the "gobbledygook" is now clear enough: if we try to understand man as he is, we fail; for by nature man is not. "So regarded man is not yet a self." The theoretical discussion of immediacy reinforces the conclusion at which the aesthete arrived existentially: immediately man is nothing but a lack (of a given self), a prospect (of acquiring himself as spirit), and a friction (between nature and freedom as the conditions of spiritual selfhool). The aesthete is described as "an existential possibility that cannot win through to existence."[6] Answering to the chaotic poetry of the aesthetic life, the aesthetic element in man ("that by which he immediately is what he is") is limned in contradictions. The force of Kierkegaard's paradoxes is to define human nature by pointing up the impossibility of defining it. His existential philosophy—which could not be written until the inhabitants of the existence-spheres had exfoliated imaginatively the richness and the poverty, the glory and the horror of human life—is a ponderous ironic epitaph over every philosphy of existence.

When Kierkegaard laid aside the role of novelist and addressed himself to the philosophical problem of man, he devised a new pseudonym, the humorist Johannes Climacus. The humorist, because he occupies a standpoint of provisional detachment from life, is able to treat of the gravest matters without prejudice to his objectivity. But at the same time, because he is a man in sympathy with men, whose disengagement is *only* provisional and *pro tem*, he is preserved from the philosophers' pretension that this objectivity is his spiritual habitation. His philosophical essays, like well-turned jokes, are to be taken quite seriously; but it is not to be supposed that they represent the personal commitments of the jokester, or that they spring from a speculative *Weltanschauung*.

It is imperative, therefore, when reading Climacus' works, to respect their avowed fragmentary and unscientific character. Above all it is necessary to take him at his word when he says he has no opinions and proposes no doctrines.[7] For the matter under discussion is human existence, concerning which the point to be made—and it can only be made humorously—is that opinions and doctrines are beside the point.

However, it is not as pseudonym that Johannes Climacus first makes his appearance in Kierkegaard's corpus, but as the blighted hero of a projected philosophical tragedy. In 1842–43 Kierkegaard made sketches for a book to be called *Johannes Climacus, or De Omnibus Dubitandum Est: A Story.* He borrowed the name for his book and his protagonist—John the Climber—from its original bearer, a Byzantine monk so-called after a work of his own on mystical theology: κλῖμαξ τοῦ παραδείσου. Kierkegaard's Johannes was a lover not of God, but of logic; his *scala paradisi* was a flight of *consequentiae,* up and down which he would gambol daylong to his soul's rapture. Not unnaturally he determined to study philosophy.

A philosopher, he quickly learned, was a man who had doubted everything. *De omnibus dubitandum est,* bound like a phylactery to the professor's brow, was the authentication of his claim to membership in the inner sanctum of the lovers of wisdom. *De omnibus dubitandum est,* like Plato's warning about geometry, was a qualification the beginner had to meet before he could enter the sacred courts. Historically *de omnibus dubitandum est* was the epitome of Descartes' propaedeutic doubt. The author of *Fear and Trembling* points out that Descartes did not recommend radical doubt to everyone as a foolproof philosophical method, but only adopted it during his own meditations as a way of dividing true from false in the dark and uncertain deliverances of his scholastic mentors. Descartes, moreover, made it abundantly clear that he never doubted those revealed truths which the Church had proclaimed *de fide,* no matter how deficient their clarity and distinctness.[8] But from the Hegelians at his university Johannes heard a different interpretation of *de omnibus dubitandum est.* Hegel had read the formula as a universal methodological imperative: the philosopher may not assume anything, he must isolate and think through all of his presuppositions so as to arrive behind them at an impregnable starting point for constructive speculation. In Hegelian hands the modest proposal of Cartesian skepticism became a charter of philosophical absolutism.

Kierkegaard knew that the program of universal doubt could never be carried through. The philosopher can no more get behind all his presuppositions than Judge Wilhelm could get behind his whole past. To do so he would have to step outside nature and history and his own intellectual skin. More than once Kierkegaard makes sport of the Hegelian claim that philosophy "begins with nothing," that is, without any unexamined or unverified assumptions:

The Dialectic of Beginning
Scene in the Underworld
Characters: Socrates, Hegel.

Socrates sits by a rippling stream, in the cool, listening to the sound of the water. Hegel is sitting at a table reading Trendelenburg's *Logische Untersuchungen,* Pt. ii, page 198, and goes across to Socrates in order to complain.

Socrates: Shall we begin by being in complete disagreement, or in agreement upon something which we will call an assumption?
Hegel:— — — —
Socrates: With what assumptions do you begin?
Hegel: From none at all.
Socrates: That is quite possible; perhaps you do not begin at all.
Hegel: I not begin, I who have written twenty-one volumes?
Socrates: Ye Gods! what a hecatomb you have sacrificed.
Hegel: But I begin from nothing.
Socrates: Is that not from anything?
Hegel: No, the inverse process. It is only understood at the end of the whole work, in which I have dealt with all sciences, the whole of universal history, etc. . . . .
Socrates: How shall I ever get over that difficulty, for many curious things must certainly have happened which would charm me. . . . And you know that I never let even Polos talk for more than five minutes, and you want to talk twenty-one volumes. [9]

Hegel's position, here ridiculed, is no more than the last and most sophisticated form of the program of modern philosophy generally. Whatever the mind of Descartes may have been, all his *epigoni* have believed (a) that philosophy must have an indubitable, because presuppositionless, foundation, and (b) that such a starting-point is to be sought in whatever element of experience is given with self-verifying evidence. Whether like the rationalist he finds his security in clear and distinct ideas, or like the empiricist in the date of sense and sentiment, or like Kant in both, the typical modern philosopher believes without question that there is and must be such an "absolute beginning." Methodological doubt is the reconnaisance by which the beginning is sighted.

139

But Kierkegaard, in the guise of the "poor existing individual" Climacus with no *grundlich und geistlich* understanding of speculation, observed that in fact there was no absolute beginning. Nothing in human experience is immediately given and self-evident, no idea is its own warrant. Our actual sense-experience, as William James was to point out somewhat later on, is a blooming, buzzing confusion. And our actual thinking, as James Joyce was to demonstrate, is a Gothic Odyssey and not a string of syllogisms in Barbara. The empiricists' sense-data and the rationalists' ideas are not the givens of experience, but abstractions from experience.

Philosophy, Climacus insists, can never begin with the immediate. At least it can never begin immediately with the immediate.[10] To do so would be to think by nature or by accident, which is absurd. But the feat is impossible in any case, for there is no immediacy to begin with. Philosophical thought gets under way only after a previous process of reflection has already been carried through, since it is by such digging that the philosopher unearths his own premises.

Hegel had seen this point and made systematic capital of it. It is, he said, exactly true that philosophy discovers its absolute starting point at the end of an exhaustive course of abstraction. *De omnibus dubitandum est*, and *omnibus dubitatis* one has one's presuppositionless beginning. Q.E.D. Universal doubt leads to self-evident truth, on which sure foundation the philosopher may proceed to reconstruct experience, all sciences, the whole of universal history, and so on, as they are seen by the speculative eye of the Absolute Spirit.

Unfortunately, interjects the poor existing individual, there is no such luck. No one by thinking ever comes to the point at which he can think no more; no one by doubting ever gets to a place where further doubt is impossible. Given any proposition whatever, even a self-evident proposition, it is always possible to imagine premises from which it might be derived. And it is equally possible to imagine premises that prove it false. Every proposition is *per se* questionable, and every alleged datum may be mooted. Reflective thought, generating as many problems as it solves, is potentially infinite. The simplest question becomes a hydra of prosyllogisms if one attempts to evoke a completely rational answer. The ordinary man succeeds in being reasonable because—irrationally—he is willing not to ask all the questions he might. He asks himself, for example, Which girl shall I marry? And when he has answered that question to his satisfaction (and hers, and the parents', and the friends' and neighbors') he is content that he has made a reasonable choice. But before he decided which girl he should marry, he should—to be altogether sure—have asked and answered the prior question, Should I marry at all? But before he can answer that he must know, What is marriage? What is this commerce of flesh and spirit that we call love? And to know this he must first know, What is flesh? What is spirit? What is the significance of the sexual difference? What is male? What female? What is man? and so on *ad infinitum*. So that in the end a man, even the most determinedly rational of men, marries—or does not marry—without sufficient reason.

Human deliberations, Climacus concluded (and here is one of the roots of his "irrationalism"), can on principle never be final. There can be no absolute beginning for philosophy. If a philosopher says he has doubted everything he is lying, and in fact the windbagging arrogance of the Hegelians proved them charlatans who never so much as meant to practice what they preached. So let the comedy begin:

> Suppose the infinite act of abstraction to be *in actu*. However, the beginning is not identical with the act of abstraction, but comes afterwards. With what do I begin, now that I have abstracted from everything? Ah, here an Hegelian will perhaps fall on my breast, overcome by deep emotion, blissfully stammering the answer: with nothing. Very well, but now I must offer my second question: *How* do I begin with nothing? Unless in fact the infinite act of abstraction is one of those tricks of legerdemain which may readily be performed two at a time; if, on the contrary, it is the most strenuous of all acts of thought, what then? Why then of course, all my strength is required to hold it fast. If I let slip any part of my strength, I no longer abstract from everything. And if under such circumstances I make a beginning, I do not begin with nothing; precisely because I did not abstract from everything when I began. That is to say, if it is at all possible for a human being to abstract from everything in his thinking, it is at any rate impossible for him to do more, since if this act does not transcend human power, it absolutely exhausts it. To grow weary of the act of abstracting, and thus to arrive at a beginning, is an explanation of the sort valid only for costermongers, who do not take a little discrepancy so seriously. [11]

141

The truth is that a man who literally doubted everything would find himself in the slough of despond, a *reductio* in which he would have to commit not only intellectual but also—lest his reflection be imperfect—bodily suicide. But no one is about to think himself to death in obedience to the philosopher's injunction, for nature, as another philosopher remarked, is always stronger than principle. [12]

> What if instead of talking or dreaming about an absolute beginning, we talked about a leap. To be content with a "mostly," an "as good as," a "you could almost say that," a "when you sleep on it until tomorrow, you can easily say that," suffices merely to betray a kinship with Trop, who, little by little, reached the point of assuming that almost having passed his examinations was the same as having passed them. We all laugh at this; but when philosophers reason in the same manner, in the kingdom of the truth and in the sanctuary of science, then it is good philosophy, genuine speculative philosophy. [13]

The "leap" of which Climacus here speaks is an act of will, the only efficacious means of breaking off a train of reflection. One does not come to certainty by systematic doubt; that way lies only confusion, disillusionment, perhaps weariness and ludicrous self-deception. But a man can *choose* to stop doubting and begin thinking constructively. And this leap, the minimal presupposition of the actual thoughts of every thinker, is always a volitional break in the inferential chain, never a necessary consequence of that process of reflection which is programmed for infinity. It is an act of will by which alone the philosopher "begins," an act of will incalculably arbitrary in relation to the infinite possibilities ever to be considered. For thought nothing is certain, because everything is possible.

All this Climacus knew, but first he had to learn it. The young Johannes, ingenuously in love with thinking and docile before his masters, resolves to try his brain on three propositions which are always in their mouths: (1) Philosophy begins with doubt; (2) One must have doubted before beginning to philosophize; and (3) Modern philosophy begins with doubt. These propositions articulate his teachers' idea of the relationship between philosophy and the maxim of universal doubt: *de omnibus dubitandum est*. Johannes subjects them to an analysis of his own, beginning with a commentary on proposition (3) *ad litteram*. The adjective "modern" suggests that the proposition merely reports a fact about a particular philosophical movement, but the eternal present "begins" hints at an intimacy between "modern" philosophy and the timeless essence of philosophy. Waiving the linguistic ambiguity and assuming that the proposition is historical, Johannes asks *how* modern philosophy began with doubt. Perhaps by accident, as by accident Columbus discovered America. From such an accident no essential consequences follow; and yet the proposition in question, so interpreted, plainly conflicts with proposition (1), which unmistakably says something about the essence of philosophy. Or perhaps it was by a different kind of accident, as by accident Newton discovered the law of gravity. That law, even before it was discovered, necessitated the "accident" of the falling apple by which it first came to light. If in this way modern philosophy begins with doubt, then proposition (3) turns straightway into proposition (1), for "modern" in that case stands only for the historical occasion which is absorbed in eternal verity before it happens. Or did modern philosophy begin with doubt of necessity? That would be a curious consequence, since its necessity would imply its continuity with previous philosophy, while doubt is a breach of continuity. Be that as it may: if modern philosophy began with doubt necessarily, because it is the nature of philosophy so to begin, then once again proposition (3) is transformed into proposition (1).

A dutiful disciple of his Hegelian mentors, Johannes decides to effect a dialectical synthesis of propositions (3) and (1). He speculates: modern philosophy begins with doubt. This is a true historical beginning. But since history itself is the unfolding in time of the eternal Idea, the historical beginning of modern philosophy is dialectically brought into perfect rapport with the Absolute. Johannes can conceive the possibility in principle of such a "mediation"; he can even suppose it a *fait accompli* like the hypostatic union of the two natures of Christ. But he cannot himself bring it about, and he cannot see how any human being might come to do so.

[I]t still was by no means clear to Johannes Climacus how he was to imagine such a combination. His anguished soul was full of unrest and forboding. He suspected that this situation must be something extraordinary. He suspected that to be a philosopher nowadays must be something indescribably difficult. If modern philosophy was like this, the individual philosopher must be the same. *He must be conscious of himself; then of his significance as a factor*

143

(moment) in modern philosophy; then modern philosophy must in turn see itself as a factor in a foregoing philosophy; and this philosophy must in turn realize that it is but a factor in the historic unfolding and development of the eternal philosophy. The mind of the philosopher must, therefore, contain the most prodigious oppositions within it: on the one hand, his own personality, and his little contribution; on the other hand, all the philosophy of the world as the unfolding of eternal philosophy.

In particular Johannes cannot understand how a mere man can be expected to have an understanding of the eternal, not by way of negation, but concretely, as it permeates the whole panorama of history. That would seem to require divinity, or in the case of a finite human being, madness. For "it was not clear to him how a factor could realize that it was merely a factor." And on the other hand,

> if a man on beginning a particular phase of his life merely regards this as a "moment" or factor in the life of one having eternal worth, then he will certainly prevent it from acquiring any significance, for he will want to annul it before it has come into existence, by wanting something which is a present fact to become in his eye something past. And if he is obstinate about this, then he really must be regarded as mad. [14]

Nevertheless Johannes attempts the mediation. And when at last he sinks and swoons under the Sisyphian burden, he almost infers that proposition (3), conceived in the grand manner of Hegel, is nonsense. But he lacks the heart to believe that his professors could command the impossible, and he turns in hope to proposition (1) *simpliciter.*

Philosophy begins with doubt. That looks like a straightforward assertion about the eternal Idea of Philosophy. But on closer inspection a difficulty presents itself. Philosophy begins with doubt. But doubt of what? Surely some philosophical principle or principles. And in that event, philosophy, by beginning with doubt, always presupposes an historical antecedent against which it polemicizes. To his dismay Johannes discovers that proposition (1) converts to the troublesome proposition (3); the alleged eternal beginning of philosophy disguises an historical succession. Johannes is further offended by the mockery which proposition (1) makes of the student-teacher relation in philosophy. For if every teacher says, *de omnibus dubitandum est,* and if every student replies, *sic de omnibus dubito,* what has become of honor and good faith? The eternal philosophy not only has a history, its history is the perpetual repetition of the Cretan Liar.

Perhaps, he reasons, one must have a proper personal relationship to proposition (1) in order to understand it. For doubt expresses no matter of fact, but an act of will. "Philosophy begins with doubt" is not an objective assertion like $2 + 2 = 4$, which is true in any mouth, whether believed or not, whether spoken with wisdom by Archimedes or babbled in uncomprehending imitation by a child. The proposition is clearly a subjective assertion, like Socrates' "Know thyself" or Jesus' "Ye believe in God, believe also in me." If his words are not to be hollow, the man who propounds it must speak with authority, in the case of "Doubt everything!" the authority one acquires only by doing what he recommends.

But suppose proposition (1) to be propounded, and that by one who (never mind how) gives due evidence of his right to propound it. How shall it be received by him who hears it? It cannot be accepted on authority, for universal doubt is a repudiation of all authority. It is not self-evident. And it cannot be imagined that Descartes has doubted for all of us, as Christ has suffered for all of us. For then philosophy would not begin with doubt for everyone, but only for Descartes, while the rest of us would begin by believing that Descartes truly doubted; just as only Christ descended into Hell, while the rest of us ride to Heaven on faith in his merits. And yet, if philosophy does begin with doubt for every philosopher, then philosophy begins anew with each new thinker, who slaughters all his predecessors with the magic sword of doubt and may look forward to his own demise at the hands of his successors. Johannes' love of logic is not strong enough to lift his hand against his teachers, and he concludes that doubt is not a part of philosophy itself but a propaedeutic designed to fit a man for the philosophic enterprise.

This brings him to the analysis of proposition (2): One must have doubted before beginning to philosophize. As a catechetical exercise, however, universal doubt is grotesquely inappropriate, since it bids the student renounce all his teachers. Or is it possible that the teachers of philosophy in their selfless wisdom have hit upon *de omnibus* as a device by which to oblige the student to learn for himself? Is the student's exposure to all the

145

perils of doubt simply a way of making him independent of his master? If that is the case, then the student is indeed put frightfully on his own. He is not led by the discipline of silence, obedience, and trust into the holy mysteries of philosophy, but commanded to find the way for himself. Sadly and reluctantly, but with resigned determination, Johannes sets out to seek his own philosophical fortune. So doing, though his innocence will not let him know it, he has for the first time doubted everything and passed his Cartesian catechism.

Eager to be a student but forced against his will to become a philosopher in his own right, feeling rather like a maiden who is married too young, Johannes undertakes to investigate the condition of the possibility of doubt in the structure of the human consciousness. That consciousness is the source of doubt he has no doubt. It is only in consciousness that the actual (immediate experience) and the ideal (thought and language) stand in opposition. Doubt is not simple uncertainty, but a deliberate suspension of judgment or a willful refusal of assent. And it is only in consciousness that a rejection of the actual by the ideal, or the reverse, can occur. But, Johannes continues, if consciousness is so constituted that the contradiction of immediacy and reflection is natural to it, how can the contradiction be reconciled and doubt overcome?

The answer is not forthcoming, for at this point Kierkegaard's manuscript breaks off. What the answer might have been can be surmised from a consideration of Kierkegaard's scattered notes and from a closer look at other features of his interrupted narrative. The title page of *Johannes Climacus* was to contain two mottos, one from Spinoza and one from St. Paul. From Spinoza's *Tractatus de intellectus emendatione:*

> Loquor de vera dubitatione in mente, et non de ea, quam passim videmus contingere, ubi scilicet verbis, quamvis animus non dubitet, dicit quis se dubitare: non est enim Methodi hoc emendare, set potius pertinet ad inquisitionem pertinaciae et ejus emendationem. [15]

Spinoza opposes real doubt, with which the science of method deals, to pretended doubt, the treatment of which demands not method but a cure for obstinacy. Kierkegaard is opposing the genuine doubt of Johannes to the obstinacy of the philosopher who "*verbis, quamvis animus non dubitet, dicit . . . se dubitare.*" The book was meant both (directly) as a cure for obstinacy and (indirectly) as a tractate on method. In the words of St. Paul, "Let no one despise your youth. . . . " (I Timothy 4:12) Johannes' teachers had contemned his youth and his sincerity by demanding of him what they would not themselves perform. Worse than the Pharisees, they bind heavy burdens on the boy, but will not lift a finger of their own to help him bear them.

> If . . . speculative philosophy, instead of objectively expounding *de omnibus dubitandum* and getting a swearing chorus to take its oath upon *de omnibus dubitandum*, had made an attempt to represent such a doubter in his existential inwardness, so that one could see to the smallest detail how he made shift to do it—had it done this, that is, had it begun upon it, it would have given it up, and perceived with shame that the great phrase which every spouter has sworn that he has realized, is not only an infinitely difficult task, but an impossibility for an existing individual. [16]

While the philosophers were always talking about doubt but never doing it, Johannes, without giving himself airs *ex cathedra*, literally doubted everything to the point of despair. And his despair was so thorough that he lost his self beyond hope of recovery. "I want," said Kierkegaard, "to strike at philosophy by means of a sombre irony," an irony which would "consist not in any particular utterance of Johannes Climacus but in the whole of his life." [17] The irony lay in the contrast between the irresponsible gabble of the philosophers about universal doubt and the honest endeavor of a man to doubt everything in reality. Its sombre color was the destruction of a human personality by an impossible task carelessly imposed and scrupulously undertaken.

The very choice of a narrative form was meant to counteract the characteristic mendacity of modern philosophers, that they never do what they say. When Johannes tries to live his philosophy, he exposes this *falsum* for the insidious betrayal it is. The narrative passages of the fragment set in contrast his own naïve love of wisdom and the sophisticated irrelevancies of his mentors. As a boy Johannes loves solitude as much as he loves thinking; closeted with dialectic he lives in ironic isolation from a world that smiles at his intensity, never divining what a mountainous pile of inferences totters on his head. His father's omnicompetent imagination, which can conjure up a whole city in their living room, and his logical agility, that can elude and upset any opponent, combine with his grammar teacher's metaphysical account *de casuum universis causis et rationibus* to weave in a born philosopher a seamless philosophic character.

But then Johannes, perfected in thought and fantasy, enters the university and encounters reality in the persons of the academic philosophers. In spite of them he retains his intellectual confidence. For he had in his father a man who had kept actual and ideal together in his own life. A wise man who wisely counted his knowledge worthless, a brilliant theologian who lived the life of a penitent, Johannes' father foils the professionals who make their knowledge precious and teach, both by precept and example! that the glory of the ideal is not to be found in the world. It was almost as if his father had doubted everything, despaired of himself, and found salvation at long last in the humiliation of faith. At the university Johannes is put off by the lack of integrity and logical consequence in academic philosophy. The philosopher deals with problems not because they are problems, but because they are current; he refutes a colleague not because the colleague is in error, but because he happens to write in a journal that the philosopher happens to read. What passes for philosophy in the schools is often no more than a pastiche of the personal idiosyncracies, petty arrogances, and professional schemings of the professors. Johannes might have sighed with the author of *Either/Or:*

> What the philosophers say about reality is often as disappointing as a sign you see in a shop window, which reads: Pressing Done Here. If you brought your clothes to be pressed, you would be fooled; for the sign is only for sale. [18]

When he takes his leave of the philosophers and sets up on his own, they mock his efforts: "You must not waste time on doubting. You must begin straight away on philosophy." But in the very next lecture: "To doubt about everything is no easy matter. It is not doubt about this, that and the other, about this thing or that, about something and something else. It is speculative doubt about everything, which is no easy matter." [19] In one breath they ask the impossible, and in the next treat it as a bagatelle. Johannes is on his own, but his ruin is sure, for he bears on his back the burden of the Pharisee, *de omnibus dubitandum est,* which no man can uphold.

148

In these narrative sections of the work there are three *personae,* or rather, since the work is a fragment, the beginnings of three *personae:* Johannes, his father, and the philosopher. If the character of Johannes' father—his imagination and his intellect balanced by his ironic and penitential self-depreciation—is a lesson in philosophic method, then the portrait of the philosopher is an inquiry into the origins and issues of obstinacy. Johannes, his youth nurtured by the one and despised by the other, is crushed between the stones. Or perhaps his reappearance as the pseudonymous author of later works indicates— what might have been the Kierkegaardian case—that he neither succumbed to the deceit of speculation nor rose to the challenge of faith, but found a provisional salvation in the temporizings of humor!

The significance of Kierkegaard's *personae* is further illumined by some of the notes he made for the book and never got to use. In particular:

Just as Actuality precedes possibility according to Aristotle (it is higher both in time and value), so does Certainty precede Doubt.

Doubt comes *either* by bringing Reality into relationship with Ideality. This is the task of cognition. If there is any question of interest, it is at its best a third thing I interest myself in, for example, Truth. *Or* by bringing Ideality in relationship with Reality. This is the ethical. What I am interested in is myself.

It is really Christianity which has brought this ethical doubt into the world, because in Christianity this self acquires importance. Doubt is not conquered by the System, but by Faith, even as Faith has brought Doubt into the world. If the System is to calm Doubt, it must be by standing higher than both faith and doubt. But in that case doubt must first of all be conquered by faith. For you cannot leap over the middle term.

In his treatise *De affectionibus* Descartes has drawn attention to the fact that there is a passion corresponding to every other. Only with Wonder is this not the case. His demonstration in general is rather weak, but it is interesting to me that he makes an exception of Wonder, just because Wonder, as everybody knows, is, according to both Plato's and Aristotle's conception, made the passion of Philosophy, and the passion with which Philosophy began. Envy, it is true, stands opposed to *admiratio,* and modern philosophy would mention doubt too. But it is just the fundamental error of modern philosophy that it begins with this negative, instead of with the positive. The positive always comes first, in exactly that sense as when one says *omnis affirmatio est negatio*. The question whether priority belongs to the positive or to the negative is of immense importance. [20]

From such notes as these we can project the likely upshot of *Johannes Climacus* and the destinies of its characters. Wonder, the immediate response of the naïve consciousness to the mystery of the given, is the beginning of philosophy. But the state of wonder, given the dual nature of consciousness, is also the possibility from which may issue, by an act of will, either doubt or faith. Faith as acceptance is the opposite of doubt as refusal, but at the same time faith is superior to doubt as the positive is superior to the negative, and superior to wonder as the actual to the potential. Doubt, as the fate of Johannes grimly shows, and as the character of his teachers shows in grimmer parody, divides and destroys. Faith, exampled in Johannes' father, reconciles a man to himself, to the world, and to God. Johannes' career was the dawn of wonder and the morning of faith, cut down by the noonday desolation of doubt and entombed in the dark night of despair.

Or rather, "was to be." For the book was never finished. In part (or so at least I believe) because Kierkegaard came to see that it was not an excess of doubt—the philosophers after all never really doubted—but an excess of assurance that was the real peril. Not skeptical modesty but the grandiloquent self-confidence of speculative thought prevented men from apprehending the contradictions of existence and the necessity of faith. And conversely Kierkegaard saw that the possibility of faith is not really inherent in the wonder with which human nature opens on its world. That there may be faith and not doubt or despair, the object of faith and the condition of believing must first be given from above. For the Wisdom of God which is the passion of faith is that which no eye has seen and no ear has heard, the miracle that has never been conceived in the heart of man, which God has prepared from all eternity for those that love Him. But that is the subject of another book.

In the wake of the Hegelian revelation, calling a book *Philosophical Fragments or a Fragment of Philosophy* was a bit like calling a treatise in geometry *Reflections on Round Squares,* so egregious was the self-contradiction. To say "philosophy" was, thanks to Hegel, to say "system;" to be "fragmentary" was possible in *belles lettres,* but a scandal in philosophy. And scandal it was. *Philosophical Fragments* is multidimensionally fragmented: each chapter begins from scratch with what looks like a new topic; the discussion is interrupted by irrelevant digressions and by imaginary conversations with an impertinent interlocutor; the book has a motto and a moral and a problem, but no conclusion; the author confesses no opinion of the matters he discusses. But at the same time these fragments succeed in being philosophical: there is in fact one subject that is pursued throughout the book, the several chapters constituting so many different approaches; the interruptions and digressions contain the heart of the argument; the motto and the moral demand a startling conclusion; and the author's indifference is necessitated by simple respect for the logic of his position.

Philosophical Fragments (ascribed to Johannes Climacus as author) poses on its full-title the question:

> Is an historical point of departure possible for an eternal consciousness; how can such a point of departure have any other than a merely historical interest; is it possible to base an eternal happiness upon historical knowledge?

In effect this is the question, Is Christianity true? though the problem is not dressed in its "historical costume." More significant is the fact that the question is not answered. In his Preface Climacus warns the reader that he is no philosopher, and that he does not even pretend to fill

> any of the various roles customarily assigned in this connection: transitional, intermediary, final, preparatory, participating, collaborating, volunteer follower, hero, or at any rate relative hero, or at the very least absolute trumpeter.

His book is only a private amusement, *"proprio Marte, propriis auspiciis, proprio stipendio,"* in which the author executes a kind of nimble dance with death in the service of thought, to the honor of God, and for his own satisfaction. The question is proposed "in ignorance, by one who does not even know what can have led him to ask it."[21]

The problem of the *Fragments* turns about the temporal nature of man and its relation to his putative eternal destiny. In Chapter I Climacus approaches the issue by way of a subsidiary question: "How far does the truth admit of being learned?"[22]

The truth in question is a (possible) eternal truth, and the learning sought is the (possible) apprehension of this eternal truth by a man who lives in time and has a history. But not even this question is answered. What is given in lieu of an answer is two hypotheses: (1) that the temporal moment in which a man glimpses eternal truth is but an episode in the career of his immortal soul; (2) that the "historical point of departure for an eternal consciousness" is a crucial instant in which the truth first comes to exist for him who learns it. These are the hypotheses, respectively, of Socrates, for whom learning is a recollection, occasionable at any time by any teacher, of truths already latent in the mind of the learner; and of Christ, for whom learning is a conversion of the soul from the willful error of Sin, by a unique Teacher who, in a moment that is the Fullness of Time, imparts both the Truth and the Faith to acknowledge it, a Teacher who is therefore Judge, Saviour, Redeemer, Atoner, God-in-Time. On the Socratic hypothesis time is of no essential significance, just because *any* moment can serve indifferently as the occasion for the recollection of eternal truth; every teacher teaches *per accidens* by stimulating the recollective disengagement from history by which a man returns to the consciousness of his Ideal unity with that same truth. On the "Christian hypothesis" (though Climacus does not identify it as such) time is of the essence. For the learner, by nature a temporal being whose free decisions shape his destiny, is by his own act alienated from the eternal truth and can only be reborn to the awareness of it by a second coming-into-being analogous to that by which he burst from his mother's womb. His teacher is no midwife, but a divine Father who can give him the understanding of truth only by engaging him in history and recreating him.

Climacus has come to stalemate. Either time or eternity. Either the truth is everlastingly immanent in man himself, or it comes to him from without in an historical person and an historical occurrence. The two hypotheses seem to be mutually exclusive. Affirmation of the former demeans the reality of time and history. The latter, even if true, could never be understood. Yet it exists, and its existence is the mystery to which Climacus is pointing. His imaginary interlocutor, who interrupts the argument at this point, accuses him of behaving

> like a lazzarone who takes money for exhibiting premises open to everybody's inspection; you are like the man who collected a fee

152

for exhibiting a ram in the afternoon, which in the forenoon could be seen gratis, grazing in the open field.

Everyone knows what Christianity is, and to pretend to elicit it hypothetically is nothing short of plagiarism. Plagiarism, Climacus asks, of whom? Not you, nor I, nor anyone can claim to be the real author of this hypothesis.

> Is it not strange that there should be something such in existence, in relation to which everyone who knows it also knows that he has not invented it, and that this "pass-me-by" neither stops nor can be stopped even if we ask all men in turn? This strange fact deeply impresses me, and casts over me a spell; for it constitutes a test of the hypothesis, and proves its truth.

At least the interlocutor may be good enough to reserve his anger for Climacus, who has "appropriated something of which no human being is the rightful owner," and reverence "the thought itself."[23] For Climacus (as for Kierkegaard) the Socratic wisdom was the *summa summarum* of all human wisdom. That there should exist a radical alternative to Socrates is the mystery which cannot be accounted for, but only wondered at, perhaps rejected in offense, or—itself a miracle—received in faith. But in no case understood. In the deceptive trappings of Climacus' "hypothesis" that which no man can think is proposed for thought, and thought is brought to a standstill.

Where intellect fails, the fancy may succeed. In Chapter II Climacus makes an "essay of the imagination" (*et digterisk Forsøg*: a poetic attempt) to comprehend the mystery that emerged from Chapter I. He imagines a great king in love with a humble maiden and desirous of union. Is there any way the king can declare his love and marry the maiden without defrauding or offending her? Is there a point of union where the "misunderstanding" that separates lofty from lowly may be overcome by love? Not by the elevation of the lowly: would the maiden feel herself loved if she knew she had first to be transformed in order to suit her lover? Nor by the appearance of the king before the maiden in the splendor of his majesty: does love covet its own glory in the worshipful admiration of the beloved? The union of love can only be effected by a humiliation of the king to the poor estate of the maiden, for love seeks not its own but ever condescends to the beloved.

Suppose now that God, eternally resolved to join himself in

love with man, encounters the "misunderstanding" of sin, an alienation more terrible than any that separates man from woman. His only recourse is to descend to the human condition and become the servant of all. The enormity of the gulf that separates Him from the beloved demands that this servant-form be "no mere outer garment" which "flutters loosely about him and betrays the king," but "his very form and figure." The divine love "desires equality with the beloved, not in jest merely, but in earnest and truth." God becomes man, experiences all things like a man, is tempted in all things, suffers all things, and endures all things—*usque ad mortem crucis*—in order that his union with man may be a genuine union and not the kindly deceit of a royal incognito. Not even this kenosis, of course, can prevent the intensified misunderstanding of offense: was not the Incarnation the seed that flowered on the tree of the Cross? But at least the Lover knows that the beloved is not deluded about His eternal purpose; and He takes consolation even from the beloved's uncomprehending rejection of His love:

O bitter cup! More bitter than wormwood is the bitterness of death for a mortal, how bitter then for an immortal! O bitter refreshment, more bitter than aloes, to be refreshed by the misunderstanding of the beloved! O solace in affliction to suffer as one who is guilty, what solace then to suffer as one who is innocent!

Thus far the poet. For the poet will not be drawn to depict the anguish of the "crucial and terrible decision" that confronts the beloved in the divine presence; he will not try his art on the terror that the beloved feels when he must—not fall to the ground at the thundering voice of God, that would be easy and natural—but sit at table with him as equal; he will not be tempted to imagine the pangs of the second birth, for "how could he find it in his heart to play frivolously with the God's sorrow, falsely poetizing his love away to poetize his wrath in!"[24]

Climacus' *bête noire* is on the mark at once: "'This poem of yours is the most wretched piece of plagiarism ever perpetrated, for it is neither more nor less than what every child knows.'" And again Climacus retorts: plagiarism of whom? I did not write the poem, nor did you, nor any man. And if no man has made the poem, we cannot suppose that mankind is the poet. Who then?

[A]h, now I understand you, it was for this reason you called my procedure the most wretched act of plagiarism, because I did not steal from any individual, nor from the race, but from the God or, as it were, stole the God away, and though I am only an individual man, aye, even a wretched thief, blasphemously pretended to be God. Now I understand you fully, dear friend, and recognize the justice of your resentment.

"But then," he continues, "my soul is filled with new wonder, *even more, with the spirit of worship;* for it would surely have been strange had this poem been a human production." To suppose that God might love man enough to become his equal! That would be a stupid thought for a human being. Or rather an impossible thought. And yet when God has given him "the sign," he may well find it "most miraculously beautiful" that such a thought, which "did not arise in my own heart," has been entrusted to him. Therefore, Climacus turns again to his interlocutor, "as you yourself involuntarily exclaim, we stand here before the *Miracle.*"

And as we both now stand before this miracle, whose solemn silence cannot be perturbed by human wrangling over mine and thine, whose awe-inspiring speech infinitely subdues all human strife about mine and thine, forgive me, I pray, the strange delusion that I was the author of this poem. It was a delusion, and the poem is so different from every human poem as not to be a poem at all, but the *Miracle.*[25]

The failure of the imagination to encompass Christianity, like the failure of the intellect to comprehend it, is turned by Climacus' wit into a testimony to its truth.

Christianity, then, is the mystery par excellence, the eternal truth which cannot be understood or even fancied, but only imparted by grace. Chapter III is a bit of metaphysical whimsy in which Climacus pauses to examine this "Absolute Paradox" (as the miracle is here called) and the "acoustic illusion" of offense produced by its resonance in the human consciousness. Without naming it he arrives at the concept of faith, that "happy passion" in which human reason and the miracle, the humble maiden and her king, Socrates and Christ, discover their mutual affinity. And affinity there is. For the opposition of Socrates the midwife to Christ the Mediator is not the opposition of human reason to the irrational, Greek philosophy versus the scandal of the Cross. The Socratic ignorance testifies that human reason is invested with the potency to transcend itself in that which is other than itself. In its passion to think a reality distinct from itself, to immolate itself in sheer transparency to its object, reason is unwittingly at one with the eternal purposes of God in the Paradox of the God-man. Man's offense at the unreasonableness of Christianity is the self-assertion of reason by which it defrauds itself of its beatitude, while faith is the happy self-surrender of reason to the Mystery of Revelation by which it is fulfilled. Christianity is not the frustration but the paradoxical satisfaction of human reason.

To be sure human reason has its limits, which are first revealed and decisively defined in its encounter with the Absolute Paradox. Yet this encounter is itself precipitated by the rational desire to think being. "Human reason," Kant had written,

> has this peculiar fate that in one species of its knowledge it is burdened by questions which, as prescribed by the very nature of reason itself, it is not able to ignore, but which, as transcending all its powers, it is also not able to answer. [26]

Climacus expands:

> [T]he highest pitch of every passion is always to will its own downfall; and so it is also the supreme passion of the reason to seek a collision, though this collision must in one way or another prove its undoing. The supreme paradox of all thought is the attempt to discover something that thought cannot think.

Climacus is speaking to Hegelian contemporaries out of his own Hegelian preconceptions. In Hegel's epistemology, thinking necessarily *hebt* the otherness of its object *auf* by transmuting the substance of what it thinks into its own spiritual dynamic. In these terms, the endeavor to think being as being, the other as other, is quite literally paradoxical. The success of the endeavor would mean the "undoing" of reason, its *Aufhebung* in the other-than-itself. For the orthodox Hegelian no such "wholly other" than reason is *possible*, because no such recalcitrant otherness is *thinkable*. Yet the rational passion to confront the *Ding-an-sich* persists; it is prescribed by the nature of reason itself and cannot be ignored. "Without rightly understanding itself, [reason] is bent upon its own downfall,"[27] just as love of self finds both its highest pitch and its absolute negation in love of another.

Suppose then *per impossibile*, Climacus continues by way of developing his caprice, that reason does collide with its own other. What shall we call this other? We can only properly call it "the unknown" since it is by definition that which thought cannot think. But let us, just for the sake of having something to say besides "X," call it God—understanding of course that this is only a label with no further significance. Surely no one will get the idea of demonstrating that this unknown X (God) exists. "For if the God does not exist it would of course be impossible to prove it; and if he does exist it would be folly to attempt it." If the reality of God were to emerge from the proof of his existence, it would shatter the conceptual framework of all thought, this proof included; and if the proof really contains the thought of God's existence, then what it thinks is not God, for a God conceived is no God at all.

> Whoever therefore attempts to demonstrate the existence of God . . . proves in lieu thereof something else, something which at times perhaps does not need a proof, and in any case needs none better; for the fool says in his heart that there is no God, but whoever says in his heart or to men: Wait just a little and I will prove it—what a rare man of wisdom is he![28]

For human reason the concept of God must ever remain a limiting concept and no more. Every attempt to understand even the otherness of the wholly other (*pace* every analogical and symbolical theology) confounds the reason and seduces it to conceive God in its own image and likeness. God is either wholly other than man; or the two are ultimately and in principle one. *Tertium non datur.* Hegel took the latter alternative and made of Christianity an illustrated popular edition of philosophy; Climacus, opting for the former, must regard Christianity as the Absolute Paradox before which the philosopher is as helpless as a Galilean fisherman.

To his interlocutor's protest that he cannot and as a reasonable man would not waste his time on such a crotchet, Climacus replies: Of course, and quite consistently so. But he adds:

> From this there would seem to follow the further consequence, that if a man is to receive any true knowledge about the Unknown

(the God) he must be made to know that it is unlike him, absolutely unlike him. This knowledge the reason cannot possibly obtain of itself; we have already seen that this would be a self-contradiction. It will therefore have to obtain this knowledge from the God. But even if it obtains such knowledge it cannot understand it, and thus is quite unable to possess such knowledge. For how should the reason be able to understand what is absolutely different from itself?

Therefore when Christianity affronts reason with the Absolute Paradox, reason is understandably offended and declares the Paradox absurd. But this very offense is only an acoustical illusion. Reason could not have discovered the absolutely irrational on its own, so that whatever it says in this vein is but an echo of the voice of the Paradox. When his interlocutor objects that he puts into the mouth of the Paradox, as expressions of offense, well-known sayings of Tertullian, Hamann, Lactantius, Shakespeare, and Luther—men of faith one and all—Climacus answers: How consequent that offense can find no better language than the language of faith! That proves my point, for "if the Paradox is *index* and *judex sui et falsi,* the offended consciousness can be taken as an indirect proof of the validity of the Paradox." Offense is just what one would expect from reason if Christianity is true. But if Christianity is false, then nothing can explain the existence of the offended consciousness. "Offense was not discovered by the reason, far from it, for then the reason must also have been able to discover the Paradox," and that is already shown to be impossible. Once again the humorist has succeeded in making a reasonable case against reason in behalf of the Miracle. The offended consciousness can say nothing good about the Absolute Paradox. And yet it speaks a language which it can only have learned from the Paradox itself, whereby in spite of itself it testifies to the possibility of faith.

> However, one merit unquestionably belongs to the offended consciousness in that it brings out the unlikeness more clearly; for in that happy passion which we have not yet given a name, the unlike is on good terms with the reason. There must be a difference if there is to be a synthesis in some third entity. But here the difference consisted in the fact that the reason yielded itself while the Paradox bestowed itself . . . , and the understanding is consummated in that happy passion which will doubtless soon find a name. . . .[29]

Such is Climacus' metaphysical whimsy. More than whimsy it never can be, for what it supposes is strictly unthinkable. The Paradox itself might suggest that reason has a higher and happier destiny than to think being; namely, to surrender itself altogether to the self-bestowing Miracle of grace in the "happy passion" of faith. But that is the sort of thing one would expect from a Paradox—and from a jokester who squanders his time and energies on nonsense.

Chapter IV resumes the poetical narrative that was begun in Chapter II and interrupted in Chapter III by Climacus' irresponsible trifling with the Miracle. God has entered the world incognito in the form of a servant. He will give some sign of his presence, for it would be inconsonant with his love to pass through life unnoticed by the men he came to redeem. Not that he is without a certain inclination to irony. Any sensible God, resolved on incarnation, around 0 A.D., would have set himself down in the capital of the Roman empire, affiliated himself to a patrician family, and attained his ends through the civil and military power structures. This one drops in on a fishing village in the backwoods, to all intents and purposes the illegitimate son of a carpenter and his fiancee, and becomes an itinerant preacher. But the supreme irony—to enter the world and leave it again without giving any notice that he was there—of that he is not capable! So he gives a sign. But what sign can he give? Presumably any he chooses. But whatever sign he gives will be as much an occasion of offense as of faith. Any sign will have to manifest itself to the direct sensory awareness of men, and direct awareness is not faith. To be an eye-witness of the Incarnation can be just the occasion for acquiring historical knowledge: "There was this man named Jesus, a native of Nazareth, etc., etc." It may serve as an occasion for the eye-witness to acquire greater self-knowledge in the Socratic sense. Or it may be the moment in which the eye-witness receives the eternal truth and the faith to embrace it from God himself.

If this last occurs the eye-witness is far beyond anything his eyes can tell him, far beyond the reach of any kind of knowledge. God-in-time, eternity shut in a span, is the Absolute Paradox. But knowledge is either knowledge of eternal verities or knowledge of mere fact, Socratic recollection or empirical collection. "No knowledge can have for its object the absurdity that the eternal is the historical."[30] Therefore no man can be the immediate contemporary of the God-man. What would it mean to be contemporary with an historical event which on principle could not happen? Only the believer is—by the "autopsy of faith"—a contemporary of the Incarnation. And one becomes a believer not by seeing and hearing, but by the gift of God. Climacus would have savored the irony of David Hume:

> [T]he *Christian Religion*, not only was at first attended with Miracles, but even at this Day cannot be believ'd by any reasonable Person without one. Mere Reason is insufficient to convince us of its Veracity: And whoever is mov'd by *Faith* to assent to it, is conscious of a continued Miracle in his own Person, which subverts all the Principles of his Understanding, and gives him a Determination to believe what is most contrary to Custom and Experience. [31]

Faith is at one with the Paradox, because in both history and eternity meet and embrace in the moment that is the fullness of time. Else we are back with Socrates.

"Then it seems," puts in the interlocutor, who has been fidgeting impatiently during this disquisition, "that the contemporary derives absolutely no advantage from his contemporaneity." Exactly, agrees Climacus, none at all. Of course there is one respect in which the immediate contemporary may be

> more fortunate than the member of some later generation. For if we assume that centuries intervene between this event and the period of a succeeding generation there will presumably have accumulated much gossip about this thing, so much foolish chatter that the untrue and confusing rumors with which the contemporary (in the immediate sense) had to contend, did not prove nearly so serious an obstacle to the realization of a right relationship. And that so much the more, since the echo of the centuries, like the echo in some of our churches, would not only have tended to surround faith with noisy chatter, but might even have transformed faith itself into chatter. . . .[32]

But for all that the immediate contemporary of the Incarnation is undisturbed by the cacophony of Christendom, his problem is the same as that of everyman. Like everyman, he is asked to find his eternal consciousness by relating himself to an historical point of departure. And if he choose not the polemic of offense, he can only respond to this demand with the irenic of faith.

Climacus is aware that the epistemological analyses of

Chapter IV have been hard going. Out of consideration for his reader he interposes before Chapter V an "Interlude," like the entr'acte of a comedy, in which he plays a few relaxing variations on the theme of becoming. The *cantus firmus* is laid down at the outset: *"Is the past more necessary than the future? or, When the possible becomes actual, is it thereby made more necessary than it was?"* The principal motif and its development may be schematized as follows. Coming-into-being is the actualization of a potentiality. It is not an alteration of the essence of that which comes to be. Otherwise nothing would come to be in the sense defined, but the world would change *de novo* in every instant. Therefore, coming-into-being is a change in the mode of existence of what comes to be. Necessary being *is* and does not come to be. Therefore, nothing comes to be of necessity, and nothing which does come to be is necessary. Necessity is a determination of essence, not of existence. Therefore, whatever comes to be does so freely, i.e., by the agency of a contingent cause. Corollary: to deny freedom and affirm determinism is to commit oneself to the view that nothing ever happens. History shows that every consistent determinist has denied the reality of time, reduced it to mere appearance, or at least found it most embarrassing.

That which comes into being is historical. Natural entities, in so far as they come into being, do so freely and therefore have a history. Nature as a whole is atemporal, since its coming-into-being assumes cyclical form. History properly so-called (development in time) takes place by a second degree of freedom within the round of nature as a setting. Historical events are noncyclical, unrepeatable, and irreversible. What has happened cannot be made not to have happened: the past is necessary in the sense of irremediable. But since they came into being, past events are not necessary in the strict ontological sense. The future is no more and no less free than the past, since all coming-into-being is contingent.

The past cannot be apprehended by an act of cognition. Its essential structure may be so apprehended, but its historicity can only be grasped by belief. This last is also true of that which happens before the very eyes of an observer: that it *is* coming to be cannot be seen but must be believed. Belief is an act of will. Since doubt (the opposite act of will) is always possible, belief contains the negated possibility of doubt, refusal refused.

The theme so developed can now be recapitulated on the

problem at Climacus' hand. The *existence* of the God-man, since it is an historical event, can be believed in the ordinary sense of belief. That he who thus exists is the *God-man*, because this involves the further complication of the union of time and eternity in history, may only be appropriated by belief in the eminent and strict sense, i.e., Christian faith. Climacus' entr'acte reviews with variations his last act. Just as there can be no immediate contemporaneity with Christ because of the discrepancy between direct awareness and the divine incognito of the Paradox, so also the uniqueness of faith is discovered against the metaphysical backdrop of becoming in general and the becoming of the God-man in particular.

Climacus' interlocutor does not appear at the end of the Interlude to put in his penny's worth. Possibly he is silenced by the clean and invincible logic of the piece. More likely he did not find the levity of this divertissement worth his serious consideration. For, as he is supposed to "have completely understood and assented to the newest philosophy," it may also be believed that he was bored by the digression on becoming with its long-winded repetition of the obvious. [33]

But he is waiting and ready at the outset of Chapter V ("The Disciple at Second Hand") to protest the division of all believers into such unequal classes as eye-witnesses and non-eye-witnesses. To pacify him Climacus considers separately two groups of "secondary disciples," the first generation after the eye-witnesses and the present generation of believers. Concerning both he asks: what does a later generation of the faithful owe to the testimony of the witnesses from whom it receives the news of the Incarnation? The answer is the same for both groups: nothing but an occasion of faith or of offense. It is true that the first generation of second-hand disciples has "the relative advantage of being nearer to the shock produced" by the Incarnation, which shock and "its reverberations will help to arouse the attention," whereas the last generation may be tranquilized by habituation to the Paradox. But this is an accidental difference that counts for nothing in Climacus' "algebraic" account; if anything it makes tradition a liability rather than an asset. [34] For the consequences of the Absolute Paradox do not alleviate but only perpetuate its paradoxical character. And the credibility of its witnesses, while it says something about them as men, does not prove the divinity of that Event to which they testify. For that Event is the Miracle, impossible by definition. And as Hume pointed out, no amount of testimony, no matter how reliable, can suffice to make a miracle credible. The disciple at second-hand, like the eye-witness, must receive the condition of faith from God himself. From the intervening generations of witnesses he takes only the occasion of his belief. There is, in short, no such thing as a "second-hand disciple" and no difference between the generations as regards their spiritual contemporaneity with the Incarnation.

When his interlocutor again objects to this levelling of the generations of Christians, Climacus reminds him that it is God, of whom it would be unworthy to "permit an accident of time to decide to whom he would grant his favor," who effects the equality by way of reconciling men to each other and to himself. When it is further objected that one must, after all, have some regard for the rapid spread of Christianity throughout the pagan world, its triumphant parade down the ages, and so on, Climacus can only admonish,

> Verily, if faith ever gets the notion of marching forward triumphantly en masse, it will not be necessary to license the singing of songs of mockery, for it would not help to forbid them to all. . . . [A] faith that celebrates its triumph is the most ridiculous thing conceivable. . . . [F]or the task is always the same, and faith is always militant.

It may be that in Heaven the Church will have leisure to sing Alleluia, but "as long as there is struggle there is always a possibility of defeat, and with respect to faith it is therefore well not to triumph before the time, that is to say, in time. . . ."

To his interlocutor's repeated complaint that he has borrowed expressions from standard Christian writers in the course of developing his "hypothesis" Climacus half-promises to clothe the problem in its historical costume in a sequel which he may write. May write, for "an author of pieces such as I am has no seriousness of purpose," and one should set no store by his promises. Nonetheless, what the historical costume will be is not hard to see, for everyone knows that only Christianity ventures an affirmative answer to the question on Climacus' title page; only Christianity offers itself to the individual as an historical point of departure for his eternal consciousness; only the "historical event" of the Incarnation has claimed to interest men more

163

than historically; only Christianity has asked men to base their eternal blessedness on an historical occurrence.

> No system of philosophy, addressing itself only to thought, no mythology, addressing itself solely to the imagination, no historical knowledge, addressing itself to the memory, has ever had this idea: of which it may be said with all possible ambiguity in this connection, that it did not arise in the heart of any man.

Climacus, however, is only a weaver of hypotheses, and something of a comedian even in this slight capacity. Whether Christianity is true he does not feel it his business to say; the proof of that pudding is in the eating. But that his hypothesis makes an advance on Socrates, of that he is certain. [35]

Climacus' point in the *Philosophical Fragments,* in so far as a humorist can be said to have a point, is that Christianity, which came into the world as the Miracle, ever remains a mystery beyond comprehension and imagination, intelligible only to a faith that is itself miraculous and God-given. But this does not mean that the act of faith entails spiritual suicide; it is rather the refusal to believe that stultifies. In any encounter of man with God—and this is what Christianity proposes—the initiative is God's. Man's only possible responses are faith or offense. And there is no way of knowing in advance which of these responses is happy and which desperate. The *Philosophical Fragments* could not be written until after Christianity had entered the world. No man would have devised such alternatives for himself, even though, as Chapter III has shown, his own reason relentlessly and unwittingly pushes him toward the choice between faithful surrender to God and offended rejection of God. "Every human life is planned religiously," says Vigilius Haufniensis in *The Concept of Dread.* [36] That is what Climacus means when he says that reason and the Paradox are at one in faith, so that reason is beatified in its surrender to the Miracle. In faith, reason has, by the grace of God, the *summum bonum* toward which its own inner teleology impels it. Faith "comes to pass when the reason and the Paradox encounter one another happily in the moment, when the reason sets itself aside and the Paradox bestows itself." [37] This is the good news of Climacus' Epistle to the Philosophers: that God lives and loves, and that by his favor it is the happy destiny of reason to be able to set itself aside.

But this is to set the *Fragments* in far too evangelical a perspective. What Climacus is getting at—hypothetically in

164

Chapter I, poetically in Chapter II, metaphysically in Chapter III and the Interlude, epistemologically in Chapters IV and V and the Appendix to III—is that the historicity of human life screws every truth, Greek or Christian, into a paradox, since truth is timeless and the truth-seeker temporal. For Socratic recollection the love of wisdom is fulfilled in the paradox: one must learn how to die. Rooted in the Miracle of Incarnation, Christian faith incurs a dialectical intensification of Socratic recollection by taking the historicity of man to be his reality and not an accident of his eternal essence.

Climacus forces his reader into a corner where he must admit—not that the Christian hypothesis is true, for that "is an entirely different question, which cannot be decided in the same breath"[38]—but that there is no honest way of understanding human existence that can avoid contradiction. The enemy of human integrity is not doubt, as Kierkegaard had thought when he began *Johannes Climacus*. Socratic recollection respects the uncertainty of human knowledge by telling likely stories and ironically postponing all conclusions until the life hereafter; faith, accepting uncertainty and transcending it in an act of assent, comprehends doubt as a threat which it constantly overcomes. The antagonist is not the man who denies the reality of eternity (the skeptic Sextus Empiricus or the sophist Protagoras),[39] for they can be met out of human resources, but the man who mitigates the reality of time in the interest of a simplistic doctrine of man. The final battle is pitched between the essentialist philosopher who views life under the aspect of eternity and the existential thinker who grapples daily with the paradoxes of his life and surmounts them in recollection or in faith. The foil to faith is the man who, already Christian by profession and consigned by historical destiny to a Christian milieu, dishonors both his heritage of revelation and his human dignity by constructing out of the data of that revelation a synthetic paganism which claims to "go beyond" Socrates but only succeeds in adulterating his humble wisdom with presumptuous folly. The only one who goes beyond Socrates is Christ, or the Christian; the only passion that exceeds the passion of philosophic reason, not frustrating but fulfilling it, is the passion of faith. "Paganism," wrote Chesterton, "was the largest thing in the world and Christianity was larger; and everything else has been comparatively small."[40] Climacus could rewrite: Socrates perfected the very considerable wisdom that is available to the understanding; Christianity brought into the world the wisdom of God that passes understanding; and everything since has been galimatias.

Even this puts the matter much too abstractly and neatly. The surface of the *Philosophical Fragments* may suggest a metaphysical reading. But Johannes Climacus—in his Preface, by his hypothetical method, and in the whimsical conversations that follow each chapter—has taken pains to disarm such an interpretation in advance. By making light of everything he says, by accusing himself of plagiarizing God, he reneges the conclusions he implies and comes up with no results after all. The book is literally fragmentary, "scrapings and parings of systematic thought."[41] To the philosophical reader who begs his theoretical opinion, Climacus' reply is firm: No, thank you, I will not have this dance.

In his *Postscript* to the *Fragments* Climacus observes that the earlier book had been reviewed in a German theological journal, and undertakes in a long footnote to review the review. Because it reveals his own understanding of the *Fragments,* the note is *"einer kurzen Besprechung nicht unwert."* Apparently Climacus' reviewer succeeded in producing a satisfactory abstract of the book. Unfortunately the abstract, "pure and unadulterated doctrination," conveyed the impression that the *Fragments* itself was a "doctrinizing" work. And this, Climacus remarks, is especially strange since the book was only reviewed *"wegen der Eigentümlichkeit ihres Verfahrens."*

> The contrast of the form; the challenging opposition between the experiment and the content; the impudence of the invention (which even invents Christianity), the only attempt made to go beyond, namely, beyond the so-called speculative construction; the unwearied incessant activity of the irony; the parody on speculative philosophy involved in the entire plan of the work; the satirical in making exertions as if *"was ganz Ausserordentliches und zwar Neues"* were to issue, and then coming out with nothing but old-fashioned orthodoxy in a suitable degree of severity: of all this the reader of the review gets not the slightest intimation.

The *Fragments,* contrary to what the German reviewer suggests, was not written to instruct people in Christian doctrine, for

> the one I introduce into the book as my interlocutor is precisely a well-informed person, which seems to indicate that the book is

written for informed readers whose misfortune is that they know too much. . . . This being the case, the art of *communication* at last becomes the art of *taking away,* of luring something away from someone. . . . When a man has his mouth so full of food that he is prevented from eating, and is like to starve in consequence, does giving him food consist in stuffing still more of it in his mouth, or does it consist in taking some of it away, so that he can begin to eat?

But it is his reviewer's concluding words which in particular lead Climacus to believe that he has not quite been understood:

"Wir enthalten uns jeder Gegenbemerkung, denn es lag uns, wie gesagt, bloss daran das eigentümliche Verfahren des Verfassers zur Anschauung zu bringe. Im Uebrigen stellen wir es dem Ermessen Jeden anheim, ob er in dieser apologetischen Dialektik Ernst oder etwa Ironie suchen will."
But my peculiar procedure, if it is this that is to be commented upon, and especially if it is to be brought to intuition, consists precisely in the contrast of the form, and by no means in the perhaps new dialectical combinations through which the problems are made clearer. It consists first and foremost and decisively in this contrast of the form, and only when this has been adequately emphasized can there be room for a moment's mention, if need be, of a bit of doctrinizing originality. When the reviewer leaves it to everyone to determine for himself whether he will seek earnest or irony in the piece, this is misleading.

When a reviewer says of a book that has obviously been written in dead earnest: God knows whether it is serious or ironic! then he has said something. But when a man who has overheard one of the ironic conversations of Socrates says: God knows whether this is irony or earnest! then he too has said something—about himself, however, and not about Socrates.

But the book was far from being pure and unadulterated earnest, it was only the review that became unmixed earnest. In so far the concluding remark might have some meaning in relation to the review, as a satire upon it, for example; but in relation to the book it is silly. . . . But from the fact that the irony is present it does not follow that the earnestness is excluded. This is something that only *Docents* assume. While they are otherwise ready to abolish the disjunctive *aut,* fearing neither God nor the devil, since they mediate everything—they make an exception of irony, that they cannot mediate.

The *Philosophical Fragments* is irony *and* earnest, unmediated. The self-contradiction in the title should have warned even a German theologian that this was to be a *paradoxical* book about the Absolute Paradox![42]

The motto of the book—a German rendition of Shakespeare's "Many a good hanging has prevented a bad marriage"—is "Better well hung than ill wed."[43] Climacus' intent is to hang his reader on the contradiction—that there is no certainty in human knowledge and that every moment is nevertheless a *kairos* that demands commitment—rather than marry him to a systematic "higher synthesis" that is eternally finished with life before life is through with the thinker. At the same time, inasmuch as it formally negates its results and imposes on its reader the necessity of decision, the book is inversely self-justifying. Otherwise, Climacus concludes, "how will we ever come to begin?" Just as the monks never finished telling the history of the world because they started anew each time with Creation, so we shall never get to live if we wait for the philosophers to explain life first.[44] To be hanged on the necessity of decision is a good hanging that prevents a bad marriage.

The details of the argument in the *Fragments,* as Climacus' interlocutor correctly points out, can all be traced back to standard philosophical and theological sources. The book is not designed to make a contribution to philosophy or theology—something that "every divinity student would be able to furnish"[45]—but to get the reader to risk his life in the service of understanding, to the glory of God, and for his own good. Insofar as it necessitates an intensified self-knowledge, it is a book in existential philosophy. And in view of the total incommensurability between essentialist speculation and Christian belief, the *Fragments* performs the only service any apologetic can render: it nails you to the incommensurability and leaves you hanging.

The *Fragments* approaches the problem of man by contrasting Socrates and Christ with each other and with the philosopher who "goes beyond" both by understanding neither. The philosopher of course is no "honest" Greek, but a "mendacious" Hegelian who makes bold to domicile human existence in the paragraphs of that "System" of "absolute knowledge" which in its completeness and finality claims to reflect unambiguously the workings of Absolute Mind. The *Concluding Unscientific Postscript* to the *Philosophical Fragments* (also by Johannes Climacus) affronts the deiform thinker outright by informing him that human life and its problems are nowhere contained in his philosophy.

Climacus is gratified that his *Fragments* have escaped the attention of "critics, reviewers, middlemen, appraisers, and the like, these tailors of the literary world, who . . . help the author cut a figure." In compliance with his motto ("Better well hung than ill wed") the author has been left hanging, his book unheralded and himself undisturbed. For, as he remarks, speaking dialectically, "it is not the negative which constitutes an encroachment, but the positive." To an admiring public the author incurs the most tiresome obligations. Simply ignored, he is free to lounge in his room, jest with his sweetheart, smoke his cigar, and generally "pursue his own way, unhampered by binding and intrusive friendships." "The social principle," he concludes, "is precisely the illiberal principle."

These prefatory misgivings presage the argument of the book, in which Climacus sets the freedom of the individual over against the "illiberal principle" of objective idealism, that the destiny of man is possessed and the human spirit fulfilled only in the communities of science and the state. Climacus would rather be well hung (i.e., left alone) than made a systematic in-law of the whole world by an unfortunate marriage with Hegelian speculation. [46]

All this is by way of introduction to Climacus' own Introduction to Christianity, an introduction which, unlike the irrelevant prolegomena offered by the scholar, the rhetorician, and the systematic philosopher, leads into the heart of the matter, "the question of the individual's relationship to Christianity."

> To put it as simply as possible, using myself by way of illustration: I, Johannes Climacus, born in this city and now thirty years old, a common ordinary human being like most people, assume that there awaits me a highest good, an eternal happiness, in the same sense that such a good awaits a servant-girl or a professor. I have heard that Christianity proposes itself as a condition for the attainment of this good, and now I ask how I may establish a proper relationship to this doctrine.

The *Fragments* defined Christianity as the Absolute Paradox without attempting to say whether or not it is true. Its afterpiece supposes that we know what Christianity is and asks, "Is it true?" Not that Climacus means to raise the question of the *objective* truth of Christianity. Book I of the *Postscript,* in which the scholar, the orator, and the systematist get their day in court, makes short shrift of that pseudoproblem. How can one determine the objective truth of a doctrine which (paradoxically) describes no objects accessible to the human mind, and (consistently) demands of its adherents not reflection and deepened understanding, but the venture of personal commitment to the absurd? Climacus is asking, "How can I—or anyone—find and sustain a *true relationship* to the Christian claim?" That is the *subjective* problem of Christian truth, with which the second and larger Book of the *Postscript* is ultimately grappling. [47]

But the proximate issue is still outstanding: What is man? How can Johannes Climacus, "an ordinary human being like most people," be sure that his humanity is properly adjusted to receive the Christian revelation? At the outset of Book II the author expresses extravagant gratitude to Lessing, who in his deathbed conversations with Jacobi refused to say whether or not he was an orthodox believer. Lessing understood

> that the religious concerned Lessing, and Lessing alone, just as it concerns every other human being in the same manner; understood that he had infinitely to do with God, and nothing, nothing to do with any man directly. This is my theme, the object of my gratitude. [48]

To be truly a man is to be alone before God. Lessing understood that the social principle is the principle of unfreedom, and he resisted with negatives of irony the positive encroachment of his friends and would-be fellow-travelers to the great beyond. Lessing had, to evoke the major theme of the *Postscript,* "become subjective."

In view of the fact that everyone is "a subject of sorts," it cannot be very instructive to tell a man that he must *become* subjective. Earnestness and "the admired wisdom of our own age" recommend that the subject "divest himself of his subjectivity in order to become more and more objective." This "objective tendency," which was in Climacus' day the gist of Hegelianism as popularly understood,

> proposes to make everyone an observer, and in its maximum to transform him into so objective an observer that he becomes almost a ghost, scarcely to be distinguished from the tremendous spirit of the historical past. . . .

170

The wisdom of *our* age might urge the adoption of a "scientific attitude" towards oneself. The advice is sensible enough, in view of

> what this guidance understands by being a subject of a sort. It understands by it quite rightly the accidental, the angular, the selfish, the eccentric, and so forth, all of which every human being can have enough of.

Christianity, Climacus allows, is no "friend of loutishness" and does not deny that such things should be eliminated. But whereas the philosophers insist that the way to eradicate loutishness is to become objective, "Christianity teaches that the way is to become subjective, i.e., to become a subject in truth."

Yet "every human being is a bit of a subject, in a sense," the objective sense in which every man is admitted to be a person (a subject-thing) rather than a thing (an object-thing). No "art or skill" is needed to be subjective in this sense. "But now to strive to become what one already is: who would take the pains to waste his time on such a task, involving the greatest imaginable degree of resignation?" To *be* what one is requires no more than the effort needed to stay alive. To *become* what one is demands a concentration of concern upon the inner disposition of the self, and a corresponding inattention to the world outside. But this necessitates renunciation of all the ambitions men ordinarily cherish. Assuming themselves adequate as subjects, they go ahead to "make something of themselves," something objective of course, such as world-historical hero, number one veterinary surgeon, or champion rifle-shot. And so their selves are scattered in the manifold. But the problem (think of the discourse on "acquiring one's soul in patience") is not, given oneself, to conquer the world, but rather to consolidate one's self, win it back from its entanglement in the world of objective concerns. Understood in this way, the task of becoming subjective is

> not directly alluring, so as to support the aspiring individual; instead, it works against him, and it needs an infinite effort on his part merely to discover that his task lies here, that this is his task. . . .[49]

To become a self means to discover and exploit one's unique possibilities (freedom) in the face of the illiberal distractions of the natural and social world.

Two ways, in general, are open for an existing individual: *Either* he can do his utmost to forget that he is an existing individual, by which he becomes a comic figure, since existence has the remarkable trait of compelling an existing individual to exist whether he wills it or not. . . . *Or* he can concentrate his entire energy upon the fact that he is an existing individual. . . . Not indeed, what it means to be a human being in general; for this is the sort of thing one might even induce a speculative philosopher to agree to; but what it means that you and I and he are human beings, each one for himself. [50]

Climacus would not be taken aback if he were told that his imperative, Become yourself! is quite empty of all content. He knows that the task of becoming what one is can only be described in the most abstract terms. But he also knows that in the case of each person the task is just as rich and concrete as the actual circumstances of that individual's life:

While the ethical is, in a certain sense, infinitely abstract, it is in another sense infinitely concrete, and there is indeed nothing more concrete, because it is subject to a dialectic that is individual to each human being precisely as this particular human being. [51]

To become what one is is to apprehend and enact the *human* in one's own particular human *being*. The important thing is not the objective facts of a man's life (its content) but his subjective bearing toward them (its form). That is why Climacus takes such pains to demonstrate the necessity of an affective disengagement from all concern with the historical significance and the worldly results of one's actions. The essential thing, from a subjective point of view, is *how* one acts, not *what* one may or may not accomplish by acting.

Objectively we consider only the matter at issue, subjectively we have regard to the subject and his subjectivity; and behold, precisely this subjectivity is the matter at issue. This must constantly be borne in mind, namely, that the subjective problem is not something about an objective issue, but is the subjectivity itself. For since the problem in question poses a decision, and since all decisiveness . . . inheres in subjectivity, it is essential that every trace of an objective issue should be eliminated. [52]

Like many of Climacus' utterances, this one is easily misread. But it is neither overstated nor simply absurd. Climacus is aware that every decision presupposes alternatives, and that these alternatives are not created by the subject but objectively given.

By the elimination of every objective issue he does not intend the denial of objective realities. Nevertheless he insists that the individual must, if he is to become himself, confront these given alternatives as possibilities. They do not impinge on him as realities but as demands for action. His problem is not What is this? but What may I do about this? That is the subjective problem.

The objectivity to be eliminated is the objectivist view that the important thing is the *what* of action rather than its *how*. Climacus is not recommending "subjectivism" in the sense of relativism. The relativist is just as objective as the absolutist or the Philistine. They all find illusory security in a supposed knowledge of the objective context of action. As the absolutist finds his security in what he takes to be "the nature of things," and the Philistine his in the narrower limits of local probability, so the relativist is set at ease by his conviction that all modes of action are objectively indifferent. Climacus will later try to show that no such objective assurances are available; for the nonce he proposes that they would be of no profit in any case. For the "way things are" does not determine the way men decide. Objective knowledge does not import subjective obligation. Climacus takes for granted that subject and object in the usual sense are real and distinct. But the reality of a self is compounded of decisions, and the fact that decisions issue from freedom and not from objects or objective subjects makes this objective content of reality secondary to the form of subjectivity itself. Because all decisiveness inheres in subjectivity, subjectivity itself is the (real) matter at issue, and every trace of an (irrelevant) objective issue must be eliminated—if a man is to become himself, i.e., fully aware of his freedom and his total responsibility for what he is and does.

Ethics, Climacus says, would be forced to despair if becoming subjective (=becoming oneself) were not the highest task imposed upon a human being. For the ethical demand—not its objective content, but its subjective form—is that a man cultivate his personal integrity in all his decisions, that he recognize and in all his actions honor the absolute distinction between good and evil, and that he concern himself "solely with the essential, the inner spirit, . . . freedom." But he forfeits his integrity if he disperses his energies among the myriad objects and events of history; for the external world quantifies every distinction, including the distinction between good and evil, to the point of relativity, and mingles the accidental and the inevitable indifferently with the essential works of freedom. In Climacus' usage "the ethical" is identical with inwardness (the inner spirit) or subjectivity. This is not the ethical "stage on life's way" occupied by Judge Wilhelm. However it may resemble the Judge's position in other ways, what Climacus calls the ethical takes a man out of nature and history, whereas the Assessor's ethics demands community and promises a reconciliation of freedom and the external world. "To be ethical" is, for Climacus, simply another way of saying "to be human."[53]

The isolation of ethical subjectivity from every objective concern is total and willful:

> The true ethical enthusiasm consists in willing to the utmost limits of one's powers, but at the same time being so uplifted in divine jest as never to think about the accomplishment. . . . A truly great ethical personality would seek to realize his life in the following manner. He would strive to develop himself with the utmost exertion of his powers; in so doing he would perhaps produce great effects in the external world. But this would not seriously engage his attention, for he would know that the external result is not in his power, and hence that it has no significance for him *pro* or *contra*. He would therefore *choose* to remain in ignorance of what he had accomplished, in order that his striving might not be retarded by a preoccupation with the external, and lest he fall into the temptation which proceeds from it. . . . He would therefore keep himself in ignorance of his accomplishment by a resolution of the will; and even in the hour of death he would will not to know that his life had any other significance than that he had ethically striven to further the development of his own self. If then the power that rules the world should so shape the circumstances that he became a world-historic figure: aye, that would be a question he would first ask jestingly in eternity, for there only is there time for carefree and frivolous questions.[54]

Certain of Climacus' phrasings have an ominous ring: "uplifted in divine jest," "even in the hour of death," "the power that rules the world," and "jestingly in eternity." The man who is isolated from the world in self-concern is *ipso facto* brought into the presence of the "power that rules the world," and by that relationship "uplifted in divine jest" over every vain hope of worldly achievement. Ethical subjectivity is the realization of freedom, the freedom of the subject establishes the uncertainty of every object, and "the Deity . . . is present as soon as the uncertainty of all things is thought infinitely."[55] The creative omnipotence of God ("God *is* that all things are possible, and that all things are possible *is* God")[56] is reflected in and temporally encountered by human freedom striving to become subjective.

> In fables and stories of adventure there is mention made of a lamp, called the wonderful; when it is rubbed, a spirit appears. Jest! But freedom is the true wonderful lamp; when a man rubs it with ethical passion, God comes into being for him. And behold, the spirit of the lamp is a servant; so wish for it then, all ye whose spirit is a wish! But whoever rubs the wonderful lamp of freedom becomes himself a servant—the Spirit is Lord.[57]

Ethical action in this sense is a man's "complicity with God," and the man who still hankers after objectivity

> seeks slyly to slip the thought into his dealings with God, that God needs him just a little. But this is stupidity, for God needs no man. It would otherwise be a highly embarrassing thing to be a creator, if the result was that the creator came to depend upon the creature. On the contrary, God may require everything of every human being, everything and for nothing. For every human being is an unprofitable servant, and the human being who is inspired by ethical enthusiasm differs from others only in knowing this, and in hating and abhorring every form of deception.[58]

By this twist of dialectic Climacus' ethical man becomes the religious man of *Either/Or,* who is edified by the thought that before God he is always in the wrong.

But Climacus is not a priest; he is not espousing and commending religion, but reporting its genesis and its import from his own sympathetic but detached observation post. To his eyes the situation of the ethical man reveals not the crisis of annihilation and restoration, but only the "sacred sportiveness of the divine madness." He expands on his congenial theme:

> God, without injustice, and without denying his nature, which is love, might create a man equipped with unexampled powers, set him down in a solitary place, and say to him: "Do you now live through and experience the human in unparalleled intensity; labor so that half the effort might suffice to transform an entire

contemporary generation. But you and I, we are to be alone about all this; your efforts are to have no significance whatever for any other human being. And yet, you understand, you are to will the ethical and you are to be enthusiastic in your striving, because this is the highest." The deceitful lover does not understand this, and much less is he capable of understanding the next: when a genuinely inspired ethical personality, earnestly stirred, lifts himself into the sacred sportiveness of the divine madness, saying: "Let me be as if created for a whim, this is the jest; and yet I propose to will the ethical with all my strength, with utmost exertion, this is earnest; and I propose to will absolutely nothing else. O insignificant significance, O sportive earnestness, O blessed fear and trembling! It is a blessed thing to be able to satisfy the divine requirement, smiling at the demands of the age; it is blessed even to despair of being able to satisfy the divine requirement, provided one does not for all that let go of God."

That, Climacus concludes, is what it means to become oneself: freely to acknowledge one's impotence before God. The ethical enthusiast draws his enthusiasm from the understanding, achieved precisely in the maximum exertion of his freedom, "that God does not need him." That was what Lessing understood, and that is why Lessing kept his mouth shut. [59]

"Whoever cannot understand this," Climacus adds, "is stupid; and if anyone dares to contradict me, I propose to make him ridiculous. . . . " However, he demurs, it may be just a peculiarity of my own person that I find this business of becoming ethical so difficult—indeed infinitely difficult, a task that will easily last as long as I do and leave me no time for larger and more world-historical undertakings. For I must confess that I am "a depraved and corrupt man" much like Socrates, who "discovered in himself, so it is related, a disposition to all sorts of evil" and felt constrained therefore to give up the study of astronomy until he had got his soul in order. For a tainted man, at least, if not for the majority, who are all such "exceptionally nice" people, the task of becoming subjective "lasts as long as life does, since it is the task of living." Even a nice man might find it strange to finish with life before life has finished with him, for "when the time itself is the task, it becomes a fault to finish before the time has transpired." And if one does find a propensity to evil in himself, the problem is rather one of beginning than of finishing the ethical enterprise. It is enough to make a man think soberly of God. And although one is a superbly nice person, has been a nice child, and then a nice youth, and now "has reached the pitch of having not only one's wife but also all one's sisters-in-law *en masse* say about one: he is verily an exceptionally nice man—" the thought of having to do with God might give him pause.

> For God is not an externality as a wife is, whom I can ask whether she is now satisfied with me; whenever it seems to me in my God-relationship that what I do is good, and omit to bring to consciousness the self-distrust of the infinite, then it is as if God were also content with me, because God is not an externality but the infinite itself, not an externality that scolds me when I do wrong, but the infinite itself which has no need to scold, but whose vengeance is terrible. . . .[60]

The key word is "infinite." Climacus' heavy reliance on this adjective here and elsewhere is a product of his long association with Romanticism. But in his usage it has the precise and always negative meaning "without determinable limits," where "determinable" means "determinable by a man." Climacus speaks always as a "poor existing individual" and never as the mouthpiece of the Absolute Spirit. Thus freedom is infinite, for no man can determine the extent of his capacity to act or the depth of his accountability, but must assume agency and responsibility in all cases; the task of becoming oneself is infinite, because no man can calculate his own possibilities or finally arbitrate the conflict of nature and freedom in his own person. Similarly, in later contexts, the uncertainty of objective knowledge is infinite, existential passion is infinite, and so on. In this negative infinity of subjectivity, which Climacus confesses is the infinite that Hegel had given a bad name (the 'bad' infinite), he finds an existential sign of the positive ('good') infinity of God. But for Climacus, who did not feel up to constructing a natural theology, this negative infinity—the "self-distrust of the infinite"— remains the whole content of man's thought about the divine. Existence is not all indeterminacy (it "has the Idea in it"), but it is in the indeterminate and indeterminable in himself that a human being encounters, if he encounters it anywhere, the reality of the Wholly Other. And that encounter will be sufficient to fill his life.

So let a man consider with himself and before God what it means that he must die, what it means that he may be immortal, what it means amid the tribulations of life that he is to thank God for His bountiful goodness, or even what it means to get married. If he honestly thinks through these problems, is brought to an extremity of passion by the contradictions he discovers therein, and glimpses the infinite uncertainty of all things mirrored in his own freedom—then he will have enough to do with God and himself and not be tempted to invite the distractions of objectivity.

> But woe unto me if the Deity were to condemn me in my most inward man for the fact that I wanted mendaciously to be systematic and world-historical, and to forget what it is to be a man, and therewith forget what it means that He is the Deity. Woe unto me. Woe unto me in time, and still more dreadfully when He gets hold of me in eternity![61]

To which peroration Climacus immediately subjoins, "This sounds almost like earnest." And many would no doubt regard it so, if only I could become red in the face and appeal to visions and revelations! But "it is not my intention to lecture, lest I habituate myself or prompt others to patter." Climacus is a humorist, not a religious man. And the palinode demanded by his profession is that he "make an apology for doing that which the authority of the first instance commands and recommends as the highest thing." It was the fortunate lot of one Dr. Hartspring, Climacus reports, to have a miracle as guarantor of his literary enterprises. For "according to his own singularly well-written account it was at Streit's Hotel in Hamburg, on Easter morning, that by a miracle (of which the waiters were unaware) he became an adherent of the Hegelian philosophy which assumes that there are no miracles." To this most singular of miracles Dr. Hartspring (in reality Climacus' contemporary, J. L. Heiberg) attributed his success as a writer of musical comedies and his eminence (so he thought) as a philosopher. Climacus has no miracles to rest on. He became a writer, he admits, by laziness and by chance. Loafing in a public resort, smoking cigars, and daydreaming, he decides he really must make something of himself. Since everyone else is making life easier, whether by omnibus and railroad and telegraph or by speedily apprehended compendia of everything worth knowing, there are no openings in that direction. So Climacus, by inclination and by accident, resolves to write a few books in which he will exhibit the arduous character of those existential problems that all his contemporaries have made so tiresomely simple. That will certainly be the easiest thing for him to do! It is after all a fit job for a lazy man with the soul of a comedian to point up the insuperable difficulty of the simplest piece of work. If, therefore, his account of the perils of becoming oneself seems excessively lurid, we may set it down to his capricious and indolent temper. [62]

His discussion of truth is a case in point. The classical definition of truth is clear enough: *adaequatio intellectus et rei,* or in the terminology of the nineteenth century, the conformity of thought and being. But Climacus manages to find ambiguities in it. He observes that this formula can be interpreted either empirically (realistically) to mean the conformity of thought with being, or idealistically to mean the conformity of being with thought. Even the terms of the definiens are equivocal. On the one hand "being" has such meanings as: the ideal, essence, the Platonic form; on the opposite hand it can signify: becoming, existence, spatio-temporal actuality. Similarly "thought" may be either the objective idea, cosmic reason, the logos; or the actual thinking of an existing human being. To discover what it means to say that truth is the conformity of thought and being, Climacus examines the permutations of the various senses of these words. The principal combinations can be represented schematically:

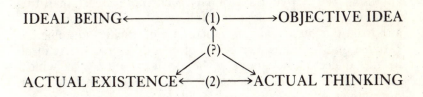

IDEAL BEING ← — (1) — → OBJECTIVE IDEA

(?)

ACTUAL EXISTENCE ← (2) → ACTUAL THINKING

The relationship designated (1) is obviously a conformity of thought and being; in fact it is the perfect conformity of tautology. But it does not exist. Being it has, in the sense of essential self-identity, but not actual existence. (2) is not even a conformity. For both actual existence and actual thought are so shaken by mutability that no correspondence between them can be fixed. In history and in the sciences truth is a *pium desideratum*

179

never attained. In Climacus' words: logical knowledge is absolutely certain, but its relationship to actual existing and actual thinking is at best hypothetical and never determinable; empirical knowledge is never more than an immeasurable approximation to an ever-receding ideal. Therefore, he concludes, there exists no such thing as truth.

Of course this analysis has limited itself to *objective* truth, truth considered from the standpoint of the objects included in its definition: thought and being. Suppose we regard not its *what* but its *how:* the "conformity" involved; and suppose we examine the relationship that is closest to Climacus' concern, the complex indicated by (?) in our diagram. The question-mark stands for what Climacus calls the subjective problem of truth: how can the eternal truth (=eternal being) be apprehended by one who exists and thinks in time? Not by means of an Hegelian reconciliation of opposites. In his early days as an apprentice philosopher Johannes had perceived that "mediation" is only a slightly deceptive name for the timeless identity of ideal being and the objective idea. It does not and cannot name an *act* whereby an existing thinker reconciles his time-ridden becoming and his discursive thinking with eternal verity. An indivdual, for example, is required to choose between good and evil, to divide truth from error. He is not abetted in this enterprise by the reflection that in logic (where no ethical questions, nor even questions of material truth or falsity, can arise) the proposition (A.-A) is just as "real" (in the logical sense) as the proposition -(A.-A). If anything, the self-contradiction is even more "real" than the tautology, since from the former follow any and all propositions, and from the latter none but equally uninformative tautologies. "Mediation" describes merely the utter indifference of the ideal to the dialectic of time ("to be or not to be") in which contradictions are not reconciled for purposes of knowledge, but discriminated for purposes of resolution and action.

Mediation turns out to be just another objectivity, but Climacus is after the truth which he says "is subjectivity." Consider: a man exists and, intermittently, he thinks. When he thinks, he thinks about idea and essence; he cannot do otherwise, since his thinking consists wholly in abstracting a certain content from its object and fixing that content in the relative stability of a concept. The object of his thought is always an idea, its dwelling-place the domain of logic. But all the while the instability of becoming infects his thinking with incalculable uncertainty. And for that reason all objective thought—thought that aims at getting a sure grasp on its object—falls short of its goal. Every objectivity as such is uncertain.

However, at cusps of decision, a man can achieve a momentary correlation of thought and being. Not by losing himself in the object. But in his own person, by means of what Climacus calls a passionate reduplication of the content of his thought in his existence. He cannot conform his temporal existence to the eternal idea, but he can make his intellectual and imaginative vision of the idea constitutive for his existence. In Climacus' phrase, he can appropriate it, literally *tilegne*: make it his *own*. Not once for all and *simpliciter*, but through a lifetime of striving and rededication he can live the idea by causing the idea to live in him. This is the only truth—the only conformity of thought and being—that *exists*, and therefore the only truth available to an *existing* human being. Since it takes place within the individual, in moments of passion, Climacus says that "truth is subjectivity." Or, what is the same thing, truth is "becoming oneself."

For, as Climacus continues, the subjective reflection "makes its way inward in inwardness." *Inderlighed* etymologically means "inwardness," but in ordinary speech "fervor" or "intensity." Therefore:

> Inwardness in an existing subject culminates in passion; corresponding to passion in the subject the truth becomes a paradox; and the fact that the truth becomes a paradox is rooted precisely in its having a relationship to an existing subject.

Almost a technical term in Climacus' vocabulary, "passion" never means simply desire or emotion, although these latter are its manifestations. The word *Lidenskab* (like the German *Leidenschaft*) is related to *Lidelse*, which (like German *Leid*) means "suffering." Passion (*passio* or *pathos*) signifies for Climacus the contradictions of existence, particularly the root-contradiction between freedom and nature in the self, experienced in the feelings, just as paradox indicates the same contradictions experienced in thought. Passion answers to paradox, and paradox to passion. Truth is the relation between passionate inwardness and paradox. But paradox designates no object, or rather it designates the peculiar aspect which objectivity wears when and only when it comes into relationship with the self-concern of an individual. Paradox is the "object" that exists only in and for a subject; it is the object absorbed in and become identical with the passion of the subject. "It is the passion of the infinite that is the decisive factor and not its content, for its content is precisely itself. In this manner subjectivity and the subjective 'how' constitute the truth." When the object (always uncertain) has *become* the subject (certain with the certainty of passion), then and then only truth *exists*.

Climacus offers a definition of subjective truth to cap his analysis:

> When subjectivity is truth, the determination of the truth must also contain an expression for the opposition to objectivity . . . , and this expression will also indicate the tension of inwardness. Here is such a definition of truth: *the objective uncertainty, held fast in the most passionate appropriation of inwardness, is the truth,* the highest truth there is for an *existing individual.* At the point where the way swings off . . . , there objective knowledge is placed in abeyance.

Objectivity and the object are not excluded from Climacus' definition. But because the object is uncertain, it cannot determine its own appropriation. Thus all concern with the objectivity of the object is placed in suspension in order that the subject may concentrate on the one thing that can be made certain, his appropriation (making his own) of the objective uncertainty.

> Thus the subject merely has, objectively, the uncertainty; but it is this which precisely increases the tension of that infinite passion which constitutes his inwardness. The truth is precisely the venture which chooses an objective uncertainty with the passion of the infinite. [63]

It is significant that Climacus refers to his formula as "such a definition" or "one such definition" of truth. He is himself a subjective thinker, and a humorist to boot, for whom it would surely be out of character confidently to offer an objective definition of subjective truth. "The objective uncertainty, held fast in the most passionate appropriation of inwardness" is the parody and the paradox that result when *adaequatio intellectus et rei* is translated into existential terms.

Recalling his earlier effort in the *Fragments,* Climacus has no trouble converting his definition of truth into a description of faith. The basic paradox (truth is subjectivity) ensues when the eternal truth comes into relation with an individual existing in time. Simply complicate this relation at both its terms and you have the Absolute Paradox. Suppose the eternal truth to be incarnate in time: then truth itself is paradoxical even before its relation to the individual. Suppose further that the individual is not initially oriented toward the truth but sinfully turned away from it, so that subjectivity is in the first instance an untruth that must be converted to truth: then the paradox is as paradoxical as it can be.

Construed as a "thought-experiment," Climacus' attempt to see how paradoxical one can get is preposterous; as a serious endeavor to produce Christianity out of his philosophical hat it is perverse. But his point is quite simple and striaghtforward. The definition of truth as subjectivity, ludicrous from the philosophical standpoint, is at least compatible with Christian faith, whereas the speculation that rules out paradox also rules out the possibility of faith. For suppose—and Climacus makes it clear that he is only supposing[64] — that Christianity really is the incomprehensible mystery it gives itself out to be. In that case the attempt to make philosophical sense of it would be stupidly and hilariously wrong. Legitimately to "explain the paradox would then mean to understand more and more profoundly what a paradox is, and that the paradox is the paradox." Climacus has no quarrel with the honest theologian who seeks to draw out the implications of faith, expounding its meaning in rational symbols but preserving therein the mysterious character of its object. Nor does he dispute the right of the philosopher to his legitimate preserve: the concept *(Tanke-Realitet)* and conceptual relations. His butt is the philosopher or the theologian enthralled to philosophy who prefers his speculative interpretation of Christianity to the thing itself.

Whether Christianity is right is another question; here we merely ask how the explanation of speculative philosophy is related to the Christianity which it explains. But if Christianity is possibly wrong, so much at least is certain: that speculative philosophy is definitely and decidedly wrong.

If one does not like Christianity, he can always remove to the Socratic or the pantheistic positions, reasonable views both of them, and always available. Climacus takes no position at all. A poor humorist has all he can do to see things as they are and set them out in their places; he would be hard put to prove rationally that the paradox, for example, is true. The production of such proofs may safely be left to the ingenuity of absent-minded philosophers. But the believer will have no truck with proofs. For to believe against the understanding is one thing,

> and to believe with the understanding cannot be done at all; for he who believes with the understanding speaks only of livelihood and wife and fields and oxen and the like, which things are not the object of faith. Faith *always* gives thanks, is *always* in peril of life, in this collision of finite and infinite which is precisely a mortal danger for him who is a composite of both. The probable is therefore so little to the taste of a believer that he fears it most of all, since he well knows that when he clings to probabilities it is because he is beginning to lose his faith. Faith has in fact two tasks: to take care in every moment to discover the improbable, the paradox; and then to hold it fast with the passion of inwardness. [65]

And with this the excursus on faith is brought back to the definition of truth whence it came; faith like truth is the objective uncertainty (what could be more uncertain than the Absolute Paradox?) held fast in the most passionate appropriation of inwardness (what inwardness so impassioned as the surrender to grace, and what appropriation so inward as the second birth?)

Once again Climacus is embarrassed by his own eloquence: "This sounds almost as if I were in earnest." If I could only allege a divine vocation and a prophetic mission to oppose speculative philosophy in the name of Christianity, then, "in lieu of considering the whole to be a fantastic reminiscence in the head of a fool," no doubt many serious men would take me seriously.

> But I can say nothing of this kind about myself. The resolve with which I began must rather be regarded as a notion that occurred to me; and in any case, it is so far from being true that any call came to me, that contrariwise the call, which, if I may so speak, I followed, did not issue to me but to another; and in relation to him was very far from being something that could in the strictest sense be described as a call. But even if a call did issue to him, I am without a call when I follow it.

Whereupon Climacus proceeds to tell another story about the formation of his authorship. During a visit to the garden of the dead, he overhears an old man conversing with his grandson, a boy of about ten. The grandfather laments the infidelity and fears the everlasting damnation of his departed son, the boy's father. In a voice whose impressiveness Climacus declares "unforgettable" he extracts from the uncomprehending grandson an oath of perpetual loyalty to his God and Saviour Jesus Christ:

> "Poor boy, you are only a child, and yet you will soon be alone in the world! Do you promise me by the memory of your dead father, who, if he could speak to you now, would speak thus, and speaks to you with my voice; do you promise me by the sight of my old age and my gray hairs; do you promise me by the solemnity of this sacred ground, by the God whose name you have learned to call upon, by the name of Jesus Christ, in whom alone there is salvation; do you promise me that you will hold fast to this faith in life and in death, that you will not permit yourself to be deceived by any illusion, however the face of the world changes—do you promise me this?" Overwhelmed by the impression, the little one threw himself down upon his knees, but the old man lifted him up and pressed him to his heart.

Climacus owns, "in deference to the truth," that this was a most moving scene. In particular he is touched by the incongruity that an "old man has in a child his only confidant, and that a sacred promise, an oath, is demanded of a child." But he is not moved "to rush forward, to express to the old man my sympathy, assuring him with tears and trembling voice that I should never forget the scene, or even begging him to pledge me in an oath." And in a long retraction buttressed by citations from Shakespeare ("No, not an oath. . . . / To think that, or our cause, or our performance/ Did need an oath.") he vents his conviction that only over-precipitate people, flighty and excitable souls, are quick to take oaths. Since they are unable to keep them, they must be ever taking them. Climacus will not swig the strong stimulant of a sacred promise. And so he goes home. And as he goes, he thinks to himself:

> "You are now tired of life's diversions, you are tired of the maidens, whom you love only in passing; you must have something fully to occupy your time. Here it is: to discover where

185

the misunderstanding lies between speculative philosophy and Christianity." This therefore became my resolve.

However, Climacus spoke to no one about his plans, and his landlady, like the waiters in Streit's Hotel in Hamburg who were ignorant of Dr. Hartspring's conversion to Hegel, took no note of any change in her lodger. That was a fortunate silence, since, as a supplement to this discussion points out, the plans Climacus had made were carried out by others before he could set pen to paper, in a series of pseudonymous books beginning with *Either/Or* and ending with *Stages on Life's Way!* A serious writer with philosophical ambitions might have taken umbrage at this preempting of his own domain, but an indolent wag like Climacus is relieved that the job is largely done, and done largely without any effort on his part. As his own belated contribution to this protracted indirect communication he offers his *Fragments* and these unscientific afterthoughts on the nature of truth and its relation to Christian faith. As for his ambitions: "I ask nothing better," he says, "than to be pointed out as the only one who *cannot* doctrinize . . . , the only one in our objective age who is incapable of being objective . . . , the only one in our serious age who is not serious."[66]

That Climacus will surely achieve this distinction is guaranteed by his summary treatment of "real or ethical subjectivity." He remarks several times in the *Postscript* that Hegel had absentmindedly neglected to include an ethics in his philosophical system.[67] By this he does not mean that Hegel had forgotten to discuss matters ethical. Hegel's absentmindedness was of a less obvious sort. In his zeal to exhibit the rationality of history, *der Gang Gottes in der Welt,* he had failed to make provision for the *subject* of ethical concerns, the existing human being. If we sit in the Hegelian grandstand and look at the human individual, regarding him simply in his particularity, he becomes a perishing irrationality, the litter cast by the Absolute along the freeways of world-history. To be sure he furthers the aims of God, but he does so chiefly in his capacity as cannon fodder. On the other hand, if we consider him in his "essential reality" and "universal truth," he is at once rapt into dialectical union with God. The soldier of the *Grande Armée,* who is (personally) splattered by a cannon ball, is (essentially) privileged to suffer the Golgotha of Absolute Spirit.

What Climacus calls "objective thought" understands any individual abstractively, by regarding it as an instance of a universal. Underscoring *instance,* the individual is as nugatory as the dissected frogs discarded by a college zoology class. With the accent on *universal,* the individual takes on the dignity of an exemplar Idea in the mind of God. This kind of analysis may be appropriate for natural entities, and even for man as regards his natural dimension. It is invevitable that scientific thought should aspire to the condition of logic and conceive its objects as universals or cases of universals. But the human person considered *subjectively* is neither a category nor a statistic. Both dimensions are present in each man—he is at once eternal verity and vanishing trifle—but present as unsettled possibilities which he is obliged to arbitrate in a lifelong process of self-becoming. Because human existence is caught in the toils of time, particularity, and finitude, this process is a perpetual and impassioned striving, spasmodically illumined by intelligence and fancy, but uncheered by any promise of millenial reconciliation, either in a life after death or in the depths of present existence. No man can give himself apocalyptic surety of immortality, though he may *believe* in it ardently enough to die for it. And no man is helped by the idealist eschatology of "pure thought" that asks him to sacrifice his self for a meaning so deeply rooted in being that it is unavailable for his personal comfort. Selfhood is neither given as an antecedent nor guaranteed as a consequent; it is a possibility which may be won or lost, but never enjoyed.

In short, speculative philosophy is of no use if a man wants wisdom to live by. If it does not misconceive human existence naturalistically in the manner of pagan realism, it seeks prematurely to quiet the raging of spirit by recourse to the "fantastic shadow-play"[68] of idealism. Frater Taciturnus writes, and Johannes Climacus would agree:

> There are three existence-spheres: the aesthetic, the ethical, the religious. The metaphysical is abstraction, there is no man who exists metaphysically. The metaphysical, ontology, *is* but does not *exist;* for when it exists it is in the aesthetic, in the ethical, in the religious, and when it *is* it is the abstraction of or the *prius* for the aesthetic, the ethical, the religious.[69]

A man can *think* metaphysically, he cannot *live* metaphysically. The philosopher who confuses life with intellection and scribbles paper answers to flesh-and-blood questions is like the poet insofar as he flees to an abstract eternity from the turmoils of time. But he lacks the poet's imaginative virtuosity, the endlessly resourceful ingenuity by which the aesthete lives his withdrawal from life. The philosopher therefore has not the poetic melancholy, and his life is not, like the poet's, tragic. He is a comic or at best a pathetic figure: the self-deceived *Privatdocent* who really believes that he breaks wind *sub specie aeternitatis*, or the drab old professor whose self is but the cast-off walking-stick of his system.

For the existing individual there is neither a home in nature nor a place of rest beyond it. Man is "an infinite existing spirit."[70] And there is, as Anti-Climacus was to say a few years later, "no such thing as immediate health of the spirit."[71] Immediately man is but the possibility of spirit, a bare "to be able"[72] anxiously placed between ideality (the domain of intellect and imagination) and reality (the spatio-temporal stretch of becoming). As spirit he is neither Platonic Idea nor positivistic fact nor the perfect splice that classical naturalism envisaged. His existence—the subjectivity that Climacus says is truth and reality[73]—is his concern to catch an evanescent possibility in the mesh of fact, and to regiment a scattered actuality under the hegemony of ideal meanings. His "ethical reality" is neither inner intent (intentions are as cheap as the aesthete's daydreams) nor outer act (the case of Judge Wilhelm shows the recalcitrance of nature to man's resolutions), but the tension of his will to move creatively from project to performance. In this tension and its pathos he has his life.

The freedom that is essential to selfhood and the skein of contradiction from which this selfhood must be woven proliferate problems that cannot even be programmed by philosophic thought; nor do they admit the kind of solutions that can be appended as a footnote to section 14 of the System, or filed for ready reference on grave occasions. They can only be apprehended by a "subjective thinking"—thinking born in passion rather than in disinterested curiosity, concerned not with the contemplation of life in general but with the conduct of this life in particular—that continually experiences the anguish of the human estate and holds out in its presence by continual resolve. The subjective thinker is like the ethical man in that he is free (the possibility of spirit) and therefore must himself integrate the given elements of personality into the unity of a person (the obligation to become oneself). But he is more dreadfully on his own than Judge Wilhelm ever dreamed of. What he is by nature (say a male American twenty-one years old) is but a cluster of ambiguous possibilities whose eventuality (husband or hermit, patriot or expatriate, believer or blasphemer, success or suicide) is determined by the man himself. In this determination he is guided by no eternal truths (the temporality of his life stains their white radiance with uncertainty and change) and by no hard facts (his self-transcendence dissolves the brutality and dense reality of fact and brings it into the whirl of possibility). Knowledge is either (like logic and metaphysics) true in the abstract but doubtful in its application to existence; or empirically problematic (like natural science and history), its truth a desideratum ever out of reach. The problem, as Climacus sees it, is one of giving

> existence the continuity without which everything simply vanishes. An abstract continuity is no continuity, and the very existence of the existing individual is sufficient to prevent his continuity from having essential stability; while passion gives him a momentary continuity, a continuity which at one and the same time is a restraining influence and a moving impulse. The goal of movement for an existing individual is to arrive at a decision and renew it.

It is Plato's image of the soul-chariot, with passion rather than reason holding the reins: "Eternity is the winged horse, infinitely fast, and time is a worn-out jade; the existing individual is the driver." [74] "Subjective thinking" must be the "double reflection" of passion that simultaneously sees the insufficiency of knowledge and holds tenaciously to its decisions.

To be man is to be, without security of nature or knowledge, compelled to make a security, a truth, for oneself. "Only the truth which edifies"—that is, builds up your self—"is truth for you." A human being is a freedom caught in the intersection of time and eternity, there constrained to mold in decision and action the integrity, the existing truth at once actual and ideal, that he does not have by nature and cannot find by taking thought. Human existence is an *interest (interesse),* a being-between the terms of a contradiction that cannot be resolved but must be resolutely endured, an unrelieved and unceasing concern with the passion, the possibility, and the predicament of becoming oneself. [75]

Neither is the individual supported, in his quest for selfhood, by the solidarity of human society.[76] The freedom which is the franchise of spirit disintegrates every natural community, splintering family, state, and race into a multitude of single human beings, each isolated with the problems, pains, and prospects of his own person. The existence of other men presents him not with a public in which he is firmly set as a part sustained by an organic whole, but only with further possibilities—beckoning, tempting, or threatening—that he must take into the gamut of his inner life. The social principle is the illiberal principle. His own inwardness is the only reality to which he has entrance without trespass, and the only reality with which he is properly occupied. The reality of others he can only know, and by knowing, distance.[77]

> With respect to every reality external to myself, I can get hold of it only through thinking it. In order to get hold of it really, I should have to be able to make myself into the other, the acting individual, and make the foreign reality my own reality, which is impossible.[78]

Every man is essentially (which for Climacus = existentially) solitary. That is not to say that he is ontologically unique. Climacus is aware that there are relationships among men and between man and nature. But the individual apprehends these realities freely ("through thinking"), and is thereby removed from every immediate engagement with others. Therefore, Climacus infers, my own subjectivity (=reality) is the only reality I can become (=exist) and it is simply irrelevant and improper (save in the exceptional case of faith, which depends absolutely upon its object)[79] to be personally concerned about the reality of others.

The parenthesis on faith instructs the interpretation of Climacus' hard sayings about the isolation of men from each other. The medievals said that God sustains no real relation to the world, whereas the world does have a real relation to its Creator. By "real" they meant (at least) "internal"; God does not depend on the world in any way for his being, but the world absolutely so depends on God. Climacus would agree: God does not need the believer, but the believer is what he is only by virtue of his adherence to God. And he would add: with respect to their inner reality, their subjectivity, men stand in "ideal" (=free) rather than "real" (=determinative) relations to each other. Whence his apotheosis of the Socratic maieutic as the acme of interpersonal relationships.

In his own language, all personal relations are "possibility-relations" and all communication among men is "indirect." His aim is not to deny or demean persons and their mutual involvements, but to point out that each person is a person on his own, and that all personal relationships are mediated by freedom. His view that human freedom intersects with the omnipotence of God, plus the fact that he calls man's relation to God a "possibility-relation," suggests that he is also delivering a warning against any compromise of the divine sovereignty. It is only for the subject in his existential isolation, released from illusions of dependence on or indispensability to other men, that God has "the role of sovereign." For the "possibility-relationship which every individual has to God" and "which is the inspiration of the ethicist in his joy over God, is God's freedom. . . . " Climacus is not offering a theoretical justification for any of the usual forms of individualism. His diatribe is directed exclusively against romantic, naturalistic, and deterministic misunderstandings of man, and his intent is only to make men aware of that minimal isolation demanded by their freedom and God's omnipotence. [80]

That a speculative philosopher will find this point of view "acosmic" is neither surprising nor terribly important. It is understandable that from his theocentric perspective he finds his self "a trifle not worth keeping," but it is also certain that he has "a very humble notion of what the ethical means to the subject." For his own subjectivity

> ought to mean more to him than heaven and earth and all that therein is, more than the six thousand years of human history, more than both astrology and the veterinary sciences or whatever it is that the age demands, all of which is aesthetically and intellectually a huge vulgarity. And if it is not so it is worse for the individual himself, for in that case he has absolutely nothing, no reality at all, since to all other things the maximum relationship attainable is a possibility. [81]

That is the radical truth about men: their freedom; and upon this foundation alone is it possible to build a solid structure of personal relationships. For whatever community of spirit is established among men is strung precariously across the chasm of possibility and made fast at the ends only in the solitude of the self-concern of each person. Sprung from nature but cut loose from her umbilical, capable of knowledge but deprived of a certainty equal to the demands of action, the existing individual also stands, in the midst of his fellow-men, essentially alone.

But this, as Climacus says whenever the philosophical rhetoric threatens to run away from him and tear through the streets like a towncrier of inwardness, sounds a little too much like earnest. [82] The *Postscript* is a humorous book. Its technique is not solemnly to define man (not even with the bizarre solemnities of existentialism), but to destroy by irony and indirection, by lyric and by lampoon, the self-confidence of those thinkers who are so thoughtless as to suppose that man can be solemnly defined. When Climacus "defines" truth as "subjectivity," "the objective uncertainty held fast in the most passionate appropriation of inwardness," [83] he is writing a satire on definition to recall his reader from the illusory certainties of knowledge to the awareness that every belief and every truth claim has no surer warrant than the freedom and the fervor of him who asserts it. When he says that every individual is isolated in his inwardness, he is not proposing a theory of human community, but reminding those men who put their trust in the ways of culture and the verdict of history that this commitment is an expression of their personal choice of themselves and not a child of the *Zeitgeist* or a mass-product of institutions and conventions. [84]

Climacus' comic muse is more prolific and expansive than these pages can suggest. Yet even these paltry few instances suffice to disclose his strategy. The *Concluding Unscientific Postscript*, faithful to the paradox of existence and the "dialectics of communication," is a funny book with a frighteningly sober purpose: to lead its reader down a broad and prodigal path of merriment to the brink of the bottomless pit of freedom and to surprise him with the absolute responsibility he bears for his own life. Read as a philosophical treatise it is nonsense; but the sense of the nonsense is to strip away every veil that covers the uncertainty of the human condition, to force the reader back on his own resources and into the awful presence of the living God.

"Subjectivity is truth, subjectivity is reality." [85] Climacus began with a polemic against the speculative identification of subject and object. At the end of his peregrination, with all their meanings dismantled and remodeled, subjectivity, truth, and reality are equated. If it be objected that this gets monotonous after a while, Climacus will own to a certain kinship with

Socrates in this regard. Like the simple wise man of antiquity, he is not able to astound the multitudes with his much learning, but must ever be repeating the same things about the same thing. As Socrates constantly recommended a therapy of the soul in preparation for eternity: learning how to die, so Climacus ever and again seduces his reader into the experience of that dreadful rebirth by which the spirit comes naked and alone into the extremity of time: becoming what one is.

In more than one respect Climacus invites comparison with Socrates. Into the concluding pages of his discussion of "real or ethical subjectivity" he inserts a bit of sage counsel about the importance of being a whole person and not neglecting any of the essential human potentialities. On the surface this is a critique of theoretical formulations that presume to rank human activities and interests hierarchically, especially the Hegelian hierarchy that ranks philosophy above religion and art. But it is also Climacus' way of warning his reader not to make an "existential system"[86] (that will-o-the-wisp of philosophers) out of the fine precisions and narrow definitions of his own treatise.

> There is an old saying that *oratio, tentatio, meditatio faciunt theologum.* Similarly there is required for a subjective thinker imagination and feeling, dialectics in existential inwardness, together with passion.

It is not the program of the subjective thinker to build a system on the empty recommendation: Become yourself! It is rather his business to provoke men into *becoming* themselves in reality and in truth. To that end he writes as a dialectician, who perceives in his own inwardness the contradictions of which existence is compounded; as a man of imagination and feeling who is able to conjure the possibility of inwardness for his readers; and as a man tensed by that passion without which "it is impossible to think about existence in existence."[87] Dialectics, imagination, and passion add up to the paradox of understanding-with-detachment that defines the humorist. As the humorist delivers a line whose punch demands to be received in the native wit of his audience, so Climacus administers a communication in the form of the possible ideally requiring itself, and then yields to the initiative of his reader by retiring behind the screen of Socratic ignorance:

> My attempt is *eo ipso* without importance and only for my own

diversion—as must be the case when a learner in the art of existence, who thus cannot want to teach others. . . , propounds something which one might in a way expect of a learner who essentially knows neither more nor less than what pretty much every man knows, only that he knows something about it more definitely and, as a set-off, with regard to much that every man knows or thinks he knows, knows definitely that he does not know it. Perhaps I should not be believed if I were to say this to anybody but you, my dear reader. For in our time, when one says, "I know all," he is believed; but he who says, "There is much I do not know," is suspected of a propensity to lie. . . . Neither in our time do I believe that it has ever failed for any speculative philosopher who says, "I know all." Ah, but the ungodly and mendacious men who say, "There is much that I do not know"—they get their just deserts in this best of worlds, yea, the best of worlds for all who get the best of it by knowing all . . . or by knowing nothing. [88]

The *Postscript,* Climacus admits the reproach, is superfluous—in the sense that a joke is superfluous for one who already knows the point, but perhaps salutary for those who need to be reminded of it—and without authority, for "to be an authority is far too burdensome an existence for a humorist." Especially, in view of the fact that the social principle is illiberal in the extreme, "may heaven preserve the book . . . from every appreciative violence. . . . " [89] The point of Climacus' disappearing act, like Socrates' irony, is not to excite admiration or dispense wisdom, but to awaken men to their precarious situation in existence and (beyond Socrates) to bring them to that exigence of pathos by which alone they are prepared to meet the One who comes to them in the midnight of their extremity:

The foolish virgins had lost the infinite passion of expectation. And so their lamps were extinguished. Then came the cry: The bridegroom cometh. Thereupon they run to the market-place to buy new oil for themselves, hoping to begin all over again, letting bygones be bygones. And so it was, to be sure, everything was forgotten. The door was shut against them, and they were left outside; when they knocked for admittance, the bridegroom said: "I do not know you." This was no mere quip in which the bridegroom indulged, but the sober truth; for they had made themselves strangers, in the spiritual sense of the word, through having lost the infinite passion. [90]

And that, it may surely be assumed, is almost in earnest.

5
VOICES OF SILENCE:
Some Versions
of Christianity

The full name of Climacus' *magnum opus* is *Concluding Unscientific Postscript to the Philosophical Fragments.* "Concluding," because at the time of writing it was to be the last of Kierkegaard's literary essays. But "concluding" also in the sense of "final": this settles the matter. The *Postscript* is Climacus' last word to the philosophers. "Unscientific" *(uvidenskabelig = unwissenschaftlich),* because like its fragmentary predecessor it is a protest against the grand illusions of absolute idealism. And "postscript," because it is the slightly redundant sequel forecast in the last pages of the *Fragments.*

The subtitle further defines the book as "A Mimic-Pathetic-Dialectic Composition, An Existential Contribution." "Mimic" in this formula has plural significations. For one thing, the author speaks from behind the mask of comedy: the title page continues "by Johannes Climacus. Published by S. Kierkegaard." Moreover, the problem to be approached (the truth of Christianity) is an old one that has been gone over many times before. And finally, the *Postscript,* as it continues and recapitulates the *Fragments,* mimics its original. [1] The book is "pathetic" because it calls attention to the suffering indigenous to Christian

195

belief, and also because its humorist author doubles as a celebrant of passion, a kind of poet. Since its author is likewise a "fearless" thinker who submits the problem of becoming a Christian to "naked . . . analysis," the *Postscript* is a "dialectical" composition.

In his Introduction Climacus contrasts his own treatment of the issue at hand with the procedures of the scholar, the orator, and the systematic philosopher in the same case. "All honor" to historical or philological "learning and scholarship," but nonetheless:

> The scholarly introduction draws the attention away from the problem by its erudition, and makes it seem as if the problem were posed at the moment when the scholarly inquiry reaches its maximum. That is to say, it seems as if the learned and critical striving toward its own ideal of perfection, were identical with the movement toward the problem.

The enterprise of scholarship provides at best approximations to historical verity; in relation to the decision of faith demanded by Christianity it is an irrelevant and never-ending parenthesis. The truth of Christianity is not attested or even touched by research into the authenticity of Holy Scripture or the continuity of apostolic succession; it is a matter of *imitatio Christi*. Climacus' own "mimicry" furnishes the "movement toward the problem" that is feigned but never really made by the "scholarly introduction."

"The rhetorical address serves to distract by intimidating the dialectician." The pulpit orator may have "rare gifts, and a great understanding of the human passions" by which to move his hearers to terror at the thought of God and divine judgment. But the hearts he so deeply disturbs he once again quiets—with words—"as a mother reassures her child with tender caresses." And the very ease with which the transition from the fear of wrath to the emoluments of love is effected shows that "the problem was not even presented, much less solved." Climacus means to replace this fantasy of sermon-rhetoric with a poetry that will depict rigorously the pathos of belief and satisfy the thinker's demand for a clear view of "the critical moment of decision" to which every believer must come. The *Concluding Unscientific Postscript* is an imaginary garden with a real Toad in it.

196

Worst of all the enemies of integrity is the systematic philosopher:

> The systematic tendency promises everything and keeps nothing. . . . The presupposition of the system that faith is given, resolves itself into a delusion in which the System has deceived itself into thinking that it knew what faith was.

As against the speculative project that would reconcile faith with absolute knowledge, Climacus offers a dialectician's intrepid definition of the Absolute Paradox which cannot be grasped by philosophic reason. All three—scholar, orator, and philosopher—produce parodies of Christianity. By his composition *(Sammenskrift)* of mimicry, poetry, and dialectics Climacus hopes to contribute to a better understanding of the Christian faith; and (because the word *Indlaeg* also signifies a lawyer's speech in court), he is making a plea for honesty with respect to the difficulty of believing. [2]

But what precisely is his "existential contribution?" The *Postscript* opens with the question, How can I, Johannes Climacus, become a Christian? How can I or any man avail himself of the eternal blessedness Christianity offers its adherents? [3] Its conclusion is apparently irrelevant, largely negative, and certainly unscientific: man exists in alienation from the world, without the consolations of objective certainty, without the uplifting arm of human community, without the vision of historical destiny, in a chaos of maybe's. For such a being the quasi-aesthetic makeshifts of the philosopher have no valence, the poet's life is but the sigh of a shadow, and the brave self-confidence of the ethical man a whistling among the tombstones.

Climacus himself admits that the book is superfluous, and yet the result is not negligible, for the man who has come up against his self in the emptiness of its need and the weight of its responsibility has also stood in the terrible presence of God. The situation of the existing individual which Climacus' philosophical works depict by the tongue-in-cheek of theoretical indirection is the same as the situation of man presupposed in the edifying discourses: before God. God is at hand, Climacus writes, whenever the uncertainty of all things is thought without limit. [4] The uncertainty of all things is the fruition of freedom, which transforms all realities into possibilities. But he who rubs the wonderful lamp of freedom and invokes the genie of possibility has called up the Spirit that is his Lord.[5] For

> God *is* that all things are possible, and that all things are possible *is* God; and only the man whose being has been so shaken that he became spirit by understanding that all things are possible, only he has had dealings with God.[6]

To live in the anxiety of freedom, without finite support or encouragement is to live by the power of God.

When he describes the human predicament in terms of paradox and insists that human freedom is absolute, Climacus is not recommending an heroic defiance of the absurdity of existence without God. The bravado of some of his epigoni would strike him as vainglorious rhetoric decorating an aesthetic refusal to face the real absurdity: that in the weakness of the finite the strength of the Infinite is given to man. His polemic against the philosophers recapitulates the wisdom of the stages: the exploitation of human freedom is the exhaustion of human potency in renunciation (of finite security), suffering (the pain of the excision of finite hope), and guilt (the total indebtedness of the finite to the Infinite). The *Postscript* is "speeches on religion to its cultured despisers," but in a spirit quite unlike that of Schleiermacher the sentimental theologian, the voluble humorist Climacus wants to call the distracted attention of the philosophers to the terse piety of the Jutland priest: there is no greater edification than that implied in the thought that as against God we are always in the wrong. Its dark humor is comprehended in the realization that the *Concluding Unscientific Postscript* is a systematic destruction of all the idols of System that come between man's want and God's abundance.

Book II, Part II, Chapter IV of the *Postscript*, which makes up a good third of the bulk of the entire work, is a new attack on the problem of the *Fragments*. The second and by far the larger section of this chapter is again subdivided into two: "A. Existential Pathos" and "B. The Dialectical." Part A, much longer and more detailed than B, traces the logic of the religious consciousness—also called "immanent religion" or "religion A"—while part B notes briefly the way in which the paradoxical logic of Christianity—"transcendent religion" or "religion B"—incorporates and transforms A. Religion A is the "universal human" experience of God; B is the special divine initiative alleged by Christianity, complicating and "potentiating" that experience.

Climacus describes three moments, or as he calls them, "expressions" of "existential pathos," each of which presumes and subsumes its predecessors. The first of these moments is *resignation,* the simultaneous maintenance of an absolute relationship to the Absolute and relative relationships to relative ends. The Absolute of which Climacus speaks, in keeping with the approach to Christianity projected in his Introduction, is an "eternal blessedness"[7] or God desired as the Absolute Good. But the identification is not crucial, since his account of religion A characterizes in completely formal terms any and every attempt on the part of a human being to effect a liaison with the Absolute however named. And the first thing necessary, if such an attempt is to succeed, is the recognition that the Absolute and the relative cannot be mediated. God cannot be understood as a further, perhaps deeper, dimension of human experience. The Absolute Good is not a quality pervading and crowning all other goods, nor is it one among them, for even the supreme member of a hierarchy of such goods would still be relative by virtue of its membership in the series. The Absolute simply resists all comparison with the relative. By its nature as absolute it demands an unqualified commitment to itself and *in potentia* at least calls for the renunciation of all goods other than itself. All relative goods, therefore, must be consigned—voluntarily by any man straining for an absolute relationship to the Absolute—to the class of expendables. This willingness to sacrifice every finite end if one's eternal blessedness requires it is what Climacus means by resignation, and it is the initial condition of the possibility of religious existence. For what would it profit a man to gain the whole world?

Climacus would not be embarrassed by the question, Why should any man want to relate himself to the Absolute in the first place? He would answer concisely that this is the *sine qua non* of an integrated personality. To be a self is to have concentrated all the passion of existing in a single unifying will, and the Absolute is the only end that will sustain total devotion. The alternative, as the essay on "Becoming Subjective" has hinted, is to lose one's soul.

But *is* there any such thing as an "eternal blessedness?"

199

That cannot be answered. The expectation of an eternal blessedness—or for that matter any commitment to the Absolute—is in the nature of the case an absolute venture and involves therefore an absolute risk. To want to know the odds before accepting the wager is (*pace* Pascal) a symptom not of existential passion but of a fondness for gambling on a sure thing. The reality of the Absolute cannot be ascertained prior to the venture by which alone it is chosen. No man is obliged to make the venture, but every man is able to do so. And no man who fails to do so has tried his humanity to the uttermost.

What is the Absolute Good? Neither can that question be answered. Because of the "infinite qualitative difference" that divides the Absolute from the relative, the Absolute cannot be given a character. Faithful to his definition of truth as subjectivity, and to the smiling reticence of his comic muse, Climacus implies that the Absolute End is definable only in terms of the *how* of its acquisition. Even if the end to which a man affixes his infinite passion is not itself absolute, the Absolute will nonetheless define itself when the infinity of the passion prescribes the renunciation of its finite object. So all roads lead to God if pursued with infinite passion. The Absolute Good is that good which is attained by the way of the absolute venture.

"Purity of heart," says one of Kierkegaard's discourses, "is to will one thing." That one thing, the discourse establishes, may be indifferently labeled "God" or "oneself."[8] Similarly the author of *Fear and Trembling* insists that a man have "the power to concentrate the whole content of life and the whole significance of reality in one single wish," for if he have not "this concentration, this intensity," then "his soul . . . is dispersed in the multifarious. . . . " And he adds that any "instance whatsoever in which the individual finds that for him the whole reality of actual existence is concentrated, may . . . be an occasion for the movement of resignation."[9] The first half of the *Postscript* defines the conditions of authentic humanity; the second half, on "existential pathos," points the way to God. Their unity is first disclosed in Climacus' analysis of resignation, according to which the ethical demand for fidelity to self and the religious demand for fidelity to the Absolute are one and the same. The Absolute is that Good to which a man cleaves only in and through the passion of inwardness by which he becomes a self; and conversely a man becomes himself only when his existential passion is so concentrated on the Absolute that all relative ends are released and renounced. When Kierkegaard in his journals remarks that the ethical is "absolutely victorious" in *Either/Or*, [10] and when Climacus says that *Either/Or* is "rounded out to a conclusion ethically," [11] they are pointing to the fact that religion A is not only a judgment on the ethics of Judge Wilhelm, but also the furthest extension of the ethical (= human) as such, its limiting possibility as well as its nemesis. For this reason the Assessor's stance *vis-a-vis* religion is an ambiguous shuffling between sympathy and antipathy: sympathy with the idea of a religious sanction for duty, but antipathy toward every suggestion of a religious *contemptus mundi.* And so Johannes Climacus, from his superior vantage point, can criticize the Judge's ethics as superficial to the extent that it shrinks from its own possibility of religious fulfillment, and at the same time describe the religion of the *Edifying Discourses* as the religion of "ethical immanence." From the perspective of the *Postscript,* "uplifted in divine jest," ethics and religion A constitute not simply an either/or, but more fundamentally a continuum. That "infinite resignation" which is the last effort of man to achieve ethical integrity is also the initiation of human freedom into its religious destiny.

Resignation, however, is the "initial" expression of existential pathos. It is not yet the whole of the religious life, but only the entrance into it. When a man perceives the necessity of an absolute relationship to the Absolute and a relative relationship to the relative, then he has made a beginning on the religious task. But the second and "essential" expression of existential pathos is *suffering.* For no man is "by nature" or "immediately" related absolutely to the Absolute. Whoever becomes aware that such a relationship is required of him also awakens to the fact that his concern is distributed among a plurality of finite goods to which he has become absolutely attached and upon which his self absolutely depends. He must therefore sever his affections from the things of this world so as to submit them to the Absolute. This dying to the world in order to be born to God entails suffering. For while he sets the whole world at naught in order to win the Absolute, while he makes even himself nothing before God, he retains his finite personality and leads his daily life amid the relative distractions of that world which he has renounced. In the experience of this contradiction is his pain.

Climacus calls this suffering the *essential* moment of the

religious consciousness. It is essential because religion is existential *pathos*, and pathos literally equals suffering. A finite human being's relation to that Absolute which infinitely differs from him is necessarily a negative relation, a relation that is expressed *passively* in existential *passion*. Over and above these etymological and quasi-ontological considerations, the suffering consequent upon the practice of *contemptus mundi* is essential in the sense of permanent. For as long as a man lives in the world he is captivated by it, and for just so long he must undertake the pain of the excision of worldly concern.

Religious suffering, in keeping with Climacus' account of the isolation of ethical subjectivity, is concealed deep within the soul. As opposed to monastic asceticism, which seeks a worldly manifestation for its contempt of the world, this existential pathos never shows. Unlike the self-tormentor, who extracts a peculiar profit and expects an extraordinary merit from his masochistic supererogations, the man who suffers God counts all his exertions worthless trifles. That is why, in the terms of Climacus' prolonged parable, it is so hard and yet so necessary for the religious man to go to Deer Park. Not of the world, he is constantly made to know that by himself he can do nothing, not even take his family on a picnic. And yet in the world, he is just as constantly asked to remember that with God's help he can do anything, even take his family on a picnic. How shall a man justify a holiday outing before the bar of the Absolute? How shall he give expression to his absolute relationship in this relativity? On the other hand, how can he presume to exclude the Absolute from his picnic? Is not the Absolute, by reason of its infinite qualitative difference from everything human, just as well-disposed to recreation and refreshment as it is to prayer and fasting? The Absolute cannot locate itself among the relativities of human life, and yet it is in this life that the absolute relationship must be instituted and maintained. This contradiction is the very substantial essence of the religious life. And, by the paradoxical logic of inwardness, the suffering induced by the contradiction is the univocal sign of the real presence of the absolute relationship to the Absolute.

But the "decisive" expression of existential pathos is the consciousness of *total guilt* consequent upon the individual's failure to perfect himself in the absolute relationship. For fail he must, and his failure decides the issue of his essay into the infinite. His failure—and his guilt—are not moral defects. They are the simple outcome of his temporality. Because his existence is stretched out in time, a man must *strive* to relate himself to the Absolute. The fact that he must be ever striving signifies that he has not yet attained. And in every moment through which he passes devoid of the absolute relationship to the Absolute he is guilty and incurring guilt. That means every moment of his life: for his task was the absolute relationship, but the prerequisite for fulfilling the task was death to the world, and now the passage of time has put and still puts him so hopelessly far behind with the prerequisite that he can never get to the task proper. The game is up as soon as the cards are dealt.

Religious guilt—Climacus echoes the leitmotif of the edifying discourses—is absolute because it is guilt toward the Absolute. It is not determined by comparison with the standings of other men: the incommensurability of the infinite with every finite computation prohibits the application of any but the Absolute norm. Even the fact that a man may be innocent in this or that particular proves him guilty on the whole. Innocence knows nothing of the distinction between guilty and not-guilty, and only he whose very existence is guilt is moved to exonerate himself.

Existence is guilt: this is the outcome of the individual's attempt to become himself by means of the absolute venture of religion. And this outcome decides the mode of his relationship to God: his absolute relationship to the Absolute is negative. He is alienated from the divine presence—"always in the wrong"—and pledged by his venture to endure this alienation with lifelong enthusiasm. In Climacus' language, the existential pathos which expects an eternal blessedness enters upon a retrograde course of renunciation and suffering whose *terminus ad quem* is the eternal recollection of guilt.

Climacus calls this religious consciousness—religion A—the religion of *immanence.* It is a religion that remains within *(immanere)* the limits of human possibility and within those limits generates the consciousness of God by infinitizing the consciousness of self. Its success is failure, for the consciousness of God so developed progressively reduces the self that develops it, through the stages of resignation, suffering, and guilt. Climacus has made a long, grim jest of the Romantic philosophy of religion with its vision of the immediate union of finite and infinite, and

203

of the Romantic theology that reposes in the sentiment of "absolute dependence."

But the joke is no less grim than it is long, and grimmest of all is the punch line: "This is not yet the worst. Christianity is *really* serious." The whole of Climacus' presentation of existential pathos is a prolegomena to "B. The Dialectical." He remarks of Magister Kierkegaard's *Edifying Discourses*—what could be said with emphasis of his own discussion of religion A—that they take on a "carefully modulated humoristic tone," which, he adds, "is doubtless the sum of what can be reached within the sphere of the immanent." [12] It may seem strange to say that the religion of immanence is humorous and Christianity serious. But for all the devastation wrought in the human personality by the immanence of God, the annihilation of the self is welcomed as the obverse of the divine sovereignty. Resignation, suffering, and guilt are the price gladly paid for the divine favor, and the finite magnitude of the cost is ludicrously incomparable with the infinite grace of the Presence. Religion A has abundant reason for good cheer, but it merely sets the stage for the entrance of religion B. And Christianity, while it does at last offer balm for the wound of religious passion, begins by widening the gulf between man and God, deepening the contradictions of existence, and intensifying the pathos of religion A. Christianity is the radical cure for the radical disease, but it insists upon making its own diagnosis of the sickness before it will administer treatment. And the pill is bitter.

The intrusion of the Absolute Paradox into "religion in general" is very briefly sketched by Climacus, as befits a dialectical revision of a pathetic text. In religion A a man presumed to be in a state of spiritual integrity endeavors to assure himself of beatitude by maximizing the "God-idea" immanent in himself. The only conflict he encounters is the contradiction between relative and Absolute, the fruits of which are his resignation, suffering, and guilt. The contradiction is never reconciled but enthusiastically endured in worship, which Climacus defines as the lucid and lifelong recognition of the infinite qualitative difference between God and man, and in the hope that at the end of this way an eternal blessedness awaits.

But religion B posits conditions external to the individual, without which he cannot hope for salvation. To wit: a God who comes into being in time and declares himself the proper object of faith; and a condition of radical non-integrity in the individual (Sin), from which he can be saved only through faith by the grace of this same God-in-time. The source and the locus of salvation are situated outside the individual's subjectivity, and he is called upon to suspend the first law of ethical and ethico-religious existence by taking an infinite personal passionate interest in the reality of another: Jesus of Nazareth, called the Christ. This violation of the human is the scandal of Christianity, but it is also the condition of the possibility of faith and the talisman of the divine origin of the Christian claim: if men are to be saved, the human must be dethroned.

Climacus enumerates three moments of the Christian dialectic, which contradict the three expressions of existential pathos. (1) As opposed to the man who resigns the temporal to gain eternity, the Christian expects an eternal blessedness already in time by relating himself to something (= some One) in time. The Absolute has entered into the relative, become wholly and miraculously one with it, and redeemed it from its alienation. (2) As opposed to the man whose suffering is the negative sign of his positive God-relationship, the Christian directly relates himself to an historical deity. The bond between man and God which in religion A is marked by *however* is because of the Incarnation signed with *therefore*. (3) As opposed to the man whose guilt is the inner barrier that separates him from God, the Christian rests his hope in the outer fact of the God-man, who has redeemed guilt by absorbing it. The Incarnation is the historical fact that can only become historical against its nature, by virtue of the absurd. That is the humorist's way of saying that the enmity between God and man has been overcome by God himself in human flesh: God was in Christ reconciling the world to himself, taking upon himself and taking away *(tollere)* the sins of the world.

But Christianity not only stands in dialectical opposition to religion A. The Absolute Paradox reacts upon the pathos of immanence and sharpens it. Guilt is displaced by the more painful consciousness of sin. The suffering of religion A is lifted, but in its place appears the possibility of offense. The Christian is not asked to renounce the world; instead he feels the smart of sympathy for those men beloved to him who have not assured their salvation by the leap of faith. So the Spirit giveth life—after it has first killed the old man. [13] Such are the rewards of faith,

205

dearly purchased at the price of the crucifixion of the understanding, the confession of sin, the swallowing of scandal, and the rupture of human fellow-feeling.

How, then, does a man become a Christian? Johannes Climacus—"John the Climber"—cannot vouch for the reality. His name and his testimony reveal that he himself is only on the way up, not yet arrived. The *Concluding Unscientific Postscript* is the *introduction* to the *problem* of becoming a Christian. Its purpose (to make things difficult!) is achieved when it has brought humanity to that condition of absolute need to which alone Christianity is relevant and meaningful. But this condition—the possibility—of becoming a Christian is well within Climacus' bailiwick: first become a man, and when you are driven by this exertion into the narrows of despair, when you have become spirit by the recognition that absolute freedom is identical with absolute dependence, when you are alone in fear and trembling, without sustenance of nature, knowledge, or community, with no recourse but God—then and only then may the threat and the promise of Christianity surge redemptively from the abyss. The whole message of the *Postscript* is that Christianity does not become a live option until every human alternative has been tried and rejected. At that point it becomes a life necessity.

But the transition from humanity to Christianity is never automatic. The leap of faith escapes Climacus' humor, as it surpasses understanding generally. Yet several of Kierkegaard's pseudonyms, albeit incapable of producing faith, offer complementary perspectival views of Christianity, some from this side of the leap and some from beyond. The intersection of these two perspectives—Christianity seen from below and from above—forms the cross that defines the way of the believer. Nothing less than this double indirection suffices to delimit Christian existence, and nothing greater is possible for a "poor existing individual" *in via*.

The view from below is described in a little book which is as deeply misunderstood as it is widely read: *Fear and Trembling*, by Johannes de Silentio. Johannes' book is an attempt to understand the story of Abraham and Isaac recounted in Genesis 22.[14] His interest, however, is not exegetical but existential. After a short Preface (of which more later) the book opens with a

206

"Prelude" or *Stemning*. The literal meaning of *Stemning* is "tuning" or "tone," so that a better translation might be "mood" or "atmosphere." For it introduces the book by establishing the mode and the tonality of the considerations to follow. In the manner of a fairy tale it begins, "Once upon a time . . . " there was a child who heard, revered, and in his simplicity comprehended the story of Abraham and Isaac, how God tempted Abraham, how he kept the faith, and how he received his son again by a miracle. But the increase of years brings about a dissociation of sensibilities. Maturity separates the passion and the reflection that are united in the pious immediacy of the child, and the man finds that the greater his enthusiasm, the less his understanding. In his disenchantment he desires to achieve an imaginative contemporaneity with Abraham in the moment of his ordeal. He does not wish for a philosophical comprehension that "goes beyond" faith by fitting it into a system of metaphysics; he simply wants to know the feeling of the reality of faith.

Johannes' character, which is part and parcel of his literary method, is presaged by the motto he has picked for his book: *"Was Tarquinius Superbus in seinem Garten mit den Mohnköpfen sprach, verstand der Sohn, aber nicht der Bote."*[15] If there is any message about faith in *Fear and Trembling*, it will be an enigmatic message. Only the sons, those who are already members of the spiritual household of Abraham, will understand it; but not the messengers, those—perhaps philosophers and theologians—who like Abraham's servants witness the mystery from a distance and even convey information about it, but do not comprehend their own witness and their own message. True to his name, Johannes de Silentio is keeping silent.

Perhaps he is silent because there is something that men need to listen for, a still small voice that cannot be heard amid the clamor of the intellectual market place. Something of the sort is indicated by his respectful Preface. In these days, he complains, faith is being sold, or sold out, at bargain prices. In fact the price is so low it is doubtful if anyone will care to buy. The intelligentsia have doubted everything, transcended faith, and understood all truth. At least they say they have, and it would be bad taste to doubt their veracity. But it is strange that they should appeal to Descartes as their patron. For Descartes was "a quiet and solitary thinker"—a man of silence—"not a bellowing night-watchman," who never doubted *de fide*. Strange, too, that

207

every philosophy professor has got beyond faith. For how many and how great are the saints and martyrs who had all they could do just to *keep* the faith until death. Nowadays, Johannes sighs, we all start where the saints and martyrs left off, and faith has gone begging for takers. As for himself:

> The present writer is nothing of a philosopher; he is, *poetice et eleganter*, an amateur writer who . . . writes because for him it is a luxury which becomes the more agreeable and more evident, the fewer there are who buy and read what he writes. He can easily foresee his fate in an age when passion has been obliterated in favor of learning, in an age when an author who wants to have readers must take care to write in such a way that the book can easily be perused during the afternoon nap. . . . He foresees his fate—that he will be entirely ignored.

There is the dissociation of sensibilities again, in the demeaning of passion by learning. There, too, is an "afternoon nap" that will make its major appearance later in more solemn and dreadful surroundings. And there is Johannes, an idler who writes for himself because he enjoys it and can afford it, retreating once more into his characteristic silence.

The words *"poetice et eleganter"* are reminiscent of the subtitle of *Fear and Trembling*, "Dialectical Lyric." A suitable translation might be "philosophical poem" or "poetic philosophy." The former is recommended by the fact that Johannes' lyric is substantive and his dialectic adjectival, though there is plenty of lyric in his dialectic (the Problemata) and an abundance of dialectic in his lyric (the Prelude and the Panegyric). With the "profoundest deference" to the philosophers, before whom he prostrates himself at the close of his Preface, Johannes de Silentio will attempt to write the poetry of faith. [16]

The attempt fails. In the remainder of the Prelude Johannes offers a series of four dramatic scenes, each of which imagines one way Abraham might respond to the divine command: "Take Isaac, thine only son, whom thou lovest . . . , and offer him . . . for a burnt offering. . . ." He may, in preparing the sacrifice, prefer to let Isaac think that his father is an idolatrous and blood-thirsty monster, rather than jeopardize the boy's faith in God by insisting upon the truth. The command may destroy Abraham's own faith and deprive him of that joy in God and in Isaac that was the substance of his life. Having obeyed the command, he may still suspect that it was not God's will but his own sinfulness that made him willing to kill his son; he becomes a perpetual penitent, his confidence in God and in himself is weakened, and he has lost Isaac forever by doubting his paternal love. Or perhaps, at the moment Abraham draws the knife, he reveals to Isaac a hand clenched in anguish and a body shuddering with terror; the ram appears and Isaac lives, but he lives in despair ever after, having lost faith in God and in his father.

> Thus and in many like ways that man of whom we are speaking thought concerning this event. Every time he returned home after wandering to Mt. Moriah, he sank down with weariness, he folded his hands and said, "No one is so great as Abraham! Who is capable of understanding him?"

Nothing the imagination puts together can contain all the data of the Biblical account: that Abraham loved Isaac and yet was willing to sacrifice him, that having given him up he could yet receive Isaac again with rejoicing and without remorse, that through it all Abraham kept faith with the God of the covenant while yet obedient to the God of the command. These are contradictions that exceed the poet's capacity for representation and stop the mouth of lyric fancy. [17]

Almost. For Johannes is not a pettifogging philosopher who measures enthusiasm and passion by the finite yardstick of the understanding. What he cannot understand he may yet admire. From his aborted essay in religious drama Johannes turns to compose a hymn of praise to Father Abraham and the power of faith which passes the power of poesy. His Panegyric opens with a meditation on heroism and poetry. Life were desperate, he writes, if there were no eternal consciousness in man, if the greatest of human achievements were but the by-product of an aimless and chaotic play of natural forces. Empty and comfortless were life, if transience were its essence and oblivion its end. But it is not so. As God created both man and woman to assure the continuance of the race, so He created the hero, that there might be no dearth of magnificence, and the poet, that the hero's renown might remain forever in the remembrance of mankind. Abraham is the hero of faith, and John of Silence the poet who will jealously guard the entrusted treasure against the assaults of time.

But how shall the poet measure the magnitude of his hero?

Every man is great in proportion to that which he loves: Abraham loved God. Every man is great in proportion to his expectation: Abraham, trusting the promises of God, expects the impossible. Every man is great in proportion to that with which he strives: Abraham strives with God. So

> Abraham was greater than all, great by reason of his power whose strength is impotence, great by reason of his wisdom whose secret is foolishness, great by reason of his hope whose form is madness, great by reason of the love which is hatred of oneself. [18]

Greater than the greatness of Jeremiah lamenting in exile is the greatness of the father of faith rejoicing in his son and seed. For it is human to weep and to grieve, greatly human to give up one's life and one's hope. But it is greater than human to believe against understanding, to hope against expectation, and to hold on to one's life with joy.

Abraham's struggle to hold fast to the promises of God in the face of His demands is a struggle against time:

> . . . Abraham believed, and believed for this life. Yea, if his faith had been only for a future life, he surely would have cast everything away in order to hasten out of this world to which he did not belong. But Abraham's faith was not of this sort, if there be such a faith; for really this is not faith but the furthest possibility of faith which has a presentiment of its object at the extremest limit of the horizon, yet is separated from it by a yawning abyss within which despair carries on its game. But Abraham believed precisely for this life, that he was to grow old in the land, honored by the people, blessed in his generation, remembered forever in Isaac. . . .

Had Abraham doubted, he would have driven the sacrificial knife into his own heart and forfeited the world for the sake of his "eternal consciousness." But Abraham believed and by believing became "the guiding star which saves the anguished." [19] Had he in irresolution discovered the ram before he drew the knife, he would have been remembered forever not as the father of faith but as the author of consternation. But he did not doubt and he did not waver: he believed, and he drew the knife, and still he believed.

The encomiast is forced to conclude that his hero is no ordinary human hero; Abraham's constancy is beyond man's capacity as it is beyond man's understanding. It was God who required of an old man his only son, the son of promise. But it was God also who gave strength to his arm to draw the knife and strength to his soul to hold onto his faith. The God of the covenant does not fail to keep his promises; the God of the trial provides that which he demands. The God of promise and the God of temptation are one God. By God's election Abraham became the father of Isaac and the father of faith, but God himself is the author and finisher of faith as He is the Father of all paternity in heaven and in earth. Johannes' title is from a Pauline text, and his lyric a rhapsody on its theme: "Work out your own salvation with fear and trembling. For it is God which worketh in you both to will and to do of his good pleasure" (Philippians 2:12-13).

The panegyric cannot continue. John of Silence is reduced to dumb apostrophe: "Venerable Father Abraham! . . . [T]hou hadst no need of a panegyric. . . . " Abraham does not need the eulogy of a poet to protect him from forgetfulness and the acids of time. In the power of faith he has already conquered time and won the temporal. "Thousands of years have run their course since those days, but thou hadst need of no tardy lover to snatch the memorial of thee from the power of oblivion, for every language calls thee to remembrance. . . ."[20] The poet has chosen a hero who wants and will suffer no poet. Not even the most reverent lover can praise a power which is impotence, a wisdom which is foolishness, a hope which is madness, and a love which is hatred of self. These are contradictions that disarm even admiration. A man can give up the temporal for the eternal, but only God can restore the temporal. It is the power of God that returns Isaac to Abraham's faith after Abraham's obedience has given him up. And no man can fitly praise God.

The lyricist is through, his powers broken against the paradox of faith. And so the dialectician, whose business it is to deal with contradictions, takes the field. Johannes the dialectician wants to examine some problems that are posed by the story of Abraham and Isaac. But there is something he must first spit out of his system before he gets to the problems themselves. Hence his Preliminary Expectoration, which is methodological preparation for the Problemata just as the Prelude provided an atmospheric setting for the Panegyric. At the beginning and end of his expectoration Johannes contrasts the function of the dialectician with the role usually assumed by the preachers when they are moved to uplift their congregations with the story of Abraham and Isaac. The dialectician ideally is an honest and honorable thinker who does not "lack the courage to think a thought whole."[21] So honest is he that, should he run across a thought that terrifies him, he will refuse to think it at all rather than tenderize it for his delicate palate. If worst comes to worst—for example, if a dialectical inquiry should disclose that Abraham is simply and solely a murderer—then the dialectician is honorable enough to keep it to himself rather than initiate others into such dreadful torments of the spirit. Not the least of the talents required in a dialectician is the ability to keep his mouth shut.

The parson, however, prates merrily away to all and sundry about the greatness of Abraham, who was willing to offer to God the best he had. Of course he takes care to keep this "best" quite vague, so that no one is troubled by the consideration that in Abraham's case the best happened to be his only son, to whom he owed the duty of solicitous paternal love and whom in fact he proposed to kill. Fortunately most of the congregation sleep through the sermon (there's that afternoon nap again), and no one is misled by his reverence's prattle. But should there be a chance insomniac in the pews who hears the sermon and goes home resolved to emulate the heroism of Abraham on his own family: in that case the parson is on the spot bright and early Monday morning to confront, accuse, convict, and convert the wretched sinner—who only wanted to murder his son in obedience to the pastor's counsel. So thoughtless that he can, without noting the discrepancy, contradict on Monday what he said on Sunday, the parson is the very opposite of the honest dialectician, who thinks a thought whole or not at all. So insensitive that he can with his ranting pro and con breed chaos in the souls of his parishioners, without observing in himself any more than a tendency to excessive perspiration and a swelling vein in the forehead, the parson is the opposite of the honorable dialectician, who turns the chaos inward and keeps his suffering to himself. It's a good thing, Johannes observes in a footnote, that there is more sense in the world than you would expect from the average sermon.[22]

Or perhaps the parson explains that Abraham's experience is only a test of his faith. Fair enough. But the preacher depicts the trial in foreshortened perspective, with the outcome deceptively assured in advance. Should a sufferer from insomnia happen to hear the sermon, he may feed on the false hope that all his own troubles are but temporary. If only I wait a moment, he thinks, I shall surely see the ram and hear the voice of the angel, just as the parson says. The parson, finding his charge in this state on Monday, might denounce his indolent optimism with the admonition that "all of life is a trial." This is so true that it may be the main point of Johannes' book. But it happens to contradict the impression that the same preacher so carefully contrived to produce on Sunday in his capacity as pulpit poet.

Johannes will have no part of these cheap editions of Abraham. If I were to preach on Abraham, he says, I would first of all take my time at it. I would drag out that three-day journey to Mt. Moriah for at least a month of Sundays. I would distill every drop of manly and paternal feeling out of Abraham's sufferings. My auditors would smell the smoke of the sacrificial wood, feel the edge of the knife, see it glint in the morning sun, hear the weeping of Isaac begging for his life on behalf of the youthful promise still hidden in his loins. In short I would do everything in my power to prevent my hearers from lightly undertaking an imitation of the dread deed of Abraham. For if a dialectician is to speak about Abraham, then he is duty-bound to be painfully clear about the incomprehensible difficulty of Abraham's case. The job of the dialectician is to keep silence in the presence of the paradox, which speaks louder and more forcefully than all the oratory of the preachers.

That the story of Abraham contains paradoxes there can be no question, in view, first of all, of the ambiguity of his motives. He proposes to offer his *son* to *God*. Ethically speaking Abraham wants to murder Isaac; religiously speaking he is prepared to sacrifice him. This contradiction between murder and sacrifice, between the ethical and the religious interpretation of his action, generates the "dread and distress, the fear and trembling" of Abraham's situation. Within the religious dimension there are further agonies. The God who—presumably, for Abraham has no surety that the voice he hears is the voice of God—asks for the sacrifice of Isaac is the same God who miraculously gave Isaac in the first place. Or again: it is possible that God—if it is God and not a demon who speaks—demands the death of Isaac only to discover if Abraham has the moral courage and the paternal devotion to refuse. If Abraham is any kind of dialectician, i.e., if

213

he is at all an honest man, he will not be able to sidestep the thought, and the prodigious dread of the thought, that he may be tempting God when he draws the knife on his son.

These and a multitude of like contradictions make up "the dialectical conflict of faith and its gigantic passion." John of Silence has encountered the *cul de sac* of dialectic:

> . . . [W]hen I have to think of Abraham, I am as though annihilated. I catch sight every moment of that enormous paradox which is the substance of Abraham's life, every moment I am repelled, and my thought in spite of all its passion cannot get a hair's-breadth further.

He cannot "think himself into" Abraham because Abraham is the paradox that repels thought. Before the paradox every honest thinker is mute. [23]

But this side of Abraham there is plenty to be understood. Though he cannot comprehend faith, Johannes can at least manage the preliminary expectoration. The movement preparatory for faith he calls "infinite resignation," and the term has roughly the same meaning for him that it has for Johannes Climacus. The novelty is the contrast with faith properly so-called. Infinite resignation means, algebraically, the renunciation of the finite and the temporal for the infinite and the eternal. Faith means, after having renounced the finite and the temporal, the confidence that one will receive them again. Abraham's willingness to sacrifice Isaac in obedience to God's command was his infinite resignation. His certainty that God would nevertheless not take Isaac was his faith.

The "knight of resignation"—who is really a devotee of religion A—believes that God transcends the world incommensurably. If need be he will evacuate his worldly life for the sake of an ideal relationship to God. If I were in Abraham's shoes, says Johannes, I would sacrifice Isaac and continue to believe that God is love. But it would be all over between God and me as far as this world is concerned. My act of renunciation would be noble and poetic, like the magnificence of a tragic hero. But it would also show that I did not love Isaac as Abraham did. And if God were to restore him to me, I would be nonplussed, as a young man who has taken monastic vows because he cannot have the girl he loves would be embarrassed to find her in his arms after the cowl is already about his ears. Abraham on the contrary receives Isaac with joy and thanksgiving. Not because he did not really give him up, for he cut the wood, bound Isaac, and drew the knife. But even while he gave him up, Abraham believed that God would not require Isaac or that, requiring him, He would yet give him back. By resignation Abraham gave up the finite, by faith he got it back again "every inch."[24] This movement of faith, Johannes confesses, I cannot understand and certainly not execute. Abraham's faith is a faith "by virtue of the absurd." By faith he receives the world, symbolized by Isaac, after he has let it go. His whole life after faith is a new creation in which he does not the least thing but "by virtue of the absurd."

"Virtue" is "power" *(Kraft).* The power by which a man makes the movement of faith is not a power indigenous or intelligible to himself. It is a power "from beyond" and therefore from the human point of view absurd and paradoxical. A man believes "by the power . . . of the absurd, by the power of the fact that with God all things are possible."[25] The only power that can save a man in Abraham's situation, a man who has drained all his own potencies in the act of resignation, is the paradoxical power of God. And this is the impossible possibility that can only be grasped by faith. "[H]e who loves God without faith reflects upon himself; he who loves God believingly reflects upon God."[26] On his own Abraham does nothing but give up Isaac; he gets him back by virtue of God.

So paradoxical is faith that Johannes the dialectician can no more talk sense about it than Johannes the poet can imagine it or praise it. And indeed no one should talk about faith at all if talking means the thoughtless babble of the preachers or the philosophers' wordy claim to total comprehension. But a dialectician may still talk, if he can by his talking make clear that faith is "a tremendous paradox . . . which is capable of transforming a murder into a holy act well-pleasing to God, a paradox which gives Isaac back to Abraham. . . ."[27] Johannes' Problemata embody his attempt at a rigorous dialectical definition of the paradox of Abraham.

Each of Johannes' three problems begins with a paragraph describing something he calls "the ethical," and the second paragraph of each problem begins with a statement that "if this is the way it is, then Hegel is right," and so on. Everything that is said about the ethical in this division of the book is qualified by the "if," for it is Johannes' intent to demonstrate that there *may be* something which escapes an ethical interpretation of human life: faith. The "ethical" in this context does not refer to any particular system of ethics, but simply to the attitude that reads all of human life in ethical terms and measures every human action by a moral yardstick.

Problem I asks, Is there a teleological suspension of the ethical? The answer is, from an ethical point of view, no. If man achieves his highest destiny in the fulfillment of moral obligation, and if this obligation applies without qualification to all men at all times and places, then there is no way a man may justifiably assert his individuality in opposition to the universal norm of ethics. The man who acts so as to set himself outside the universal is simply evil. And since, on this supposition, the moral universal is the highest court of appeal, there is no possible redemption and no conceivable pardon for such an "exception."

But the story of Abraham suggests that in the situation of faith the individual does find a justified standpoint outside the universal. Abraham (the particular) was faithful to the universal (his duty to his son) until it broke against the command of God. Through his fidelity to the universal he entered into that "absolute relationship to the absolute" by which he became "the individual who as the particular is superior to the universal."

> Faith is precisely this paradox, that the individual as the particular is higher than the universal, is justified over against it, is not subordinate but superior—yet in such a way, be it observed, that it is the particular individual who, after he has been subordinated as the particular to the universal, now through the universal becomes the individual who as the particular is superior to the universal, for the fact that the individual as the particular stands in an absolute relation to the absolute. [28]

It should not surprise anyone that Johannes' description of faith is full of contradiction, for faith is a "teleological suspension of the ethical," a suspension of the ethical imperative for the sake of a higher telos. In Abraham's case the father's duty to his son is lifted for the sake of his obedience to God. From the ethical point of view that is absolutely paradoxical. Johannes, here as everywhere a man of silence, has nothing to say about this claim of faith. He only wants to clarify the absolute disjunction: *either* there is such a suspension of the ethical, in which case the ethical is not the norm of human striving; *or* "if this be not faith, then

Abraham is lost, then faith has never existed in the world . . . because it has always existed."[29] If there is no teleological suspension of the ethical, then the position of supremacy claimed by faith is in fact occupied by ethics, and there is no faith because faith—i.e., the highest telos—has always existed in the form of ethical action.

Johannes repeatedly argues that Abraham cannot be mediated; his action cannot be reconciled with the universal it violates. He remains forever alone with God in the dread and distress of his trial. Significantly the only figures Johannes can find to compare with Abraham are the Mother of God who, although she was highly favored among women, was also Our Lady of incomparable Sorrows, and those disciples of the Lord who, in spite of the scandal and the offense, sat at meat with Him, believed in Him, and became the Apostles of the Crucified. Like Abraham these cannot be mediated; they too are beyond human understanding, and their faith a miracle beyond human working.

Problem I suggests Problem II: Is there an absolute duty toward God? Johannes' solution is again simple: If a man's ethical obligations define his whole duty, then these are the only divinity there is. The ethical norm is the supreme power to which man owes his allegiance, and compliance with it the last end toward which he strives. But the claim of faith is that the individual—as an individual and not as an instance of the universal—has an absolute duty toward God—the Absolute Individual and not the ethical universal—which reduces his moral duties to relativities. Thus Abraham's duty to God supercedes his duty to his son.

This is a paradoxical kind of duty. Duty by definition is universal, but the particularity of the bond between God and Abraham defies reduction to universality and mocks the ethical understanding of obligation. Yet if this paradox does not hold, there is no such thing as faith. Worse: the inclination to faith is a temptation that every man is morally bound to avoid. But the alternatives are clear: *either* faith, *or* Abraham is a murderer and there's an end of it.

In this connection Johannes quotes a parallel from the New Testament, Luke 14:26. The verse, following directly upon the parable of the great supper and the little excuses, introduces its own interpretation:

26. If any man come to me, and hate not his father, and mother, and wife, and children, and brethren, and sisters, yea, and his own life also, he cannot be my disciple.

27. And whosoever doth not bear his cross, and come after me, cannot be my disciple.

28. For which of you, intending to build a tower, sitteth not down first, and counteth the cost, whether he have sufficient to finish it?

29. Lest haply, after he hath laid the foundation, and is not able to finish it, all that behold it begin to mock him,

30. Saying, This man began to build, and was not able to finish.

31. Or what king, going to make war against another king, sitteth not down first, and consulteth whether he be able with ten thousand to meet him that cometh against him with twenty thousand?

32. Or else, while the other is yet a great way off, he sendeth an ambassage, and desireth conditions of peace.

33. So likewise, whosoever he be of you that forsaketh not all that he hath, he cannot be my disciple.

Johannes argues, against a euphemistic exegesis, that in this context the word "hate" is meant in a strong sense. If "hate" is softened to *"minus diligo, posthabeo, non colo, nihili facio,"* one arrives at the curious notion that an absolute devotion to God enjoins pallid halfheartedness toward self, kindred, and fellows. That love for God should demand the renunciation of all other affections is credible and a "worthy conception of the Deity." But no man would be so stupid or conceited as to regard defective filial devotion in his wife as a proof of connubial passion. Shall the sign of religious commitment be a lukewarm fellow-feeling? Johannes' own exegesis is more rigorous:

The absolute duty may cause one to do what ethics would forbid, but by no means can it cause the knight of faith to cease to love. This is shown by Abraham. The instant he is ready to sacrifice Isaac the ethical expression for what he does is this: he hates Isaac. But if he really hates Isaac, he can be sure that God does not require this, for Cain and Abraham are not identical. Isaac he must love with his whole soul; when God requires Isaac he must love him if possible even more dearly, and only on this condition can he *sacrifice* him; for in fact it is this love for Isaac which, by its paradoxical opposition to his love for God, makes his act a sacrifice. . . . Only at the moment when his act is in absolute contradiction to his feeling is his act a sacrifice, but the reality of

218

his act is the factor by which he belongs to the universal, and in that aspect he is and remains a murderer. [30]

The man who recognizes an absolute duty toward God does not cease to love what is other than God. He does not cease, for example, to acknowledge his moral obligations. Otherwise his infinite resignation is a sham. But by his duty to God he is bound to be prepared to do things which, objectively and in reality, have the moral character of evil.

Most men think in terms of two categories of practical reason: the ethical (the universal) and the selfish (the particular). Faith claims, and the proper understanding of Abraham requires, that there is a third category: that of the individual who does not by self-interest sink beneath the universal, but through the universal rises to a particularity superior to the universal. At the sub-ethical level there is Cain, who killed Abel out of self-interest and hatred. At the ethical level there is the tragic hero who, whatever sacrifices he may have to make, reposes securely in the universal. And at the level of faith: Abraham. Such at least is the claim of faith. Whether the claim is true no one can say. But unless it is true, Abraham is condemned, and "faith" is a terrible temptation to be resisted with all possible vigor.

Of course, Johannes adds, there is a mark whereby one can distinguish the genuine knight of faith from the counterfeit. To wit, the true knight is always incommunicado. He keeps to himself, whereas the false knights are great sectarians, always clubbing together for mutual encouragement and plotting holy wars against the infidel. Johannes sports with the Rotarian temper of the pseudo-knights of faith, but a sober reader may wonder who is really the butt of this joke. The sole criterion by which to tell a knight of faith is his silence and his secrecy. Is this not the most futile of all criteria, that a knight of faith can be recognized only by the fact that he cannot be recognized? So it is, and this becomes the subject of Johannes' Problem III.

The problem is, Was Abraham justified in keeping silent about his purpose before Sarah, Eleazar, and Isaac? The moral imperative demands revelation. Every man shall be prepared to declare to his fellows the purpose and intent of his actions. Only thieves, murderers, and adulterers need the cover of night to obscure their deeds. The honest man acts openly in the light of day. Readiness for community is part of the universal good commanded by ethics.

But Abraham keeps silent. He has to keep silent, for there is no way he can explain to anyone else what he intends to do with Isaac on Mt. Moriah. His only recorded utterances are instinct with the most terrible irony. To his servants at the foot of the mount he says: "I and the lad will go yonder and worship, and come again to you." (Genesis 22:5) The remark is true, but it says nothing about his real intentions. More terrible still is the dialogue with Isaac at the place of sacrifice:

> And Isaac spake unto Abraham his father, and said, My father: and he said, Here am I, my son. And he said, Behold the fire and the wood: but where is the lamb for a burnt offering?—And Abraham said, My son, God will provide himself a lamb for a burnt offering. (Genesis 22:7-8)

Jehovah-jireh: the Lord will provide.[31] That, of course, is the whole import of the story of Abraham and Isaac. The irony of Abraham is a holy irony, but it is no less ironical for all that. *Jehovah-jireh* tells Isaac precisely nothing; for all practical and moral purposes Abraham is silent.

Faith paradoxically asserts that there is a silence and a concealment superior to ethical community and revelation. Either this paradox, or else faith is a demonic temptation. That there are many kinds of silence is the theme of Johannes' protracted digression on aesthetics. There is an innocent silence that seeks to spare the feelings of others: for example, *de mortuis nihil nisi bonum.* There is the frivolous secrecy beloved by comic playwrights: the mistaken identity, for example, without which very few comedies could be written. And there is demonic silence: the enforced secrecy of a man committed to evil. John the Seducer is bound to silence by his nefarious purpose; his way of life includes a commitment to that silence without which he cannot carry through his program of betrayal.

The ethical verdict on all such forms of silence is easily arrived at. Of the innocent silence ethics says that it is the product of a misconceived and misdirected sympathy; better to have the matter out than to presume to shield another from the truth. The secrecy employed by the comedian is a nugatory fiction unworthy of ethical consideration. The silence of the demon is unqualified evil. He must be compelled to speak, even as Christ caused the dumb to speak by casting out the devil that possessed him. For if the demoniac is made to reveal himself in public utterance his demonia will be annulled by the community of the good.

If the ethical is coterminous with the human, Abraham's silence is the involuntary silence of the demon. And yet faith sees his reserve as the sign of his complicity not with the devil but with God. Either there is a silence that is justified over against ethical revelation, or Abraham is lost and the incommunicado of faith is but the horrible and vacuous isolation of the demoniac. Johannes once again gets no farther than to faith. Not even that far, for he always ends short of faith with his monotonous either/or: either there is a teleological suspension of the ethical, an absolute duty toward God, and a justified silence, or—. Either faith, or—the rest *is* silence.

It might be supposed, from his constant reference to "the ethical," that the terms of Johannes' disjunction are faith and ethics. Either faith or ethics provides the guide for human life and the norm for human achievement. *Fear and Trembling* has often been read as a comment on the discrepancy between ethics and religion. But there is that mighty "if" that qualifies everything John of Silence says about "the ethical." His conviction— which he holds with exceptional vigor and tenacity—that infinite resignation (religion A) is the supreme act of man shows that his book has nothing to do with those questions about the propriety of waiving ethical rules which his commentators have so often foisted upon him. Equally irrelevant are all attempts to parallel the case of Abraham with made-up instances of unmotivated evil or real examples of supererogatory sanctity. John of Silence is not concerned at all with sanctions, human or divine, and the paradox he poses is not religion versus ethics. A man on trial, an Abraham, could never parcel out his dilemma in these tidy compartments. The real alternative is: either faith/or despair. His analysis of Abraham ironically dissembles Johannes' belief that a faith which passes understanding and exceeds human agency is the only alternative to a resignation that heroically expires in an apotheosis of impotence.

Or in the language of Climacus: Christianity is the only power that can extricate a man from the predicament of suffering and guilt into which he precipitates himself by his own efforts to secure his God-relationship. It is not without reason that John of

221

Silence has introduced New Testament allusions into his discussion at several critical points. His reference to the Blessed Virgin and the disciples of the Lord, as well as his analysis of Luke 14:26 and his citation of the dumb demoniac, not only illumine the situation of Abraham; they also suggest the use Johannes wants to make of his patriarch-hero. These, plus the text from which the title of his book is lifted ("*Work out your own salvation* with fear and trembling, for *it is God which worketh* in you. . . ."), show clearly enough that whatever Johannes says about Abraham is to be understood obliquely of the Christian believer.

There are two other passages in the New Testament that are decisive in this connection. Although he does not wish to be classed as a "learned exegete," Johannes has betrayed no slight expertise *in sacra pagina,* and it may be supposed that he knows the verses in question. First from the Epistle to the Hebrews:

> By faith Abraham, when he was tried, offered up Isaac: and he that had received the promises offered up his only begotten son, Of whom it was said, That in Isaac shall thy seed be called: Accounting that God was able to raise him up, even from the dead; from whence also he received him in a figure. (Hebrews 11:17-19)

The second is from St. Paul's explanation of Abraham, "our father, as pertaining to the flesh," in his letter to the Christians at Rome:

> He staggered not at the promise of God through unbelief; but was strong in faith, giving glory to God; and being fully persuaded that, what he had promised, he was able also to perform. And therefore it was imputed to him for righteousness. Now it was not written for his sake alone, that it was imputed to him; But for us also, to whom it shall be imputed, if we believe on him that raised up Jesus our Lord from the dead; who was delivered for our offenses, and was raised again for our justification. (Romans 4:20-25)

The words that stand out in the passage from Hebrews are the words "in a figure." It is reasonable to suppose that *Fear and Trembling,* in its own lyric and dialectical way, is an essay in the figural reading of the Old Testament. Abraham is the "father of faith" because he is a type or figure of faith, foreshadowing the faith of the New Covenant. The typology is reduplicated in *Fear and Trembling* itself: whatever John of Silence says about Abraham is also to be understood as "in a figure." To be sure the figure is presented by understatement and dissemblance. But the clues are there, and for all its irony this problematic book demands typological resolution.

Along with this general observation it is necessary to look more closely at the *kind* of figural interpretation found in *Fear and Trembling.* According to the predominant medieval tradition, a Scriptural text, besides its literal meaning, may carry three modes of spiritual significance: the allegorical, the moral, and the anagogical. At the literal level, the story of Abraham and Isaac probably has something to do with the elimination of human sacrifice as a cultic element in primitive Semitic religion. Johannes de Silentio may or may not have known about this, but in any case it is clear that he is not interested in that dimension of the Biblical record. In the allegorical reading favored by the author of the Epistle to the Hebrews, the sacrifice and restitution of Isaac prefigures the redemption of the world by the Passion and Resurrection of Our Lord Jesus Christ. But neither is Johannes concerned to read the story at this level. His reading is guided by the words of the Pauline text: "Now it was not written for his sake alone . . . , But *for us also* . . . , *if we believe*. . . ." (Romans 4:23-24. My emphasis.) It is the moral sense alone that interests John of Silence. Abraham's faith is the pattern after which the Christian must model his own belief. Or as Johannes says, Abraham is the *paradigm* of faith according to which all instances are to be declined in all cases. Not for his sake alone, but for us also if we believe, God is able to perform what He has promised.

A "learned exegete" in the middle ages, expounding the faith of Abraham tropologically, would have viewed it from above, as a confirmed believer examining the sources and prophecies of his own salvation. His lyric-dialectic character, his profession of unfaith, and his running polemic against the parsons and theologians besotted with philosophy exclude Johannes from the aerie of churchly theology. But from his inferior standpoint he casts up a few hints as to the Christian-moral significance he glimpses in the saga of Abraham and Isaac. In the course of Problem III, after sifting through a handful of literary parrallels, Johannes notes that none of these is strictly analogous to Abraham's case. He continues:

> If there might be any analogy, this must be found in the paradox of sin, but this again lies in another sphere and cannot explain Abraham and is itself far easier to explain than Abraham. [32]

223

This is a typical twist of irony, better suited to unsettle than to satisfy the understanding. For the condition of the sinner who needs forgiveness and can only have it by virtue of the absurd is, *mutatis mutandis*, exactly the analogy Johannes is trying to draw. Earlier in Problem III he says as much, though again in an off-hand way as an ironist might. In the course of reviewing the legend of Ágnes and the Merman[33] he speculates that the merman (a demonic figure) might be saved for marriage with Agnes, but only by

> recourse to the paradox. For when the individual by his guilt has gone outside the universal he can return to it only by virtue of having come as the individual into an absolute relationship with the absolute.

The sentence immediately following says: "Here I will make an observation by which I say more than was said at any point in the foregoing discussion." A footnote explains:

> In the foregoing discussion I have intentionally refrained from any consideration of sin and its reality. The whole discussion points to Abraham, and him I can still approach by immediate categories—in so far, that is to say, as I am able to understand him. As soon as sin makes its appearance ethics comes to grief precisely upon repentance; for repentance is the highest ethical expression, but precisely as such it is the deepest ethical self-contradiction.

From other pseudonyms and from the *Edifying Discourses:* repentance (or the eternal recollection of guilt) is the "highest expression" of that religion which itself is only a tensing of ethical passion to the uttermost. But the uttermost is the breaking-point. Repentance not only sums up all that a man can do to bind himself to God; it also reveals that his God-relationship is consummated negatively in self-denial, and is therefore the "deepest ethical self-contradiction."

> Sin is not the first immediacy, sin is a later immediacy. By sin the individual is already higher (in the direction of the demoniacal paradox) than the universal, because it is a contradiction on the part of the universal to impose itself upon a man who lacks the *conditio sine qua non*. . . . An ethics which disregards sin is a perfectly idle science; but if it asserts sin, it is *eo ipso* well beyond itself.

Sin is the paradoxical Christian obverse, the transcendent

224

dialectical reversal, of the immanent and pathetic consciousness of guilt. It is not the "first immediacy" of creation, to which Abraham belongs. That immediacy is exhausted in the strenuous exercises of religion A, but Abraham has not yet reached the *terminus ad quem* of total guilt. His trial is, so to speak, a special case. Sin is the prologue to the "later immediacy," the new dispensation of grace by which a man is returned in virtue of the absurd to the unity and simplicity of childhood wistfully recalled in Johannes' Prelude. The man originally flawed by sin is beyond the end of his ethical rope and beyond the reach of the universal imperative. He is already higher—demonically—than the universal and may through faith be reconciled to the universal by his "absolute relationship with the absolute." But

> what is said here does not by any means explain Abraham; for it was not by sin Abraham became the individual, on the contrary, he was a righteous man, he is God's elect. So the analogy to Abraham will not appear until after the individual has been brought to the point of being able to accomplish the universal, and then the paradox repeats itself.[34]

More irony. Of course sin does not explain Abraham. But Abraham, with his lesser problem and his patriarchal promise, does explain, as a figure explains that of which it is a figure, the predicament of the man for whom the ethical is permanently suspended by sin and to whom is given, by virtue of the absurd, the promise of the grace of forgiveness. And in such a knight of faith—the Christian believer—the paradox of Abraham will repeat itself when he attempts to live the new life that is given to him beyond the extremity of guilt and condemnation.

In an Epilogue that harks back to the "clearance sale" of his Preface, Johannes tells of a trick once hit upon by the merchants of Holland to improve the market in spices.

> One time in Holland when the market was rather dull for spices the merchants had several cargoes dumped into the sea to peg up prices. This was a pardonable, perhaps a necessary device for deluding people. Is it something like that we need now in the world of spirit? Are we so thoroughly convinced that we have attained the highest point that there is nothing left for us but to make ourselves believe piously that we have not got so far—just for the sake of having something left to occupy our time? Is it such a self-deception the present generation has need of, does it need to be trained to virtuosity in self-deception, or is it not

rather sufficiently perfected already in the art of deceiving itself? Or rather is not the thing most needed an honest seriousness which dauntlessly and incorruptibly points to the tasks, an honest seriousness which lovingly watches over the tasks, which does not frighten men into being over hasty in getting the highest tasks accomplished, but keeps the tasks young and beautiful and charming to look upon and yet difficult withal and appealing to noble minds.

Is *Fear and Trembling* an exercise in pious self-deception or an honest and serious call to the task of believing? Johannes' irony suggests the former, but his lyric and dialectical intensity belies the latter. Perhaps the case is Socratic. For if the suspicion is correct that our age, which has gone far beyond faith, is already sufficiently self-deceived, then to deceive this generation out of its self-deception is the best service an honest seriousness can render to the times. In a figure and for us also, deception and seriousness may be the same thing. In a world where all men stand on their heads an upright man is bound to look queer. One thing is sure in any case:

> Faith is the highest passion in a man. There are perhaps many in every generation who do not even reach it, but no one gets further. Whether there be many in our age who do not discover it, I will not decide, I dare only appeal to myself as a witness who makes no secret that the prospects for him are not the best, without for all that wanting to delude himself and to betray the great thing which is faith by reducing it to an insignificance, to an ailment of childhood which one must wish to get over as soon as possible. But for the man also who does not so much as reach faith life has tasks enough, and if one loves them sincerely, life will by no means be wasted, even though it never is comparable to the life of those who sensed and grasped the highest.

The parson spoke more truly than he knew: all of life is a trial. Those who finish with life before life has had its way with them are like children who finish playing before their holiday is over: as these are wretched and deficient children, so those are miserable and unprofitable servants. Even the man who does not get as far as faith will find occupation enough for a lifetime. But the high passion of faith is like the speed of light: the only absolute in a world of relativities. And the man who is too eager to exceed it may find himself moving steadily backwards. [35]

Like Johannes Climacus, John of Silence can only approach

Christianity from below. The prospects for him as for his namesake are "not the best." Like Climacus, Johannes de Silentio can only catch a far-off glimpse of the *possibility* of faith, imminent just over the edge of his imaginative and intellectual horizons. Neither of them can testify to its reality. The *actuality* of Christianity, its annihilating word of condemnation and its comfortable word of reconciliation, is the theme of Climacus' opposite number, the "ideal Christian" Anti-Climacus. His superiority as a believer enables him to view Christianity "from above." In the first part of *Training in Christianity* Anti-Climacus, following the *Fragments,* defines Christian faith as contemporaneity with Christ. He develops this definition in a rhapsody on the text, "Come hither to me, all ye that labor and are heavy laden, I will give you rest" (Matthew 11:28). He who issues this invitation is Christ, and in order to appreciate the invitation it is necessary to know more about the identity of the inviter.

The Christian Church has enshrined its dogmatic understanding of Christ in the Nicene Creed:

". . . one Lord Jesus Christ, the only-begotten Son of God; Begotten of the Father before all ages, God from God, Light from Light, Very God from Very God; Begotten not made; Consubstantial with the Father; Through whom all things were made: Who for us men and for our salvation came down from heaven, And was incarnate by the Holy Ghost of the Virgin Mary, And was made man. . . ."

But the symbolic formula sets its object at the distance of cognition. It is in the New Testament that Jesus of Nazareth, his appearance as a man to men, may be more readily approached. The contending attractions and repulsions of his personality compel that "infinite interest" in his reality that is forbidden to the "possibility-relations" of ordinary human intercourse. [36]

Anti-Climacus is sensitive to the attractions of Jesus' person. In contrast to human charity, which must insist upon its due if it is not to become condescension, He offers his aid gratuitously to all who labor and are laden. Unlike human sympathy, which must retain its superiority to evil lest it become impotent, his compassion is a self-emptying by which He undertakes the sufferings of the wretched of the earth. Ignoring the distinctions which human affection must make if it is not to

227

become effete, his invitation is extended to all who travail. No man can be the bond of another's peace, but here the Helper is the Help, He is himself the rest He offers: "Abide with me, for in abiding with me there is rest."

The mercy of God poured out through the Christ, transcending the inevitable and legitimate limitations of human solicitude, proffers healing and refuge to all men. Wherefore Anti-Climacus' repeated exclamation, Wonderful! That repose of the spirit always longed for and never attained, that ideal of love which in human relations is but a deceitful romance, is here truth and reality. Wonderful! [37]

But this very "Wonderful!" sows the seed of offense. Approached by another human being with the words, "Come to me, and I will be everything to you, your joy, peace, light, health, and comfort!" who would not draw back in suspicion? What man, disillusioned by his trial of human love, would not smell fraud? All experience warns against the allurement here offered; all experience testifies that the promise cannot be kept. What man, presented with this invitation, would not, sadly no doubt, but wisely and firmly, send his regrets?

This is what men have done. [38] But they have done it dishonestly. The comfortable promise of Christianity is contained in the invitation, "Come hither to me, all ye that labor and are heavy laden, and I will give you rest." The offense of Christianity is that the invitation—which only God has the right and the might to make—was given by one whom his biographers describe as an itinerant teacher of dubious origin and ignominious end. This is the Absolute Paradox of which the *Fragments* speak: that God assumed the unlovely form of a servant, made himself intimate with every grief and shame that break the human heart, and won beatitude for men by assuming the penalty of their guilt. The comfort of Christianity is promised only to those who can surmount their offense at the Absurdity of Christianity: that the historical son of Mary is the eternal Son of God.

Naturally men wanted the blessedness and the consolation of Christianity, but they wanted it without the offense. Instead of rejecting outright the unpleasant Galilean and his invitation, they pretended to accept Him, but in fact put in his place a set of convenient illusions. The name of this pretense and these illusions is Christendom.

One of the pleasantest of Christendom's self-deceits is the fantasy that Anti-Climacus calls the illusion of "Christ in glory." According to orthodox Christian belief the crucified, risen, and ascended Christ now sits in majesty *ad dexteram patris.* So be it. But it was not the glorified Christ who issued the invitation, "Come hither to me. . . ." Christianity did not enter the world as an authoritatively magnificent communication wafted to earth from realms of heavenly splendor, and to this day Christ has uttered not a word from his celestial throne. The Christ who speaks in the Gospels—the only Christ who has ever spoken to men—is the man of sorrows, mocked, scourged, spit upon, and slaughtered, the repellent Nazarene with no form nor comeliness that men should desire Him.

"Christ in glory" is only a promise and an expectation. He is not and never has been a reality present among men. To ascribe the gospel to the glorified Christ is a revision of Christianity that misrepresents it as a divinely beautiful poem. It is natural that a militant Church should anticipate its own triumph, natural even that it should be sometimes deceived by its longings. The picture of Christ in glory is theologically correct and aesthetically proper, as an expression of the believer's hope and the groaning of the creation for redemption. But it is a deceit if it puts a fairy-tale prince in place of the sign of offense as the object of faith. Christianity demands no less than a "contemporaneous" meeting of human pride with Christ in his humiliation. It does not flatter men with the lie that they can transcend their terrestrial limitations and aspire to God, but offends them with the good news ("Come hither to me. . . .") that God has condescended to the littleness of their finitude and the pinch of their predicament. [39]

Equally illusive and equally common is the notion that the consequences of the life of Jesus, especially the centuries-long continuity of the Church, demonstrate the truth of the claim that He is divine. But even if perfect knowledge of the "historical Jesus" were not impossible, it would still not amount to a knowledge of the Christ, the subject of Peter's confession and the object of the Christian's trust. Historical research necessarily remains within the framework of the presupposition that men are only men. One may prove—or try to, since historical evidence is never more than approximation to proof—that Caesar was a hero or a scoundrel. But no historian would argue

229

that he was a ghost or an angel or an avatar of the Buddha, or even for that matter a man. Reincarnations and free-floating spirits are outside the historian's domain. His province, marked out in advance and so conditioning but never established by the historical method, is human action. Assuming that his subjects are men, he endeavors to show from the consequences of their lives their relative significance within the bounds of that assumption.

By no means then could one demonstrate historically that Caesar (or Jesus) was (or was not) *God.* Because of the absolute difference between God and man, the project would be, from the historian's point of view, vain, and from the believer's perspective, blasphemous. The God-man is not only an historical event in the usual sense, but is "furthermore of such a character as to include in its composition that which by virtue of its essence cannot become historical, and must therefore become such by virtue of an absurdity."[40] The belief that Jesus of Nazareth is God will not be made less paradoxical by centuries upon centuries of ecclesiastical success. Until the beatific vision it will remain an article of faith to which no historical evidence is even remotely relevant.[41]

When the inherent repugnance of the Christian claim and the limitations of historical knowledge are not respected, men are hoodwinked by the illusion of familiarity, which Anti-Climacus calls the "misfortune of Christendom." The sign of offense (Christ in his humiliation) is replaced by the standard of victory (Christ in triumph) and whittled to the dimensions of human ingenuity (the proof of the centuries). Christianity becomes a culture phenomenon, a folk religion, and a second nature for all men (save Jews) who are born in Christendom. The advent of "Christian civilization"—Christendom—is the end of Christianity. For Christendom *(Christenhed),* and in particular its supreme monument the Established Church, is the politesse with which men who will not make the honest surrender of faith or the honest refusal of offense have shown Christianity *(Christendom)* the door. Christendom, especially emancipated Protestant Christendom, and more especially (Kierkegaard thought) Lutheranism in Denmark, is either simple worldliness *(Wer liebt nicht Weib, Wein, und Gesang, Der bleibt ein Narr sein Leben lang)* or else worldliness plus a high intellectual culture, decked out in the vestments of Christian language and Christian worship but ignorant of the perils of the imitation of Christ and therefore undeserving the solaces of grace. Anti-Climacus is determined to expose the rejection of Christianity that lies concealed under the vestments of Christendom, and to turn these festive garments to shirts of flame. In place of Thorvaldsen's effete imitation-classic and super-life-size Christ, extending his arms in invitation above the high altar of the cathedral Church of Our Lady, he sets a bloody crucifix. "Come unto me, all ye that labor and are heavy laden" becomes in his jeremiad *"Procul, o procul, esto profani!"*

Not only is the Christ politely and ceremoniously excluded from Christendom; he is made a commodity to be sold and a shibboleth to be mouthed by the factions that contend with each other in Christian society. The bishops and priests of the Church, along with countless other lesser civil servants, market Christ to the multitudes and live off the profit of his Body. The man who was numbered among the malefactors becomes, for a bourgeois middle-class, the symbol of the *status quo* of those who profess the faith out of the depth of the insecurity of their own privilege, and for the disinherited *illuminati* of that society, the rallying point of social change. "Better well-hanged than ill-wed," was the motto of Climacus. His opposite number might gloss: better to be crucified with Christ than be made familiar of the mass of corruption and untruth that calls itself Christian civilization. For Christendom is only a perverse sort of pantheism, an "acoustical illusion which confuses *vox populi* and *vox dei* as when the cry was heard: crucify him, crucify him—*vox populi.*"[42] Once his cause is espoused by human intelligence and imagination, Christ becomes whatever men want him to be by dint of ceasing to be the one thing He is: a scandal and a stone of stumbling.[43]

The contemporaries of Jesus were more consistent: they were offended and they put him to death, out of human honesty and godly fear. They could not fail to notice the absurdity that so plainly declared itself: the son of the carpenter and the maiden, conceived out of wedlock, familiar of whores and tax-collectors, says that He is the Son of God. It was not the riff-raff of Judaea, but the pillars of state and church, that crucified Jesus, thinking they did God service. Humanity essentially and at its best rebels against his person and his profession. The contradictions may be softened for us by our historical and spiritual distance from 30 A.D., but to the men of

231

Jesus' time they were sharp enough. He promises eternal life (wonderful!), but He cannot keep his own skin. "Cast not your pearls before swine," He warns his disciples, but what are these followers of his if not the most swinish of the vulgar herd? He preaches in the synagogue—in order to damn the Establishment. This undistinguished man, who says that God does not dwell in the temple at Jerusalem, accepts divine honors from the crowd. He grandly forgives the sins of slatterns and denounces the Pharisees, who of all men honor the law with meticulous observance. He is immoral (Except a man hate father and mother . . .), imprudent (Take no thought for the morrow . . .), and silly (The meek shall inherit the earth!).

So He came to a bad end, just as anyone with a scrap of sense might have predicted: this is madness and will come to a bad end. Losing the patronage of the mob, running afoul of the authorities, getting himself executed, He vindicates every negative judgment ever laid against him, including the consummate accusation: pity. If He really were the Son of God, He would surely come down from the cross, but He doesn't. He saved others, himself He cannot save. Therefore He was wrong, and now He is lost. Poor man. [44]

This is the logic of offense. Once a man is disabused of the trumperies of theological fantasy and the irrelevancies of historical criticism, once he makes himself contemporaneous with Jesus, then offense is his only natural and reasonable response. Anti-Climacus takes the polemic between man and the God of Christianity to be absolute. There is no passage from the human to the divine, and the divine itself appearing in the human milieu can only fester opposition to itself. It was no accident that Jesus was crucified; crucifixion would be at any time and in any place the consistent—and from a purely human point of view justifiable—rejoinder of men to the claim made by and about the Christ. Man crucifies God: this is the truth about man and about his relationship to Christianity.

But if the logic of offense is unexceptionable, how is *faith* possible? If Golgotha is a necessary truth, what is the sense of Christianity? Let Anti-Climacus reply:

> Christianity did not come into the world . . . as an admirable example of the gentle art of consolation—but as *the absolute*. It is out of love God wills it so, but also it is God who wills it, and He wills what He will. . . . But what, then, is the use of Christi-

anity? It is, then, merely a plague to us! Ah, yes, that too can be said: relatively understood, the absolute is the greatest plague. . . . Christianity seems madness, since it is incommensurable with any finite wherefore. What is the use of it, then? The answer is: Hold thy peace! It is the absolute!

To become a Christian demands, in view of the absolute difference between God and man and the absolute impossibility of assimilating the divine to the human, that one "be transformed into likeness with God." But this can happen only if a man has first become contemporary with Christ, the Absolute invading the realm of the relative. "For in relation to the absolute there is only one tense: the present."

> Christ is . . . not at all a merely historical person, since as the Paradox [the Eternal-in-time] He is an extremely unhistorical person. . . . What really occurred (the past) is not . . . the real. It lacks the determinant of truth (as inwardness) and of all religiousness, the *for thee.* The past is not reality—for me: only the contemporary is reality for me. What thou dost live contemporaneous with is reality—for thee. [45]

As "the historical event which on principle could not happen,"[46] Christ is not himself a homogeneous part of human history. He is the irruption of the Absolute into history, and for that reason the "sign of contradiction"[47] and the signal for offense. But He is also and for the same reason a possible object of faith. Reality is *that which is present for you.* Christ as the Absolute is never past, but perpetually present, so that any man at any time can become his contemporary.

A man becomes the contemporary of Christ and is transformed into the likeness of God only if he participates in the life of Christ. And this he does if, like the God-man himself, he suffers the offense and the contradiction of God and man in his own person.

> If thou canst not endure contemporaneousness, canst not endure the sight in reality, if thou art unable to go out in the street and perceive that it is God in this horrible procession, and that this is thy case wert thou to fall down and worship Him—then thou art not *essentially* a Christian.

To have faith is like Simon to bend publicly under the cross of Christ in the dead march down the street of sorrows and out to the place of skulls. *Via crucis:* that is the true contemporaneity

233

with Christ, the true participation in his abjection, transformation into the only likeness of God that God has ever vouchsafed us. That is the embarrassment of faith.

And if a man has not faith, then

> What thou hast to do . . . is unconditionally to admit this to thyself, so that above all thou mayest preserve humility and fear and trembling with relation to what it means in truth to be a Christian. For that is the way thou must take to learn and to get training in fleeing to grace in such a wise that thou dost not take it in vain.

The "training in Christianity" which Anti-Climacus recommends is simply honesty before God and with oneself about one's inability to be a Christian. The condition for becoming a Christian, said Climacus, is that one first become a man. The practice of Christianity, says Anti-Climacus, begins with the candid confession of offense:

> In how far a man may succeed essentially in becoming a Christian, no one can tell him. But dread and fear and despair are of no avail. Candor before God is the first and last. Candidly to admit to oneself where one is, with candor before God holding the task in view—however slowly it goes, though one only creeps forward: yet one thing a man has, he is in the right position. . . . [48]

Offense is the natural human reaction to Christ; the honest avowal that one is offended is the only contribution a man can make toward his own participation in the promises of Christ. The faith of Magdalen and of Peter is not as instructive as Thomas' unbelief. Strictly speaking it is not within a man's power to believe; faith is a divine visitation for which the only preparation he can make is the admission of his own unworthiness. The prevenience and the prerogative belong to God. [49] Let a man recognize the absolute claim that God has made in the person of Jesus, and then let him acknowledge without evasion that he cannot meet this claim.

> And then no further; then for the rest let him attend to his work, be glad in it, love his wife, be glad in her, bring up his children with joyfulness, love his fellowmen, rejoice in life. [50]

The only power a man has before God is the capacity to admit his impotence; this is what Christianity calls the *consciousness of sin.* Abraham's trial was a "transitional phase," but the abiding teleological suspension of the ethical, the "terrible emancipation from the requirement of realizing the ethical, the heterogeneity of the individual with the ethical . . . , is *Sin,* considered as the state in which a human being is."[51] The power of God to make good man's failure is *grace.* "Only the consciousness of sin is the expression of absolute respect" for God (worship), and "only consciousness of sin is the way of entrance, is the vision, which, by being absolute respect, can see the gentleness, loving-kindness, and compassion of Christianity."[52]

The religion of the edifying discourses Climacus labels "Religion A." Its worship is man's enthusiastic endurance of his alienation from God, renouncing the world, suffering the pain of this severance, and ending in the everlasting recollection of guilt (total indebtedness) against God. The religion of the discourses is the immanent expression of the discrepancy between the finite and the infinite. Christianity ("Religion B") transforms this "religion of immanence" dialectically with its claim that God has entered time in order to reconcile the world to himself.[53] God gives himself to men, and men refuse him; therefore Christianity proclaims that men's alienation from God is self-incurred. Sin is the paradoxical Christian inversion of guilt. In the wake of the originality of sin, the suffering of Religion A is grotesquely inapropos: "dread and fear and despair are of no avail." Not spiritual debauch, but straight-faced confession of sin, is the entry into grace. Nor is the renunciation of the world demanded; the salvation of the Christian (the forgiveness of sin) is God's permission to be—not in "hidden inwardness" but in the publicity of the marketplace—the man he is: to attend to his work, be glad in his wife, bring up his children, love his fellowmen, and enjoy life. Here is the relevance of the Christian Absurdity: that which a man's burning wish and his determined resolution cannot effect, the pearl of price without which all else is vanity, is here granted. Christianity is the Absolute Paradox. That is not to say that man is *required* to believe an absurdity, for that itself would be an absurd thing to do. Rather, he is *permitted* by the power of the Absurd to believe what he must with all his passion *want* to believe if only he may. The miracle of faith is that a man *may* believe that with God all things are possible, even his own life. His self—the self that is dissipated in aesthetics, dissembled in ethics, and suffered in religion—is restored *in*

235

statum pristinum in the life of faith. To the man racked on the contradictions of existence and worn out in the struggle to become himself, Christianity offers in this world the "new immediacy" of life by grace, and the hope of Paradise in the world beyond.

In his determination not to sell the consolations of Christianity too cheap, Kierkegaard more often dwells on the consciousness of sin than on the emoluments of grace. Because of his resolution to respect the boundaries of thought, Kierkegaard never allows himself to fancy the wonders of Heaven. But in "three godly discourses" on the lilies of the field and the birds of the air he counters the resignation, suffering, and guilt of Religion A with a meditation on the silence, obedience, and joy in which the Christian relinquishes the project of becoming himself and receives his being from the hand of God.

Published simultaneously with the second edition of *Either/Or,* these discourses offer the Christian reality answering to the wishful dream of the poet. The poet longs for the carefree life of the lilies and the birds, and yet he "cannot come to an understanding with the Gospel. For at bottom the poet's life is despair of being able to become the thing he wishes; and this despair begets 'the wish'." While the poet is "the child of eternity," he "lacks the seriousness of eternity." But the Gospel soberly commands, Thou *shalt* become as a little child, thou *shalt* consider the lilies and the birds and model thy life on their demeanor. For they teach "what it is to be man, and what in a godly understanding of it is the requirement for being man— . . . silence, obedience, joy!"[54] The Gospel (in this case Matthew 6:24-34) is the "repetition" in fact of that simple self-identity which the poet vainly seeks in fancy.[55]

The Gospel enjoins *silence.* Be not anxious for life, meat, drink, or raiment, which is to say: Be not anxious for the morrow. It is "the next day" that is the object of all anxiety; for anxiety dreads the "nothing" of possibility, and possibility is concrete in the future.[56] Preoccupation with the morrow pervades human discourse, and the clamor of this preoccupation makes it difficult to learn and easy to forget "in society with men . . . , there in the human swarm"[57] the essential conditions of humanity. The power of speech shows man's superiority over the lilies and the birds; but the wanton exercise of this power may cause him to lose sight of that which the lily and the bird constantly and voicelessly declare: that the destiny of the creature is to keep silent before the Creator. It is by means of speech that man projects himself in possibility out of the present into the future, and by much speaking he lives always ahead of himself in plans and anticipation. Yet between the wish and its fulfillment there is, as the melancholy of the poet reveals, a great gulf fixed.

> And although the whole world were not big enough to contain thy plans when thou wouldst unfold them—from the lilies and the birds as teachers thou shalt learn before God to be able to fold up all thy plans together very simply in what requires less room than a point and makes less fuss than the most insignificant trifle—in silence. . . . Yea, if thou couldst learn from the lilies and the birds to become perfectly silent before God, what might not the Gospel help thee to accomplish, then nothing would be impossible for thee! [58]

Silence is the language of reverence and worship, the only language man may address to God: in His presence every mouth is stopped. And it is only before God, for whose omnipotence all things are possible, that man receives his heritage and enjoys the satisfaction of his creaturely longings. What the freedom of man can wish for only the power of God can supply.

But the Gospel immediately adds to silence, *obedience*. No man can serve two masters, God and mammon; therefore seek first God's kingdom and his righteousness. The lily and the bird are absolutely care-free because they are absolutely obedient to God. Man alone is subjected to the self-destroying cares of reckoning, deliberating, and choosing. But if the mute creation is of necessity obedient to its Creator, then

> thou mightest also succeed in making a virtue of necessity. Thou too art subjected to necessity; God's will is done nevertheless, so strive to make a virtue of necessity by submitting with absolute obedience to God's will. . . .

Perhaps the lily was cut down by the scythe in the very instant that, obedient to the Lord of nature, it unfolded to the sun. Yet it was "absolutely obedient . . . , it became actually its whole possibility, undisturbed, absolutely undisturbed. . . ." So in submitting his freedom to the discipline of obedience taught by the lilies and the birds the believer may "embrace the instant,

237

absolutely undisturbed by the next instant" and become without ambiguity of self-will "mere simplicity before God." In the simple present action of unconditional obedience, the man of faith serves the one Master and is given the beauty and the freedom from care which he can attain in no other way. The service of God—the "solemn divine service" of obedience—is perfect freedom. [59]

The issue of silence and obedience is *joy*. The grass of the field "today is," and to him who seeks the kingdom and the righteousness of God in silence and obedience even this shall be added, that *he* today *is*. This presence to himself of the true believer is unconditional joy, the perfect repose of the soul in Him who is immutably at rest in Himself.

> What is joy? or what is it to be joyful? It is to be present to oneself; but to be truly present to oneself is this thing of 'today', that is, this thing of *being* today, of truly *being today*. And in the same degree that it is more true that *thou* art today, in the same degree that thou art quite present to thyself in being today, in that very same degree is the baleful tomorrow non-existent for thee. Joy is the present tense, with the whole emphasis upon the *present*. Therefore it is that God is blessed, who eternally says, Today.

The Christian's joy is rooted in the eternal presence of God. Only the contemporary of God is contemporary with himself. But this joy is also the fruit of the believer's silence and obedience in the divine presence:

> There is a today. Upon the word '*is*' there falls an infinite emphasis. There is a today—and again, there is no concern at all for the morrow or for the day after. This is not frivolity on the part of the lilies and the birds, but it is the joy of silence and obedience. For when thou dost hold thy peace in the solemn silence which prevails in nature, the morrow is non-existent; and when thou dost obey as the creatures obey, the morrow is nonexistent—that baleful day which is the invention of chattering and disobedience. But when by reason of silence and obedience the morrow is non-existent, today is, it *is*—and then there is joy, as there is in the lilies and the birds.

The eternal presence of God, and the believer's worshipful and obedient silence before Him: these are not two, but one and the same. For silence and obedience are the Christian's participation in the divine repose, his joy is the *unio caritatis*. What is usually called "living for the moment" is in truth distractedness and dissipation; the *today* of silence, obedience, and joy is a "'collectedness'" possible only to the faithful who cast "all care absolutely . . . upon God."[60]

Kierkegaard's discourse concludes with an imaginative exegesis of the doxology of the Lord's prayer: for thine is the kingdom, and the power, and the glory, forever. The allusion with which he illustrates this analysis reminds the Christian that he is called to contemporaneity with an abject and crucified God, while the doxology itself points to the glory that is pledged to be revealed in him:

> Only hold fast therefore to this, that His is the kingdom and the power and the glory in eternity, and thus for thee there is a day which never comes to an end, a day in which thou canst remain eternally present to thyself. . . . Consider what applies to thee, if not as a man, at least as a Christian, that even the danger of death is for thee so unimportant that it is said, 'Even now today art thou in Paradise,' and thus the transition from time to eternity (the greatest possible transition) is so swift—and though it were to occur in the midst of universal destruction, it is yet so swift that thou even now today art in Paradise, for the fact that thou dost Christianly *remain* in God. For if thou dost remain in God, then whether thou dost live or die, and whether it goes well with thee or ill whilst thou livest, whether thou diest today or only after seventy years, or whether thou findest thy death at the bottom of the sea where it is deepest, or thou art scattered in the air—thou dost not find thyself outside of God, thou *remainest*, and so thou remainest present to thyself in God, and art therefore at the day of thy death even now today in Paradise.[61]

Without irony the silence, obedience, and joy of the Christian believer recapitulate this side of the Incarnation the silence of Father Abraham, his unconditional obedience to the divine command, and his joy at receiving Isaac again by the new provision of Mt. Moriah. No longer the "unhappiest man" lost in recollection and anticipation, nor the ethical man straining to pull past and future together in resolution, nor the religious man with his Now drained into eternity, the contemporary of Christ who seeks not himself but "God's kingdom and his righteousness" dwells in the power and the glory of the presence of that kingdom, its everlasting Today.

But it is the consciousness of sin and that alone through

which a man may enter into Christianity. The Paradox of Christ—that tormented manhood that nevertheless enjoyed the consubstantial presence of the Father—is the Pattern for the life of the believer, and that life is, for all its joy, a *Via crucis*. The Way of the Cross—*imitatio Christi*—extends until the eschaton, in the hope of a blessedness beyond time and existence and man's ability to conceive, a Resurrection whose reality rests inscrutably in the depths of the divine power and love, a depth which not even faith can fathom, and about which therefore both Kierkegaard and his pseudonyms are silent.

6
A KIND OF POET...

"Every divinity student" would presumably be able to furnish the information that the Christianity of Anti-Climacus is incomplete and tendentious. Its substitution of absurdity for mystery draws a Nestorian cloud over the Incarnation and darkens the understanding of Sacrament. Anti-Climacus' compulsion for a contemporaneity that leaps the centuries all but pushes the history out of sacred history; not the historical Jesus but the historicity of Jesus becomes the sting of the Christian Paradox. The eternal presence of Christ, which makes contemporaneity possible, renders the Church of Christ and all but the barest bones of Scripture embarrassingly superfluous.[1]

The critique can be made yet more devastating. It can be argued that the problem of becoming a Christian, as defined by Anti-Climacus and his lesser brother Climacus, is wholly artificial. No one can doubt that mystery and miracle are essential to Christianity, that the revelation of God calls for a mode of acceptance quite out of the ordinary, and that this very acceptance is a work of grace. But the Kierkegaardian Christian is crippled at the outset by the presumption of an absolute

241

opposition between time and eternity, truths of reason and truths of fact;[2] he is deprived of the divine immanence implicit in the classical doctrine of creation and left with unapproachable transcendence; and he is invested with a depravity so total that it has altogether corroded the *imago Dei*. In the hands of Kierkegaard's pseudonyms the mystery and the miracle of Christianity have degenerated to contradiction and nonsense. Christianity has become not difficult to believe, but completely incredible.

Even belief in God, waiving the special difficulties imported by the Christian claim, is edged out of the domain of reason by the peculiar presuppositions of the Kierkegaardian dialectic. Classical Christian theology, beginning from a Platonic-Aristotelian notion of the intellect and a belief in the goodness of Creation, supposes reason initially illumined and reformed in believers by the light of special revelation dispelling the shadows of a fallen world. Kierkegaard's pseudonyms take their concept of reason from Hegel, an all-comprehending and all-creating reason that brooks no object distinct from itself; post-Scholastic and ultra-voluntarist, they presume no "general revelation"; in a fine Protestant frenzy they credit original sin with power to nullify whatever natural awareness of God the Creation might have established in the sons of Adam. It is for this reason that Climacus gives short shrift to the proofs of God and discounts the possibility of any positive natural theology. And it is for this reason that Anti-Climacus sees no plausible alternative to offense in the encounter of man with God.

Such are the objections that might be brought against the partisan and unnecessary artificiality of the presentation of Christianity in the Kierkegaardian literature. A number of defenses might be made, and some of them have been made by the Kierkegaardian rescue corps. It has been observed, for example, that in the *Fragments* Climacus develops Christian definitions hypothetically by taking minimal exception to the idealist understanding of Socrates. This method of proceeding, justified by the pedagogic purpose of the book, accounts for Climacus' emphasis on the absolute dichotomy between God and man, his recasting of hypostatic union as Absolute Paradox, and his omission of such theological staples as the Trinity and the sanctifying work of the Holy Spirit. On this view the Hegelian shape of his thinking is not a symptom of philosophical shortsightedness, but a tactic necessitated by his determination to meet idealism on its own anthropocentric ground and make it face up to the Christian opposition. In the same way one could warrant his defense of the "infinite qualitative difference" against all manner of mediation and his insistence on the sovereignty and majesty of a God who quite literally "needs no man." So also with Anti-Climacus' identification of human honesty and sincerity with the candid admission of offense and the confession of sin.

As against the appearance of excessive Protestantism in Kierkegaard's Christianity it has been noted that there is a deep strain of Catholicism and a correspondingly deep critique of Lutheranism running through his later works. It is going too far to say that he was a latent Catholic, or that he might have become a Catholic openly had he lived longer. But there is no questioning Anti-Climacus' disdain for the abuses of *sola fide* in Denmark, and there is no mistaking the medieval character of his demand for an imitation of Christ. His distinction of the Christian requirement from the Christian indulgence—on the one hand following Christ the Pattern, and on the other confessing sin and imploring forgiveness—reflects the traditional Catholic distinction between the *consilia* of perfection and the *praecepta* of the minimal Christian life. In his pseudonymous presentation of Christianity, as well as in his own late writings, Kierkegaard prepared an antidote for Protestantism which often incorporated elements of the Catholic heritage.

There is justice in these defenses, and in the many others like them that may be imagined. They take Kierkegaard and his pseudonyms seriously, and treat them all as honest and sober men. But the fact remains that Kierkegaardian Christianity is imbalanced and excessive. And the decisive fact, still outstanding, is that Kierkegaard knew it and meant it that way. To all such friendly apologetics, as well as to all the proper protests of his accusers, Kierkegaard would reply that *Training in Christianity*, *Fear and Trembling*, the *Fragments*, the *Postscript*, and all the rest were but "correctives" recommended to the complacent debility of "the present age."[3]

The works of Anti-Climacus in particular are a volley of thoughts that wound from behind, aimed at "revival and increase of inwardness"[4] among Christians, not at a theological synthesis for the benefit of the professors of Christianity. Theologians may doubt the apologetic wisdom of mounting Calvary in Tivoli

Gardens to shock the merrymakers, but Anti-Climacus will excuse his loud insistence on the Crucifixion and his casual suppression of the Resurrection by reference to his incendiary purpose. His aim is not to present Christianity as if it were a reasonable doctrine. The history of theology and of Biblical scholarship reveal that not even the meaning of Christianity can be determined by the techniques of objectivity; the very content of the Christian's belief is given with his decision to believe. What Anti-Climacus writes is not theology or criticism, but rhetoric designed to introduce his reader into the presence of the "sign of contradiction" and to evoke a decision. When it is a question, not of introducing Christianity to pagans, but of reintroducing Christianity in all its majesty and terror to self-assured matter-of-fact mass-produced Christians who have waxed overconfident in their possession of this great treasure, then only the shock of contradiction will do.

In a passage of his *Postscript* Johannes Climacus explains the "plan of the *Fragments*," and in particular his reasons for choosing a point of departure in the pagan consciousness. What he says could as well be said, *mutatis mutandis*, by Anti-Climacus of his own works. The "piece," he writes, "was not doctrinal but experimental," because its problem was not "logical" but "pathetic" and "existential." Men have become so philosophical that they have almost, in their speculative enthusiasm, ceased to be men. A magic spell is needed to turn them from pure Egos back into human beings before they can appreciate the "existential communication" of Christianity. The *Fragments* was to be this "powerful formula of incantation."

Corresponding to the degeneration of the subject, there has been a softening of the concepts of Christian dogmatics by philosophical speculation; for example, the careless use of the concept of "reconciliation" or "mediation" in logic. The *Fragments* endeavored to put muscle back into these notions, so that the human intellect and will might have something to try their teeth on. Christianity has become use and wont; the *Fragments* restored its shock value in order that it might be treated with the respect it merits, even though that respect take the form of offense. A case in point is the reduction of the sacrament of Baptism to an operation performed indiscriminately upon all infants and assumed to be mechanically effective. Trivialized in this way, *ex opere operato* suggests that the passionate personal appropriation of faith is in bad taste and out of order in a Christian society. If it is difficult to become a Christian when one is a pagan, it is virtually impossible if one is already a guaranteed Christian, whether by birth or by rubber-stamp rebirth. Therefore the *Fragments* began with the contrast between pagan and Christian, in order to make the demand and the promise of Christianity stand out from the mediocre piety of the age and show men what they were missing.

> Under such circumstances in Christendom . . . it becomes more and more difficult to find a point of departure, when it is desired to determine what Christianity is. . . . For this reason I had recourse to paganism, and to Greece as the representative of the intellectual, and to Socrates as its greatest hero. After thus having made sure of paganism *I sought to find as decisive a difference as possible. Whether the content of the experiment really was Christianity is another question.* . . .

Climacus meant to delineate Christianity as decisively as possible, not necessarily as accurately as possible, and certainly not as moderately as possible. The problem is not doctrinal but personal, and Climacus' presentation is therefore not theological radicalism or fundamentalism. Rather it is informed by a rhetoric of awakening, designed not to improve doctrine but to stun men into a salutary awareness of the absolute claim of Christianity and to remind them of their own defection from this claim.

After the crisis of guilt that Climacus discovers on his climb to Religion A, from which he animadverts into humor, Christianity with its message of forgiveness comes as something of an anti-climax. But it is a let-down only too eagerly desired by those naturalized Christians who crave no salvation more strenuous than confirmation in their own insouciance. And so Anti-Climacus, like Climacus, has a double purpose: in part to "explain what Christianity is," but in greater part to make it "difficult to become a Christian." And since the latter is the major—because personally decisive—issue, "the only possible introduction must be a repellent one, thus precisely calling attention to the absolute decision."[5]

In other words, Anti-Climacus is a pseudonymous *persona*. He is that "ideal Christian" that never was and never will be. From the aerie of his faith he perceives that what he administers is not the Christianity of the New Testament *toute entière,* but an attack on a Christendom grown prosperously fat and philosophically flatulent. Apropos the publication of *The Sickness Unto Death,* by Anti-Climacus, Kierkegaard wrote in his journal this reflection on the newly created pseudonym:

> Like the river Guadalquivir . . . which at one point plunges underground, so there is a stretch (the devotional) which bears my name. There is something lower (the aesthetic), which is pseudonymous, and something higher, which also is pseudonymous because my personality does not correspond to it.
>
> The pseudonym is called Johannes Anti-Climacus in contrast to Johannes Climacus who said he was not a Christian. Anti-Climacus is the opposite extreme, being a Christian in an extraordinary degree. . . .[6]

Accordingly the Preface to *Training in Christianity* by the "editor," S. Kierkegaard, warns that in "this little book . . . , the requirement for being a Christian is strained by the pseudonym to the highest degree of reality."[7] Kierkegaard's introduction to Christianity via Anti-Climacus is deliberately artificial ("to show that I do not proclaim myself to be an exceptional Christian") and without authority ("to denote that I do not lay others under an obligation, or judge them").[8] Kierkegaard was not always able to make in his own person the distinction between poet and apostle[9]; to his own discredit he forgot it in the broadsides that he nailed to the doors of the Establishment in his last days.[10] But Anti-Climacus is clear: this is not the New Reformation, it is an outrageous exaggeration "for edification and awakening."[11]

The pseudonymous extravagance of Anti-Climacus forces into the foreground the problem of hermeneutics. Every reader of Kierkegaard's works knows that he declares them to be "indirect communications"; yet it is by no means patent what the indirectness consists in and what it communicates. It is easy to see what direct communication might be. A man with knowledge of certain realities forms concepts that are the mental symbols of those realities, and expresses what he thinks by means of words which are the spoken or written signs of his concepts. When a hearer or reader apprehends the verbal symbols, translates them into the concepts they stand for, and these in turn into the realities signified, the process is complete. The communication is direct because both communicator and recipient are capable of the same knowledge of the same realities, and in order to share that knowledge need avail themselves only of symbolic vehicles the being of which is exclusively their translucence to the tenor of the knowledge in question. The direct route from mind to mind is a segment of that larger communion in which minds are bound to each other within the intelligible totality of being. [12]

The centrality of freedom in "human nature" and in Kierkegaard's "message"—the freedom that sets both these classical entities in scarequotes—riddles the totality and intelligibility of being, dismembers the community of men with each other and the cosmos, and deflects all existential discourse into the detour of indirection. Pseudonymity is the most striking of the devices by which this diaspora is acknowledged in Kierkegaard's writings.

Kierkegaard's misbegotten attempt to deceive Regine about his real character should not be confused with his literary employment of pseudonyms. A Kierkegaardian pseudonym is a *persona,* an imaginary person created by the author for artistic purposes, not a *nom de plume,* a fictitious name used to protect his personal identity from the threats and embarrassments of publicity. When Kierkegaard signed his books with impossible names like Johannes de Silentio (John of Silence) and Vigilius Haufniensis (Watchman of Copenhagen), no one in the gossipy little world of Danish letters had any doubt about their origin. Nor did he mean they should; his purpose was not mystification but distance. By refusing to answer for his writings he detached them from his personality so as to let their form protect the freedom that was their theme.

The effects of this pseudonymity are many and subtle. At the first level of analysis the attribution of the works to representative characters permits these spokesmen of the existence-spheres a liberty they would not have as expressions of the opinions of Kierkegaard. Sometimes Kierkegaard opposed his pseudonymity to the direct utterance in which Hegel communicated his philosophical system; as against Hegel, he had no philosophy of his own to offer, only a warning against system (which could hardly be delivered in systematic form) and a reminder that "subjectivity is truth, subjectivity is reality" [13]

247

(which could hardly be propounded objectively and directly as a doctrine). In "A First and Last Declaration" which accompanied the *Postscript* Kierkegaard wrote:

> My pseudonymity or polynymity has not had a casual ground in my person . . . , but it has an *essential* ground in the character of the *production*, which for the sake of the lines ascribed to the authors and the psychologically varied distinctions of the individualities poetically required complete regardlessness in the direction of good and evil, of contrition and high spirits, of despair and presumption, of suffering and exultation, etc., which is bounded only ideally by psychological consistency, and which real actual persons in the actual moral limitations of reality dare not permit themselves to indulge in, nor could wish to.

As for the pseudonyms themselves,

> . . . their importance (be it *in reality* what it may) absolutely does not consist in making any new proposal, any unheard-of discovery, or in forming a new party, or wanting to go further, but, precisely on the contrary, consists in wanting to have no importance, in wanting (at a distance which is the remoteness of double reflection) to read solo the original text of the individual, human existence-relationship, the old text, well-known, handed down from the fathers—to read it through yet once more, if possible in a more heartfelt way.

On other occasions Kierkegaard contrasted his pseudonymous works with his own direct communications of the religious point of view:

> Therefore, whereas surely everyone who has felt the least concern about such things has as a matter of course hitherto regarded me as the author of the pseudonymous books . . . I, who after all must know best, am the only one that very doubtfully and ambiguously regards me as the author, for the reason that I am figuratively the author, whereas on the contrary I am quite literally the author of the Edifying Discourses, and of every word in them. [14]

The contrast within Kierkegaard's works between direct and pseudonymous writings is fully as important as the opposition between the pseudonyms of Kierkegaard and the professional ego of Hegel. From his early "aesthetic" writings Kierkegaard is altogether absent, and the pseudonyms are entirely on their own. To be sure Kierkegaard's name was listed on the Stationer's Register in Copenhagen, and he assumed full legal responsibility for the publication of *Either/Or, Repetition*, the *Stages*, and the rest. But he wanted to be sure that he was not held personally responsible for their contents. What is taken for granted in the case of an ordinary poet (that Shakespeare, for example, is not to be charged with the sins of Lady Macbeth) must be guaranteed by artifice in the case of a poetic philosopher or philosophical poet. [15]

In his middle and later works—chiefly *Philosophical Fragments, Concluding Unscientific Postscript, The Sickness Unto Death*, and *Training in Christianity*—Kierkegaard is visibly at hand on the title page, as "editor." By this designation he gave notice that he was both legally and morally accountable for the dissemination of the views expressed in these books. But the editorial mask, covering the proper person of the author, declares that Kierkegaard is still not speaking for himself. Only in two series of his publications (excluding the posthumous) did Kierkegaard take the role of author without qualification: the edifying discourses, and the pamphlet assault on the Established Church of Denmark. The former set forth without hint of artful dissemblance the religious convictions for which Kierkegaard felt he could give collateral in his own person. In the latter he sets himself as confessor and would-be martyr against what he took to be Babylon and its great whore: Christendom and the Church.

The presence in the Kierkegaardian corpus of these subclasses of direct communications is of crucial importance for his literary program. The direct writings provide the ultimate *what* and the ultimate *why* of the pseudonymous books, while these latter supply the *how*. The edifying discourses and the Christian witness define the religious end to which the aesthetic and philosophical works are the means. And conversely, the distinction between pseudonymous and direct writings establishes the independence of the poetic production. Because they can be opposed to the known intent of Kierkegaard, the works of the pseudonymous *personae* are protected against biographical and psychological snoopery. Neither symptoms nor simulacra of any living person, they stand by themselves and take their autonomous literary effect.

The difference between *personae* and persons is crucial: the pseudonyms are not mouthpieces through which Kierkegaard hopes to get a hearing for his views, but fictive personalities whose lives are poetically observed and reported. As the poet is silent in his poem, so Kierkegaard is silent in his books: "I always stand," he wrote, "in an altogether poetic relationship to my works, and I am, therefore, a pseudonym."[16] This is the second level of pseudonymity: the disappearance of the poet behind the *persona.* By contemplating his *persona* in the fulguration of possibility—infinitely ambiguous and dialectical—the poet guarantees the *persona* objectivity and himself the silence that seals that objectivity.[17]

Reviewing the pseudonymous production prior to his own *Fragments* Johannes Climacus twice avers that he is "only a reader" of these books, the authors of which he admires for the fact that they

> . . . have themselves said nothing, nor misused a preface to assume an official attitude toward the production, as if an author were in a purely legal sense the best interpreter of his own words; or as if it could help a reader that an author had intended this or that, if it was not realized; or as if it were certain that it was realized because the author himself says so in the preface; or as if an existential misdirection could be corrected by being brought to a finite decision, in the form of madness, suicide, and the like, which feminine authors are especially prone to, and that so quickly that they almost begin with it; or as if an author were served by having a reader who precisely because of the author's clumsiness knew all about the book.[18]

The relation between an author's person and his book should be mutual independence, and Kierkegaard took pains to see that he remained "external" and "indifferent" to his own works. His definitive statement merits extended quotation:

> What is written. . . is in fact mine, but only in so far as I put into the mouth of the poetically actual individuality whom I *produced,* his life-view expressed in audible lines. For my relation is even more external than that of a poet, who poetizes characters, and yet in the preface is himself the author. For I am impersonal in the second person, a *souffleur* who has poetically produced the *authors,* whose preface in turn is their own production, as are even their own names. So in the pseudonymous works there is not a single word which is mine, I have no opinion about these works except as a third person, no knowledge of their meaning except as a reader, not the remotest private relation to them, since such a

thing is impossible in the case of a doubly reflected communication. . . . So I am in a position of indifference: that is
to say, it is a matter of indifference what and how I am, precisely
because in its turn the question whether in my inmost man it is
indifferent to me what and how I am, is for this production
absolutely irrelevant. . . . From the beginning I perceived very
clearly and do still perceive that my personal reality is an
embarrassment which the pseudonyms with pathetic self-
assertion might wish to be rid of, the sooner the better, or to have
reduced to the least possible significance, and yet again with
ironic courtesy might wish to have in their company as a repellent
contrast. [19]

Thus Kierkegaard's pseudonymity first releases the creatures of
his imagination from their creator; and second, in order that they
may do their maieutic work unhampered, it diminishes his
personal identity as author toward the vanishing point.

Because the imagination is dialectically agile to traverse
possibilities without end, a third level of pseudonymity discovers itself: the distinction of poet and *persona* not only qualifies
the relation of Kierkegaard to his books, but is repeated and
complicated within the books themselves. [20]

Perhaps the exemplary instance of tangled pseudonyms is
Stages on Life's Way. "Collected, forwarded to the press and
published" by one Hilarius, a bookbinder, the *Stages* consists of
"studies by sundry persons." The papers of which it is composed
were left in Hilarius' shop, possibly but not certainly for
binding, by a "literatus" now dead. On his departed wife's
advice, which he followed meticulously in all things, Hilarius
used the manuscripts as handwriting models for his son to copy.
They are later discovered in this employment by a young
seminarist-poet-candidate in philosophy who is engaged as tutor
for Hilarius' boy. The seminarist supposes that the papers are
the work of a literary society of which the deceased literatus was
"caput or leader," and recommends to Hilarius that he publish
them—for which counsel he requires nothing but (in
"'consideration of the expected capital gain'") "'$10 down and a
half-pint of wine at dinner on Sundays and holidays.'" [21]

So Hilarius Bookbinder comes upon his manuscripts by an
elaborate concatenation of accidents, and resolves to use them for
what they are worth. The papers thus discovered and published
are attributed to three pseudonyms, each of whom carefully

shrouds his identity in yet greater mystery. The first division of the papers, *"In Vino Veritas,"* is a "recollection" *(Erindring)* "subsequently related" *(efterfortalt)* by William Afham. In his prefatory note *(Forerindring)* he credits his work to the poetic power of recollection, though, as we have seen, he almost admits ("I sometimes feel as though . . .") he has invented and not experienced the banquet he describes. [22] The participants in the banquet, each of whom speaks in his own person, are Johannes the Seducer, Victor Eremita, Constantin Constantius, an anonymous young man, and a *couturier.* William Afham does not give himself out as one of the party; for he is "something already passed (therefore 'a recollection')" who "cannot disappear entirely." [23] He is possibly but not definitely identical with the non-entity who, after the banquet, observes the party spying on Judge Wilhelm and his wife at morning coffee in their arbor, notices Victor Eremita's theft of a manuscript from the Assessor's house, steals the manuscript from Victor and determines to publish it himself. [24] The fact that his plans for publication were somehow thwarted (possibly by the dead "literatus") and inadvertently furthered by Hilarius merely confounds an already confused state of affairs.

The second part of the *Stages* is the manuscript stolen by Victor Eremita, stolen again by William Afham, and finally made public by Hilarius Bookbinder. "Various Observations about Marriage in Reply to Objections" is by "a Married Man," [25] who does not reveal his identity, though it is clear from the end of the preceding section that he must be Judge Wilhelm. William Afham has a way of writing the works he claims only to publish, but apart from that (and the unexplained intervention of Hilarius and the literatus) Judge Wilhelm's authorship of the "Observations" is uncontested.

The third and by far the longest division of the *Stages,* "Guilty?/Not Guilty?", is described on the title page as "a psychological experiment" by Frater Taciturnus. In an "Advertisement" the quiet brother apprises the reader that he has discovered the manuscript of his "experiment" quite by chance. He had, it appears, accompanied a naturalist friend the previous summer on an exploratory expedition to Søeborg Lake. There, reclining in a rowboat and toying with his friend's marine equipment, he fished up from the bottom a rosewood box, wrapped in oilskin, sealed and locked with the key inside. Opened by force the box yielded a gold ring, sundry jewels and trinkets, other mementoes of a love affair and engagement—and the manuscript of Quidam's diary which Frater Taciturnus published as "Guilty?/Not Guilty?" At the end of this story, the Frater hints that he may have doctored the papers a bit by way of dating the entries in the diary:

> [O]ne might, for all I care, assume that a poor devil of a psychologist who can count upon but scanty sympathy for psychological experiments and unsubstantial constructions has made an attempt to give them both a little life by adding a touch of romanticism, the fiction that the thing belonged to a past age.

And he goes on to acknowledge, though with a reticence appropriate to his name and a vagueness proper to his doubtful identity, that merging of "psychological experiment" with poetry that we have earlier noted in the case of Constantin Constantius:

> For a sketch, however psychologically correct, which does not inquire whether such a person ever lived, is perhaps of less interest to our age, when even poetry has snatched at the expedient of trying to produce the effect of reality. A little psychology, a little so–called observation of real men they still want to have, but when this science or art follows its own devices, when it looks away from the manifold expressions of psychic states which reality offers, when it slips away in order by itself alone to construct an individuality by means of its own knowledge, and to find in this individuality an object for its observations, then many people grow weary. As a matter of fact, in real life passions, psychic states, etc., are only carried to a certain point. This too delights the psychologist, but he has a different sort of delight in seeing passion carried to its utmost limits.

To the story of Quidam's unhappy love Frater Taciturnus appends an "Epistle to the Reader" in which he openly confesses that he has invented Quidam and composed his diary in order to illustrate the religious life by means of a demonic approximation to it. A psychological experiment is a "thought–experiment," and the experimenter himself an "enthusiast for the understanding" who comprehends the meaning of religion without being religious. His dwelling-place, he adds, is in "the metaphysical," the neverland which, it will be recalled, is also the home of poets. Like all poets the Frater tends to multiply the possibilities of himself in his creations, and conversely to model himself after the shape of his creatures:

253

> The reader who is acquainted with the little book by Constantin Constantius will perceive that I resemble in a way that author but yet am very different, and he who experiments ought always to fashion himself in conformity with the experiment.

Frater Taciturnus and his "subject" begin to blend, and as the edges of their figures blur so their corporate identity grows ever vaguer. At last the meaningful non-name Quidam (Someone) stands simply for man, faced with the possibility and the need of religion but suspended in indecision at the moment of God's approach. The quiet brother finally defines himself as a sophist who sees the religious and forbears to enact it: "The religious man, according to my view, is the wise man. . . . I see the religious on all sides, but what makes me a sophist is that I do not become a religious man. The least in the sphere of religion is greater than the greatest sophist." Certain that he has held no reader to the last, Frater Taciturnus ends as a monologist who uses his "wit" and "reflection" in the service of religion lest the gods deprive him of that little he has.[26]

But it is typical of Kierkegaard to throw the problem of every book back on the reader and so Frater Taciturnus allows some imaginary "countrymen" to conclude his book by damning him, along with all poets, as "the most dangerous sort of seducer" and warning all comers to "let him go for what he is, a scoffer and a fanatic *in uno*, a Philistine *in toto*, a deceiver, the pure negation." And this, as the Frater suggests with his last words, not only comments ironically on his countrymen and throws Br'er Rabbit back into the briar patch; it also puts every man in his proper place:

> Ah, what luck that there is no reader who reads the whole thing through! And if so be, the injury done a man by leaving him to shift for himself, when that is the only thing he wishes, is like the Wise Men of Gotham punishing the eel by throwing it into the water. *Dixi.*[27]

The inclusion of pseudonym within pseudonym, and the superfetation of commentaries by pseudonyms upon pseudonyms, reproduces the dialectic of inner and outer that polarizes all human existence. Every inside has an outside, which in turn can become inside for yet another outside. Only God has no outside, for

> God is pure subjectivity, ideal, pure subjectivity; He has not a bit of objectivity in Him; for everything that has such objectivity falls into the domain of relativities. [28]

The lived subjectivity of a man is as inviolate as the transcendence of God. But inwardness imagined is only one possibility among others: in possibility everything is possible. No human perspective attains the absoluteness of pure subjectivity, not even the perspective of faith. Every human attitude is diffracted immediately into a host of relativities, for the literary presentation of which Kierkegaard's device of multiple interlocked pseudonyms was the happiest available instrument.

In sum: the use of pseudonyms first severs Kierkegaard's *personae* from Kierkegaard. At the second level pseudonymity obliterates Kierkegaard the poet. Finally the identities of the pseudonyms themselves are so scrambled that they become masks without faces, their works self-standing objects unbuttressed by human subjects. The blank calling card inserted in *Repetition*, the concluding exordium of *Either/Or* ("Only the truth which edifies is truth for you"), [29] and like hints in the other books, direct the reader to supply the necessary personal identity: his own. So the form of Kierkegaard's writings insinuates their content: subjectivity, inwardness, the passionate appropriation of objective uncertainty, is the only truth possible for an existing individual.

But for all the weight it pulls in Kierkegaard's practice, pseudonymity as such is only a gambit, a powerful but not isolated tactic in the overall strategy of indirect communication. It is the principal though not the only *species Kierkegaardiana* of the genus image. Billeskov Jansen accounts imagistic thinking the chief formal characteristic of the writings: "Kierkegaard felt a manifest satisfaction . . . when he could unite an idea and a figure. Kierkegaard thought in types; therefore he became both poet and philosopher." In all of Kierkegaard's writings, he points out, there is a union of concept and image. But while the image (especially the *persona*) bears the major burden in the "aesthetic" works, it is the conceptual problem that is to the fore in the "philosophic" writings. [30] Compare the intricate web of pseudonyms, whose figural interrelations are the whole point of *Either/Or* and the *Stages*, with the monotonic pseudonymity of

Climacus' *Fragments* and *Postscript.* Yet even in these latter the image is not absent: the fable of the king and the maiden in the *Fragments* is image inflated to myth; in the *Postscript* the asides on Lessing, the story of the conversion of Dr. Hartspring with its inversion in Climacus' experience, and the author's not-so-charismatic moment in the garden of the dead are only more obvious instances of the many images with which these works are laced.

But it is not the mere *presence* of images that counts; what matters is that the images are internal to the meaning of the books in which they appear. Lessing's reticence about his God-relationship demonstrates as coercively as any syllogism that subjectivity is truth. The garden of the dead, reflected in the eyes of a humorist, is irrefutable proof of the equality and equal solitude of individuals before God. The interlocutor of the *Fragments* is the ironic foil without whom that book would be, in "unmixed earnest," the most tiresome and pedestrian piece of routine apologetics.[31] In defense of the "aesthetic validity of marriage" and the salutary effect of matrimony on the beauty of woman, Judge Wilhelm offers literary equivalents of those genre pictures of hearth and home which so confirmed the bourgeoisie of the nineteenth century in the rightness of their ascendancy. Anti-Climacus develops the logic of offense in a series of thumbnail sketches that present, in their reaction to the Christ, the philosopher, the churchman of the Establishment, the solid citizen, the statesman, the mocker, and a handful of the "wise and prudent." The anachronism of these figures—that they are more Danish and nineteenth century than they are Galilean and first century A.D.—only drives home more effectively Anti-Climacus' point about contemporaneity.

Even the stark dialectic of the *Edifying Discourses* is advanced in the main by similes and epic images drawn from the common life of "my listener."[32] The Jutland priest draws the edification of total guilt out of a tale of unhappy love. Images of shifting prosperity and adversity reflect the immutable Father of Lights from whom comes every good and perfect gift. The acquisition and possession of one's soul in patience is meticulously contrasted with the anxious and uncertain ownership of worldly "goods." Images that appear but briefly in the gospels—the bread and the fish, the lilies and the birds, the woman who was a sinner—are in Kierkegaard's discourses time and again elaborated into figural proofs of the greatness of God, the littleness of man, and their perfect reciprocity in the religious life.

The pervasiveness of *argumentum ad imaginem* in Kierkegaard's works, especially in the religious discourses, has metaphysical and theological implications. Image, simile, fable, and myth constitute demonstrations only in a world that is itself organized exemplaristically. If human affairs can stand for divine things, if the relation of man to beast can represent the relation of God to man, then the universe, from the highest angel to the lowest creature, is a hierarchic chain of proportioned images of the Divine Original. When Kierkegaard argues analogically in the logical and poetic sense, he also argues analogically in the metaphysical sense of *analogia entis.*

Such notions would seem to be out of bounds for a man who thinks of God as the Wholly Other exceeding human thought and imagination. But that is to take too literally the statements of one pseudonym, a humorist at that, and to ignore the cautions and correctives which he and his brothers strew about their devious paths. The edifying discourses make clear Kierkegaard's belief that God can be experienced inwardly even though that experience cannot find adequate representation in public symbols. When the symbols are used, therefore, they are accompanied by a warning to the reader: Do not be deceived, no finite image can contain God; if you would estimate the worth of this figure, first divide it by infinity, for the pattern is true but the scale immeasurably small. In particular Kierkegaard and his pseudonyms call attention to the fact that all differences within the created world—between man and man, man and beast, the king and the maiden, and so on—are relative and quantitative differences, whereas the difference between God and the world is an absolute and qualitative difference.

But the best warning of all is internal to the image itself. The negative, in earthly and human relations, is the sign of the positive, in matters heavenly and godly: the fact that he suffers signifies to the religious man that God loves him. Therefore, when he uses an earthly or human image to represent a heavenly or godly reality, Kierkegaard characteristically inverts the normal structure of the image. The love of the king for the maiden is not the beginning of a Cinderella myth that ends with the elevation of the maiden to royal magnificence; in Climacus' hands it preludes the humiliation of God turned suffering servant. Prosperity and adversity are leveled, their ordinary values upended or interchanged. Knowledge is made the off-spring of doubt, and protestations of innocence become proof of guilt, as the imagery of Kierkegaard's discourses unfolds. Folk sayings, the *bons mots* of current common sense, even the language and narrative of Holy Scripture, are invested with a significance far distant from and often hostile to their ordinary acceptation. What Anti-Climacus does with "Come hither, all ye that labor . . ." is only one, albeit a startling, instance of Kierkegaard's way of recasting old images to serve new and radical purposes.

Aquinas remarks, paraphrasing the pseudo-Areopagite, that Holy Scripture fittingly expounds divine truth under the figure of less noble bodies. Not only are the things of God thereby protected from the unworthy; but men are kept from error, for "then it is clear that these things are not literal descriptions of divine truths, which might have been open to doubt had they been expressed under figure of nobler bodies." And moreover, since we know better what God is not than what He is, "similitudes drawn from things farthest away from God form within us a truer estimate that God is above whatsoever we may say or think of Him."[33] Kierkegaard chose his images from among lowly and common things, often the very figures found in Scripture, and revaluating them according to his peculiar version of *via remotionis*, came up with the topsy-turvy world of the *Discourses*.

But the recognition of such techniques still leaves the question of principle unanswered. To my knowledge the apparent contradiction between Kierkegaard's negative theology and his habit of thinking in images, similes, and analogies has never been officially noticed. But unless it is reconciled, it opens a gap between theory and practice that undermines Kierkegaard's whole program of "reduplicated" truth and "double reflection." I am convinced that the path to reconciliation lies not through a *univocal* conception of the *content* of Kierkegaard's statements, formed in accordance with some reader's notion of what a philosopher and Christian apologist ought to mean by the things he says. Reconciliation, however, may be accomplished if all of Kierkegaard's statements, taken as *formal* entities, are understood by reference to their situation within the organic wholes of the works in which they occur, and by reference to their location within the whole corpus. So understood, the statements that seem to assert (univocally) an exclusively negative theology become (analogically) formal constituents of Climacus' rhetoric in ridicule of Hegelian philosophical theology. They are themselves polemic images, or elements of the *persona*-image of the poor existing humorist trying vainly to find his way through the trackless maze of Absolute Knowledge.

The philosophical and theological propositions in Kierkegaard's writings may consistently be read as articulations of a formal totality. They are elements of style that contribute to the larger design of the individual works and the entire literature. And they can only be understood within the context of the formal significance of these larger designs, a significance that discloses itself to a comprehensive literary study but not to a purely logical analysis. The opposite procedure will not succeed: the literary techniques of Kierkegaard cannot be interpreted as devices for the expression of a content independently intelligible. Every attempt to isolate such a content leads either to the supression of ideas inconsistent with the scholar's image of Kierkegaard, or to the conclusion that Kierkegaard contradicted himself wildly and foolishly. Which would be the equivalent of, on the one hand, writing off Shakespeare's comedies on the grounds that he had a tragic view of human life, or on the other, inferring an inconsistency in Shakespeare from the differences between *Hamlet* and *Macbeth*. In Kierkegaard's works, as in the works of any literary artist, "content" is a dimension of "form," "form" is not an adventitious mechanism for the communication of a separate and shapeless "content." From first to last everything in the writings, including "content," is an element of form, which for that reason may stand on its own without the apology of inverted commas.

In a word, Kierkegaard is not a philosopher and theologian who puts up poetic advertisements to recommend his product. More Dante than Thomas Aquinas, he is a poet whose orientation is primarily philosophical and theological. His writing, even the most ostensibly theoretical, is not syllogistic but figural. The unity and consistency of his thought, not at all apparent to logical scrutiny, is a metaphoric unity.

By metaphor I mean a term or expression or system of expressions that groups plural meanings about some central

259

organizing principle. The principle may be stated (as in the case of simile) or left tacit (as in metaphor *stricte sic dictu*). It may be relatively abstract (like proportion or proportionality in Thomistic analogy) or relatively concrete (like the image). In Kierkegaard's case the principle responsible for metaphoric unity is most often the single *persona* representing a whole way of life. In any metaphor its multiple meanings must be consistent with the organizing principle of that figure, though they need not be consistent with or by the "laws of thought." For the so-called laws of thought are only the laws of one rather limited kind of thinking, traditionally but somewhat tendentiously called logic. In this regard, "logical" argument is taken to be a minimal or limiting case of metaphor, its "validity" a restricted form of analogical unity, explicit and abstract, never perfectly achieved but sometimes desirable and always desired by mathematical and quasi-mathematical forms of thought. A syllogism is (ideally) a metaphor all of whose terms are univocal and whose basis of comparison is univocally stateable. By contrast Kierkegaard's paradox is the supermaximal limiting case: the unimaginable metaphor traditionally employed by Christian poets and thinkers to articulate the mysteries of their faith. "The thinker without a paradox"—a philosopher who is not a poet?—"is like a lover without feeling: a paltry mediocrity." The difference between metaphor *beyond* imagination (mystery) and metaphor that breaks *against* the imagination (paradox) is a function of the different contexts, classical-realist and Hegelian-idealist, within which the ancients and Kierkegaard respectively assert the Christian claim. His recognition of the ultimacy of metaphor (this side of Vision) makes Kierkegaard a poet; his recourse to *broken* metaphor makes him a "peculiar kind of poet."

A philosophical system, to the extent that it is couched in univocal terms, unambiguous propositions, and "strict inferences," is bound to its terms and to the law of contradiction. Metaphoric language at large, because it is fundamentally analogical, contains diversity within itself: its terms admit of many senses, and its propositions interact in ways not open to the statements of logical discourse. The difference between them may be a matter of degree, since logical purity is an ideal and not a fact, but it is nonetheless notable. Logical unity is strict and for that reason relatively barren: $-(A.-A)$. Metaphoric unity is multivalent and for that reason incomparably richer: "O rose, thou art sick. . . ." Modern philosophers by and large have preferred to follow the thin thread of logic, in emulation of the great precision and slight compass of scientific discourse. Kierkegaard, whose aim was the communication of subjectivity, had to become a poet. Human existence has unity, but it is not the unity of logic, and for that reason "what it means to exist" cannot be said in the language of a world-view conceived and expressed in syllogistic terms. The unity of human life is an analogical unity, which can only be represented by the unity of artistic form. [34]

The metaphoric structure of the works and their parts is our only guide to the world they image and the truth they convey. There is some truth to be found in the mouth of each of the pseudonyms. In a sense the whole truth, as Kierkegaard understood it, is found in each of the works. But it is seen in each from a different point of view, and for that reason is not truth simply, but truth plus the distortion of partiality: A, Judge Wilhelm, Climacus, and the Kierkegaard of the discourses all understand religion, but each of them comes to it from his own preoccupations under the impetus of his own ruling passion. Truth of a sort everywhere, but truth absolute, *sub specie aeternitatis,* nowhere. Whatever truth and reality is imagined in the Kierkegaardian corpus must be sought in the internal organization of the several works and in the reciprocal limitation and reinforcement they offer each other. The epistemological and metaphysical extravaganzas of Johannes Climacus do not represent "the views of Kierkegaard." But neither, for all the sincerity with which they forward his religious purpose, do the edifying discourses of Magister Kierkegaard. The whole story about man and his world—it is a measure of Kierkegaard's greatness as a poet that he discerned and respected this fact—is larger and richer than even its optimum statement. The whole story, to the extent that Kierkegaard could tell it, is the metaphoric texture of that poetic anagoge he called his "literature."

It is not my purpose in this chapter or in this book to state once and for all *extensive* the unitary "meaning" of Kierkegaard's work. That would be impossible in any case, for the meaning of a poetic corpus is never exhausted. But it is possible to offer an example of the analogic structure that shapes and supports his writings. [35] The analogicity of one of his leading concepts is explicitly acknowledged by Kierkegaard, [36] and its contextual variations made the armature of an entire book. The book and the concept are both called "repetition." The motto chosen for his "experiment" by the pseudonymous author, Constantine Constantius, is from Philostratus' *Stories of Heroes:* "On wild trees the flowers are fragrant; on cultivated trees, the fruits."[37] Conformable with this division, the book itself has two sections, the first of which depicts the fragrant but unwholesome flowers of a "wild" (i.e., aesthetic) personality, while the second imagines the savory and nourishing fruits of the "cultivated" (i.e., ethically and religiously matured) individual. Both flowers and fruits are forms, inauthentic and authentic respectively, of repetition.

The young man who appears at the beginning of Part First is a potential poet, in actuality a virtuoso of recollection. Deeply in love, but temperamentally incapable of marriage, he cannot achieve repetition in the ethical sense—the lifelong day-to-day renewal of love in the medium of duty. The ethical way of life, here called simply "the universal," makes its appearance at the outset and continues to hover in the background of the narrative as a possibility which, though refused for good reason, nevertheless focuses and organizes the "exceptions" with which the book is principally concerned.

The young man is in love, but he can neither marry the girl nor honorably rid himself of her and regain his primal innocence. Constantine's proposal—that he deceive the girl into renouncing him as a rascal, by utilizing the services of a demimonde Constantine has engaged for the job—is a device for producing repetition in the sense of a recovery of immediacy. The proposal fails, not only because the youth lacks gall for such deceit, but more significantly because innocence once lost can never by regained by guile.

His confidence in himself as a practical aesthete (experimental psychologist) somewhat disturbed by the young man's failure, Constantine decides to try a repetition in his own person. He takes a trip to Berlin, hoping to repeat the pleasures of a former sojourn in the city. But Berlin, its haunts and habitants, has changed irremediably (his sometime bachelor landlord, for example, has taken a wife), and Constantine concludes that "there is no such thing as repetition." Not even his return to Copenhagen is a genuine repetition, for in his absence his servant has rearranged the living quarters to his master's immense chagrin. Constantine's account of the unhappy expedition to

Berlin incorporates two major digressions: one on the shadow-play of possibilities in which every man's life is cast; and the other on the farce, which by bringing together the ideal and the accidental, faithfully mirrors the random essence of actuality. The resources of cleverness are inadequate to discipline the fecklessness of chance and guarantee a repetition of past delights; or as Constantine puts it, life "takes back again" *(tager igjen)* "insistently and perfidiously all that it gave, without giving a repetition" *(Gjentagelse).* [38] So Part First ends, in resignation, with Constantine's apostrophe to the post-horn, symbol of transience, his farewell to youth, strength, and pleasure, and his invitation to death, the fulfillment of transience and perhaps the only repetition in the offing for one whose life is nullity.

To indicate, however, that the subject of the book is about to be taken up again, the title, *Repetition,* is repeated as the subtitle of Part Second. The supreme instance of repetition, passionately and longingly described in the young man's letters to Constantine, is Job, who took himself again from the hand of God after his probational torment. No Job, the young man is released from his predicament when his beloved betroths herself to another, and restores her first love to himself. Now happy in his devotion to "the Idea," he becomes in act what he always was in potency: a poet. Where cleverness and contriving failed, the power of God and the magnanimity of woman have succeeded in cultivating the fruits of a true repetition.

There are many ways of "taking oneself again," all linked together by the common proportionality that informs the self's varied relations to itself. The normal and normative version is the reduplication of the universal human in the individual person, through a lifetime of renewed commitment to the ideal. Below this norm stands the vain hope of innocence gone but not forgotten to redeem itself from the bondage of Adam, and the equally vain attempt of sophistication to reconstitute by intelligent design pleasures originally bestowed by fortune. Above the norm are the "justified exceptions": the poet who is recovered for the ideal by a default of the actual, and the religious man who is reconciled to himself by the grace of God. Within the narrow confines of his experiment, Constantine Constantius has exfoliated the diversity in unity of this most analogous of Kierkegaard's analogical notions. All by itself, *Repetition* is an epitome of the metaphoric unity of Kierkegaard's thought and of the poetic fusion of content and form in his literary practice.

The roster of his techniques establishes Kierkegaard's identity as a poetic thinker. But in order to understand him fully, we must pinpoint his *peculiar* poetic character. And to this end, it is necessary to survey the reasons why he chose to philosophize poetically. These reasons, already touched on above,[39] grow out of Kierkegaard's unique relationship to the modern philosophical tradition. Since Descartes philosophers have made two assumptions which are responsible for the methodological monotony of their thought, a monotony far more important and deep-rooted than the variety of doctrines. To wit: (1) philosophy must build on a presuppositionless foundation, and (2) such a foundation exists. Differences among modern systems of philosophy are largely the outcropping of different notions about the nature of this bedrock of experience. For rationalists, clear and distinct ideas provide the foundation for philosophical thought; for empiricists, sense data; for Kant, a consciousness modelled *a priori* on the structure of scientific experiment; and for Hegel, the articulated totality of the developed self-consciousness of Absolute Spirit: the identity of Subject and Substance. Even contemporary existential philosophers, though they draw many of their problems, themes, and concerns from a reading of Kierkegaard, are the legitimate heirs, methodologically, of the Cartesian tradition. Jaspers' subject-matter is out of Kierkegaard and Nietzsche, but his architectonic is straight from Kant's critiques. Sartre and Heidegger by different ways go to Edmund Husserl, *Cartesius redivivus,* for their philosophical methods. In the hands of the early Heidegger the self-evident data of the phenomenologically reduced consciousness become the Being which, though drowned in the chatter of everyday and hidden beneath the minutiae of daily usages, is ever present and giving itself as it is in itself to the philosopher who has ears to hear and eyes to see. *Pour soi* and *en soi* (sometime "subject" and "object" purified and fortified by phenomenological tempering) are the supports from which the whole edifice of *Being and Nothingness* is suspended; at least as much of the old as of the new Descartes went into Sartre's construction.

From all these thinkers Kierkegaard differs in one crucial respect. While he agrees that systematic philosophy requires a presuppositionless starting-point, he denies categorically that such a starting point is available to the finite intellect. However internally rigorous, a man's thinking is always perspectival. It

264

exhibits the bias of a starting point which he has chosen out of a welter of genuine alternatives. No matter what premises he assumes for the purposes of his particular intellectual enterprise, there is always a potential infinity and an actual plurality of others. Because he is free, everything is possible to the thinker; because he is both free and finite, nothing is certain.

And thereby hangs his problem. For does not the ambiguous conjunction of freedom and finitude, that unsettles human existence and makes it impossible for a man to escape either the bonds of his situation or the implications of his liberty, poison the wells of philosophical reflection? In lieu of the Archimedean point, where shall the philosopher stand? The dearth of self-evident principles would seem to be for the philosopher a failure of the *conditio sine qua non.* So it would seem, at least, to a philosopher of the house and lineage of Descartes, for whom an indubitable starting-point would be an absolute prerequisite. And so it seemed to Kierkegaard, who agreed that absolute beginnings were needed but denied that they could be had. With respect to the *nature* of philosophy he follows the modern tradition, but he departs from that tradition on the question of the *possibility* of systematic speculation. And so he insisted that he was not a philosopher, for he could not be a philosopher in the sense understood both by himself and by his contemporaries. The list of his passages in mockery not of philosophy in general, not of the philosophers of Greece, and certainly not of Socrates, but of modern and especially German-inspired idealist speculation, would make up an index to his *Collected Works.*

In a fragment of dialogue quoted earlier, Socrates in Hades chides Hegel for "starting with nothing" and building thereon a system that ran to twenty-one volumes. [40] In view of the fourteen volumes of his own works and the eighteen volumes of journals, one might anticipate for Kierkegaard a like reprimand in the underworld. From a man who disallowed the very possibility of philosophy, one might have been justified in expecting silence. But the inconsistency is only apparent. And the key to its resolution is the recognition that Kierkegaard, for all his loquacity about matters philosophical, never wrote a word of systematic philosophy. In his Preface to *Two Discourses at the Communion on Friday,* which quotes the First and Last Declaration of the *Postscript,* Kierkegaard capsulizes his own purpose and practice in these words:

> . . . The author . . . calls himself . . . only a peculiar kind of
> poet or thinker, who "without authority" has nothing new to
> bring, but "would read through yet once more the original text of
> the individual human existence-relationship—the old, well-
> known, handed down from the fathers—if possible in a more
> heartfelt way."[41]

What this says is that in Kierkegaard *philosophy becomes poetry*.
Modern philosophers have always thought it possible to be
objective; that is, they have claimed to occupy an existentially
neutral standpoint, to view reality from the perspective of the
angels. Kierkegaard counters: every standpoint is in fact not
neutral but biased, not objective but subjective, not angelic but
human and finite. Philosophy as understood by the modern
tradition is impossible.

But that does not mean that all thought and all communication are impossible. One may still read the old and well-known
document, the existential heritage of every human being, and
read it now in a more heartfelt way than ever before. It was
Kierkegaard's belief that the possibility of honest human thinking and truthful human discourse first becomes apparent at this
dead-end of modern philosophical speculation. Johannes Climacus writes:

> In the world of the spirit the various stages are not like towns on a
> route of travel, which it is quite in order for the traveller to tell
> about directly. . . . Such a traveller changes places but not
> himself, and hence it is in order that he tells about it in the direct
> unaltered form, and thus *relates* the change. But in the world of
> spirit a change of place means a change in oneself, for which
> reason all direct assurances about having reached this or that stage
> are attempts *à la* Münchhausen. That a man has arrived at this or
> that distant place in the world of the spirit is proved by the mode
> of presentation itself. . . .[42]

Direct asseverations of a spiritual content, without the testimony
of an appropriate form, are the lying travelogues of an armchair
voyager. The passions of Othello and Lady Macbeth are guaranteed not by their speeches alone but by their actions also, and the
scenes in which their words are uttered. The plot, not thought or
diction, is the life and soul of tragedy. Only the "mode of
presentation" gives authenticity and authority to the spiritual
message. Content must find and merge with its proper form,

266

language must become gesture and symbolic action; where subjectivity is truth, truth like subjectivity must be plotted and dramatically enacted.

But the proper expression of subjective truth is not a simple disgorging of emotion. An earnest statement of his feelings and convictions, backed up by a pledge of sincerity, would not have been sufficient to communicate what Kierkegaard called "inwardness":

> Inwardness cannot be directly communicated, for its direct expression is precisely externality, its direction being outward, not inward. The direct expression of inwardness is no proof of its presence; the direct effusion of feeling does not prove its possession, but the tension of the contrasting form is the measure of the intensity of inwardness. [43]

To Kierkegaard, still inundated by the backwash of *Sturm und Drang,* the "tension of contrasting form" seemed like a paradox: that poetry, the most objective and disengaged form of utterance, should be the vehicle for the communication of subjective and passionately appropriated truths. But the "objective correlative" is a commonplace of twentieth-century criticism, the clinical objectivity of Prufrock conveys an intensity of feeling and a conviction of reality that are only dissipated and attenuated by the rhetorical ragings of Allen Ginsberg. Kierkegaard had discovered, with little help and much hindrance from his contemporaries, that as all honest thinking is subjective, so all truthful communication takes place via the objectivity of indirect discourse. Which is to say that all humane speech is poetic.

All speech is poetic. There is of course a difference between poetic discourse and philosophic discourse in the usual sense of the terms. But it is not a difference in essence, only a difference in emphasis. Both poetry and philosophy use signs to embody and communicate meaning. The difference between poetry and philosophy is a function of the duality that is latent in every sign. Every sign has two dimensions: it is both a thing *(res)* itself and a significance *(signum);* as thing it reposes ontologically in itself, as significance it points beyond itself to its referent. Philosophy strives toward pure *theoria,* and so stresses the significance of its signs. Poetry aims at pure *poiesis,* and so looks upon the sign chiefly as thing. Yet neither poetry nor philosophy can afford to neglect the other dimension of signs, for all theoretic vision is communicated *via* things, and all things, including things made, signify. So Kierkegaard, who was a "kind of . . . thinker," had also to be a "kind of poet. . . ."

As "a kind of poet" Kierkegaard is perhaps the most extreme antiphilosopher of modern times, even more at odds with the tradition than those positivists and analysts who adopt, respectively, its rationalist and empiricist methods and merely restrict the range of its subject-matter. But it is also true that in parting company with modern philosophy, Kierkegaard rejoined the *philosophia perennis.* Alongside his vitriolic critique of German speculation must be set Kierkegaard's veneration for the Greeks, and in particular his devotion to Socrates, outranked only by his devotion to Christ. In antiquity and the Middle Ages philosophy was still poetic, since philosophy had not yet made the claim to absolute knowledge and poetry had not yet been consigned to the asylum of irrationality. Philosophers still "understood themselves in" their philosophizing, and they knew the art of indirect communication. [44] Witness the first and still the greatest philosophical writer of the West, who produced no treatises but only dialogues which serve the same purpose as Kierkegaard's poetry of inwardness: they deliver no ready-made wisdom, but admonish the reader to tend his own soul. Aristotle's high opinion of poetry and rhetoric is evident not only from his explicit praise of these disciplines, but even more from the tragic rhythm that imbues his own theoretical and practical philosophizing with the dark humor of mortality. [45] Plato's greatest follower, inspired by the Christian revelation and illumined by faith, instituted by precept and example a thousand years of preoccupation with and exploitation of the possibilities of symbolic thought. In everything, from the created world, which is the poetry of God, to human artifacts, poems of word or deed, St. Augustine and his successors saw a tissue of divinely ordained and empowered metaphors serviceable for wisdom and beatitude. Even the later scholastics, for all the hardening of their intellectual arteries, continued to think by figure and by analogy. They were sure of their Christian faith, but they never forgot that they had this truth on trust and not by sight; though it was occasionally criminal, it was never unintelligent, to harbor unorthodox notions.

But all that came to an end, and—with due allowance for the many subtleties here suppressed—modern philosophy entered the world with its demand for absolute truths expressed in simple and univocal terms. In a sense not altogether perverse it was William Ockham who, with his insistence on the utter univocity of the concept of being, first turned philosophy into prose. The effect of Ockham's razor was to cut away all analogical complexity from the realm of being and leave philosophers with nothing but the skeleton of logic on which to exercise their (now severely constrained if not emasculated) ingenuity. Ockham is in this sense the first modern philosopher, at least the legitimate grandfather of Descartes. Kierkegaard's rejection of the modern tradition is rooted in his recognition of the poverty of univocity. The apotheosis of univocity, made in the interests of canonizing scientific method and repudiating scholastic theology, had destroyed poetry along with theology and reduced philosophy to near-starvation. By refusing the demand for univocity, by turning philosophy into poetry, Kierkegaard was—to the extent that his powers and his situation permitted—reconverting it to its ancient form. He opposed the course of modern philosophy to the end that he might reinstate philosophy itself in its historic and poetic destiny. His own writings offer not ideas about the thing—certainly not clear and distinct ideas—but, through the resplendence of images and the refractions of indirect communication, a way to the thing itself.

This is the philosophic rationale for Kierkegaard's poetic program and procedure. But there was also a religious ground, as there was for everything he did. Niels Thulstrup has remarked that the central motif in the *Concluding Unscientific Postscript*, as in all Kierkegaard's works, is the doctrine of creation. This doctrine, which governs the biblical world-view, includes in the Kierkegaardian version three interrelated elements: the omnipotence of God, the freedom of man, and a stress upon the ethical-practical aspects of life rather than the cognitive-theoretical. God has made men free in order that his infinite creative will may be done in the finite created order. Man's task, therefore, is to do God's will in the world, a task he can only fulfill if he first "becomes himself" by getting his relationship to God in proper focus. In Kierkegaard's language, the infinite qualitative difference between Creator and creature is the "possibility-relation" that links divine omnipotence and human freedom and stretches human life from here to eternity into a "perpetual striving" after God.

A Kind of Poet . . .

In a journal entry of 1854 God's tolerance of wickedness and indifference is explained, classically enough, by analogy with the relationship of the poet to his works:

> My thought is this: God is like a poet. From this is to be explained the fact that he puts up with evil and all the nonsense and the wretchedness of insignificance and mediocrity etc. That is also the relation of a poet to his productions (which are also called his creations), he allows it to come forth. But just as one would be profoundly mistaken if one were to believe that what the individual persons in the poem said or did were the poet's personal opinion: so too one is mistaken if one supposes that what happens receives God's approbation simply by happening. Oh no, he has his own opinion. But poetically he allows everything possible to happen, he himself is present everywhere, looks on, continues to create poetically, in a sense impersonally, at the same time observant of everything, in another sense personally, marking the most terrible difference, the difference between good and evil, between willing as he wills and not willing as he wills etc. [46]

Johannes Climacus reverses the direction of the analogy so as to explain his own methods by reference to the creative activity of God. Scarcely hidden in his words is the suggestion that God (whose initials are alleged by some to be J. C.) may be, like Johannes Climacus, a bit of a humorist as well as a poet.

> For no anonymous author can more cunningly conceal himself, no practitioner of the maieutic art can more carefully withdraw himself from the direct relationship, than God. He is in the creation, and present everywhere in it, but directly He is not there; and only when the individual turns to his inner self, and hence only in the inwardness of self-activity, does he have his attention aroused, and is enabled to see God. . . . Nature is, indeed, the work of God, but only the handiwork is directly present, not God. Is not this to behave, in His relationship to the individual, like an elusive author who nowhere sets down his result in large type, or gives it to the reader beforehand in a preface?

God's motive, like that of Climacus himself, is respect for the freedom of men and for that truth which can only be formed in inwardness:

> And why is God elusive? Precisely because He is the truth, and by being elusive desires to keep men from error. . . . Nature, the

270

totality of created things, is the work of God. And yet God is not there; but within the individual man there is a possibility [*Mulighed*] (man is potentially [*efter sin Mulighed*] spirit) which is awakened in inwardness to become a God-relationship, and then it becomes possible to see God everywhere. . . . Is this not as if an author wrote one hundred and sixty-six folio volumes, and a reader read and read, just as people look and look at nature, but did not discover that the meaning of this tremendous literature lay in himself. . . .

It may seem to be arrogance when Climacus thus compares himself to God. But it may also be the mark of humble piety to cultivate that reticence which even God displays before the wills of his creatures.

> To communicate in this manner constitutes the most beautiful triumph of the resigned inwardness. And therefore no one is so resigned as God; for He communicates in creating, so as by creating to *give* independence over against Himself. The highest degree of resignation that a human being can reach is to acknowledge the given independence in every man, and after the measure of his ability do all that can in truth be done to help someone preserve it.

It is hardly possible to imagine a greater self-restraint than that shown by God on Calvary. Some teachers of religion, Climacus notes, cut a fine figure in the pulpit and in the tailor's shop; some have fat livings and some get slim pickings; and then "some teachers of religion are crucified—but the religion is quite the same." The fact is that a "direct relationship between one spiritual being and another, with respect to the essential truth, is unthinkable." Both God and Climacus, by keeping an elusive silence, merely respect this fact in relation to their respective creations. [47]

Elsewhere Johannes Climacus defines the humorist as a man who perceives the contradictions of existence, in particular the contradiction between actual and ideal, the real and the true, and laughs in sympathy with those who suffer these contradictions. He laughs in sympathy because he himself stands in the midst of existence and knows its smart, while the ironist laughs *at* existence from a standpoint above the conflict. The extent of Climacus' own humor is evident from his playful comparison of his and God's indirect methods of communication. No ironist

271

would make such a comparison; for his own quasi-divine transcendence is far too close to him, too serious a thing to be made a subject of jest. It is this circumstance which suggests that God himself may be something of a humorist who does not take his transcendence with too much gravity. An ironical God would never have created a world, for without a sense of humor how could he bear it? Or if he did create a world, he would doubtless enter it in the form of a man eighteen feet tall, or in "the figure of a very rare and tremendously large green bird, with a red beak, sitting in a tree on the mound, and perhaps even whistling in an unheard of manner,"[48] to make sure that the serious people of the world noticed his presence. But God, like Johannes Climacus and his subjective thinker, is too uplifted in divine jest for that sort of thing. According to the testimony of Holy Scripture and the Doctors of the Church, God created the world in play. By treating grave matters so lightly, Climacus—and *his* poet—are most piously and reverently imitating the ultimate Maker.

All poetic discourse is indirect: it conveys the most intensely subjective content by means of the most objective linguistic correlates of image, simile, and metaphor. Kierkegaardian communication is doubly indirect. For the philosophic and religious reasons just stated, it does not seek a one-to-one correlation of form and content nor vary its vehicle in direct proportion to its tenor. Subjective certainty is not induced by objectively self-evident axioms and rigorous deductions therefrom; earnestness is not expressed in solemn words and deep organ tones of rhetoric; God does not assume the form of a very large and powerful man; and so on. Herein lies the peculiar character of Kierkegaard's poetics. Feelings and thoughts can be adequately communicated by the first indirection of analogy. But when the content to be communicated is already poetic, when it involves, as Kierkegaard would say, a "reduplication" in itself, then its expression must be poetic at a second remove of obliquity. Such is the case with subjective truth. The special content that Kierkegaard desired to convey demanded the further indirection of the broken image, the distorted simile, and the metaphor whose logic has gone awry.

His idiosyncratic handling of imagery has already been briefly mentioned. It remains to survey the principal forms of distortion to which his language is subject: irony, humor, and parody. Billeskov Jansen has suggested that Kierkegaard's three stages on life's way may correspond to the three stages on Dante's way of salvation: Hell, Purgatory, and Heaven. There is no evidence in Kierkegaard's writings to suggest that he might have taken the *Commedia* as his literary model for the stages or the *Stages*. But the first and more incisive reaction to Billeskov Jansen's conjecture is that the analogy fails. For Kierkegaard's aesthete can always be saved and his Christian damned, while there is no release from Dante's strictly orthodox Inferno and no damnation to them that are in Christ eternally. Nevertheless the likeness is close enough to point up a typical Kierkegaardian gambit. He will elect, consciously or not, a familiar literary object as the model for one of his works, and then, by making a critical (though not always obvious) readjustment in its configuration, write what amounts to a parody on his model. The parody is not always satiric or whimsical in effect, but it invariably represents what is for Kierkegaard a closer approximation than its original to the existential truth, and the discovery of the parody can produce in his reader a shock that alerts him to radically different and radically Kierkegaardian modes of self-understanding. It may be, therefore, that the stages on life's way are Kierkegaard's rendition of the Christian's earthly and temporal pilgrimage, the sting of which, in opposition to Dante's excursion through the afterworld, is its anxious unfinality: no matter how desperately low you have sunk, no matter how sublimely high you may rise, take care! for your destiny is not yet decided.

In the earlier chapters of this book I have analyzed in some detail *Either/Or,* the first book in the official canon of Kierkegaard's "literature." That book, which I have called a novel, is obviously a deficient sort of novel, at least by traditional standards. [49] Kierkegaard was impressed by *Wilhelm Meister,* which he regarded as the one great universal novel, universal because it compassed all other literary forms in its vast ambit, and universally human because it was the record of a whole man. There is reason to believe that *Either/Or* is modelled on Goethe's masterwork. Like *Wilhelm Meister, Either/Or* was to be a *Bildungsroman,* a novel of the formation of human personality, unfolding and shaping the manifold potentialities of its protagonist, and exploiting all the Romantic conventions: the narrative, the letter, the aphorism, the essay, and the monologue.

But when Kierkegaard set about writing a *Bildungsroman*

273

there had to be some changes made. His view of human nature and in particular of human freedom necessitated a parodic imitation. For if each stage on life's way represents a radical self-choice from which there is no exit save by way of another equally radical choice of a radically different self, then it follows that there is no necessary continuity in human personality. And this breach of continuity—the transition from aesthetic to ethical, ethical to religious, or vice versa—cannot be represented unambiguously in fiction. The free election of an existential *possibility* cannot be exhibited without distortion in a fictional mode committed to the principle of the natural evolution of human *potentialities.* It must therefore be left out.

Either/Or is incomplete and necessarily so. It is unfinished and open-ended in the same way that man is infinite and always exposed to further possibilities. It has not one protagonist, but two, three, who-knows-how-many *personae,* none of whom is any sort of hero. Each *persona* stands for an existential option which he has taken up, and no author with superior insight evaluates his choice *vis-à-vis* those of the others. There is no narrative resolution of the stretto among A, Judge Wilhelm, the priest from Jutland, and all the real or putative others. Each is stuck fast in his own categories, by his own choice; none of them develops; their actions merely reiterate their choices. The novel in which they live is a *Bildungsroman,* but without *Bildung.* Kierkegaard has exaggerated the technical variety of the universal novel in such a way as to prevent its unity.

The parody was of course deliberate. And it was aggravated by the fact that Kierkegaard accompanied the publication of *Either/Or* (as he accompanied all his "aesthetic" works) with the publication of a set of edifying discourses, direct communications by which *in propria persona* he recommended his own preference for the religious life. He remarks that he offered the world edifying discourses in his right hand and aesthetic writings in his left; the world, taken in by the deception but hardly edified by it, grasped eagerly with its right hand what he offered with his left.

Yet even in the left hand there was edification if a man could find it where it lay. In lieu of the flowering personality of a clearly designated protagonist, *Either/Or* contained a number of obtuse indications that *Bildung* was to be sought, not in the novel but in its readers. The priest's last sentence alone—"Only the truth that edifies is truth for you"—should have alerted the perspicacious reader not to look for an account of normative human personality in the structure of the book, but to effect the reality of his own human person by the agency of his freedom. Yet the main point—the cardinal indirection—was the absence of any main point. The trick of *Either/Or* was to leave conspicuously undone what no book can possibly do—the concrete universal is a person, never a *persona*—in the hope that the reader might notice the omission and act accordingly.

The lack of plot thread in *Either/Or* is a necessary and integral part of the Goethe-parody. Kierkegaard's conviction of the all-decisiveness of freedom converts the *Bildungsroman,* leading its hero's potentialities through time to fulfillment in happy union with his preordained fate, into *Either/Or,* an ineluctable present alternative confronting not a novelistic *persona* but the reader himself. And it is this conviction, finding its adequate formal vehicle, that breaks up the spatial unity, telescopes the temporal continuity, and eliminates the plotted narrative of the traditional novel. [50]

Goethe, for whom Kierkegaard felt attraction and repulsion in equal measures, is never far from his mind or his works. Judge Wilhelm's essay in the *Stages* is critical of *Dichtung und Wahrheit,* but his letters in *Either/Or* II interpret sympathetically Goethe's *Wahlverwandtschaften,* the novel and more especially the notion. In accord with his own view that marriage is based in natural affection ("romantic love") and *aufgehoben* by choice into the realm of duty, the Assessor separates the *Wahl* from the *Verwandtschaften* and construes their dialectic with most un-Goethean results: only the election of freedom validates erotic affinities, by translating them into the sacred bond of Christian marriage. In the first volume of the same work and also in the *Stages* Johannes the Seducer makes sport of the elective affinities with his observation, against marriage, that "for every woman there is a corresponding seducer. Her good fortune consists in encountering precisely him." [51] It is appropriate that the name of Johannes' principal victim is Cordelia Wahl: the choice that issues from the heart; for it is, on his own admission, his heart's choice whom he destroys. This little skirmish between the Seducer and the Judge is the whole disjunction of *Either/Or* writ small: either the choice of the heart which is death, or the choice of freedom which is life and happiness.

275

One last and rather striking case, again involving Goethe, should suffice to demonstrate the parodic slant of Kierkegaard's style. *Die Leiden des jungen Werthers* provoked, as is well known, more than literary reactions from the youth of the day. Kierkegaard's works abound in rejections of suicide, especially suicide as a way out of an unhappy love affair. Most explicitly anti-Werther is *Repetition.* Like all of Kierkegaard's woeful protagonists, the youth of that book is not kept from his beloved by adamant parents, social inequity, or an inconvenient husband, but by an insuperable misunderstanding rooted in his spiritual disparity with the girl. He contemplates suicide, and in an original draft shoots himself. After Regine Olsen had announced her engagement to Fritz Schlegel, Kierkegaard devised the present ending, salvation by the magnanimity of woman. The young man neither kills himself nor becomes a man of faith, but takes himself again as the poet he always was. So the novel becomes a tragi-comic answer to Goethe's moribund hero. It displays the possibility of a religious exit from melancholy; in the case of Job, the burden of suffering is undertaken as guilt and lifted by the hand of God. But it concludes with a whimsical aesthetic recovery of innocence. As against suicide it offers both the new immediacy of faith and the mock immediacy of poetry. Werther lacked sufficient ethical resolve to become religious (saved by grace) and sufficient aesthetic buoyancy to ride the crest of the wave of fantasy (saved by the magnanimity of woman). Storm and stress is parodically displaced in *Repetition,* either by the superior levity of poetry or by the superior earnest of religion. [52]

But parody, though omnipresent in the Kierkegaardian corpus, is like pseudonymity only a special technique, one detail in a larger pattern of poetic distortion. Its import is expanded by a consideration of Kierkegaard's discussions of irony and humor. These modes of obliquity are said to be *confinia* bounding the stages on life's way, irony separating the aesthetic from the ethical, humor dividing the ethical from the religious. As such they open halfway houses to people in progress: the aesthete who is disenchanted with aestheticism but not yet gathered for ethical choice will look with ironic duplicity on his own life; the ethicist who is disabused of his moral self-confidence but not yet ready for religion will smile good-humoredly at his eagerness in well-doing. After their respective leaps have been made, the aesthete-turned-ethicist and the ethicist-become-religious will continue to wear irony and humor as incognitos in which to go among their erstwhile peers. Knowing the gulf that parts him from his former friends, the newly-arrived ethicist will hide his eternal validity under a bushel of irony when he addresses them. The religious man's converse with his ethical associates will take the form of a jest the humor of which dissembles his own suffering.

That irony may express ethical commitment, and humor, religious devotion, is explained in the *Postscript* by reference to the close association of jest and earnest in human existence:

> The relative difference which exists for the immediate conscious-ness between the comic and the tragic, vanishes in the doubly reflected consciousness where the difference becomes infinite, thereby positing their identity.

Should this Hegelian formulation leave the matter still some-what obscure, Climacus adds a plainer word: "What lies at the root of both the comic and the tragic . . . is the discrepancy, the contradiction, between the infinite and the finite, the eternal and that which becomes." The difference between comic and tragic becomes a matter of existential orientation supervening upon their essential identity:

> When viewed from a direction looking toward the Idea, the apprehension of the discrepancy is pathos; when viewed with the Idea behind one, the apprehension is comic. When the subjective existing thinker turns his face toward the Idea, his apprehension of the discrepancy is pathetic; when he turns his back to the Idea and lets this throw a light from behind over the same discrepancy, the apprehension is in terms of the comic.

An instance of this existential *double entendre* is the serio-comical character of time itself as the medium of existence:

> Existence itself, the act of existing, is a striving, and is both pathetic and comic in the same degree. It is pathetic because the striving is infinite; that is, it is directed toward the infinite, being an actualization of infinitude, a transformation which involves a self-contradiction. Viewed pathetically, a single second has infin-ite value; viewed comically, ten thousand years are but a trifle, like yesterday when it is gone.[53]

The duplicity of existence itself, plus the capacity of freedom to shift its interpretive bias, makes possible the duplicity of indirect communication.

Later in the *Postscript*, Climacus interrupts his meditation on religion to offer a genealogy of irony and humor. Comedy and tragedy, he repeats, have a common root in the contradictions of existence:

> The comical is present in every stage of life (only that the relative positions are different), for wherever there is life there is contradiction, and wherever there is contradiction, the comical is present. The tragic and the comic are the same, in so far as both are based on contradiction; but *the tragic is the suffering contradiction, the comical, the painless contradiction.*

The tragic sufferer is stuck in the contradictions of existence, and this is the source of his tragedy. Even though, as in the case of the traditional tragic hero, his suffering is meaningful at some social, moral or religious level of evaluation, the awareness of this meaning does not annul or abate his pain. Comedy, however, is "painless" because, in Climacus' words, the contradiction and the suffering it brings are "non-essential," "viewed as cancelled." While the tragedian evokes the contradictions of life in order to exploit their pathos, the "comic apprehension" has "in mind a way out, which is why the contradiction is painless." All humor is in one sense "sick," for the commonplaces of comedy are the universal loci of human pain: sex, religion, death. But the comic apprehension, from its superior stance, draws the teeth of contradiction and renders it harmlessly amusing.

Within the sphere of the comic Climacus makes a further distinction, between *being* comic and *perceiving* the comic.

> The law for the comical is quite simple: it exists wherever there is contradiction, and where the contradiction is painless because it is viewed as cancelled; for the comical does not indeed cancel the contradiction, but a legitimate comic apprehension can do so, otherwise it is not legitimate.

In formal Hegelian array, the comic object is the comic *an sich*, the comic apprehension is the comic *für sich*, and (one might project) a humorist like Climacus who makes jest of himself is the comic *an und für sich*. In any case it is the comic apprehension and not the butt of comedy with which Climacus is presently concerned.[54]

There are, subdividing once more, two modes in which the comic may be apprehended and expressed: irony and humor. Irony is the mode of comic apprehension which views the comic object from the standpoint of the ethical ideal. Humor views the object from the standpoint of religious experience. Both irony and humor experience, express, but immediately *revoke* the contradiction wherein the comic consists. They "call back" the contradiction to the perspective of a contemplative eternity. Apropos his own effort in the *Fragments* Climacus writes:

> The humoristic makes its appearance when the problem of the *Fragments,* "Can there be an historical point of departure for an eternal happiness?" is answered not with the yes or no of decision, but with a smile of sadness (this is the lyrical in humor), which means that both the aged individual's seventy years, and the almost stillborn child's half an hour of life, are too little to become decisive for an eternity. Just as one might voluptuously tuck one's head under the pillow and not give a fig for the whole world, so the humorist tucks himself away, with the aid of immanence, into the eternity of recollection behind him, and smiles with sadness at decision. The humorist does not indoctrinate immorality, far from it; he holds the moral in all honor, and does for his part all he can, and then again smiles at himself. But he is femininely in love with immanence, and recollection is his happy marriage, as recollection is also his happy longing. A humorist might very well conceive the notion, and also actually realize it, of working with greater zeal than anyone, of being as miserly with his time as a laborer on duty. But if this labor were to have the least significance in relation to the decision of an eternal happiness, he would smile. The temporal life is for him a fugitive episode having a very dubious significance; and in time it is only a foretaste of his happiness that he has his eternity assured behind him, by way of a recollection that takes him out of the temporal.[55]

Humor and irony, which is like humor in this respect, are therefore quasi-aesthetic devices because they (temporarily at least) hold the urgencies of temporal existence in abeyance and retreat by way of recollection to an anticipated eternity.

Their function within the Kierkegaardian schema of the stages reflects two aspects of the aesthetic character of irony and humor. As moments of suspension between two spheres of existence, they are aesthetic in the sense of uncommitted. They are essentially *confinia*—borderline situations—not self-sufficient existential stages. They cannot be lived in like houses, but only stopped at like motels; they cannot be worn like daily garments, but only put on like costumes. As incognitos, irony and humor are aesthetic in the sense of poetic and rhetorical instrumentalities. They are modes of communication secretively arch rather than conventionally sincere. As the ethicist thinks to master existence by resolve, so his irony scrutinizes the contradictions of life through the stern jaundice of the ideal; the religious man, resigned to suffer what he cannot subdue, wrings his humor out of a compassion with those contradictions. In both cases irony and humor disengage the communication from the communicator so as to signalize and charge the gap between communicator and recipient. Between two freedoms they insert a "doubly-reflected" work of artfulness condensing the inwardness of the communicator into an explosive shock of recognition for the recipient.

Of the two, humor is the superior mode of indirection; first because, while irony is negative in its attitude to the comic object, humor is affirmative.

> Thecomical is always the mark of maturity; but it is important that the new shoot should be ready to appear under this maturity, and that the *vis comica* should not stifle the pathetic, but rather serve as indication that a new pathos is beginning. . . . The power to wield the weapon of the comic is the policeman's shield, the badge of authority, which every agent who in our time really is an agent must carry. But this comic spirit is not wild or vehement, its laughter is not shrill; on the contrary, it is careful of the immediacy that it sets aside. . . . This comic spirit is essentially humor. When the comic is cold and comfortless it is a sign that there is no new immediacy in the shoot, and then the comical does not function as a harvest, but as the contentless passion of an unfruitful wind raging over the naked ground. [56]

Because of the solicitude with which humor handles the first immediacy (the *an sich* of its object) it leaves intact the soil and the seed from which the second immediacy (the pathos of religion) can grow, and so becomes not merely a confine of the religious but a propaedeutic for it.

As incognito of the religious, humor is again superior to the irony that masks the ethical. Johannes de Silentio remarks that "irony and humor reflect . . . upon themselves, and therefore belong within the sphere of the infinite resignation."[57] Climacus, slicing thinner, believes that the "carefully modulated humoristic tone" of the edifying discourses is "doubtless the sum of what can be reached within the sphere of the immanent."

> While the ethical requirement is maintained, while life and existence is accentuated as a toilsome way, the decision is not posited in a paradox, and the metaphysical retirement by way of recollection into the eternal is always possible, and gives to this immanent sphere the color of humor. . . .[58]

Humor, as an option within the religious life, shares in man's highest spiritual achievement short of the paradoxical decision of Christian faith.

It is for this reason, undoubtedly, that humor pervades and determines the texture of Kierkegaard's work. As religious man and poet of the religious, it is appropriate that he should appear in the aesthetic guise of humor. While Kierkegaard never, within individual books, compromises the integrity of his pseudonymous *personae,* the whole corpus, seen from the vantage of his religious intent, assumes a humorous form and aspect.

Humor, abetted by occasional irony, felicitously serves Kierkegaard's religious purpose. But his poetic practice of indirect communication absolutely demands their obliquity. All writing for the public is an aesthetic activity. But while the aesthete can portray himself, as A and his cohorts do, while the ethicist can reveal himself in his letters and papers, and while the religious man can speak directly to an imaginary auditor, no stage of life transcends itself sufficiently to characterize disinterestedly the other spheres of existence. Humor and irony provide semi-detached viewpoints which mediate imaginatively between the stages, oases of momentary disengagement from which the stages may be observed and compared. So the most comprehensive Kierkegaardian pseudonyms tend to be humorists, of whom the prince is Johannes Climacus. Kierkegaard's commitment to religion, plus the location of humor almost within the forecourts of the temple, make Climacus the pseudonym closest to Kierkegaard himself. But he is nevertheless not quite Kierkegaard, for that would make him, as an extension of Kierkegaard's own person, a spokesman *simpliciter* for the religious.

Central to the Hegelian system are the idea of the unity of

281

subject and object (self and world, subject and substance, thought and being, and so on) and its corollary notion, that the principle of contradiction is superceded at the highest levels of thought by the principle of mediation. Climacus' polemic against Hegel amounts to an insistence that the subject-object distinction is absolute and the principle of contradiction inviolate. The special character of his polemic is a function of his role as humorist, or conversely, it was only in the role of humorist that he could enforce his opposition to Hegel. The humorist depends for his material on the fact of contradiction, and for the exercise of his craft upon his ability as subject to transcend any and every comic object. That Climacus is not identical with Kierkegaard or with any of his other *personae* is shown by the fact that in the *Edifying Discourses* and in the Christianity of various pseudonyms the principle of contradiction is set aside by the (dogmatic) principle of reconciliation, the subject-object distinction overwhelmed by the union of God and man at the moment of most intense religious passion.

The special capability of the humorist is his power to speak with understanding of the religious without having to be its advocate. For "the religious individual is not a humorist, but a humorist only in his outward appearance." And again,

> the humorist earns his justification by having his life in his humor. Against religiosity only it is not justified, but it is justified against everything that courts recognition as religiosity. The religiosity which has humor as its incognito can also see the humoristic as comical, but preserves its justification only by constantly keeping itself in religious passion with respect to the God-relationship, and hence it sees the comic aspect of humor only vanishingly. [59]

The humorist, lightly playing with the pathos of religion, is pitted victoriously against everyone who solemnly "courts recognition" as religious; for example, the nominally Christian preacher whose working categories are aesthetic. As a religiously sophisticated poet, the humorist is nemesis for the speculative thinker who bungles even the business of poetry; immanently discerning the comic he is free from its dominion, while the systematic philosopher becomes comic by his very presumption of transcendence.

> If ever there should be any question of such a thing, Danish philosophy would differ from German philosophy in this: that it

would not begin with nothing, or without assumptions, or explain everything through mediation, on the contrary it would begin with the proposition: that there are many things in heaven and earth which no philosopher has explained.

Taken up into philosophy that proposition would produce the necessary corrective and at the same time introduce a humorous and edifying feeling into everything. [60]

That could stand as a precis of Climacus' program and his achievement in the *Postscript:* the construction of an honest "Danish" philosophy that honors the pious wisdom of Hamlet over the boasting folly of Hegel. Humor is the Kierkegaardian replacement for philosophic objectivity. It treats without distortion existential problems from which speculation can only abstract and by abstracting confound. In his Appendix to the *Postscript*, "for an understanding with the reader," Climacus writes:

> . . . I have no opinion and wish to have none, being content and delighted with things as they are. As in Catholic books, especially those of an earlier age, one finds at the back of the volume a note which informs the reader that everything is to be understood conformably with the doctrine of the Holy Catholic Mother Church—so what I write contains also a piece of information to the effect that everything is so to be understood that it is understood to be revoked, and the book has not only a Conclusion but a Revocation. More than that no one can require, either before or after. [61]

Climacus' "revocation" is the humorist's eternal self-recall from his engagement with the sufferings of men. He has no opinion—does not occupy a stage on life's way—and desires none; satisfied with seeing "things as they are," he is uniquely fitted to make his mimic-pathetic-dialectic contribution to the elucidation of human existence. His peculiar combination of sympathetic understanding and provisional noncommitment enables the humorist to produce a poetic vehicle which communicates the tenor of subjectivity without subjective prejudice across the chasm of infinite possibility.

So the meaning of indirect communication emerges as the pattern of existential involvement, personal detachment, and artistic mediation woven into the motley of Kierkegaard's works and exemplified by such instances as parody, irony, and humor. The pattern is visible in the superficially argumentative but fundamentally satiric texture of *Philosophical Fragments* and *Concluding Unscientific Postscript;* it can also be traced in such diverse fabrics as the "dialectical lyric" of *Fear and Trembling,* the psychological microscopy of *The Sickness Unto Death,* and the pedantic posturing of *The Concept of Dread.* Its genres are as illimitable as possibility and as devious as imagination. But the essence is the same in all its manifestations: to interpose between author and reader an anonymous object so articulated by the author that it deploys upon contact into a phalanx of possibilities for the reader. Such communication is indirect because it turns author and reader away from each other toward "some third thing, something more abstract, which neither of them is." Indirect communication uses the example [image] "to turn the spectator's eye in upon himself, and thus repel him through placing the possibility between the example and the spectator as something they both have in common. . . ."[62] Such indirection is a communication of subjective truth because the impersonality of the object returns the reader to the arena where the possibilities it displays must be acted on: his inwardness.

The method of indirection is prefigured in the peirastics, anatreptics, and maieutics of the Socratic dialogues. Kierkegaard discovered it there and in what he took to be the compassionate cunning of the Incarnation. More immediately he was impelled to wield the Romantic irony as a weapon against the pretensions of the Romantic philosophers and their theological imitators. His own practice of indirect communication, which he describes as "elusive and artistic,"[63] is not unlike the techniques evolved (or rediscovered) by modern poets and familiar to contemporary literary critics. It is a commonplace of twentieth-century criticism to distinguish sharply between poetic language and prosaic discourse. The terms of the distinction are differently defined by different critics, but the theme is not lost amid their partisan variations on it. In "direct" or prosaic language, words are straightforward expressions of the writer's meaning; his language is a symbolic extension of his mind, as unambiguous as he can keep it. The speech of a poet, on the other hand, does not utter his inner states, but rather builds meanings into a free standing structure of language. Paradox, self-concealment, plural connotations, distentions of metaphor and the like are shears by which he clips the umbilical of his fancy's child and sends it out on its own. His art is not the externalizing of himself, but the objectifying of a work of words: *poiesis.*

What the poet produces is a verbal object *(poiema)* in which meanings, released from any personal interest he may vest in them, are neither affirmed nor denied, but simply placed. A poem in this sense does not *mean*—it does not urge the feelings and opinions of the poet on the reader. It *is*—as a thing made it is self-sufficient *(perfectum)* and bears no message not indigenous to its perfection.

But the poetic object, however much it dispatches the poet's words from the poet, is nevertheless an object *(objectum, Gegenstand)* and as such commands a response. A direct communication (indicative prose utterance) is a request for assent, and the proper response is some degree of belief or disbelief: one swears by a religious dogma, abandons a moral conviction, gives moderate credence to a scientific hypothesis, denies a factual allegation, and so on. But it would be out of place to believe in, to doubt, or to disaver a poem, since the poet makes no claim to which such attitudes would be relevant. At the same time a poem is not a bit of mute decor that is adequately appreciated when savored. Its locutions embody meanings, and its sensuousness addresses the intelligence. Kierkegaard would say that a poetic object, like any object, but with the preternatural vivacity induced by art, functions as a possibility when it is apprehended by a subject. And that in two distinct but related ways: as a term of knowing and as a challenge to action. [64]

A poem calls not for belief but for knowledge, not for admiration but for personal appropriation. We have already examined the primary rationale for Kierkegaard's use of indirect communication. Climacus proposes a further reason when he argues that all communication of subjectivity must be couched in terms of the possible. For

> existential reality is incommunicable, and the subjective thinker finds his reality in his own ethical existence. When reality is apprehended by an outsider it can be understood only as possibility. Everyone who makes a communication, in so far as he becomes conscious of this fact, will therefore be careful to give his existential communication the form of a possibility, precisely in order that it may have a relationship to existence. A communication in the form of a possibility compels the recipient to face the problem of existing in it, so far as this is possible between man

and man. . . . Whatever is great in the sphere of the universally human must therefore not be communicated as a subject for admiration, but as an ethical *requirement.* In the form of a possibility it becomes a requirement. [65]

In the schema suggested by Climacus a reality (for example, the reality of the God-man or of a human being) is always an object of belief, while a possibility is an object of knowledge and a spur to action. This alignment defines yet more closely the sense in which Kierkegaard's work is properly described as poetic.

Aristotle established a tradition when he declared that poetry is "more philosophical" than history, because it tells what might have happened or what should have happened whereas history only relates what did happen. [66] Climacus adduces this classical dictum in support of his contention that, "From the poetic and intellectual standpoint, possibility is higher than reality, the aesthetic and the intellectual being disinterested." The Stagirite is hereby linked with the sage of Königsberg and his doctrine of the disinterestedness of aesthetic experience.

> Art and poetry have been called anticipations of the eternal. If one desires to speak in this fashion, one must nevertheless note that art and poetry are not essentially related to an existing individual; for their contemplative enjoyment, the joy over what is beautiful, is disinterested, and the spectator of the work of art is contemplatively outside himself *qua* existing individual.

This disinterestedness of poetry sets it in opposition to what Climacus calls "the ethical," for there is "only one interest, the interest in existing." Poetry, along with metaphysics which is a species of poetry, stands over against that inward reality which it is the obligation of every man to cultivate. [67]

Kierkegaard parallels Aristotle's distinction of possibility (poetry) and actuality (history) with a distinction of his own between poetic "experiment" and the "historically-actual." Climacus explains:

> *Repetition* was called "a psychological experiment" on the title-page. That this was a doubly reflected communication-form soon became clear to me. By taking place in the form of an experiment, the communication creates opposition for itself, and the experiment establishes a yawning chasm between reader and author, posits the separation of inwardness between them, so that an immediate understanding is rendered impossible.

The aesthetic distance of the experiment prevents the reader from seeing in its surface only an image of himself with all his accumulated prejudices and preoccupations, and opens the way for an unimpeded communication of possibilities:

> When a man knows everything, but knows it by rote, the experimental form is a good instrument of exploration; one may tell him even what he knows in this form, and he will not recognize it.

The detachment of the work from its author and its reader, which releases it for contemplation and cognition, also allows to author and reader alike the freedom by which they may make the final existential appropriation of the possibilities it embodies:

> If the utterance is earnest in the writer, he preserves the earnestness essentially for himself; if the recipient apprehends it as earnest, he does it essentially by himself, and this is precisely the earnestness. [68]

Not only the personal reality of the poet and his reader, but also the factuality of the poetic utterance is aesthetically irrelevant:

> In connection with the aesthetic and the intellectual, to ask whether this or that is real, whether it really has happened, is a misunderstanding. So to ask betrays a failure to conceive the aesthetic and the intellectual ideality as a possibility, and forgets that to determine a scale of values for the aesthetic and the intellectual in this manner, is like ranking sensation higher than thought.

A theory, a doctrine, a statement of fact purport to say something about realities, and for that reason must be believed or doubted or rejected. A poem gives insight into possibilities by fashioning them in words; as a symbol that incarnates what it symbolizes such a verbal structure is the avenue and the object of an act of gnosis.

The fulfillment of the cognitive act—the satisfaction of intellect and imagination by a vision of the possible—is a condition for the shift to personal, ethical appropriation:

> In *Stages on Life's Way* occurs the following: "It is intelligent to ask two questions: (1) Is it possible? (2) Can I do it? But it is unintelligent to ask these two questions: (1) Is it real? (2) Has my

neighbor Christopherson done it? has he really done it?" In this passage reality is accentuated ethically. It is fatuous from the aesthetic and the intellectual point of view to raise the question of reality. . . . But when the ethical question is raised in connection with my own reality, I ask about possibility; only that this possibility is not an aesthetically and intellectually disinterested possibility, but as being a conceived reality it is related as a possibility to my own reality, so that I may be able to realize it. [69]

Possibility is a Janus which turns one face—the face of contemplative calm—on the imagination and the intellect, and the other—the face of moral earnest and exhortation—on the will. The peculiar task of the will, the reduplication of thought in existence, demands a definition of reality in ethical terms as "becoming subjective"; for such a reality the works of the poet are *possibilities.* But the intellect and the imagination are perfected in seeing and enjoying, so that from their side the possibilities enshrined in poetry are *realities,* the only realities conceivable by and interesting to an aesthetic point of view.

"Being" is a continuum variously interpretable; to rank entities as "abstract" or "concrete," "possible" or "actual," is to formulate the orientation induced by perspective bias. Thus when Climacus says that aesthetically regarded possibility is "higher" than actuality, he is speaking in the *persona* of an ethico-religiously inclined humorist and noting that the aesthetic orientation simply inverts the ethicist's hierarchy. What the ethicist calls possibility the aestheticist calls reality, and vice versa. So long as men are free to alter their perspectives, so long as life can accomodate diverse biases, the ethical and the aesthetic orientations are not in conflict with each other. [70] And so long as the individual keeps his perspectives well sorted and duly disciplined within the larger tensions of his existence, neither poetry nor ethics need be confused by alien values. Ideally the inordinate claims which each is tempted to lay on the other may be settled equitably if the two are seen as complementary halves of a double way. The poem, which for an aesthetic concern is end (reality), is for an ethical interest only the beginning (possibility) of action. And the reality which satisfies ethical passion merely provides aesthetics with an occasion of poetry. Poetry and ethical action are distinct; if the distinction is muddled, existence itself is confounded. But they are both legitimate, and if either is lacking existence is impoverished.

Climacus summarizes all these complex relationships in the following passage of the *Postscript:*

> Is the real then the same as the external? By no means. Aesthetically and intellectually it is usual and proper to stress the principle that the external is merely a deception for one who does not grasp the ideality involved. Frater Taciturnus says: "Mere knowledge of the historical helps simply to produce an illusion, in which the mind is beguiled by the raw material of the externality. What is it that I can know historically? The external detail. The ideality I can know only by myself, and if I do not know it by myself I do not know it at all; mere historical knowledge avails nothing. Ideality is not a chattel which can be transported from one person to another, nor is it something to be had gratis when buying in large quantities. If I know that Caesar was a great man, I know what greatness is, and it is on this knowledge that I base my judgment of Caesar; otherwise I do not know that Caesar was great. The testimony of history, the assurances of responsible people that no risk is involved in accepting this opinion, the certainty of the conclusion that he was great because the results of his life demonstrate it—all this helps not a jot. To believe an ideality on the word of another is like laughing at a joke because someone has said that it was funny, not because one has understood it. In such case the witticism might as well be left unsaid; for anyone who laughs at it because of the respect he entertains for some guarantor, and on the ground of his faith in him, could laugh with the same emphasis notwithstanding." What then is the real? It is the ideality. But aesthetically and intellectually the ideality is the possible (the translation from *esse ad posse*). Ethically the ideality is the real within the individual himself. The real is an inwardness that is infinitely interested in existing. . . .

Kierkegaard's work is poetry because it traffics in possibilities. It is the poetry of existence because the possibilities it exhibits for contemplation are also idealities that challenge the will to the ethical activity of realization. "A communication in the form of the possible operates in terms of the ideal man (not the differential ideal, but the universal ideal), whose relationship to every individual man is that of a requirement."[71]

The two faces of possibility effect an identity of poetry and rhetoric in Kierkegaard's works. Poetry generally consists of verbal structures predominantly centripetal (inner-directed); rhetoric on the other hand is largely centrifugal (outer-directed). A poem leads you deeper into itself; a rhetorical address points you beyond itself. Kierkegaard's writings, as a presentation of possibility, are at once poetry and rhetoric. As possibility seen from the perspective of an aesthetical concern, they are poetry. As possibility seen from an ethical bias, they are rhetoric. Kierkegaard intended both poetry and rhetoric; more specifically he meant to drive his reader *through* poetic apprehension *to* ethical appropriation.

Climacus' correlation of reality with belief and of possibility with knowledge and action instructs the interpretation of Kierkegaard's poetry of indirect communication. His books, *poiemata* and not statements of his views on human life, are out of the reach of the ordinary distinction of truth and falsity, which strictly applies only to the yeas and nays of the intellect compounding and dividing. Yet they open ways for understanding; they are seeds of possibility fecund with meaning, buds that flower perennially for the reflective imagination. Because they are works of irony and humor, they deftly evade the kind of evaluation that suits the generalizations of scientists and the theories of theorizing philosophers. Poems like jokes may be refused; they are never refuted. They may be rich or sparse, superficial or penetrating, estimable in a variety of ways, but they are never propositionally right or wrong. As poetry Kierkegaard's works fertilize the seeing intellect and bring to birth the offspring of the visionary fancy; as poetic irony and poetic humor they survive the misplaced and ineffectual assaults of a literal-minded and prosaic critique.

Not to mention the misplaced and impotent embrace of a literal-minded and prosaic espousal. The heresy of paraphrase and the intentional fallacy tempt the reader of Kierkegaard as they tempt readers of poetry generally. The pitfalls of the latter trap those earnest endeavors to determine what Kierkegaard "really means"—which, if they do not conveniently leave out everything that conflicts with what the scholar thinks Kierkegaard ought to mean, conclude either that Kierkegaard is a fool deaf to the most resounding self-contradictions or that he is saying something so precious and so deep that it can't help sounding silly. Taken as instruments of his intent, his works add up to magnificent nonsense. But the truth is that Kierkegaard the poet of inwardness did not "really mean" anything. His "intent" is to exfoliate existential possibilities, not to offer a systematic appraisal of reality as seen from his point of view; like all poets he is concerned not with mentioning but with making.

That it is heretical to paraphrase Kierkegaard is equally noteworthy. The "arguments" of his pseudonyms on behalf of religion and Christianity make abundantly clear by their unpersuasive formality just how important is the contextual setting of the originals. Any paraphrase of Kierkegaard must carry a disclaimer and an injunction to return to the source. It is for this reason that the influence of Kierkegaard on contemporary existential philosophy and theology is so questionable in spite of its vast publicity value for the Dane. Existential theologians tend to offer in place of the historic faith of the historical Church in the historical Incarnation an abstract of the dialectic of Climacus—an ersatz congenial to a disinherited generation oppressed by life and incapable of supernatural faith. But it was manifestly not part of Kierkegaard's program to found a school of theology on the barren crisis of despair, only to recall men to the divine imperative and to the conditions of faith in their own sufferings and their own freedom.

My purpose, he often says, is *"without authority, to call attention . . . ,"* or "to make aware."[72] That in a way is the purpose of every poet: not to tell the truth, nor yet to insinuate fabulous lies, but to make men aware of the options so that the emergence of truth within the individual is not hindered by the conceit of knowledge or the tangle of error. Knowledge there must be, and Kierkegaard will provide it if need be. But his ulterior aim is always "to engender inwardness"; that is a "task relative to one who may be presumed essentially to have knowledge, and hence not in need of having this conveyed to him, but rather needing to be personally affected."[73] In this sense Kierkegaard's poetry of inwardness is a poetry to drive men away from poetry back to the concern of top priority: becoming themselves. The passage quoted above ends ". . . to *call attention* to religion, to Christianity . . . ," which points directly to the extreme possibility. Climacus is more general, and more eloquent:

> The reception of inwardness does not consist in a direct reflection of the content communicated, for this is echo. But the reproduction of inwardness in the recipient constitutes the resonance by reason of which the thing said remains absent, like Mary when she *hid* the words as a treasure in the beautiful setting of a comely heart, but inwardness is when the thing said belongs to the recipient as if it were his own—and now it is his own.[74]

To read Kierkegaard aright is not to pick his brain (or his psyche) nor to produce an outline, however careful, of his argument. Neither in fact can be done without the impropriety of presuming to read his mind or the injustice of disregarding his own solicitude for form. Kierkegaard's writings are public domain, and as such they may and will be made to serve a variety of purposes. But they are most consistently and rewardingly understood as a poetry which opens to the inquiring intellect, the avid imagination, and the restless will the infinite wealth of possibility that is the material of human selfhood.

By the philosophers Kierkegaard has been prolifically pilfered from, his paradoxes have been twisted into doctrinal parodies of themselves, his mischievous recalcitrance to system chastised and solemnly invested with systematic dignity. There is no private property in the realm of the spirit, and there is no reason why everyone should not take from Kierkegaard what serves his turn. But it is impossible not to imagine Kierkegaard sharpening his wit and going to hilarious work on those contemporary ontologies of freedom that are determined to make inwardness academically respectable. The mysteries of the epoché and the disdain of the *existentiale* thinker for his *existentielle* gaucheries would impress Kierkegaard as so many new attempts—only slightly less honest than Hegel's—to give human existence the dubious prestige of professorial sanction. He would insist—and the form of his insistence would reduplicate the content—that system enslaves and that only poetry can adequately communicate inwardness in such a way as to emancipate the recipient. [75] Only *poiesis,* which cuts the tie that binds words and men and things, joints a verbal framework tough enough to contain the negativity of freedom without breaking; only poetry can crystallize limitless possibilities in an object capable of engaging the understanding and enticing the imagination ("making aware") without seducing or prostituting the spirit.

Kierkegaard's practice may throw some light on the vexed critical question of "poetry and belief." The problem may be put in this way: how can Kierkegaard, a man of grave religious conviction striving to become a Christian, have any real sympathy with the wildly irreligious and unChristian possibilities projected in his pseudonyms? The same problem, *mutatis mutandis,* should perplex his readers and in fact has often confounded

292

them. It is not, I think, resolved by appeal to a "willing suspension of disbelief." That would be make-believe, and Kierkegaard is in earnest. Nor does he eliminate the issue by simply removing poetry from the domain of cognitive concern: poetry, especially philosophical poetry, demands a cognitive response.

I think that in Kierkegaard's work the problem is foreclosed by his recognition that "belief" itself is an analogous state of mind. Were it an unambiguous and univocal attitude, then there would be a problem: you could not at once believe A and seriously entertain –A. Belief is a resolution of the will, but it is also the supreme effort of the imagination. One believes as he thinks, imaginatively and metaphorically. Kierkegaard says that faith always incorporates doubt as a sublated moment; so a belief in Christianity does not exclude but rather demands a real imaginative participation in paganism. The names a man chooses for his beliefs (Christian, humanist, and so on) do not fix their objects as clear and distinct ideas. They denominate a dominant perspective of the imagination and a ruling passion of the will, a perspective and a passion that do not shut out the possibility of others quite unlike them. Without the constant co-presence of other possibilities, the reality of belief condenses to blind dogmatism or evaporates into vapid fancy. Poetry, the imaginative cultivation of multiple perspectives, is the condition, the environment, and the source of belief. So Kierkegaard not only *could* but *had to* hold fast to his own convictions, and simultaneously elaborate all the alternatives in his pseudonymous poetry.

The theories of the systematic thinker—it was Hegel's genius that he saw this fact and his perversity that he exploited it—inevitably tend to set up as ends and to usurp the place of the realities they should serve. The poetic object, however, not only rejoices the mind with its objectivity; it also, by its repellent aloofness, challenges its reader to his own activity of self-becoming. The success of an indirect communication depends upon its capability to awaken in the recipient an awareness that the possibilities it objectifies—alluring, exciting, or frightening—are his own. He has not received the communication until he has read the concluding *de te fabula narratur* that can turn him from the wonder of the object to an engagement with the urgency and the unfinality of his own existence.

Kierkegaard's poetic is at once a rhetoric designed to coerce its reader to freedom. By the impassioned detachment with which it marshalls the resources of spirit, it lays on him the necessity to act and deprives him of any warrant for action except his own freedom. The Kierkegaardian corpus can neither be "believed" nor "followed": it is and was meant to be—poetically—the impetus, the occasion, and the demand for the reader's own advance to selfhood and to a solitary meeting with the divine. Not by exhorting him to this or that line of conduct, not by offering him the chance to let knowledge or admiration go proxy for decision, but by vividly summoning before him the richness and the risk ingredient in his freedom, Kierkegaard's works impart to "that individual" who is their true reader the opportunity and the need of achieving himself in the sight of God.

It was remarked above that when Kierkegaard turned philosophy into poetry he was only returning philosophy from its post-Cartesian to its traditional form. The view that philosophy and poetry are in reality the same thing, perhaps seen from different angles, is recommended by Climacus' association of the "aesthetic" with the "intellectual." An even more persuasive argument is suggested by his thesis that all communication of human reality is necessarily indirect:

> A double reflection is implicit in the very idea of communication. Communication assumes that the subject who exists in the isolation of his inwardness, and who desires through this inwardness to express the life of eternity (the ideal, the possible), where sociality and fellowship is unthinkable, since everyone must be assumed essentially to possess all, nevertheless wishes to impart himself; and hence desires at one and the same time to have his thinking in the inwardness of his subjective existence, and yet also to put himself into communication with others. This contradiction cannot possibly . . . find expression in a direct form.

The form which such a pervasive contradiction—the contradiction between the actual and the ideal which racks all existence—must take is a form that will "embody artistically as much of reflection as he himself has when existing in his thought. In an artistic manner, please note; for the secret does not lie in a direct assertion of the double reflection; such a direct expression of it is precisely a contradiction." "Objective thinking"—of the sort proper to mathematics, science, and history, and believed appropriate to philosophy in Kierkegaard's century—

is wholly indifferent to subjectivity, and hence also to inwardness and appropriation; its mode of communication is therefore direct. . . and lacks the godly and human solicitude in communicating which belongs to subjective thinking. It can be understood directly and recited by rote. Objective thinking is hence conscious only of itself, and is not in the strict sense of the word a form of communication at all.

In opposition to which: "The greater the artistry, the greater the inwardness." For wherever "the subjective is of importance in knowledge, and where appropriation thus constitutes the crux of the matter, the process of communication is a work of art, and doubly reflected."[76]

The implication is that any philosophy which deals with matters vital to human beings must communicate itself indirectly. Not only the special poetic philosophy of Kierkegaard, but all humane philosophy is a poetic and for that very reason an indirect communication. Poetry implies indirection, and indirection poetry. Unless the philosopher is content to restrict his operations to the pseudo-linguistics of language analysis, the quasi-mathematics of symbolic logic, or the strange mixture of geometry and mysticism that makes up most phenomenology, he must become a poet. The philosophers of the Western tradition, consistently preoccupied with the problems of human life, have always been poetic philosophers. And when modern thinkers reject the form of poetry they also renounce their ancient birthright and their humanistic heritage.

Not so Kierkegaard, and that is what makes him a stranger to his own and to our century. He was and is ". . . a peculiar kind of poet and thinker who . . . has nothing new to bring but would read the original text of the individual, human existence-relationship, the old, well-known, handed down from the fathers—would read it through yet once again, if possible in a more heartfelt way."[77] The conjunction of "poet and thinker" is essential. His philosophy *is* poetry because it centers in man. The ambiguity of human existence is reflected in the analogical (not univocal) unity of his thought, which in turn finds expression in the metaphoric (not literal) mode of utterance. The contradictions of human existence are acknowledged by the distention of all his metaphors: pseudonymity dispersed in polynymity and subverted to anonymity, imagery undercut by irony and humor, imitation screwed into parody—all the resources of poetry made doubly resourceful by indirection.

For although Kierkegaard's thought centers on man, it does not in the last analysis find its repose in him. And for that reason, though it holds itself proudly and objectively aloof from every reduction to human intentions and human affects, his "literature" cannot and will not claim that autonomy which modern critics in their enthusiasm for poetics and their envy of science are wont to attribute to all poetry. To the mind of Kierkegaard, all things human and finite are but relative, their reality derivative, their unity equivocal, and their freedom constrained. Absolute reality, unqualified unity, and unlimited freedom are to be found only in God, to whose perfection no thought or speech can hope to attain. God is the ultimate reason of poetry as of all things: His Being everywhere imaged in the creation makes poetic communication possible; His image everywhere distorted by the creation makes the obliquity of poetry necessary. Before the throne of that Reality, that Unity, and that Freedom even the most gorgeous poetry must abase itself in humble adoration and willing service. To understand Kierkegaard is to explore the sense in which he is "a kind of poet . . ."—and to remember constantly that every word he wrote was dedicated to the glorification of that Father of lights from whom come all good and perfect gifts, without whom poetry would neither be possible nor necessary. In his own concluding words to posterity:

> The dialectical structure he brought to completion, of which the several parts are whole works, he could not ascribe to any man, least of all would he ascribe it to himself; if he were to ascribe it to anyone, it would be to Providence, to whom it was in fact ascribed, day after day and year after year, by the author, who historically died of a mortal disease, but poetically died of longing for eternity, where uninterruptedly he would have nothing else to do but to thank God. [78]

BIBLIOGRAPHY

I. Kierkegaard's Works

A. DANISH

Afsluttende uvidenskabelig Efterskrift. Udgivet med Indledning og Kommentar af Niels Thulstrup. B. I–II. København: Gyldendalske Boghandel Nordisk Forlag, 1962.

Breve og Aktstykker vedrørende Søren Kierkegaard. Udgivne ved Niels Thulstrup. B. I–II. København: Ejnar Munksgaard, 1953–1954.

Philosophiske Smuler. Udgivet med Indledning og Kommentar af Niels Thulstrup. København: Ejnar Munksgaard, 1955.

Søren Kierkegaards Bibliotek. En bibliografi ved Niels Thulstrup. København: Ejnar Munksgaard, 1957.

Søren Kierkegaards Papirer. Anden forøgede Udgave ved Niels Thulstrup. B. I–XIII. Kjøbenhavn: Gyldendalske Boghandel Nordisk Forlag, 1968–1970. (Except for volumes XII and XIII, which contain new material, this is identical with the first edition prepared by P. A. Heiberg, V. Kuhr, and E. Torsting, and published by the same publisher, 1909–1948.)

Søren Kierkegaards Samlede Vaerker. Anden Udgave. Udgivne af A. B. Drachmann, J. L. Heiberg, og H. O. Lange. B. I–XV. Kjøbenhavn: Gyldendalske Boghandel Nordisk Forlag, 1920–1936. (This edition, "gennemset og ajourført af Peter P. Rohde," was reprinted by the same publisher in 20 volumes, 1962–1964.)

297

Bibliography

B. ENGLISH

Armed Neutrality and An Open Letter. Ed. and trans. H. V. and E. H. Hong. Bloomington: Indiana University Press, 1968.

Attack Upon Christendom. Trans. W. Lowrie. Princeton: Princeton University Press, 1946.

Christian Discourses. Trans. W. Lowrie. London: Oxford University Press, 1940.

The Concept of Dread. Second Edition. Trans. W. Lowrie. Princeton: Princeton University Press, 1957.

The Concept of Irony. Trans. L. M. Capel. New York: Harper and Row, 1965.

Concluding Unscientific Postscript. Trans. D. F. Swensen and W. Lowrie. Princeton: Princeton University Press, 1944.

Crisis in the Life of an Actress and Other Essays on Drama. Trans. S. D. Crites. New York: Harper and Row, 1967.

Edifying Discourses. Vols. I-IV. Trans. D. F. and L. M. Swenson. Minneapolis: Augsburg Publishing House, 1962.

Either/Or. Vols. I–II. Trans. D. F. and L. M. Swensen and W. Lowrie, revised by H. A. Johnson. Princeton, N. J.: Princeton University Press, 1959.

Fear and Trembling and The Sickness Unto Death. Trans. W. Lowrie. Princeton, N. J.: Princeton University Press, 1954.

For Self-Examination and Judge for Yourselves! Trans. W. Lowrie. London: Oxford University Press, 1944.

The Gospel of Suffering and The Lilies of the Field. Trans. D. F. and L. M. Swenson. Minneapolis: Augsburg Publishing House, 1948.

Johannes Climacus or, De Omnibus Dubitandum Est. Trans. T. H. Croxall. Stanford: Stanford University Press, 1958.

The Journals of Søren Kierkegaard. A selection edited and translated by A. Dru. London: Oxford University Press, 1938.

The Last Years: Journals 1853–1855. Ed. and trans. R. G. Smith. New York: Harper and Row, 1965.

On Authority and Revelation. Trans. W. Lowrie. Princeton: Princeton University Press, 1955.

Philosophical Fragments. Trans. D. F. Swenson, introduction and commentary by Niels Thulstrup, translation revised and commentary trans. by H. V. Hong. Princeton: Princeton University Press, 1962.

The Point of View. Trans. W. Lowrie. London: Oxford University Press, 1939.

The Present Age. Trans. A. Dru and W. Lowrie. London: Oxford University Press, 1940.

298

Purity of Heart. Trans. D. V. Steere. New York: Harper and Row, 1948.

Repetition. Trans. W. Lowrie. New York: Harper and Row, 1964.

Stages on Life's Way. Trans. W. Lowrie. Princeton: Princeton University Press, 1945.

Søren Kierkegaard's Journals and Papers. Vols. I-II. Ed. and trans. H. V. and E. H. Hong. Bloomington: Indiana University Press, 1967, 1970.

Thoughts on Crucial Situations in Human Life. Trans. D. F. Swenson. Minneapolis: Augsburg Publishing House, 1941.

Training in Christianity. Trans. W. Lowrie. Princeton: Princeton University Press, 1947.

Works of Love. Trans. H. V. and E. H. Hong. New York: Harper and Row, 1962.

II. Books about Kierkegaard

A. DANISH

Billeskov Jansen, F. J. *Studier i Søren Kierkegaards litteraere Kunst.* København: Rosenkilde og Bagger, 1951.

Brandt, Frithiof. *Syv Kierkegaard Studier.* København: Ejnar Munksgaard, 1962.

Geismar, Eduard. *Søren Kierkegaard: Livsudvikling og Forfattervirksomhed.* B. I–VI. København: G. E. C. Gads Forlag, 1926–1928.

Hansen, Knud. *Søren Kierkegaard: Ideens Digter.* København: Gyldendalske Boghandel Nordisk Forlag, 1954.

Henriksen, Aage. *Kierkegaards Romaner.* København: Gyldendalske Boghandel Nordisk Forlag, 1954.

Høffding, Harald. *Søren Kierkegaard som Filosof.* Anden Udgave. København: Gyldendalske Boghandel Nordisk Forlag, 1919.

Hohlenberg, Johannes. *Den Ensommes Vej.* København: H. Hagerup, 1948.

Holm, Søren. *Søren Kierkegaards Historiefilosofi.* København: Nyt Nordisk Forlag Arnold Busck, 1952.

Jørgensen, Carl. *Søren Kierkegaard: en Biografi.* B. I–V. København: Nyt Nordisk Forlag Arnold Busck, 1964.

Kuhr, Victor. *Modsigelsens Grundsaetning. Kierkegaard Studier,* n. II. København: Gyldendalske Boghandel Nordisk Forlag, 1915.

Lønning, Per. *"Samtidighedens Situation."* Oslo: Forlaget Land og Kirke, 1954.

Malantschuk, Gregor. *Dialektik og Eksistens hos Søren Kierkegaard.* København: Hans Reitzels Forlag, 1968.

Roos, Carl. *Kierkegaard og Goethe.* København: G. E. C. Gads Forlag, 1955.

Bibliography

B. ENGLISH

Brandt, Frithiof. *Søren Kierkegaard*. Copenhagen: Det Danske Selskab, 1963.

Collins, James. *The Mind of Kierkegaard*. Chicago: Henry Regnery, 1953.

Croxall, T. H. *Glimpses and Impressions of Kierkegaard*. Digwell Place, Welwyn, Herts.: James Nisbet and Co. Ltd., 1959.

Croxall, T. H. *Kierkegaard·Commentary*. New York: Harper and Brothers, 1956.

Croxall, T. H. *Kierkegaard Studies*. London: Lutterworth Press, 1948.

Diem, Hermann. *Kierkegaard's Dialectic of Existence*. Edinburgh: Oliver and Boyd, 1959.

Dupré, Louis. *Kierkegaard as Theologian*. New York: Sheed and Ward, 1963.

Garelick, Herbert M. *The Anti–Christianity of Kierkegaard*. The Hague: Martinus Nijhoff, 1965.

Geismar, Eduard. *Lectures on the Religious Thought of Søren Kierkegaard*. Minneapolis: Augsburg Publishing House, 1938.

George, A. G. *The First Sphere: A Study in Kierkegaardian Aesthetics*. London: Asia Publishing House, 1965.

Gill, Jerry H., ed. *Essays on Kierkegaard*. Minneapolis: Burgess Publishing Co., 1969.

Hanna, Thomas. *The Lyrical Existentialists*. New York: Atheneum, 1962.

Heinecken, Martin J. *The Moment Before God*. Philadelphia: Muhlenberg Press, 1956.

Henriksen, Aage. *Methods and Results of Kierkegaard Studies in Scandinavia*. Publications of the Kierkegaard Society, Copenhagen, Vol. I. Copenhagen: Ejnar Munksgaard, 1951.

Hohlenberg, Johannes. *Søren Kierkegaard*. New York: Pantheon Books, 1954.

Johnson, Howard A., and Thulstrup, Niels, eds. *A Kierkegaard Critique*. New York: Harper and Brothers, 1962.

Jolivet, Regis. *Introduction to Kierkegaard*. New York: E. P. Dutton and Co., Inc., undated.

Lowrie, Walter. *Kierkegaard*. London: Oxford University Press, 1938.

Lowrie, Walter. *A Short Life of Kierkegaard*. Princeton: Princeton University Press, 1942.

LeFevre, Perry D. *The Prayers of Kierkegaard*. Chicago: The University of Chicago Press, 1956.

Malantschuk, Gregor. *Kierkegaard's Way to the Truth*. Minneapolis: Augsburg Publishing House, 1963.

Miller, Libuse Lukas. *In Search of the Self*. Philadelphia: Muhlenberg Press, 1962.

Price, George. *The Narrow Pass*. New York: McGraw-Hill Book Co., Inc., 1963.

Shestov, Lev. *Kierkegaard and the Existential Philosophy*. Athens: Ohio University Press, 1971.

Swenson, David F. *The Faith of a Scholar*. Philadelphia: The Westminster Press, 1949.

Swenson, David F. *Something about Kierkegaard*. Minneapolis: Augsburg Publishing House, 1941.

Thomas, J. Heywood. *Subjectivity and Paradox*. Oxford: Basil Blackwell, 1957.

Thompson, Josiah. *The Lonely Labyrinth: Kierkegaard's Pseudonymous Works*. Carbondale: Southern Illinois University Press, 1967.

Thomte, Reidar. *Kierkegaard's Philosophy of Religion*. Princeton: Princeton University Press, 1949.

Wyschogrod, Michael. *Kierkegaard and Heidegger: The Ontology of Existence*. New York: The Humanities Press, Inc., 1954.

C. FRENCH

Wahl, Jean. *Etudes Kierkegaardiennes*. Paris: J. Vrin, 1949.

III. Journals and Articles

A. JOURNALS

Inquiry. Vol. 8, no. 1, special Kierkegaard number. Oslo: Universitetsforlaget, 1965.

Kierkegaardiana. Udgivne af Søren Kierkegaard Selskabet. København: Ejnar Munksgaard, 1955ff.

Symposion Kierkegaardianum. *Orbis Litterarum* Tome X Fasc. 1–2. Copenhague: Ejnar Munksgaard, 1955.

B. ARTICLES

Allison, Henry E., "Christianity and Nonsense." *The Review of Metaphysics*, Vol. XX, no. 3 (March, 1967), pp. 432–460.

Allison, Henry E., "Kierkegaard's Dialectic." *Union Seminary Quarterly Review*, Vol. XX, no. 3 (March 1965), pp. 225–233.

Cumming, Robert, "Existence and Communication." *Ethics*, Vol. LXV, no. 2 (January, 1955), pp. 79–101.

Durfee, Harold A., "The Second Stage of Kierkegaardian Scholarship in America." *International Philosophical Quarterly*, Vol. 3 (February, 1963), pp. 121–139.

Bibliography

Hess, M. Whitcomb, "Kierkegaard and Socrates." *The Christian Century*, Vol. LXXXII, no. 23 (June 9, 1965), pp. 736–738.

Henriksen, Aage, "Kierkegaard's Reviews of Literature." *Symposion Kierkegaardianum* (see III.A. above).

Holmer, Paul L., "Kierkegaard and Ethical Theory." *Ethics*, Vol. LXIII, no. 3 (April, 1953).

Holmer, Paul L., "Kierkegaard and Logic." *Kierkegaardiana*, Vol. II, 1957 (see III.A. above).

Holmer, Paul L., "On Understanding Kierkegaard." *Symposion Kierkegaardianum* (see III.A. above).

Kroner, Richard, "Kierkegaard or Hegel?" *Revue Internationale de Philosophie*, no. 19 (1952), pp. 1–18.

Mackey, Louis, "The Analysis of the Good in Kierkegaard's *Purity of Heart*." Lieb, I. C., ed., *Experience, Existence, and the Good*. Carbondale: Southern Illinois University Press, 1961, pp. 260–274.

Mackey, Louis, "Kierkegaard and the Problem of Existential Philosophy," I and II. *The Review of Metaphysics*, March and June, 1956. (Reprinted in Gill, Jerry H., ed., *op. cit.* in II.B. above.)

Mackey, Louis, "Kierkegaard's Lyric of Faith: A Look at *Fear and Trembling*." *The Rice Institute Pamphlet*, Vol. XLVII, no. 2 (July, 1960), pp. 30–47.

Mackey, Louis, "The Loss of the World in Kierkegaard's Ethics." *The Review of Metaphysics*, Vol. XV, no. 4 (June, 1962), pp. 602–620.

Mackey, Louis, "Philosophy and Poetry in Kierkegaard." *The Review of Metaphysics*, Vol. XXIII, no. 2 (December, 1969), pp. 316–332.

Mackey, Louis, "Some Versions of the Aesthete: Kierkegaard's *Either/Or*." *Rice University Studies*, Vol. 50, no. 1 (Winter, 1964), pp. 39–54.

Mackey, Louis, "Søren Kierkegaard: The Poetry of Inwardness." Schrader, George A., Jr., ed., *Existential Philosophers: Kierkegaard to Merleau-Ponty*. New York: McGraw-Hill Book Co., 1967, pp. 45–107.

McInerny, Ralph, "Ethics and Persuasion: Kierkegaard's Existential Dialectic." *The Modern Schoolman*, Vol. XXXIII (May, 1956), pp. 219–239.

McKinnon, Alastair, "Kierkegaard's Pseudonyms: A New Hierarchy." *American Philosophical Quarterly*, Vol. 6, no. 2 (April, 1969), pp. 116–126.

Popkin, Richard H., "Kierkegaard and Scepticism." *Algemeen Nederlands Tijdschrift voor Wijsbegeerte en Psychologie*, Vol. 51, no. 3, pp. 123–141.

Ramsey, Paul, "*Existenz* and the Existence of God: A Study of Kierkegaard and Hegel." *The Journal of Religion*, Vol. XXVIII, no. 3 (July, 1948), pp. 157–176.

Weiss, Paul, "Existenz and Hegel." *Philosophy and Phenomenological Research*, Vol. VIII, no. 2 (December, 1947), pp. 206–216.

NOTES

The following abbreviations have been used for the English translations of Kierkegaard's works:

CD: *Christian Discourses.* Trans. Walter Lowrie. London: Oxford University Press, 1940.

COD: *The Concept of Dread.* Trans. Walter Lowrie. Princeton: Princeton University Press, 1957.

CUP: *Concluding Unscientific Postscript.* Trans. D. F. Swenson and Walter Lowrie. Princeton: Princeton University Press, 1944.

Dru: Alexander Dru, ed. and trans., *The Journals of Søren Kierkegaard.* London: Oxford University Press, 1938. (Reference is to entry numbers, not page numbers.)

ED: *Edifying Discourses.* Trans. David F. and Lillian M. Swenson. Minneapolis: Augsburg Publishing House, 1962. (References will carry a volume number and page numbers. E.g., ED I 46 stands for *Edifying Discourses*, volume I, page 46.)

E/O: *Either/Or.* Trans. D. F. Swenson, L. M. Swenson, and Walter Lowrie. Princeton, N.J.: Princeton University Press, 1959. (References will carry volume and page numbers, as for ED above.)

FAT: *Fear and Trembling and The Sickness unto Death.* Trans. Walter
SUD: Lowrie. Princeton, N.J.: Princeton University Press, 1954.

JC: *Johannes Climacus: or, de omnibus dubitandum est.* Trans. T. H. Croxall. Stanford: Stanford University Press, 1958.

PF: *Philosophical Fragments.* Trans. D. F. Swenson. Princeton: Princeton University Press, 1962.

POV: *The Point of View.* Trans. Walter Lowrie. London: Oxford University Press, 1939.

Rep: *Repetition.* Trans. Walter Lowrie. New York: Harper and Row, 1964.

SOLW: *Stages on Life's Way.* Trans. Walter Lowrie. Princeton: Princeton University Press, 1945.

TIC: *Training in Christianity.* Trans. Walter Lowrie. Princeton: Princeton University Press, 1947.

References to less frequently cited works of Kierkegaard will be given in full. Although I have on a few occasions altered the existing English translations, I have not made reference to the Danish text of Kierkegaard. For the many who do not read Danish, such references would be a cumbersome and confounding futility. The few who do read Danish will find it easy to check the sources without my help. For these few, however, I note here the Danish editions I made use of.

For the works I have used *Søren Kierkegaards Samlede Vaerker*, Anden Udgave, udgivne af A. B. Drachmann, J. L. Heiberg, og H. O. Lange. Kjøbenhavn: Gyldendalske Boghandel Nordisk Forlag, 1920-1936.

For the Journals I have used *Søren Kierkegaards Papirer*, Anden forøgede Udgave ved Niels Thulstrup. Kjøbenhavn: Gyldendalske Boghandel Nordisk Forlag, 1968-1970. Except for volumes XII and XIII, this is identical with the first edition prepared by P. A. Heiberg, V. Kuhr, and E. Torsting, 1909-1948.

CHAPTER 1: Some Versions of the Aesthete

1. Dru 367. Kierkegaard is slightly misquoting *Aeneid*, II, 3: *Infandum, regina, jubes renovare dolorem.* "Thou biddest me, O Queen, renew an unspeakable grief." In another entry (Dru 717) Kierkegaard writes, "By a strange freemasonry I can make these words of the poet a motto for part of my life's suffering: *Infandum me jubes* Regina *renovare dolorem.*"

2. Dru 22, 70; Rep 126-127; Dru 626, 1191, 1252, 1333, 1334, 1260, 1275, plus numerous notes from the year 1852 on; POV 100-102.

3. Dru 641, 921, 952, 1299, plus index references to "melancholy"; Dru 767. The Latin means, "I had perished, had I not perished."

4. SOLW 187; E/O I 135, 163, 215.

5. E/O I 19.

6. E/O II 182.

7. The references in this paragraph are to E/O I 45-134, especially 47; and to Lorenzo da Ponte's libretto for Mozart's *Don Giovanni*, Act I, scene 2, Leporello's "catalogue" aria: "If only she wears a petticoat, you know what he does." In A's interpretation of *Don Giovanni*, the Commendatore is not part of the unity of the opera, but a voice of divine judgment morally shattering this unity *ab extra.*

8. E/O I 52-55, 63-72, 100.

9. E/O I 17-42, 279-296.

10. The references in the preceding three paragraphs are to E/O I 19-20, 27, 30, 1, 18, 164, 37-39.

11. The references in this paragraph are to E/O I 288, 290-291, 295-296.

12. E/O I 229-277. Cf. D. F. Swenson's "Translator's Introduction" to PF, p. xx.

13. The references in the preceding two paragraphs are to E/O I 162-213, 135-162, 215-228, 20, 165.

14. The references in the preceding two paragraphs are to E/O I 215, 165-167, 149-151, 172-174, 228. Cf. Eduard Geismar, *Lectures on the Religious Thought of Søren Kierkegaard* (Minneapolis, 1937), p. 29. A whole phalanx of antitheses suggests that the *symparanekromenoi* are meant as a deliberate parody on the Christian Church. E.g., they are the fellowship of those who are dead even while they live, as opposed to the fellowship of those who though dead have been revivified by the death of Christ; as Christian pilgrims seek the empty tomb of the risen Christ, so the *symparanekromenoi* seek the empty tomb of the "unhappiest man" who has never been alive (E/O I 218); as Christians are gathered by the grace of God into a community that shall endure forever, so the *symparanekromenoi* are a non-community of scattered and fragmentary men (*ibid.);* as Christians quest for eternal beatitude, so the *symparanekromenoi* believe in nothing but misfortune and expect only misery.

15. The quotations in this paragraph are from Rep 33, 38-39, 135.

16. The references in the preceding two paragraphs are to E/O I 40, 165.

17. Dru 467; cf. CUP 226.

18. Dante, *Inferno,* III, 9: "All hope abandon, ye who enter here."

19. E/O I 20-21, 35.

20. E/O I 19.

21. The references in the preceding three paragraphs are to SOLW 25, 27-30, 32,34. Cf. Ovid, *Tristia,* III, 4, 25.

22. SOLW 36. My translation loses the pun on "blessed."

23. The quotations in this paragraph are from SOLW 26, 30-32. Cf. Georg Christoph Lichtenberg, *Vermischte Schriften* (Göttingen, 1844), B. IV, s. 40.

24. The references in the preceding four paragraphs are to Rep 29, 33-36, 38-39, 43, 49, 58-61, 66-67, 101-103, 109-118, 125-127.

25. SOLW 60-67.

26. Rep 49-50; for this paragraph in general, cf. Rep 47-48, 51-52, 71-73.

27. Cf. Plato, *Phaedrus*, 270B-272B. Kierkegaard was influenced by Karl Rosenkranz, *Psychologie* (Königsberg, 1837). Cf. COD 28 n, 131-132.

28. COD 16 n. Cf. CUP 235, where Johannes Climacus mistakenly attributes this expression to Constantin Constantius himself.

29. Rep 31, 129, 131, 134, 137. The phrase translated "a fictitious figure" is really *en poetisk Person,* "a poetical person."

30. E/O I 297-440. The essay on *Don Giovanni* is not strictly the first essay in *Either/Or* I; the *Diapsalmata* enjoy that distinction. However, Victor Eremita remarks (E/O I 7-8) that in editing A's writings he left them in the order in which A had arranged them *with one exception.* The *Diapsalmata,* which he found on separate sheets scattered throughout A's papers, he collected and placed together at the head of the volume. They do not constitute an integral member of the body of A's papers; rather, they stand as a key signature before the volume and fix the tonality for the whole work. The essay on *Don Giovanni* remains the first essay, as such, in the papers, and its significant symmetry with the Seducer's Diary is preserved.

31. E/O I 432.

32. Dru 472.

33. The references in the preceding three paragraphs are to E/O I 98, 107, 298, 303-305, 308-309, 341, 432. The Italian is again from *Don Giovanni,* I, 2, the "catalogue": "His ruling passion is the fresh young girl."

34. The quotations in this paragraph are from SOLW 31, 82.

35. E/O I 440.

36. The quotations in this paragraph are from SOLW 87.

37. The references in this paragraph are to E/O I 177-178, 305-306, 308-309, and to D. F. Swenson, *op. cit.,* PF xii.

38. The references in the preceding three paragraphs are to E/O I 299, 304-306.

39. The references in the preceding two paragraphs are to E/O I 3-4, 9, 300. Cf. CUP 263 n: "Even the 'Diary of the Seducer' was only a possibility of terror which the aesthete in his fumbling existence had evoked, precisely because without actually being anything he had to try himself in everything in possibility."

40. The references in this paragraph are to E/O I 13-14.

41. SOLW 43-44.

42. CUP 253 n. Cf. Dru 533: "V. Eremita [has said] that he will never more praise *Don Juan* in words."

43. CUP 226.

44. With this compare John Keats' famous letters, to George and Thomas Keats (21, 27? December 1817), and to Richard Woodhouse (27 October 1818), on "negative capability" and the "poetic character." Douglas Bush, ed., *John Keats: Selected Poems and Letters* (Boston, 1959), pp. 260-261, 279-280.

45. SOLW 38.

46. Cf. COD, ch. I, section 5.

47. The references in the preceding four paragraphs are to SOLW 38-41, 44-88.

48. SOLW 93.

49. This and the immediately preceding citations are from Rep 131, 134-135, 137.

50. E/O I 14-15.

51. E/O I 13. Cf. F. J. Billeskov Jansen, "The Literary Art of Kierkegaard," in H. A. Johnson and N. Thulstrup, eds., *A Kierkegaard Critique* (New York, 1962), p. 14.

CHAPTER 2: World Enough and Time

1. The quotations in the preceding two paragraphs are from E/O II 7-8, 11-15.

2. E/O II 161-164.

3. E/O II 17.

4. The references in the preceding two paragraphs are to FAT 92-93, 95-96.

5. E/O II 180.

6. E/O II 171.

7. SOLW 153.

8. This and the previous citation are from E/O II 167, 169.

9. For the previous quotation and for this paragraph in general, cf. E/O II 163-167.

10. The references in the preceding five paragraphs are to E/O II 24-25, 182, 184-195, 197-199, 215, 240.

11. E/O II 193.

12. CD 320.

13. E/O II 217-218.

14. SOLW 95-178.

15. The references in the preceding three paragraphs are to SOLW 112-114, 116-119, 121.

16. E/O II 219-220.

17. This and the previous quotation are from E/O II 144-146.

18. For this paragraph, see E/O II 220-223, 229, 236, 244, 252-253.

19. The references in this paragraph are to E/O II 221-222.

20. The references in the preceding four paragraphs are to E/O II 99-100, 171-173, 254-255, 257-275.

21. The references in the preceding two paragraphs are to SOLW 155, 157-158, 160-161.

22. SOLW 159.

23. PF 100-105.

24. SUD 173-174.

25. COD 140-141.

26. The two preceding quotations are from SOLW 159-160.

27. FAT 46-58.

28. SOLW 159, 161.

29. E/O II 259-266.

30. E/O II 327.

31. Dru 473.

32. E/O II 245-259.

33. The quotations in this paragraph are from SOLW 166.

34. The quotations in this paragraph are from Rep 133-134.

35. The references in the preceding three paragraphs are to SOLW 170-177.

36. Cf. chapter 5 below; also Louis H. Mackey, "Kierkegaard's Lyric of Faith: A Look at *Fear and Trembling*," in *The Rice Institute Pamphlet*, XLVII, 2 (July, 1960), pp. 30-47.

37. SOLW 177.

38. The references in the preceding three paragraphs are to E/O II 285-287, 292-293, 297-298, 301-302.

39. E/O II 302-321.

40. E/O II 309-310.

41. The references in the preceding three paragraphs are to E/O II 9-10, 19-22, 36.

42. The references in the preceding three paragraphs are to E/O II 9-10, 31, 33, 35, 37, 42-43.

43. The references in the preceding three paragraphs are to E/O II 44, 46-47, 50-51.

44. The references in the preceding three paragraphs are to E/O II 55-59, 61-62.

45. This and the quotations in the preceding paragraph are from E/O II 62-63, 89.

46. E/O II 95. *Forklarelse* (glorification) also means "transfiguration" and is related to the word for "explanation" (*Forklaring*).

47. The references in the preceding three paragraphs are to E/O II 96, 98, 133-137, 140-141.

48. The references in this paragraph are to SOLW 123-144.

49. E/O II 5-6.

50. E/O I 6-8.

51. E/O II 328.

52. E/O II 207.

53. Dru 467.

54. E/O II 1.

55. E/O I 1.

56. E/O II 359 (note by H. A. Johnson, ed.)

57. SOLW 96. Cf. Gorgias, Fragment 23, in K. Freeman, *Ancilla to the Pre-Socratic Philosophers* (Oxford, 1952), p. 138. In the passage quoted Gorgias is speaking of the aesthetic deception involved in the presentation and enjoyment of tragedy. "Tragedy, by means of legends and emotions, creates a deception in which the deceiver is more honest than the non-deceiver, and the deceived is wiser than the non-deceived." Judge Wilhelm's use of this particular passage against the aesthete is especially pointed.

58. SOLW 162.

CHAPTER 3: That God May Be All in All

1. E/O II 155. For Judge Wilhelm's rapturous estimate of his own marriage, see in particular the introductory remarks to his observations about marriage, SOLW 97-104.

2. SOLW 162-163.

3. E/O II 83.

4. E/O II 183.

5. CUP 161.

6. The references in this paragraph are to E/O II 341-342. Concerned to discover structural symmetry between the two parts of *Either/Or*, one may muse on the possibility that Judge Wilhelm himself is the author of the sermon, and that the Jutland priest is a fiction like Johannes the Seducer. Certainly the Assessor claims the contents of the sermon for his own with a warmth that might bespeak the amateur preacher. On the other hand, due observance of the relative proprieties of the aesthetic and ethical ways of life might demand that while A is haunted by a ghost of his own imagining, the ethical man must be confronted by a living threat to his security. The ingenuousness with which the Judge describes his clerical friend suggests that he is a real "other" and not a poetic appendage of himself. But the matter is ambiguous and perhaps deliberately so.

7. Cf. E/O II 243-244 for Judge Wilhelm's use of this same text against the aesthete. It is standard practice for Kierkegaard's pseudonyms to comment on each other, often with the effect of reciprocal or transitive irony. See chapter 6 below.

8. E/O II 349-350. For an extended and detailed analysis of the God-man relationship in terms in the analogy of human love, see Kierkegaard, "The Joy in the Thought that in Relation to God a Man Always Suffers as Being Guilty," in *The Gospel of Suffering*, trans. D. F. and L. M. Swenson (Minneapolis, 1948), pp. 65-96.

9. SOLW 119.

10. SOLW 405. To remain suspended in indecision is demonic. This is the case with the Quidam whose lugubrious journal forms the "passion narrative," "Guilty?/Not Guilty?" in *Stages on Life's Way*. He never decides the question of guilt but continues to revolve it—and suffer it—inwardly year after year, solemnly observing the feasts and fast days of his love affair in parody of the Church, who faithfully repeats her calendar year after year *donec veniat*. Though the "experimental psychologist"—and of course author—of Quidam's diary, Frater Taciturnus, can regard this as a "tragi-comedy" and take from it a "solemn pleasure, the dialectic pleasure of beholding equilibrium" (SOLW 407), he is objectively alert enough to recognize that his subject is in demonia and can only rescue himself by a religious act of repentance.

11. E/O II 350-353.

12. *Søren Kierkegaards Papirer*, Vol. IV, Group A, entry 256. My italics. Cf. *The Koran*, trans. N. J. Dawood (Baltimore, 1956), p. 42. Joseph says: "Not that I am free from sin: man's soul is prone to evil, except his to whom Allah has shown mercy."

13. This and the previous quotation are from E/O II 222, 346-348, 353-354.

14. This and the previous quotation are from SOLW 394-395, 430. On the matters discussed in this paragraph, cf. W. O. Doescher, "Kant's Postulate of Practical Freedom," in G. T. Whitney and D. F. Bowers, eds., *The Heritage of Kant* (Princeton, 1939), pp. 197-225; also Louis Mackey, "The Analysis of the Good in Kierkegaard's *Purity of Heart*," in I. C. Lieb, ed., *Experience, Existence, and the Good* (Carbondale, 1961), pp. 260-274.

15. CUP 230. However, see also CUP 450 n: "The ethicist in *Either/Or* has already directly and indirectly protested against this (the 'derelict Hegelian ethics', with its desperate attempt to make the State the court of last resort'); indirectly at the close of the essay on the equilibrium between the aesthetic and the ethical in the personality, where he himself is compelled to make concessions in the direction of the religious; and again at the close of the article on 'Marriage' in the *Stages*, where even from the point of view of the ethics which he champions, which is quite the opposite of the Hegelian, he does indeed raise the price of the religious to as high a level as possible, but nevertheless makes room for it."

16. The references in this paragraph are to E/O II 50-51, 56, 58-59, 91, 125, 241-243, 255.

17. CUP 262.

18. This and the previous quotation are from SOLW 375, 383.

19. FAT 59. Kierkegaard scholars have commonly assumed that *Either/Or* presents a simple contrast between the aesthetic and the ethical with no more than a flavoring of religion. On this interpretation the sermon of the Jutland priest is not a challenge to Judge Wilhelm, but only a rounding out of his point of view well within the confines of the ethical. They are confirmed in this opinion by some of Kierkegaard's own statements in his journals; and there is a perspective from which, as we shall see in chapter 5, their opinion is absolutely correct. But the content of the *Ultimatum* itself, not to mention the stylistic hints that are strewn in its path, counsel reservation. The sermon can be consistently read as an admonition to the Assessor, but there is some straining required to read it as expressing his own mind. Moreover, there is a note by Kierkegaard which definitely ties the *Ultimatum* to his indubitably religious writings: "In *Either/Or* the aesthetic factor was present in opposition to ethics and the choice made from the struggle was ethics. There were therefore only two factors, and the Assessor absolutely victorious, even though the book ended with a sermon and with the observation that only the truth which edifies is truth for me (Inwardness—the starting point for my Edifying Discourses)." (Dru 519) This note is part of a longer journal entry comparing *Either/Or* with *Stages on Life's Way*. And it is true in this setting that ethics is triumphant in the former. For the letters of Judge Wilhelm occupy 340 of 360 pages of its second

volume, with the sermon as a quasi-appendix; whereas in the *Stages* the proportions of ethics and religion are almost inverted, and there is no doubt that a religious choice is demanded by the struggle. But what is interesting about this note is, first, the concessive status of the last clause—which certainly qualifies the Judge's absolute victory—and, second, the parenthetic reference to the *Edifying Discourses*. For it is in the discourses that Kierkegaard unfolds most explicitly his vision of the religious life.

20. CUP 256.

21. This theme runs throughout all of Kierkegaard's writings. For a concise statement, cf. PF, ch. III. See also chapter 4 below.

22. CUP 239-240; cf. CUP 369.

23. ED I 200.

24. ED II 252-253.

25. The references in this paragraph are to ED I 45, 57, 61-64.

26. The references in this paragraph are to ED I 67-68. Cf. Kierkegaard, *Purity of Heart*, trans. D. V. Steere (New York, 1938), *passim;* and Mackey, *op. cit.*, n. 14 above.

27. ED I 51, 53, 59, 66, 71.

28. The references in these two paragraphs are to ED I 191-192, 194-195, 203-204, 209. Cf. Luke 21: 19.

29. ED I 197.

30. ED I 116.

31. ED I 197-198.

32. ED I 198.

33. The quotations in the preceding three paragraphs are from ED I 199-201, 205-206.

34. The quotations in the preceding two paragraphs are from ED I 23, 31-33.

35. In the following discussion, the similarity with Martin Heidegger's view of time is so striking that it cannot be entirely coincidental. Heidegger has acknowledged his debt to the *Edifying Discourses*. Cf. *Being and Time* (London, 1962), p. 494, note vi to Division Two, Section 45.

36. ED I 34.

37. The references in this paragraph are to ED I 35-37.

38. ED I 37-38.

39. SUD 170-175.

40. COD 94.

41. Boethius, *De Consolatione Philosophiae*, V, *prosa* 6. Cf. Knud Hansen, *Søren Kierkegaard: Ideens Digter* (Copenhagen, 1954), pp. 188-190. The Latin says, "Eternity is the total, simultaneous, and perfect possession of endless life."

42. Dru 416.

43. ED I 42.

44. This and the previous quotation are from ED I 43, 47-48.

45. The references in this paragraph are to SOLW 400-403.

46. The citations in the preceding five paragraphs are from ED I 151-154, 157-161, 163-164. Cf. Luke 11: 13.

47. CUP 179 n.

48. The citations in the preceding three paragraphs are from ED II 125-129, 134-135, 137-139.

49. Cf. ED II 142 ff.

50. With this, compare Nietzsche's dogma that man must be surpassed. The Danish critic, Georg Brandes, tried to get Nietzsche to read Kierkegaard, but Nietzsche was already too far into his madness to read anything.

51. The quotations in this paragraph are from ED II 154-157.

52. CUP 369.

53. Kierkegaard, *The Gospel of Suffering*, p. 212.

54. The quotations in this paragraph are from ED II 158-160, 251-252.

55. SUD 158.

56. The quotations in this paragraph are from Rep 110-113, 117, 135-136.

57. E/O I 3.

58. E/O II 356.

59. SOLW 388.

60. Cf. F. J. Billeskov Jansen, *Studier i Søren Kierkegaards litteraere Kunst* (Copenhagen, 1951), p. 59.

61. *Søren Kierkegaards Papirer*, Vol. IV, Group B, entry 59. Cf. W. Lowrie, *Kierkegaard* (New York, 1962), p. 240.

62. The quotations in the preceding two paragraphs are from SOLW 411, 413-415, 422.

63. SOLW 425, 430.

64. This and the preceding quotation are from E/O I 143-144.

65. Cf. Rep 117, 133; also FAT 31.

66. Kierkegaard, *Thoughts on Crucial Situations in Human Life*, trans. D. F. Swenson (Minneapolis, 1941), p. 33.

CHAPTER 4: Almost in Earnest

1. CUP 164-167.

2. CUP 223-224.

3. SUD 146.

4. See Plato, *Phaedrus* 246A ff. and *Republic* 434D-441C, and Aristotle, *De Anima*, II, 1, 2; and cf. COD 20, 96-97, 99-101.

5. For these three paragraphs, see CUP 74-86, 177-178, 276-278, 313-314.

6. CUP 226; cf. CUP 262-264.

7. CUP 545-550, PF 5-7.

8. FAT 22-23.

9. Dru 552.

10. CUP 101 ff.

11. CUP 104.

12. David Hume, *An Inquiry Concerning Human Understanding*, Section XII, Part II.

13. CUP 105.

14. The citations in this paragraph are to JC 124, 125, 126.

15. R. H. M. Elwes, trans., *The Chief Works of Benedict de Spinoza* (New York, 1951), Vol. II, p. 29: "I speak of real doubt existing in the mind, not of such doubt as we see exemplified when a man says that he doubts, though his mind does not really hesitate. The cure of the latter does not fall within the province of method, it belongs rather to inquiries concerning obstinacy and its cure."

16. CUP 228.

17. JC 101.

18. E/O I 31.

19. JC 144, 145.

20. JC 180, 187-188.

21. The references in this paragraph are, in order, to PF iii, 137, 3, 6, 9.

22. PF 11.

23. The references in this paragraph are to PF 26, 27.

24. The references in this paragraph are to PF 39, 42.

25. The references in this paragraph are to PF 44 (my italics), 45.

26. Immanuel Kant, *Critique of Pure Reason*, Preface to First Edition, Avii.

27. PF 46, 48.

28. PF 49, 54.

29. References in this paragraph are to PF 57, 63, 67.

30. PF 76.

31. Hume, *op. cit.*, Section X.

32. PF 88.

33. PF 89, 90.

34. PF 114, 116.

35. References in the two preceding paragraphs are to PF 134-138.

36. COD 94.

37. PF 72-73.

38. PF 139.

39. PF 47-48.

40. G. K. Chesterton, *The Catholic Church and Conversion*, cited in A. C. Pegis, ed., *The Wisdom of Catholicism* (New York, 1949), p. 861.

41. CUP 2.

42. The citations in this paragraph are from CUP 245 n-246 n.

43. PF 2.

44. PF 138.

45. CUP 14

46. The references in the preceding two paragraphs are to CUP 3-6.

47. The references in this paragraph are to CUP 18-19, 330-340.

48. CUP 61.

49. The references in the preceding two paragraphs are to CUP 116-118.

50. CUP 109.

51. CUP 138.

315

52. CUP 115.

53. The references in this paragraph are to CUP 119-121.

54. CUP 121.

55. CUP 80.

56. SUD 173-174.

57. CUP 124.

58. CUP 122.

59. The citations in this paragraph are from CUP 122-123, 140.

60. The citations in this paragraph are from CUP 125, 144-146, 148.

61. CUP 163.

62. The quotations in this paragraph are from CUP 160, 163. J. L. Heiberg's own story of his conversion to Hegel, here parodied, is almost a parody of itself. While staying at the "*König von England*" in Hamburg, "*mit Hegel auf meinem Tisch und Hegel in meinen Gedanken,*" Heiberg was seized by an inner light ("*es war wie ein Blitzstrahl*") that illumined Hegel and the universe for good. The miracle took place to the accompaniment of choral music wafted from the nearby Church of St. Peter. Cf. the excerpts from his "*Autobiographischen Fragmenten*" quoted in *Søren Kierkegaard in Selbstzeugnissen und Bilddokumenten,* dargestellt von P. P. Rohde (Hamburg, 1959), pp. 20-22, from which my own citations here are taken.

63. The citations in this paragraph are from CUP 177-178, 181-182.

64. Cf. CUP 191-192, 194.

65. The quotations in this paragraph are from CUP 197, 203, 208-209.

66. The quotations in this paragraph are from CUP 210, 213-214, 216, 251. The Shakespeare passage is from *Julius Caesar,* Act II, Scene i.

67. CUP 108, 110, 119. Cf. SOLW 219.

68. CUP 292.

69. SOLW 430.

70. CUP 75.

71. SUD 158.

72. COD 40, 44.

73. CUP 306.

74. The quotations in this paragraph are from CUP 276-277.

75. Cf. CUP 84-85, 279.

76. See Kierkegaard, *The Present Age,* trans. A. Dru (London, 1940), pp. 3-70; and "Two Notes about 'The Individual'" in POV 105-140.

77. Cf. CUP 67-74, 282-292, 320-322.

78. CUP 285.

79. CUP 290.

80. The references in this paragraph are to CUP 139-140.

81. The quotations in this paragraph are from CUP 305.

82. CUP 163, 210.

83. CUP 182.

84. Cf. CUP 115-163.

85. CUP 306.

86. Cf. CUP 99, 107-113.

87. This and the preceding quotation are from CUP 313.

88. CUP 550.

89. These two quotations are from CUP 546.

90. CUP 20.

CHAPTER 5: Voices of Silence

1. CUP 20.

2. The citations in the preceding three paragraphs are from CUP 15, 16, 18.

3. CUP 19.

4. CUP 80.

5. CUP 124.

6. SUD 173-174.

7. CUP 19.

8. Kierkegaard, *Purity of Heart,* trans. D. V. Steere (New York, 1948). Cf. Louis Mackey, "The Analysis of the Good in Kierkegaard's *Purity of Heart,"* in I. C. Lieb, ed., *Experience, Existence, and the Good* (Carbondale, 1961), pp. 260-274.

9. FAT 52 n, 53.

10. Dru 519.

11. CUP 261.

12. CUP 241.

13. Cf. Kierkegaard, *For Self-Examination and Judge for Yourselves!*, trans. W. Lowrie (Princeton, 1944), pp. 91-106.

14. For the story of Abraham, see Genesis 12-25. For an illuminating literary treatment of the Isaac episode, see Erich Auerbach, *Mimesis* (Garden City, 1957), chapter 1. See also Louis H. Mackey, "Kierkegaard's Lyric of Faith: A Look at *Fear and Trembling,*" *Rice Institute Pamphlet*, XLVII, 2 (July, 1960), pp. 30-47.

15. FAT 21. "What Tarquinius Superbus spoke in the garden by means of the poppies, the son understood, but not the messenger." Tarquin, king of Rome, was bent on the destruction of Gabii. His son, having worked his way into the confidence of its people, sent to his father asking what to do next. Tarquin, distrustful of the messenger, took him into the garden, where he proceeded to cut off the heads of the tallest poppies with his sword. This was reported to the son, who understood thereby that he was to cause the death of the leading citizens of Gabii, and went straight to the task.

16. The citations in the preceding two paragraphs are from FAT 22, 24.

17. The quotations in this paragraph are from FAT 27 (Genesis 22:2), 29.

18. FAT 31.

19. The quotations in this paragraph are from FAT 34-35.

20. These quotations are from FAT 37.

21. FAT 41.

22. FAT 40 n.

23. The quotations in this paragraph are from FAT 43-44.

24. FAT 48.

25. FAT 57.

26. FAT 47.

27. FAT 64.

28. FAT 66.

29. FAT 65.

30. The quotations in this paragraph are from FAT 82, 84.

31. Cf. also Genesis 22: 14.

32. FAT 121.

33. The legend of Agnes and the Merman is enshrined in the ballad, "Agnete hun stander på højelandsbro," which may be found in B. Bramsen and E.

318

Larsen, eds., *Danske Sange* (Copenhagen, 1954), pp. 6-7. See also Matthew Arnold's poem, "The Forsaken Merman," which is based on this legend.

34. The preceding quotations are all from FAT 108, 108 n.

35. The quotations in this paragraph are from FAT 129-131.

36. CUP 289-291.

37. TIC 10-15.

38. TIC 25.

39. TIC 26-28.

40. CUP 345.

41. TIC 28-34.

42. Dru 817.

43. TIC 37-39.

44. TIC 40-60.

45. The preceding quotations are from TIC 66-68.

46. Cf. PF 107-110, 124-126; CUP 512-513.

47. Cf. TIC 124-127.

48. The three quotations preceding are from TIC 69-70.

49. Cf. PF 17-22, 68-88, 111-132.

50. TIC 71.

51. CUP 238-239.

52. TIC 71-72.

53. CUP 493-519.

54. These quotations are from CD 315, 320.

55. Cf. Rep 53.

56. Cf. COD 40; CUP 272.

57. CD 315.

58. CD 329-330.

59. The references in this paragraph are to CD 339-341, 344.

60. The references in this paragraph are to CD 348-350, 353. Cf. St. Augustine, *Confessiones*, I, 1: *"Tu nos fecisti ad te, Domine, et cor nostrum inquietum est donec requiescat in te."*

61. CD 355.

CHAPTER 6: A Kind of Poet . . .

1. Cf. PF 130-131.

2. Cf. CUP 86-97.

3. Dru 1141; POV 162.

4. CD 167 and TIC 5.

5. The references in the three paragraphs preceding are to CUP 323-325, 329 (my italics), 339, 343.

6. Dru 936.

7. TIC 7.

8. Dru 891, and cf. 1060.

9. Cf. Kierkegaard, *On Authority and Revelation,* trans. W. Lowrie (Princeton, 1955), *passim;* and Kierkegaard, "Of the Difference between a Genius and an Apostle," trans. A. Dru, in *The Present Age* (London, 1940), pp. 137-163.

10. Cf. Kierkegaard, *Attack upon "Christendom,"* trans. W. Lowrie (Princeton, 1946), *passim.*

11. SUD 141.

12. CUP 76.

13. CUP 306.

14. These three quotations are from CUP, "A First and Last Declaration," unpaged = pp. 551, 552, 554.

15. That there was a discrepancy between the views of the aesthetic *personae* and Kierkegaard himself is clear from (to choose only one instance) his private reasons for selecting Victor Eremita as pseudonymous editor for *Either/Or.* That name, which has disclosed so many levels of significance, expressed for Kierkegaard the man that he was already living in the cloister—that the religious had triumphed in him, and that he dwelt in solitude with God—at the time he wrote his celebration of the poetic life and his exhortation to ethical publicity.

16. Dru 484.

17. Silence and secrecy appear as themes in more than one of Kierkegaard's books. It could almost be said that silence is the major subject of *Fear and Trembling.* Nor is it an accident that so many of the pseudonyms bear names indicative of concealment and reticence: Victor Eremita, Johannes de Silentio, Frater Taciturnus. Victor plays with the implications of his own name:

> "It is a matter of indifference whether somebody uses gold or silver or paper money, but the man who never pays out a farthing unless it is false will understand what I mean. The man for whom every direct expression is only a *falsum* is better insured than if he entered a monastery, he continues to be a

hermit even though he rides day and night in an omnibus."
(SOLW 75-76)

Likewise the author who understands that there is no "'immediate' expression for spirit" builds a poetic hermitage in his works even though he may be the most notorious writer in all Denmark.—On the same track: Victor Eremita's anti-Hegelian thesis concerning the discrepancy between inner essence and outer expression is reduplicated not only in the overall pattern of *Either/Or*, but by images within images. Into his Preface alone Victor packs three concretions of this particular universal: the secretary with its secret compartment; the confessional in which the priest hears the outpourings of the soul but cannot discern the disposition of the penitent's face and form; and the pistol case in which Victor carries, not duelling equipment, as he lets his innkeeper believe, but the manuscript of *Either/Or*.—Details like this could be multiplied almost endlessly.

18. CUP 225-226, 249.

19. CUP, "A First and Last Declaration," unpaged=pp. 551-552.

20. In *Either/Or* Victor Eremita edits (or does he write?) the papers of A and Judge Wilhelm; the Judge holds a mirror up to A at the same time that he transcribes and is transfixed by the sermon of the Jutland priest; A examines the complex entanglements of (among many others) Mozart, Don Juan, Leporello, and the Don's victims, while simultaneously he authors his own undoing in the diary of Johannes the Seducer. The writers are interlocked with each other like the pieces in a Chinese puzzle, and the reader is never certain who is being seen through whose eyes—who is poet and who persona—at any moment.—According to his own account Victor Eremita acquires the papers of A and Judge Wilhelm quite by accident. Prompted by irrational impulse he purchases a secretary which he has long coveted where it stood in a dealer's window. Later in his apartment, when a drawer of the secretary refuses to open, Victor, frustrated to the point of violence, smashes the secretary with a hatchet. The drawer in question is not loosed, but another and hitherto unsuspected compartment springs open discovering the papers that make up *Either/Or*. Having come upon the papers by chance Victor proceeds to make the most of them.—This is Victor's own explanation. The fortuitous origin of his book is the beginning of that ambiguity of authorship which is further complicated by the suggestion, examined in chapter 1, that Victor Eremita is responsible for *Either/Or* in more than an editorial capacity. The book as a whole is either his discovery or his creation, just which is not certain.—This ambiguity is multiplied throughout the internal structure of the work. All the essays in Volume I save the last are by A edited by Victor Eremita. Or depending on Victor's role, by Victor through A as pseudonym. The Diary of the Seducer is by Johannes the Seducer edited by A, reedited by Victor Eremita. Or is it by A, edited by Victor with Johannes as *persona?* Or is it simply by Victor *via* A as pseudonym and Johannes as sub-pseudonym? In Volume II, the two long letters are written by Judge Wilhelm and made public by Victor Eremita, or, it may be, written by Victor and attributed to the Assessor. The Ultimatum is by the Jutland priest, copied out and forwarded to A by Judge Wilhelm, discovered and published by Victor Eremita; or perhaps

it is the work of the Assessor which he attributes to the priest; or perhaps the whole thing is by Victor wearing two more masks. The sum of these ambiguities is a work all or various parts of which may or may not be attributed to one, two, or three authors or editors.—Equally intricate but more compressed is the network of *personae* in *Repetition*. Ostensibly the work is a casebook novel in which Constantin Constantius, the experimental psychologist and dilettante author, reports the history of a Kierkegaardian young man who falls in love, realizes that he cannot marry the girl, nearly achieves a religious reconciliation to his sorrow by reading *Job*, but is at last made a poet by the girl's magnanimity in marrying someone else. "Really" the book investigates the possibility of "repetition"—of restoring a personality to integrity after it has been broken by grief and guilt. With an irony appropriate to the investigation the two pseudonyms are diffracted into a series of masks that satirize themselves and each other (several times over) and finally the reader, who is presented at the end with a calling card, bearing a blank space for his name, and an admonition to be reconciled to the flippancy and incoherence of the book. The reader who recovers *himself* from the farcical shadowplay of the novel will have achieved repetition, and the heretics eager to ascertain the author's position will get nothing to run with.

21. The references are to SOLW 17, 21, 23-24.

22. SOLW 25, 27-32.

23. Dru 519.

24. SOLW 92-93.

25. SOLW 95.

26. The citations in this paragraph are from SOLW 179, 184, 363-365, 367, 388-389, 395-396, 398, 437.

27. The quotations in this paragraph are from SOLW 442, 444. It is easy enough to complain that Kierkegaard's writing is over-wrought and over-rich, his style too turgid, his artifice too elaborately articulated, and his books too long. But this itself is a bit of existential maieutic, a deliberate surfeit calculated to awaken the reader's attention even at the risk of insulting him. No view of life (existence-sphere) can be established or refuted in a way that is both logically and existentially efficacious. Therefore the pseudonyms illustrate and explain their stages on life's way at such length and with such richness and purity that the reader is over-filled. The reader who is already committed to a given view of life will revel in its presentation by the Kierkegaardian pseudonym. He who is not committed may well become sick of it and throw it all up. Whether he like it or lump it, he will have got the message, and the book in question will have done its work, not to advance a doctrine but only "to make aware."

28. R. G. Smith, ed. and trans., *The Last Years: Søren Kierkegaard, Journals 1853-1855* (New York, 1965), p. 213.

29. E/O II 356.

30. F. J. Billeskov Jansen, *Studier i Søren Kierkegaards litteraere Kunst* (Copenhagen, 1951), pp. 21, 45-46. See also the same author's "The Literary Art of Kierkegaard" in H. A. Johnson and N. Thulstrup, eds., *A Kierkegaard Critique* (New York, 1962), pp. 11-21.

31. CUP 246 n.

32. Cf. Billeskov Jansen, *Studier i Søren Kierkegaards litteraere Kunst*, chapter IV.

33. *Summa Theologiae*, Ia, q. I, a. 9, *ad* 3.

34. Thus, e.g., the unity of the aesthetic life ("immediate" human nature) is a metaphoric complex in which A is the comprehensive organizing *persona* and every other aesthete synecdoche for the totality he represents in anonymous outline. A similar relation obtains among William Afham and the company of aesthetes his recollection assembles at the banquet in *Stages on Life's Way.*— What holds within the individual works holds also of their interrelationships. Each of Kierkegaard's books explores the entire domain of his thought; the dialectic of the stages is rehearsed in each from a different poetic angle. Each work is thus self-contained, and the whole Kierkegaard may be read out of any of them by a sufficiently close perusal. But at the same time, the different angles from which they are written make of each book a perspective reference to all the others, and endow each with the perspectival interpretations provided by all the rest. Each is at once *Abschattung* for every other and a microcosm of the whole.

35. There are many other instances. E.g., Kierkegaard's use of "religious language." On the one hand he insists that the edifying discourses do not appeal to specific Christian categories; Johannes Climacus complains of the Hegelian abuse of dogmatic terminology, laments the shortage of precise Christian definitions, and even goes so far as to delimit Christian faith *sensu strictissimo* from strong conviction, ethical resolution, wishful thinking, and belief in general. On the other hand, Judge Wilhelm makes the freest use of Holy Scripture, Christian theology, liturgics, and ecclesiastical tradition to build his ethical case for marriage; the edifying discourses quote and expound the Bible in the language of orthodox Lutheranism; even the aesthete refers to Christian history and doctrine in his literary essays. The only alternative to confusion is the supposition that such terms as "faith" and "sin" and the like are used equivocally and not univocally in the Kierkegaardian corpus. In character, Judge Wilhelm uses "faith" to stand for the extreme exertion of freedom resolving itself *in sempiternum*. The "expectation of faith" of the edifying discourses is not the paradoxical and God-given contemporaneity with Christ of Climacus and Anti-Climacus, but the capacity, immanent in man, to submit himself wholly to the sovereignty of God. Each *persona*, speaking in and to a Christian culture, uses the honorifics of that culture to represent the ultimate possibilities of his own way of life. In like manner pejoratives such as "sin" can denominate the *bêtes noires* of each stage on life's way, though the specific Christian usage is underlined in other contexts. Religious (and other) words that appear throughout the body of Kierkegaard's writings are therefore meant

to be taken metaphorically rather than literally. Their meanings—always manifold—are not defined by convention or stipulation (except occasionally by individual pseudonyms, and only within the provenance of their own works), but determined by context.—Equivocity of terms is matched by an analogy of concepts. E.g., recollection is the aesthetic analogue of repentance. Recollection is an ideal revision of the past in the interest of aesthetic satisfaction; repentance is an ideal revision of the past in the interest of moral integrity. Neither succeeds, and when it fails, each opens the possibility of ascent to a higher level of self-understanding. The analogy in this case is a structural uniformity that cuts across the division of the stages on life's way, a likeness of form exhibited in a difference of context and content.—Another instance of this kind of analogy is the pattern of "withdrawal and return" that is repeated at every level of human life. At the aesthetic stage, it appears as the dialectic of the rotation method: *nil admirari* countered by arbitrariness. In the domain of ethics, it is the tension of repentance and duty. In religion A, the negative movement of resignation, suffering, and guilt is answered by the enthusiastic endurance of worship. And beyond the leap of faith, in religion B, the "double movement" of subjectivity is fulfilled in the paradox of sin and forgiveness. The ubiquity of such a pattern, at once unifying the spheres of existence and diversified by them, is part of what Kierkegaard means when he says that human life is immediately aesthetic. The fact that the exemplary and consummatory expression of this pattern—its primary analogue—is found at the level of Christianity testifies to the truth of Vigilius Haufniensis' contention that every human life is religiously planned.—Related to this pattern of withdrawal and return is the separation effected by freedom between inner life and outer manifestation, a separation enjoyed aesthetically in the form of melancholy, surmounted ethically by resolution, religiously experienced as suffering, and resolved in principle by the Christian identification of *sola gratia* and *imitatio Christi.*

36. Cf. *Søren Kierkegaards Papirer*, Vol. IV, Group B, entries 110-120.

37. Rep 31.

38. The references in this paragraph are to Rep 74, 76, 77.

39. Cf. above, chapter 5, pp. 138-142.

40. Dru 552.

41. Kierkegaard, *For Self-Examination and Judge for Yourselves!*, p. 5. Cf. CUP, "A First and Last Declaration," unpaged = p. 554.

42. CUP 250.

43. CUP 232.

44. Cf. among many other references CUP 273: "If philosophical reflection had not in our time become something queer, highly artificial, and capable of being learned by rote, thinkers would make quite a different impression upon people, as was the case in Greece, where a thinker was an existing individual stimulated by his reflection to a passionate enthusiasm; and as was also once the

case in Christendom when a thinker was a believer who strove enthusiastically to understand himself in the existence of faith."

45. Cf. *Metaphysics* I, 2; *Nicomachean Ethics* X, 7-8.

46. Dru 1377.

47. The quotations in this paragraph are from CUP 218, 220-222, 232-233. Cf. Dru 616.

48. CUP 219.

49. In what follows as regards Kierkegaard's parodies of Goethe, I am greatly indebted to Carl Roos' exhaustive study, *Kierkegaard og Goethe* (Copenhagen, 1955).

50. For a brilliant discussion of Kierkegaard as a novelist, see Aage Henriksen, *Kierkegaards Romaner* (Copenhagen, 1954). I have learned more from this book than a few footnotes could indicate.—Elsewhere than in *Either/Or,* the conventions of time-place-and-plot are differently manipulated, but always conformably with the import of the book in hand. *Repetition,* e.g., is plotted differentially for the narrator (Constantin Constantius) and his hero (the young man). Constantin's whereabouts are always known, but his life is a succession of distinct temporal moments containing random experiences which add up to nothing—as befits a man who cannot achieve repetition, but drifts from Copenhagen to Berlin and back again in execution of the terms of his fundamental aesthetic self-choice. The spatial location of the young man is often vague and sometimes unknown, since he as a poet and (for a while) potentially religious man is not really of this world. But his time, like that of Job, is the redemptive time in which, dramatically by the hand of God or farcically by the volatile will of a woman, a *redintegratio in statum pristinum* is effected.—*Guilty?/Not Guilty?* is precisely timed—even dated—but the whole tenor of Quidam's story makes it evident that his time is an endless and aimless cycle reflecting his perpetual stasis before the religious choice that he will never make.—Within *Either/Or,* a compendious work in more ways than one, further parodies appear. The Diary of the Seducer is alleged to have as its real prototype Kierkegaard's sometime associate, the notorious libertine P. L. Møller. No doubt Kierkegaard had an eye for his own contemporaries when he wrote, but the interpretation of Johannes' diary as a *roman à clef* is a thing of very limited interest and value. More informative are the striking parallels between the Seducer's diary and Choderlos de Laclos' *Les Liaisons Dangereuses.* But whereas the French novel of intrigue arranges, somewhat incongruously and unconvincingly, to have its seducer and his accomplice justly punished for their misdeeds—the Viscomte de Valmont is killed in a duel by his victim's true lover, and the Marquise de Merteuil is disfigured by smallpox—, Kierkegaard's Seducer, unscathed by so much as a nasty rumor, runs from one adventure to the next with no nemesis in sight. The effect is at once less moralizing and morally more shaking, since the question of seduction gets "no finite decision in particular personalities." (E/O I 14)

51. SOLW 87.

52. The parody would be apparent to none but Danes, and few of them any more, but even Kierkegaard's edifying discourses rework a contemporary pattern: the sermons of Jakop Peter Mynster, Bishop of Sealand, Primate of Denmark, Michael Kierkegaard's confessor, his son's erstwhile spiritual guide, eventually his enemy, and at all times the highly acclaimed interpreter of Christianity to the overprivileged upper middle class of Copenhagen. The style of Kierkegaard's discourses is that of Mynster's sermons, with one difference: while the sole effect of the latter is to impress the seal of Gospel approval on the hearts of his audience, to console them that need no consolation and encourage them with the comfortable assurance of their own sanctity, Kierkegaard's discourses attack this prosperous bourgeois Christendom from the rear and rout its illusions with the devastating dialectic of the religious life. Mynster's rhetoric is nothing but rhetoric; the *Edifying Discourses* conceal an iron fist of godly logic in their velvet glove of fable and homely wisdom. When he insisted that his discourses were not sermons, but only lay addresses that might prove edifying to the single individual who read them with application, Kierkegaard was simply respecting the orthodox dogma of apostolic ministry. Orthodoxy became ironic comment on the state of religion in Denmark when Kierkegaard's contemporaries failed to understand his distinction.—A comparable instance is *The Concept of Dread* by Vigilius Haufniensis. This book, a "simple psychological deliberation oriented in the direction of the dogmatic problem of original sin," (COD 1) is to say the least pedantic in form. The author divides his work scholastically into chapters, sub-divisions, and paragraphs; he cites and discusses the relevant theological authorities; and he exhibits the most fastidious concern for conceptual precision and the proper delimitation of the spheres of the various *Geisteswissenschaften.* (COD, motto, 9-21) The language throughout is pedestrian. If *Philosophical Fragments* is entirely Greek, almost a Socratic dialogue, then *The Concept of Dread* is pure academic Latin. It was in fact a parody on the theological textbooks to which Kierkegaard was subjected by his professors in divinity, a parody because it employs the cathedral manner to insinuate doubts about the adequacy of the orthodox doctrine of original sin. (Cf. Billeskov Jansen, *Studier i Søren Kierkegaards litteraere Kunst,* pp. 48-49.) It points beyond theological symbol and Biblical myth to the anxiety of freedom as the source of man's first disobedience and the fall. The later history of this work, unique in the influence it has exerted on secular existentialists (e.g., Heidegger and Sartre), faithfully and ironically reflects its combination of strict academic form and wildly heterodox content.—Carl Roos finds a *Trutz-Werther* in *The Sickness Unto Death,* which establishes theoretically that bodily death is not to be compared to death of the spirit, and that the will to do away with oneself in the flesh is jest compared to spiritual self-annihilation. (Roos, *op. cit.,* pp. 50-53.) The hero of *Guilty?/Not Guilty?,* prevented by his own melancholy from marrying the girl he loves, refuses the release of suicide in favor of perpetual indecision with an option of religion. (Roos, p. 44.)—It has been suggested to me that Goethe's *Werther* was itself an ironic mockery of *Sturm und Drang.* That may be. But no one at the time, including Kierkegaard, read it that way.

53. The quotations in this paragraph are from CUP 82-83, 84-85.

54. The references in the two preceding paragraphs are to CUP 459, 459 n, 462-463, 466.

55. CUP 241 n-242 n.

56. CUP 250-251.

57. FAT 62.

58. CUP 241.

59. CUP 448, 465.

60. Dru 489.

61. CUP 547.

62. CUP 321.

63. CUP 73.

64. Cf. Ralph McInerny, "Ethics and Persuasion: Kierkegaard's Existential Dialectic" in *The Modern Schoolman,* XXXIII, May, 1956, pp. 219-239. Prof. McInerny maintains that for Thomas Aquinas, as for Kierkegaard, poetry functioned as indirect communication in the realm of ethics.

65. CUP 320.

66. *Poetics* 9.

67. The references in this paragraph are to CUP 277 n, 282, 296-297. Cf. COD 16 n.

68. The quotations in this paragraph are from CUP 235-236. Cf. CUP 447 n.

69. This and the previous citation are from CUP 286-287.

70. Cf. CUP 307-312.

71. The quotations in this paragraph are from CUP 288-289, 321.

72. POV 155, 138.

73. CUP 241.

74. CUP 232.

75. CUP 69.

76. The references in this paragraph are to CUP 68 n, 68-70, 72-73.

77. TIC 5.

78. POV 103.